CLASSIC
CARS
OF THE WORLD

CLASSIC CARS
OF THE WORLD

OVER 600 WORLD-CLASS AUTOMOBILES

RICHARD NICHOLLS & CRAIG CHEETHAM

amber
BOOKS

First published in 2004 by
Amber Books Ltd
Bradley's Close
74–77 White Lion Street
London N1 9PF
www.amberbooks.co.uk

ISBN 1-904687-008

Printed in Singapore

Picture credits
All pictures courtesy of Art-Tech Ltd
except pages 7 and 8 courtesy of TRH Pictures Ltd/John Cadman.

Contents

Introduction

Although it may be said that Frenchman Nicholas Cugnot's experiments in 1769 with a steam-driven vehicle marked the beginning of the car's history, it was not until the internal combustion engine first appeared in 1860 that a practical power unit was available for road vehicles, and even then it relied on coal gas, which was difficult to store.

A German engineer, Nikolaus-August Otto, developed a four-stroke internal combustion engine, which was converted to run on petrol by Gottlieb Daimler in the 1870s. After inventing the motorbike, in 1886 Daimler built a four-wheeled vehicle from a horse-drawn carriage with a steering column and the engine mounted below the rear seat. A four-speed gearbox drove the back wheels using a belt mechanism. However, distracted by other demands in his business, Daimler did not manufacture another car design until 1889.

At the same time Karl Benz used a lightweight steel frame to anchor the body and wheels of his own three-wheeled car design in 1885. In January 1886 Benz decided to

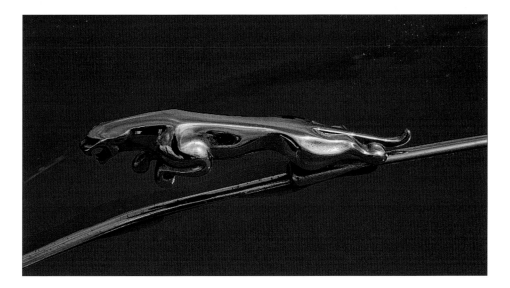

The distinctive emblem of Jaguar, a sports car manufacturer now owned by Ford but first founded by Sir Richard Lyons in 1933 as SS Cars Ltd.

Introduction

The AC Ace was transformed into a fearsome racing machine when Carroll Shelby put a Ford V8 engine into its chassis.

market his car, and he exhibited it at the Paris Exposition of 1887, where Emile Roger, a French cycle maker, bought the rights to manufacture it in France. However the first actual French car was built in 1890 by the firm of Panhard et Levassor who had bought and adapted Daimler's design, introducing brakes and a front-mounted engine. Benz then launched a four-wheeled car in 1892 which he named the 'Viktoria' that had great success, although his two-seat car called the 'Velo' – launched in 1894 – quickly surpassed the 'Viktoria' with his best sales yet. Benz himself drove a 'Velo' in the first recorded car race from Paris to Rouen.

Throughout Europe, America and even distant Australia, various engineers and enthusiasts began designing their own vehicles. Louis Renault built his first car in 1898, while FIAT established its first car factory in Italy in 1899. Daimler's firm built its first Mercedes – named after the daughter of one of his financial backers – in 1901. Napiers and Lanchesters were the cars to own in Britain, but in 1907 Rolls-Royce emerged on the scene with its famous Silver Ghost. Arguably none of these manufacturers were to have as significant an impact as Henry Ford with his Model T motorcar, which dominated the American market until 1927. Of the 12 million cars registered in the USA in the early 1920s, over half of them were Model Ts.

Racing fuelled the interest in motor cars, and it soon became commonplace for cars to exceed 100mph on the new tracks that were being built. World War I slowed the market for cars, and only the wealthy could afford the Duesenbergs and Cords now available in the USA. The stock market crash and the worldwide depression that followed ruined many manufacturers and small cars like the Austin Seven became popular. Car manufacturing did not really recover until after World War II, when the USA entered a boom period, and the cars of the time reflected that. Chrome was everywhere, and there were new car names to whisper in awe: Cadillac, Corvette and Thunderbird. Europe too had its successes, with the Jaguar XK120 and the emergence of Ferrari as a force to be reckoned with.

In the 1960s the American car market continued to seek greater power or 'muscle' in its cars, epitomised by the Pontiac GTO and Ford Mustang, both of which spawned a host of competitors. Porsche launched its 911, which would remain in production for decades, and Jaguar's E-type took people's breath away. Volkswagen's Beetle became a car of the people, as did the popular Austin Mini and, perhaps unexpectedly, the Citroen 2CV. Lotus, Lamborghini and Maserati challenged Ferrari's dominance of the sports car market, while Rolls-Royce's Silver Shadow was *the* luxury car to own.

FUEL CRISIS

The fuel crisis of the 1970s ruined the car market for many, as manufacturers were forced to offer economical models that lacked the performance of their predecessors. Famous names went under, or were bought by other companies; it was a time for survival of the fittest, although the Triumph and MG models were minor success stories for the beleaguered British manufacturers. The Japanese, too, were beginning to make their mark, offering a viable alternative to car buyers with models from Toyota, Nissan and, later, Mitsubishi. Computerisation and engine management software in the 1980s meant that the good times were back, with new generation models from the American car makers and flashes of inspiration from the Italians, such as the Lamborghini Countach. In the 1990s Lotus was revived, and Jaguar, now owned by Ford, has re-emerged, while such famous names as Chevrolet, Ford, Pontiac, Chrysler, BMW, Bentley, Porsche – the list goes on – are enjoying a period of creativity and profitability. Mercedes-Benz, the firm formed by the merger of Gottleib Daimler's firm with that of Karl Benz in the 1920s, isn't doing too badly, either.

AC Cobra 289

This car launched thousands of replicas and it was Carroll Shelby who started it all. He approached the Hurlock brothers at AC in 1961 – who were then producing the six-cylinder AC Ace – with the idea of putting Ford's compact and lightweight V8 into the car. AC jumped at the chance and in 1962 production began. At first, Shelby installed the 260ci (4.3-litre) but only the first 75 cars had this engine. In 1963 Shelby switched to the 289ci (4.7-litre) V8 and changed the steering to rack and pinion. The result in this lightweight roaster was sensational. The Cobra was the fastest accelerating car in the 1960s, but required nerves of steel because of the basic twin tube chassis. Its saving features were all-round independent wishbone suspension and large disc brakes. The bare essentials inside the roadster kept weight well under a ton and 100mph (160km/h) could be reached in just 14 seconds.

Top speed:	140 mph (224 km/h)
0–60 mph (0–95 km/h):	5.5 sec
Engine type:	V8
Displacement:	289 ci (4,735 cc)
Transmission	4-speed manual
Max power:	271 bhp (202 kW) @ 5,750 rpm
Max torque:	285 lb ft (386 Nm) @ 4,500 rpm
Weight:	2,024 lb (920 kg)
Economy:	15 mpg (5.3 km/l)

AC Cobra MkIV

The original AC Ace, modified by Shelby American to produce the AC Cobra in 1962, was every inch a muscle machine. In the mid-1980s AC Cars of Surrey, England, was emulating those early cars with a modern version of the Cobra, the MkIV. Still using a Mustang V8, this time it was the Phase 3 Mustang's 5.0 HO motor with sequential fuel injection and a lightweight engine block to keep the weight down. Through a manual gearbox it gave the MkIV almost the same acceleration as the original car, but with more fuel economy and better road manners. Underneath there were double wishbones front and rear to keep the suspension quick reacting, while 11-inch (280mm) discs provided awesome stopping ability on the roadster. Inside the car was hardly different even after all those years, with the bare minimum of analogue dials required just to keep the driver informed.

Top speed:	135 mph (216 km/h)
0–60 mph (0–95 km/h):	5.3 sec
Engine type:	V8
Displacement:	302 ci (4,942 cc)
Transmission	5-speed manual
Max power:	225 bhp (168 kW) @ 4,200 rpm
Max torque:	300lb ft (406 Nm) @ 3,200 rpm
Weight:	2,468 lb (1,122 kg)
Economy:	17 mpg (6 km/l)

AC Superblower

The Superblower was a re-creation of what Carroll Shelby had done in the early 1960s, only this time it had more bite. Like its predecessors, the Superblower was hand-built and even used a similar chassis with twin round tubes running the length of the car and smaller tubes between. Unequal-length wishbones front and rear made the handling good, and at each corner were huge discs. But most people were interested in the 'go' of the Superblower and the power was exceptional. Like the Cobras of the past, the car used a Mustang V8, this time the 5.0L from the 1987–1995 models, but with a Ford SVT (Special Vehicle Team) centrifugal blower to boost power up from the standard engine's 225bhp (167kW) and 300lb ft (406Nm) torque. The body was still hand-fabricated by craftsmen in aluminium alloy, while inside there was a modern interpretation of the original multi-dial dash.

Top speed:	155 mph (248 km/h)
0-60 mph (0–95 km/h):	4.2 sec
Engine type:	V8
Displacement:	302 ci (4,942 cc)
Transmission	5-speed manual
Max power:	355 bhp (250 kW) @ 5,700 rpm
Max torque:	385 lb ft (521 Nm) @ 3,750 rpm
Weight:	2,558 lb (1,163 kg)
Economy:	14 mpg (20 km/l)

AC Ace

After a long battle in the boardroom, the AC Ace name was revived and the car launched in 1997. A version of the Ace had been designed by International Automotive Design in 1991, and the prototype used a Cosworth turbo four-cylinder engine, which was replaced in production with a modified Ford V6. The model didn't do well, with 48 sold before AC went into receivership. Pride Automotive Group later acquired the company and came up with the current Ace, with smoother body lines. The exterior was aluminium and composite, bonded to the stainless steel chassis to form a very stiff structure. Suspension consisted of double wishbones front and rear, with 10–inch (282mm) discs all around covered by wide 17-inch (436mm) alloys. Under the hood was all Mustang V8 again, as with the 1960s Shelby-built AC Cobra, though this time with sequential fuel injection and a supercharger.

Top speed:	165 mph (264 km/h)
0–60 mph (0–95 km/h):	5.5 sec
Engine type:	V8
Displacement:	302 ci (4,942 cc)
Transmission	5-speed manual
Max power:	340 bhp (254 kW) @ 5,700 rpm
Max torque:	385 lb ft (522 Nm) @ 3,500 rpm
Weight:	3,330 lb (1,514 kg)
Economy:	17 mpg (6 km/l)

Acura Integra Type R

The Integra Type R was launched in 1997, though its roots can be traced back years before that. In 1994 Honda debuted an all-wheel drive Integra prototype to the world's press, but it never went into production because of weight and cost. Instead, the design team concentrated on a lightweight, front-wheel-drive only vehicle and put into practice all their technology from the F1. The 110ci (1.8-litre) engine used their variable camshaft timing VTEC technology, low-friction pistons, high-volume intake, a bigger free-flow exhaust and a compression ratio of 11.1:1 for 195bhp (145kW), though being at 8,000rpm, the motor needed to be kept buzzing for best results. A stiffened bodyshell, full independent suspension with MacPherson struts up front, plus a helical gear-type limited-slip differential kept the power down and made it one of the best-handling front-wheel-drive cars ever.

Top speed:	143 mph (228 km/h)
0—60 mph (0–95 km/h):	6.7 sec
Engine type:	In-line four
Displacement:	105 ci (1,797 cc)
Transmission	5-speed
Max power:	195 bhp (145 kW) @ 8,000 rpm
Max torque:	130 lb ft (176 Nm) @ 7,300 rpm
Weight:	2,427 lb (1,103 kg)
Economy:	26 mpg (10 km/l)

Alfa Romeo 1750 GTV

The forerunner to the 1967 1750 GTV, the Sprint Coupe, debuted in 1963 as part of the Giulia family of cars which included saloons and Spiders designed by Giorgetto Giugiaro, was distinctive and handsome. The GTV (GT Veloce) was the fast version of the Sprint and shared the same mechanicals as other models in the range. Independent front suspension using double wishbones and an anti-roll bar, together with a live axle with trailing arms and anti-roll bar, made for fantastic handling with just a slight hint of understeer. Best of all was the all-aluminium engine twin-overhead cam which used larger valves and a modified intake to increase power. Though it started out as a 98ci (1.6-litre), in 1967 the engine was increased to 120ci (1.7 litre) and this is regarded as the high point in its development; it was such a sweet revver, even if not as powerful as the 120ci (1.9-litre) unit of 1971.

Top speed:	116 mph (185 km/h)
0–60 mph (0–95 km/h):	9.3 sec
Engine type:	In-line four
Displacement:	108 ci (1,779 cc)
Transmission	5-speed manual
Max power:	132 bhp (98 kW) @ 5,500 rpm
Max torque:	137 lb ft (186 Nm) @ 2,900 rpm
Weight:	2,239 lb (1,018 kg)
Economy:	20 mpg (13 km/l)

Alfa Romeo Alfasud

If only the Alfasud had been better built, it could have been an enormous success. Hailed at launch as the finest compact family car in Europe, the Alfa combined characterful flat-four engines with a chassis that wouldn't have been out of place on a sports car. It might have been competing against the likes of the Fiat 124 and Opel Kadett, but the Sud was a driver's dream. Unfortunately, it was terribly put together. It was manufactured in a new factory in Naples, Southern Italy, thanks to a Italian government subsidy to bring employment to the deprived regions of the country. Unfortunately, low-cost labour and cheap bought-in metal meant production standards were shoddy, and most Alfasuds rusted away within the first few years of ownership. Later cars were better, but by then it was too late to save the car's reputation.

Top speed:	106 mph (169 km/h)
0–60 mph (0–95 km/h):	11.8 sec
Engine type:	Flat four
Displacement:	78.4ci (1,286cc)
Transmission:	5-speed manual
Max power:	76 bhp (57 kW) at 6,000 rpm
Max torque:	76 lb-ft (103 Nm) at 3,500 rpm
Weight:	1,848 lb (831 kg)
Economy:	30 mpg (10.7 km/l)

Alfa Romeo GTV6

Styling by Giorgetto Giugiaro made the GTV attractive and with its low front nose, steeply raked windscreen and sharply cut-off fastback, it was ahead of its time in the mid-1970s. Back then it ran a 122ci (2-litre) at best, but all changed in 1981 when the GTV6 joined the line-up. The following year a GTV6 won the first of four consecutive European Touring Car titles before production of the car came to an end in 1986. It was originally based on the 1972 Alfetta, with the wheelbase shortened by just over 4 inches (102mm) to suit the GT. The motor was first used in Alfa's Six saloon in 1979, and it became their defining modular engine of the 1980s. The all-alloy unit ran a single cam-per-bank, with Bosch multi-point fuel injection, and the spread of torque made the GTV6 so satisfying to drive, especially with the V6's high rpm howl. A rear-mounted gearbox kept weight distribution near perfect.

Top speed:	132 mph (211 km/h)
0–60 mph (0–95 km/h):	8.8 sec
Engine type:	V6
Displacement:	152 ci (2,492 cc)
Transmission	5-speed manual
Max power:	154 bhp (115 kW) @ 5,500 rpm
Max torque:	152 lb ft (206 Nm) @ 3,200 rpm
Weight:	2,840 lb (1,291 kg)
Economy:	25 mpg (11 km/l)

Alfa Romeo SZ

The bulldog looks promised much, but the SZ, Alfa's foray into sportscar territory in 1989, was not as quick many expected. However, what it lacked in out-and-out performance, the car more than made up for in handling and grip once out on the road. This it achieved through the rear-mounted transmission which distributed the weight perfectly. Based on the Alfa 75 Saloon, the SZ differed in that it used a composite body bonded to a steel frame, therefore making the chassis very solid, stable and predictable. The all-aluminium V6 ran a single cam-per-bank for 210bhp (175kW), and gave a glorious multi-cylinder howl. Combined with the torsion bar front suspension and de Dion rear end, the on-the-limit cornering ability of the Alfa is how it's best remembered. With less than 1,000 produced, the SZ was a rare sight on the road, but part of the attraction of the car was its exclusivity.

Top speed:	153 mph (245 km/h)
0–60 mph (0–95 km/h):	7.2 sec
Engine type:	V6
Displacement:	180ci (2,959 cc)
Transmission	5-speed manual
Max power:	210 bhp (157 kW) @ 6,200 rpm
Max torque:	181 lb ft (245 Nm) @ 4,500 rpm
Weight:	2,778 lb (1,263 kg)
Economy:	20.8 mpg (7 km/l)

Alfa Romeo Spider

The wedge shape of the Spider can be traced back to the SZ which was launched in 1989, and more still to the Proteo concept car which Alfa showed at the Geneva Motor Show two years later. It was 1994 before the public got to see the actual Spider, but it was worth the wait. With a dramatic wedge waistline running down the car and beautifully sculptured grille flanked by twin headlamps (actually one big lamp behind), the Spider was instantly recognizable as an Italian classic. Even with front-wheel drive, unusual for an Alfa sports car, it used the power well, thanks to MacPherson struts at the front and a multi-link rear, again both new, as the cars previously used double wishbones and a live rear axle. The Twin Spark engine from other Alfa models was used and with balancer shafts plus 16 valves, it gave a smooth power delivery which would buzz eagerly to the 7,000rpm redline.

Top speed:	130 mph (208 km/h)
0–60 mph (0–95 km/h):	8.9 sec
Engine type:	In-line four
Displacement:	120 ci (1,970 cc)
Transmission	5-speed manual
Max power:	150 bhp (112 kW) @ 6,200 rpm
Max torque:	137 lb ft (185 Nm) @ 4,000 rpm
Weight:	3,020 lb (1,373 kg)
Economy:	29.4 mpg (9.5 km/l)

Alfa Romeo 156

A fter years of decline, the 156 marked a turning point for Alfa Romeo's fortunes. For decades, the Italian marque had suffered at the hands of poor product placement, below average reliability and terrible build quality – yet suddenly here was a car that could take on the likes of BMW and Mercedes-Benz, and put up a good fight. Launched in 1998, the 156 was instantly referred to as a modern classic thanks to its beautiful, pure Italian styling. It was a fine drive, too, with exceptional handling and a first-rate line up of Alfa's Twin Spark four-cylinder and silky smooth V6 engines. The 156 took the Car of the Year award in the UK, beating its rival Mercedes A-class. A neat estate model appeared in 1999 to further strengthen the Alfa's cause, and already immaculate examples are being sought out and preserved by Alfa enthusiasts.

Top speed:	141 mph (225 km/h)
0–60 mph (0–95 km/h):	7.3 sec
Engine type:	V6
Displacement:	152ci (2,492cc)
Transmission:	Six-speed manual
Max power:	190 bhp (141.5 kW) at 6,300 rpm
Max torque:	164 lb-ft (223 Nm) at 5,000 rpm
Weight:	2,932 lb (1,319 kg)
Economy:	26 mpg (9.2 km/l)

Allard J2

The J2 was conceived after Sidney Allard made a visit to the USA in the late 1940s and saw how effective a powerful American V8 could be in a lightweight roadster. He chose the Mercury V8 modified by Ardun for 267ci (4.3 litres), though some cars were shipped to America without any engines and ended up with one of two favourites: the Cadillac V8 or 331ci (5.4-litre) Chrysler Hemi. While the J2 was a lightweight, its tubular cross-braced chassis was also flexible, and this didn't help handling. The other downfall was the split front axle which gave positive camber, though the de Dion rear improved things. The car was very quick and a handful on the circuit, with a huge steering wheel, widely spaced pedals and awkward gearshift hampering rapid progress in anything but a straight line. The later J2X, with its extended nose to house much-improved suspension, was a better machine.

Top speed:	110 mph (176 km/h)
0–60 mph (0–95 km/h):	8.0 sec
Engine type:	V8
Displacement:	267ci (4,375 cc)
Transmission	3-speed manual
Max power:	140 bhp (104 kW) @ 4,000 rpm
Max torque:	225 lb ft (305 Nm) @ 2,500 rpm
Weight:	2,072 lb (942 kg)
Economy:	14 mpg (5 km/l)

Alvis TD21

British luxury car maker Alvis turned to Graber of Switzerland to supply bodies for its new luxury GT in 1958 – and the result was a car that looked absolutely stunning. As well as the sleek, elegant two-door coupé, an even prettier drophead variant was introduced. Although designed by Graber, the bodies were built in England, first by Willowbrook in Loughborough and later by Park Ward of London. Series II models, from 1962, had disc brakes on all four wheels and a five-speed manual gearbox, or optional three-speed automatic. The TD21 evolved into the TE21 and TF21 until 1967, when production was stopped by Alvis' parent company Rover, who wanted Alvis to concentrate on building military vehicles instead. Alvis remains an important manufacturer of military vehicles to this day, although it is no longer part of Rover.

Top speed:	106 mph (170 km/h)
0–60 mph (0–95 km/h):	13.5 sec
Engine type:	in-line six
Displacement:	182 ci (2,993 cc)
Transmission:	4-speed manual
Max power:	115 bhp (86 kW) at 4,000 rpm
Max torque:	152 lb ft (206 Nm) at 2,500 rpm
Weight:	3,360 lb (1,512 kg)
Economy:	22 mpg (7.8 km/l)

AM General Hummer

The High Mobility Multi-purpose Wheeled Vehicle, otherwise known as the HMMWV or Humvee for short, started life in 1980 with tests in the Nevada desert after being designed just 11 months earlier. The American Army were so impressed they ordered 55,000 vehicles in 1983, but it wasn't until 1993, after the Gulf War where the Humvee starred, that the car was sold to the general public. It started public life with a gasoline small-block Chevy engine, but this was replaced in 1994 by GM's new 378ci (6.4-litre) turbo diesel V8 which gave out massive torque. The car was designed to be tough for military use, so weight was not an issue, hence there's a massive ladder-style chassis. Independent suspension is used with a lot of travel and huge ground clearance, while four-wheel drive was mandatory with a four-speed auto transmitting to a two-speed transfer case and centre differential.

Top speed:	87 mph (140 km/h)
0–60 mph (0–95 km/h):	17.3 sec
Engine type:	V8 diesel
Displacement:	395 ci (6,472 cc)
Transmission	4-speed auto
Max power:	195 bhp (145 kW) @ 3,400 rpm
Max torque:	430 lb ft (582 Nm) @ 1,700 rpm
Weight:	6,620 lb (3,009 kg)
Economy:	10.7 mpg (4 km/l)

AMC AMX

The 1968 AMX was basically a shortened Javelin, and was the first American two-passenger steel-bodied production sportscar since the 1957 Ford T-bird. AMX stood for 'American Motors Experimental' and it came in base-model form with a 290ci (4.8-litre) V8, though did have a 343ci (5.6-litre) option and monster 390ci (6.6-litre) V8 which turned it into a screamer. When Craig Breedlove took a 390ci AMX to Goodyear's Texas test track in February 1968, he established 106 World Speed Records. AMC even made 50 Breedlove specials with red, white and blue paint jobs to celebrate, but they only came with the 290ci (4.75-litre) engine. Independent front suspension with an anti-roll bar were part of the good handling set-up, along with quick-rack power steering, front disc brakes and a limited-slip differential, so the AMX was as capable through the twists as pounding down the drag strip.

Top speed:	125 mph (200 km/h)
0–60 mph (0–95 km/h):	6.6 sec
Engine type:	V8
Displacement:	390 ci (6,390 cc)
Transmission	3-speed auto
Max power:	315 bhp (235 kW) @ 4,600 rpm
Max torque:	425 lb ft (575 Nm) @ 3,200 rpm
Weight:	3,400 lb (1,545 kg)
Economy:	13 mpg (4 km/l)

AMC Rebel Machine (1970)

AMC were small compared to the big three muscle-car producers in 1970. They'd released the patriotic-coloured SC Rambler in conjunction with Hurst in 1969 which packed 315bhp (235kW) for 14-second quarter-miles, but only 1,512 were made. In 1970 the SC/Rambler replaced it, but again it only lasted for a year and just 2,326 were made. The Rambler was a good muscle car, and AMC stuffed their largest engine into the new mid-sized saloon. It was a strong motor with a forged steel crank and it could spring the car to mid-14-second times on the quarter, through a Borg Warner Muncie gearbox. At the rear a 3.54:1 moderate gear was fitted, but AMC offered up to 5.00:1 acceleration gears and a Twin Grip limited-slip differential for racers. The Rambler had very stiff suspension, and grossly overpowered steering, which didn't help reviews and, hence, sales.

Top speed:	115 mph (184 km/h)
0–60 mph (0–96 km/h):	6.4 sec
Engine type:	V8
Displacement:	390 ci (6,390 cc)
Transmission	4-speed manual
Max power:	340 bhp (254 kW) @ 5,100 rpm
Max torque:	430 lb ft (583 Nm) @ 3,600 rpm
Weight:	3,650 lb (1,659 kg)
Economy:	11 mpg (3.89 km/l)

AMC Javelin AMX (1971)

While the new-for-1971 Javelin wasn't as small nor as sharp looking as its previous incarnation, with the range of V8s available, it could still be made to perform. The new car was bigger than the previous model which meant four seats instead of two, and rode on a 1-inch (25mm) longer wheelbase. The 'Go Package' gave it heavy-duty suspension, power front disc brakes, a cowl induction set-up and 7x15-inch (178x381mm) rims with Goodyear tyres. The AMX was the high-performance version of the Javelin so had the option of either a 360ci (5,899cc) or 401ci (6,571cc) V8, the top model producing 335bhp (250kW) and 360lb ft (487Nm) torque. Javelins came with a 3-speed manual transmission, but a 4-speed was optional and recommended for the bigger engines. A Shift Command automatic option was available, buyers choosing between floor or column shift.

Top speed:	114 mph (182 km/h)
0–60 mph (0–96 km/h):	6.9 sec
Engine type:	V8
Displacement:	360 ci (5,899 cc)
Transmission:	4-speed manual
Max power:	285 bhp (213 kW) @ 5,000 rpm
Max torque:	315 lb ft (427 Nm) @ 3,400 rpm
Weight:	3,244 lb (1,474 kg)
Economy:	10 mpg (3.54 km/l)

Amphicar

It might have been a novelty, but the Amphicar wasn't as daft an idea as it sounds. The brainchild of German inventor Hans Trippel, who had experience of building successful amphibian vehicles during World War II for the German army, the Amphicar was designed to double up as a car and a boat. It came with two engines – a Triumph Herald unit for road use and a Hermes outboard motor for aquatic use, powering twin propellers. But while brilliant in concept, the Amphicar was a disaster in execution. Its design was too compromised in too many ways, and it was neither brilliant on the road nor in water, and thus unappealing to drive. Poor rust proofing didn't help the car's reputation, either. Owners who forgot to dry their Amphicars off after a swim found them rotting away or – even worse – sinking due to water ingress.

Top speed:	65 mph (104 km/h)
0–60 mph (0–95 km/h):	43.0 sec
Engine type:	in-line four
Displacement:	70 ci (1,147 cc)
Transmission:	4-speed manual
Max power:	43 bhp (32 kW) at 4,750 rpm
Max torque:	61 lb ft (85 Nm) at 2,250 rpm
Weight:	2,312 lb (1,040 kg)
Economy:	35 mpg (12 km/l)

Anglia Gasser

As drag-racing grew ever-more popular in the 1950s, racers looked for smaller and lighter cars in which to put big engines. Ford's little 'sit-up-and-beg' car, which began life in 1939 as the Anglia EO4A and went through from 1953 to 1959 as the Popular, proved to be ideal for the big engine swap. Its already basic interior could easily be replaced with aluminium panels to lose weight, while inside the front was deceptively large once the inner wings were cut away. With basic suspension, racers could get their car's weight right down, and modifying a V8 would see the power-to-weight ratio way beyond any supercar. As cars and racing developed, roll cages were added for safety, special drag-racing suspension was installed and the power increased with either superchargers or nitrous oxide. Such cars represent a nod to past racers, giving as much excitement, but more safety.

Top speed:	170 mph (272 km/h)
0–60 mph (0–95 km/h):	2.4 sec
Engine type:	V8
Displacement:	350 ci (5,735 cc)
Transmission	4-speed clutchless manual
Max power:	775 bhp (578 kW) @ 6,200 rpm
Max torque:	680 lb ft (921 Nm) @ 4,000 rpm
Weight:	1,870 lb (850 kg)
Economy:	4 mpg (1.42 km/l)

Aston Martin DB5

Most famous for its role in the James Bond film 'Goldfinger' the DB5 was more than just a movie star. It is widely regard as one of the most beautiful Astons and was an exceptional grand tourer, thanks to its power ride. Underneath was a strong steel platform with steel tubes to support the hand-formed aluminium bodywork. A double wishbone front with coil springs and telescopic dampers was complemented by a live rear axle well located with a Watts linkage and radius arms, again using coils. The all-alloy straight-six engine was first debuted in the DB4, but engineer Tadek Marek reworked it for 244ci (4-litre) displacement in the DB5. With twin overhead camshafts and triple SU carburettors, it was powerful enough, but with triple Webers, its output was raised to 314bhp (234kW) in the Vantage. All after the first 90 cars used a ZF five-speed transmission, and had front/rear disc brakes.

Top speed:	143 mph (229 km/h)
0–60 mph (0–95 km/h):	8.6 sec
Engine type:	In-line six
Displacement:	244 ci (3,995 cc)
Transmission	5-speed manual
Max power:	282 bhp (210 kW) @ 5,550 rpm
Max torque:	280 lb ft (379 Nm) @ 4,500 rpm
Weight:	3,450 lb (1,568 kg)
Economy:	15 mpg (5.3 km/l)

Aston Martin DB6

The 1966 DB6 replaced the DB5 and was a much updated car. Underneath, out went the steel platform construction and in came a modern monocoque design with steel inner panels and floorpan covered with the aluminium body. Though longer by 3.7 inches (94mm) in the wheelbase, which gave a slightly better ride quality, the DB6 used the same suspension layout as the DB5 with double wishbones at the front and a Watts linkage/trailing arm live axle rear. The engine was also the DB5's, but slightly up in power especially in Vantage form which had 325bhp (242kW). While similar in the nose, the DB6 had a distinct cut-off rear which was accentuated by a raised rear lip which doubled as a spoiler. It made the car more aerodynamic, increasing downforce and high speed stability. The interior had Wilton carpet, leather seats, multiple gauges and a wood/aluminium wheel.

Top speed:	150 mph (240 km/h)
0—60 mph (0–95 km/h):	6.7 sec
Engine type:	In-line six
Displacement:	244 ci (3,995 cc)
Transmission	5-speed manual
Max power:	325 bhp (242 kW) @ 5,750 rpm
Max torque:	290 lb ft (393 Nm) @ 4,500 rpm
Weight:	3,417 lb (1,553 kg)
Economy:	10.7 mpg (3.8 km/l)

Aston Martin DBS

Bearing in mind its previous cars had all been curvaceous and nimble, the DBS came as a bit of a shock to Aston Martin's loyal fans. The new car was built to American principles, meaning it was big, bold and brash. Powered by a 4.0-litre (244 cu in) straight six, or latterly a 5.3-litre (326 cu in) V8 engine, it offered phenomenal performance, but was based on the chassis of previous Astons, meaning it felt dated compared to many contemporary performance cars and could prove tricky to handle in the wet. The huge weight didn't help either, giving terrible fuel economy and taking away much of the car's sportiness. As for the styling, you either loved it or loathed it. In profile, it resembled an American muscle car, and those used to their understated, elegant Astons were shocked by the new car's uncompromising appearance.

Top speed:	160 mph (256 km/h)
0–60 mph (0–95 km/h):	5.9 sec
Engine type:	V8
Displacement:	325 ci (5,340 cc)
Transmission:	5-speed manual
Max power:	320 bhp (238 kW) at 5,000 rpm
Max torque:	360 lb ft (488 Nm) at 4,000 rpm
Weight:	3,800 lb (1,710 kg)
Economy:	12 mpg (4.3 km/l)

Aston Martin Lagonda

A ston Martin's chief designer, William Towns, had yet another surprise in store
with the 1976 Lagonda. Reviving a glorious name from the past, the new car
was billed as a technical tour de force. Based on a stretched AM V8 chassis, the car
had a complex digital dashboard and automatic locking. But its most talked about
feature was its distinctive wedge-shaped styling. Never before had a four-door
sedan been built with such striking lines, and there was no way you could mistake
the Lagonda for anything else on the road. Early cars were appalling, <u>with electrical</u>
glitches aplenty and, in some cases, the automatic locking trapping owners either
inside or outside their vehicles. But the Lagonda had its fans, and that ensured a
production run of 14 years, with the last cars being delivered to those who adored
its appearance more than anything in 1990.

Top speed:	144 mph (231 km/h)
0–60 mph (0–95 km/h):	8.8 sec
Engine type:	V8
Displacement:	325 ci (5,340 cc)
Transmission:	3-speed auto
Max power:	325 bhp (242 kW) at 5,600 rpm
Max torque:	375 lb ft (509 Nm) at 4,500 rpm
Weight:	4,630 lb (2,083 kg)
Economy:	14 mpg (5.0 km/l)

Aston Martin Zagato

The first Zagatos were produced in the early 1960s, and a meeting in 1984 between AM chairman Victor Gauntlett and Gianni Zagato led to the idea of recreating that Zagato styling magic on a new Aston to revive the line-up. It was 1986 that production of the Zagato began, with almost $7 million taken in orders based on the sketches alone. Underneath the car used the V8 Vantage floorpan shortened by 16 inches (406mm). It had a double wishbone front and a de Dion rear, which allowed the huge rear vented discs to be moved inboard for quicker suspension movement. The short-stroke all-alloy V8 dated back to 1969 but had been steadily improved, featuring twin overhead chain-driven camshafts, four Weber carbs, Cosworth pistons and a less restrictive intake and exhaust. The Zagato was every bit a supercar with a claimed 180mph (290km/h) top speed, but only 75 were produced.

Top speed:	183 mph (292 km/h)
0–60 mph (0–95 km/h):	4.8 sec
Engine type:	V8
Displacement:	326 ci (5,340 cc)
Transmission	5-speed auto
Max power:	432 bhp (322 kW) @ 6,200 rpm
Max torque:	395 lb ft (534 Nm) @ 5,100 rpm
Weight:	3,630 lb (1,650 kg)
Economy:	12 mpg (4.2 km/l)

Aston Martin Virage

A ston's 1988 Virage was the successor to the DBS which had been introduced in the late1960s. The chassis was modernized using a steel semi-monocoque frame to make it stiffer. However, the suspension configuration was much the same as previous Astons with double wishbones and an alloy de Dion rear with Watts linkage and alloy trailing arms. Massive 13 and 11-inch (330 and 279mm) discs were fitted to cope with the extra pace available from the heavyweight tourer. The engine's head were re-designed by Corvette tuner Reeves Calloway, who put the valves closer together to improve flow and packaging of the huge V8. The modifications gave an extra 32bhp (24kW) through a heavy-shifting ZF five-speed manual. Luxury was evident inside with leather and walnut, and the outer styling won many fans, despite Audi 100 headlights and VW Scirocco tail lamps.

Top speed:	157 mph (251 km/h)
0–60 mph (0–95 km/h):	7.0 sec
Engine type:	V8
Displacement:	326 ci (5,340 cc)
Transmission	5-speed manual
Max power:	330 bhp (360 kW) @ 6,000 rpm
Max torque:	340 lb ft (246 Nm) @ 3,700 rpm
Weight:	3,940 lb (1,791 kg)
Economy:	13.1 mpg (4.6 km/l)

Aston Martin DB7

A takeover of Aston Martin by Ford in 1992, and the subsequent access to plenty of development cash, meant Aston Martin could at long last produce a worthy successor to the famed DB6 model. Underneath, the DB7 was closely related to the XJS of Jaguar, also owned by Ford, though the engine was all new. Developed with the help of famed motorsport company TWR, the 195ci (3.2-litre) all-alloy straight-six produced more than 100bhp (74kW) per litre thanks to four valves per cylinder, sequential fuel injection and an Eaton supercharger. The body broke from Aston Martin tradition in that instead of hand-formed aluminium, it used composite panels, though it featured retro touches such as the vents behind the front wheels. Massive vented discs behind 18-inch (457mm) alloy rims ensured speed was wiped off quickly, while leather and wood were inside as a benchmark of British quality.

Top speed:	157 mph (251 km/h)
0–60 mph (0–95 km/h):	6.0 sec
Engine type:	In-line six
Displacement:	198 ci (3,239 cc)
Transmission:	5-speed manual
Max power:	335 bhp (250 kW) @ 5,750 rpm
Max torque:	400 lb ft (542 Nm) @ 3,000 rpm
Weight:	3,859 lb (1,754 kg)
Economy:	13.8 mpg (4.9 km/l)

Auburn Speedster

Hollywood glitz and glamour was the main *raison d'être* behind the Auburn. Built by the Eckhardt Carriage Company of Auburn, Indiana, the car was specifically designed for the super-rich of America in the inter-war period. The brutal yet handsome machines had 12-cylinder engines and hand-tailored cabins, and for three years was America's most expensive car. Eckhardt suffered badly during the Great Depression as incomes tumbled, but the Auburn car was kept alive by the motoring visionary Erret Cord, who founded his own company famed for making dramatic and distinctive machinery for well-heeled owners. Only 500 Auburns were built in total before the company finally failed in 1937, but it is remembered today as one of the true greats and remains one of the most collectable cars in the world.

Top speed:	108 mph (173 km/h)
0–60 mph (0–95 km/h):	10.0 sec
Engine type:	straight-eight
Displacement:	280 ci (4,589 cc)
Transmission:	3-speed manual
Max power:	50 bhp (111 kW) at 4,000 rpm
Max torque:	n/a
Weight:	3,753 lb (1,688 kg)
Economy:	12.4 mpg (4.42 km/l)

Audi Quattro SWB

Highly regarded as the car of the 1980s, the cutting-edge Quattro turbo brought 4WD to the sportscar market in 1983. In 1981 the car had been homologated for rallying and it took fifth place that year, going on to win Audi its first constructor's rally championship in 1982. The Quattro dominated mid-1980s rally action, especially with this later short wheelbase 306bhp (228kW) 20-valve Sport Quattro. The road-going car was put together using many parts already in the Audi range, such as a 200 turbo front end, the Coupe floorpan and the rear differential from sister company VW. The combination of MacPherson strut suspension all-around plus four-wheel drive made it virtually impossible to unstick a Quattro on the road. The Sport Quattro used Kevlar and glass-fibre panels to reduce weight, while underneath it had Porsche brakes to cope with the extreme performance.

Top speed:	154 mph (246 km/h)
0–60 mph (0–95 km/h):	5.0 sec
Engine type:	In-line five
Displacement:	130 ci (2,133 cc)
Transmission	5-speed manual
Max power:	306 bhp (228 kW) @ 6,700 rpm
Max torque:	258 lb ft (349 Nm) @ 3,700 rpm
Weight:	2,867 lb (1,303 kg)
Economy:	13.1 mpg (4.67 km/l)

Audi V8 Quattro

With its successful 4WD system proven years earlier, Audi applied its technology to the interesting V8 Quattro in 1989. The world-class sports saloon took on the competition from BMW and Mercedes and offered a fantastic package. While the body and chassis' roots could be traced back to the early 1980s, the Quattro four-wheel-drive system with front and rear differentials connected via a viscous coupling was state-of-the-art. Same goes for the engine, Audi's first eight-cylinder engine in a mainstream production car. The technological masterpiece was all-aluminium with four belt-driven overhead camshafts and 32 valves. Originally in 225ci (3.7-litre) form, it went to 256ci (4.2 litres) in later models. Wide BBS cross-spoked alloys distinguished the later Quattro V8 4.2 models available from 1992 to 1994, and these represented good value for money as a sport/luxury saloon built for all seasons.

Top speed:	145 mph (232 km/h)
0–60 mph (0–95 km/h):	6.6 sec
Engine type:	V8
Displacement:	217 ci (3,562 cc)
Transmission	4-speed auto
Max power:	240 bhp (179 kW) @ 5,800 rpm
Max torque:	245 lb ft (331 Nm) @ 4,400 rpm
Weight:	3,898 lb (1,772 kg)
Economy:	16 mpg (5.7 km/l)

Audi S2 Quattro

The S2 was the first of a new breed of Audis, developed to rival the likes of BMW's M-Power and Mercedes-Benz's AMG model ranges. Based on the standard 80 Coupé, the S2 had tuned suspension and a turbocharged 2.2-litre (136 cu in) engine, developing 220 bhp. That was enough to power the Audi from 0–60 mph in less than 60 seconds and give it a top speed of almost 150 mph. S cars were easily identified by their unique colour schemes and chrome-effect door mirrors, which distinguished them from more ordinary models. Initially, the Quattro badging was left off the cars in deference to the UR Quattro, which ceased production in the year the S2 was launched. But it made a comeback in 1992, when Audi expanded the S2 designation to the saloon and Avant versions of the 80. An even wilder model, the RS2, appeared in 1994 and was developed with the help of Porsche.

Top speed:	147 mph (235 km/h)
0–60 mph (0–95 km/h):	5.7 sec
Engine type:	in-line five
Displacement:	135 ci (2,226 cc)
Transmission:	5-speed manual/6-speed auto
Max power:	230 bhp (171 kW) at 5,900 rpm
Max torque:	275 lb ft (373 Nm) at 1,950 rpm
Weight:	3,248 lb (1,461 kg)
Economy:	24 mpg (8.5 km/l)

Audi RS2

M ost remember the RS2 so well that few can recall its predecessor, the 230bhp (172kW) S2 Avant which made the Audi 80 wagon into a very quick yet practical car. However, the RS2 took performance to a whole new level with much involvement from Porsche in its engineering. Starting with an Audi 80 wagon, Porsche tweaked the all strut suspension and added race-spec anti-roll bars and Bilstein shocks. The permanent four-wheel drive system used a central Torsen-type differential to ensure the best grip, and a six-speed close-ratio gearbox was fitted. The brakes were vented discs with four-pot callipers, all from Porsche's 968 model, while the 8x17-inch (203x432mm) rims were straight off a 911. The five-cylinder was Audi, but Porsche added a larger intercooler on the KKK turbo (giving out 16psi boost), larger injectors, a 911 fuel pump, high-lift cams and a low-pressure exhaust.

Top speed:	158 mph (253 km/h)
0–60 mph (0–95 km/h):	4.8 sec
Engine type:	In-line five
Displacement:	136 ci (2,226 cc)
Transmission	6-speed manual
Max power:	315 bhp (235 kW)@ 6,500 rpm
Max torque:	302 lb ft (409 Nm) @ 3,000 rpm
Weight:	3,510 lb (1,595 kg)
Economy:	20 mpg (7.1 km/l)

Audi A4 BTCC

The British Touring Car Championship was the most hotly contested race series of the 1990s, so when Audi decided to compete, they had to be good. They entered in 1996 and instantly made an impression with a pole position and two wins at the opening rounds, then that season dominated with eight wins, twice as many as any other manufacturer. The secret to Audi's success was their 4WD system which offered immense traction and cornering speed, even with a 275lb (125kg) weight penalty over other cars with 2WD only. The car used an ultra stiff multi-point roll cage with double wishbones and struts, plus 13-inch (330mm) disc brakes with alloy callipers that gave immensely powerful yet lightweight brakes. The all-alloy engine displaced 122ci (1.9 litres) and used four valves per cylinder. Wheels were 8.2x19-inch (208x483mm) OZ forged alloys with slick Dunlops.

Top speed:	152 mph (243 km/h)
0–60 mph (0–95 km/h):	4.9 sec
Engine type:	In-line four
Displacement:	122ci (1,998 cc)
Transmission	6-speed sequential
Max power:	296 bhp (221 kW) @ 8,250 rpm
Max torque:	189 lb ft (225 Nm) @ 7,000rpm
Weight:	2,292 lb (1,042kg)
Economy:	5 mpg (1.78 km/l)

Audi A8 Quattro

Audi stunned crowds at the 1993 Geneva Motor Show with its A8 concept car, which showed just how far vehicle structure had developed over the past three decades. Much of the prototype's hull was made from stress-moulded aluminium, giving it a rigidity that no steel car could muster, the ability to resist corrosion and the added benefit of extremely light weight. Nobody believed it could be a production reality, but Audi shocked the motoring world even further when the car went into production the following year as the A8. It was offered with a choice of two- or four-wheel drive transmissions and either V6 or V8 engines, both of which gave it the ability to reach 130mph (208km/h) plus. The A8 was one of the first cars to install airbags for the rear seat passengers, although if a passenger is not present the car will not deploy the relevant airbag.

Top speed:	130 mph (208 km/h)
0–60 mph (0–95 km/h):	6.9 sec
Engine type:	V8
Displacement:	254ci (4,172cc)
Transmission:	6-speed auto
Max power:	300 bhp (223 kW) at 6,000 rpm
Max torque:	295 lb ft (400 Nm) at 3,300 rpm
Weight:	3,902 lb (1,755 kg)
Economy:	21.2 mpg (7.6 km/l)

Audi S4

As Audi's 4WD cars developed, it became apparent they were shooting at a more performance-orientated market. The S4 was one of the most recent cars to harness all-wheel power and it was also one of their most powerful yet stress-free drives. It was basically an A4 sedan, but with the transverse engine removed and a longitudinal V6 mounted in its place. Audi concentrated on making low down power with the new motor, so gave it a small turbo per bank and thus made lag non-existent. It had over 250lb ft (338Nm) from 1,850 through to 3,600 where most street driving is done. Power was put down through a Torsen centre differential and rear limited-slip differential. Double wishbones and fully independent suspension ensured the best cornering on the six-spoke 7.5x17 (203x431mm) alloys with 45-series tyres, while 10 - and 12-inch (254 and 305mm) vented and ABS-assisted discs stopped it very rapidly.

Top speed:	143 mph (230 km/h)
0—60 mph (0–95 km/h):	5.9 sec
Engine type:	V6
Displacement:	163 ci (2,671 cc)
Transmission	6-speed manual
Max power:	250 bhp (186 kW) @ 5,800 rpm
Max torque:	258 lb ft (349 Nm) @ 1,850 rpm
Weight:	3,593 lb (1,633 kg)
Economy:	22 mpg (7.8 km/l)

Audi TT

Fitting a shortened Golf floorpan underneath their sportscar, Audi created a masterpiece in design with the TT. From the sharp-edged looks through to the heavily stitched leather interior, the car was instantly recognizable as Audi in design. The exterior harked back to the pre-WW2 Auto Union racers, while huge 17-inch (432mm) diameter rims pushed to each corner gave the car an almost futuristic feel. The base engine in the TT was the 110ci (1.8-litre) turbo unit as used in the VW and Audi range, though top was the Quattro with five-valves per cylinder, a KKK K04 turbocharger, new intake manifolds plus a six-speed gearbox to make the most of the 225bhp (168kW). MacPherson struts and a double wishbone rear on the Quattro made for fantastic handling with tremendous grip. However, even the base model offered good road-holding and performance from the punchy turbo motor.

Top speed:	130 mph (208 km/h)
0–60 mph (0–95 km/h):	7.4 sec
Engine type:	In-line four
Displacement:	109 ci (1,781 cc)
Transmission	5-speed manual
Max power:	180 bhp (134 kW) @ 5,500 rpm
Max torque:	173 lb ft (234 Nm) @ 1,950 rpm
Weight:	2,910 lb (1,323 kg)
Economy:	31 mpg (11.07 km/l)

Austin 7

If the Ford Model T transformed motoring in the USA, then the Austin Seven did the same for Great Britain. Built for 17 years, the baby Austin was the ideal choice for family motorists on a tight budget. Power came from a tiny sidevalve engine of just 696cc (42 cu in), but was later enlarged to 747cc (46 cu in). The formula was a success, and by 1929 the Seven enjoyed enormous success, accounting for 37 per cent of new car sales in Britain. It was also built under license in Germany as the Rosengart and BMW Dixi, as well as in America as the American Austin. Although it wasn't intended to ever be a sporting car, the Seven enjoyed enormous track success as many owners chopped the original bodywork to create lightweight specials. Even today, the 750 motor club – named after the car's engine size – races Seven-based specials on a regular basis at meetings throughout the UK.

Top speed:	48 mph (77 km/h)
0–60 mph (0–95 km/h):	n/a
Engine type:	in-line four
Displacement:	45 ci (747 cc)
Transmission:	3-speed manual
Max power:	4 bhp (18 kW)
Max torque:	n/a
Weight:	n/a
Economy:	1 mpg (1.46 km/l)

Austin Atlantic

With post-war Britain having to 'Export or die', attention turned away from the indigenous market and towards more profitable sales arenas in order to generate much-needed cash for the British economy. The A90 Atlantic was Austin's attempt to exploit the booming and profitable American market, and the Stateside influences were evident in it styling. Its designer, Dick Burzi, tried his best to emulate the glitzy appearance of contemporary US models, including three headlamps at the front, ornate chrome strips on the bonnet and front wings, wheel spats and gold-faced dashboard gauges. The A90, however, wasn't a sales success. The awkward handling, heavy steering and leisurely performance didn't appeal to US buyers and the car was withdrawn in 1952, after less than 8,000 examples had been built over a four-year life cycle.

Top speed:	86 mph (138 km/h)
0–60 mph (0–95 km/h):	17.6 sec
Engine type:	in-line four
Displacement:	162 ci (2,660 cc)
Transmission:	3-speed auto
Max power:	88 bhp (66 kW) at 4,000 rpm
Max torque:	140 lb ft (190 Nm) at 2,500 rpm
Weight:	3,056 lb (1,375 kg)
Economy:	19 mpg (6.8 km/l)

Austin Mini (modified)

In the UK the Mini has been the most popular car to modify for the past 40 years. Its combination of cute looks, great handling and pure simplicity has put it in the top five of British people's most loved car, and its long production run from 1959 to 2000 proves this. During its time, many modified versions have come from the factory but it's the home tuners who have pushed the little car's limits the most. Because of this, a huge aftermarket has grown around the car. This roadster version is perhaps one of the most extreme both in looks and performance. Its roof has been cut off and the body reduced by 3 inches (76mm) in height, as well as being made into a two-seater. The car features a highly tuned engine which, due to the light weight of the car, can get it down the quarter-mile faster than most American muscle car models.

Top speed:	136 mph (218 km/h)
0–60 mph (0–95 km/h):	5.4 sec
Engine type:	In-line four
Displacement:	85 ci (1,400 cc)
Transmission	4-speed manual
Max power:	125 bhp (93 kW) @ 6,500 rpm
Max torque:	95 lb ft (128 Nm) @ 4,000 rpm
Weight:	1,300 lb (591 kg)
Economy:	18 mpg (6.4 km/l)

Austin Healey 3000

The Donald Healey Motor Company debuted its stunning little sportscar, the 100, at the 1952 Earls Court Motor Show. Using the four-cylinder 159ci (2.6-litre) Austin Atlantic engine, the roadster was competition to Triumph's TR2. Four years later the 100 turned into the 100-Six using Austin's six-cylinder 159ci (2.6-litre) engine. The Austin Healey 3000 MkI came in 1959 with an output of 124bhp (92.5kW). While looking like a sports roadster, Pat Moss proved what a worthy rally car the Healey was too by winning the Liege-Rome-Liege Rally. A re-styled MkII followed for 1961 with a curved screen, wind-up side windows and vertical grille slats. The final MkIII version (1964–1969) was the best, with 150bhp (112kW) and servo brakes. All the Healeys used a ladder-frame cross-braced chassis with wishbone and hard leaf spring suspension. They were a handful, with understeer which could very quickly switch to oversteer.

Top speed:	121 mph (193 km/h)
0–60 mph (0–95 km/h):	10.1 sec
Engine type:	In-line six
Displacement:	178 ci (2,912 cc)
Transmission	4-speed manual with overdrive
Max power:	148 bhp (110 kW) @ 5,250 rpm
Max torque:	165 lb ft (223 Nm) @ 3,500 rpm
Weight:	2,549 lb (1,159 kg)
Economy:	16.8 mpg (6 km/l)

Bentley Continental R

The handsome 1952 Continental R's fastback styling stopped show-goers in their tracks at the London Motor Show that same year. Such was the cost at the time, however, being many times the average annual wage, it was out of reach to all but the super rich, and in three years of production just 207 were made. The Continental shared its underpinnings with the MkVI Bentley saloon. Independent wishbones suspension at the front and leaf springs out back made a ride that was leisurely, though the car could turn on the pace when required and was remarkably quiet with it, even over the 100mph (160km/h) mark. A 280ci (4.6-litre) straight-six with intake valves mounted overhead and exhaust valves to the side was described by Bentley as 'adequate' and that it was, within a swift but silent grace. Inside was typically gentleman's club, awash with hide and walnut, and extreme luxury.

Top speed:	117 mph (187 km/h)
0–60 mph (0–95 km/h):	13.5 sec
Engine type:	In-line six
Displacement:	278 ci (4,566 cc)
Transmission	4-speed manual
Max power:	N/A
Max torque:	N/A
Weight:	3,543 lb (1,610 kg)
Economy:	16 mpg (5.7 km/l)

Bentley Corniche

Although a convertible version of the Bentley T1 was available from 1967, it wasn't until 1971 that the model became recognised in its own right – as the Bentley Corniche. The model was almost identical to its sister car, the Rolls-Royce Corniche, but was tailored more to suit traditional Bentley buyers. That meant it had to be more sporty and less ostentatious than the Rolls-Royce offering, with firmer springing and a different steering ratio. Cruise control and ventilated disc brakes appeared in 1972, while those built from 1977 onwards came with thicker impact absorbent bumpers and a rubber front spoiler. But some Bentley buyers felt short-changed by the Corniche, preferring their cars to be bespoke as opposed to badge-engineered Rolls-Royces. Only 149 Bentley Corniches were built over a 13-year period, including a handful of two-door saloon models.

Top speed:	122 mph (195 km/h)
0–60 mph (0–95 km/h):	9.6 sec
Engine type:	V8
Displacement:	411 ci (6,750 cc)
Transmission:	4-speed auto
Max power:	Not quoted
Max torque:	Not quoted
Weight:	4,815 lb (2,166 kg)
Economy:	15 mpg (5.35 km/l)

Bentley Turbo R/T

Bentley's history is associated with luxury and grace, but another attribute that could be added is high performance. Up until 1982 the company had been more concerned with producing the best car money could buy, but then it turbocharged the Mulsanne. The car was a phenomenal performer for such a heavyweight, and the R/T continued that tradition. To make such a big, luxurious and heavy car go so fast, a lot of power was needed, and thanks to a V8, albeit a basic one with a single in-block cam and two overhead valves per cylinder, displacing close to 427ci (7 litres) and breathed on by a Garret turbo, the R/T goes at the pace you'd expect of a low-slung supercar. Stiff suspension and electronically controlled shocks kept the ride smooth, though the handling was exceptional too. Big 18-inch (457mm) rims went against tradition, but run 265/45 ZR-rated tyres in the R/T's sporting theme.

Top speed:	152 mph (243 km/h)
0–60 mph (0–95 km/h):	6.7 sec
Engine type:	V8
Displacement:	412 ci (6,750 cc)
Transmission	4-speed auto
Max power:	400 bhp (298 kW) @ 4,000 rpm
Max torque:	490 lb ft (663 Nm) @ 2,000 rpm
Weight:	5,450 lb (2,477 kg)
Economy:	12.4 mpg (4.4 km/l)

Bentley Azure

Using the Continental R as a base, Bentley collaborated with the Italian stylist Pininfarina to come up with the luxurious 1995 two-door convertible Azure. Pininfarina also helped design the folding roof which stowed away neatly behind the rear seats. The car used a strengthened version of the Continental R's monocoque chassis, and to keep their new ideal of 'spirited driving' alive, Bentley put adaptive shock absorbers at each corner and self-levelling suspension at the rear. Braking was handled by 13.4-inch (340mm) discs brakes which were assisted by Bosch ABS. The engine was all about torque, being a turbocharged version of the long-running Cosworth tuned Rolls Royce V8, the Garret turbo running an intercooler too. This remains one of the torquiest production engines ever. It was also one of the biggest four seaters you could buy, being 17.5ft (5.3m) long.

Top speed:	150 mph (240 km/h)
0–60 mph (0–95 km/h):	6.3 sec
Engine type:	V8
Displacement:	412 ci (6,750 cc)
Transmission	4-speed auto
Max power:	385 bhp (287 kW) @ 4,000 rpm
Max torque:	553 lb ft (748 Nm) @ 2,000 rpm
Weight:	5,754 lb (2,615 kg)
Economy:	16 mpg (5.7 km/l)

BMW 2002 Turbo

It was in 1969 that BMW won the European Touring Car Championship with their turbocharged 2002, and it was from that car they developed a street-going version with the 2002 Turbo. The flared arches and racing stripes made it very obviously a circuit-inspired street car, and this was one of few cars at the time to use fuel injection. The street manners weren't so good and tractability wasn't the car's strong point, with the large turbo giving little power until the engine hit 3,800rpm, though by then it summoned an extra 46lb ft (63Nm) of torque (one-third more power) for an incredible hit in the back. This put the car into sub-8-sec territory for the 0–60mph dash, almost unheard of then from anything but a top sportscar. Suspension – MacPherson struts up front and a semi-trailing arm rear with anti-roll bars both ends – kept the car planted on the street, as did the wide alloy wheels.

Top speed:	130 mph (208 km/h)
0–60 mph (0–95 km/h):	7.6 sec
Engine type:	In-line four
Displacement:	121 ci (1,990 cc)
Transmission	5-speed manual
Max power:	170 bhp (126 kW) @ 5,800 rpm
Max torque:	177 lb ft (240 Nm) @ 4,500 rpm
Weight:	2,381 lb (1,082 kg)
Economy:	18.1 mpg (6.4 km/l)

BMW 3.0 CSL

The 1971 CSL was the ultimate derivative of the handsome CSi coupe, made for the European Touring Car Championship. Just 1,000 street versions were needed for homologation and they made them lightweight. An alloy hood, trunk lid and door skins saved weight, while inside fixed bucket seats were fitted along with a sport wheel. The independent suspension was as per the CSi, with MacPherson front struts and a trailing arm rear plus anti-roll bars both ends. The straight-six engine used a single overhead cam and Bosch fuel injection to get 200bhp (268kW), though later racer versions with twin cams and 24 valves had 370bhp (276kW). The aerodynamics were where this car scored best with a huge trunk spoiler to give downforce. The front air dam limited air flow under the car, rubber fins over the hood. Wide 7x14-inch (178x356mm) alloys and 195 tyres gave great roadholding.

Top speed:	133 mph (212 km/h)
0–60 mph (0–95 km/h):	7.6 sec
Engine type:	in-line six
Displacement:	183 ci (3,003 cc)
Transmission	4-speed manual
Max power:	200 bhp (149 kW) @ 5,500 rpm
Max torque:	199 lb ft (269 Nm) @ 4,300 rpm
Weight:	2,889 lb (1,313 kg)
Economy:	16.8 mpg (6 km/l)

BMW M1

Started in 1972 with the intention of making a Group 4 endurance racing car, the M1 stumbled off the blocks with a re-design just months after the original concept drawings. Giorgetto Giugiaro came up with the M1's production look and it was launched in 1978. Unfortunately, due to the steel chassis and sheet steel reinforcement, even with a glass-fibre body the car was too heavy for competition. On the street the mid-mounted engine was mildly tuned to 277bhp (207kW), being the straight-six from the 1960s models, which had proved immensely strong. In race tune up to 700bhp (522kW) was possible in turbo form for Group 5 racing. Race suspension on the M1 consisted of adjustable double wishbones all around, and though the clutch and brake pedals were hard, the steering feel and response was typically BMW, and so very good, while the ride quality was firm.

Top speed:	162 mph (260 km/h)
0–60 mph (0--95 km/h):	5.7 sec
Engine type:	In-line six
Displacement:	211 ci (3,453 cc)
Transmission	5-speed manual
Max power:	277 bhp (207 kW) @ 6,500 rpm
Max torque:	239 lb ft (323 Nm) @ 5,000 rpm
Weight:	3,122 lb (1,419 kg)
Economy:	12.9 mpg (4.6 km/l)

BMW M6

BMW's top 6-series model, the 635CSi, was a looker and performer when it was launched in 1983. Using that car as a basis, BMW's Motorsport division revamped it and produced the M6, also known as the M635CSi throughout Europe. Underneath the suspension was re-calibrated with Bilstein gas shocks, stiffer springs and anti-roll bars. A lower ride-height increased stability in corners and a re-located battery (to the trunk) helped weight distribution. The 24-valve engine, taken from the defunct M1 supercar, used a light-alloy head with central spark plugs for maximum combustion power. MacPherson struts and a multi-link rear kept the handling predictable, while a close-ratio transmission kept the engine in the power band. Bringing the most powerful BMW of the 1980s down in speed was the job of 11-inch (280mm) discs. Inside the car had air-con, on-board computer and leather.

Top speed:	158 mph (253 km/h)
0–60 mph (0–95 km/h):	6.0 sec
Engine type:	In-line six
Displacement:	210 ci (3,453 cc)
Transmission	5-speed manual
Max power:	286 bhp (213 kW) @ 6,500 rpm
Max torque:	251 lb ft (340 Nm) @ 4,500 rpm
Weight:	3,329 lb (1,513 kg)
Economy:	18 mpg (6.4 km/l)

BMW M5 (1985)

Though an M535i was launched in 1980 with the same body style, it had very little Motorsport division technical input. That version had only a single cam, but for the 1985 M5, the engine from the M1 supercar was used, albeit without dry sump lubrication. It had a high compression ratio, cross-flow aluminium cylinder head with larger inlet and exhaust ports, twin overhead camshafts, Bosch fuel injection, an oil cooler and low restriction dual exhaust. It was too much for the standard 5-speed, so BMW had Getrag produce a special close-ratio version with dog-leg first gear. The suspension used a patented Track Link system at rear, but was conventional MacPherson strut up front with shorter springs and uprated shocks all around. Massive four-wheel vented discs with ABS meant excellent stopping power. Inside the driving position was perfect and there were power seats plus air-con.

Top speed:	147 mph (235 km/h)
0–60 mph (0–95 km/h):	6.0 sec
Engine type:	In-line six
Displacement:	210 ci (3,453 cc)
Transmission	5-speed manual
Max power:	256 bhp (191 kW) @ 6,500 rpm
Max torque:	243 lb ft (329 Nm) @ 4,500 rpm
Weight:	3,420 lb (1,554 kg)
Economy:	20 mpg (7.1 km/l)

BMW M3 1987

To homologate their car for Group A racing, BMW were required to build 5,000 road-going versions of their M3. The car appeared with a 192bhp (143kW) four-cylinder and was a success. The independent suspension layout is the same as the regular 3 Series, with MacPherson struts and a semi-trailing arm rear design, but the springs, shocks and bushes were uprated, along with the anti-roll bars, while up front the castor was increased to improve high-speed stability. The vented disc brakes were also increased in size and finally a limited slip differential was added. The engine had a forged steel crank, all-new alloy head with four valves per cylinder, and with short stroke/ large bore design, it could rev beyond 7,000 rpm. Side blister helped cover the wider wheels, but what isn't so obvious is the re-angled rear screen and fatter pillars, which gave a stiffer bodyshell.

Top speed:	141 mph (225 km/h)
0–60 mph (0–95 km/h):	6.9 sec
Engine type:	In-line four
Displacement:	140 ci (2,302 cc(
Transmission	5-speed manual
Max power:	192 bhp (143 kW) @ 6,750 rpm
Max torque:	170 lb ft (230 Nm) @ 4,750 rpm
Weight:	2,857 lb (1,299 kg)
Economy:	22 mpg (7.8 km/l)

BMW Alpina B10

In 1988 BMW launched their all-new 5 Series and soon after that Alpina, a German tuning firm specializing in BMWs, set about a 535i model. Starting with the suspension, they lowered it by half an inch then added Bilstein shocks and stronger anti-roll bars. To further improve the handling, Alpina 8x17-inch (203x432mm) 20-spoke alloys were fitted, which made the car stand out as the 535i came with 15-inch (381mm) wheels. Body styling was kept to a minimum, with a deep front spoiler and subtle trunk spoiler plus Alpina badges. The drive train was modified by taking the engine up in compression and giving it a hotter camshaft and hand-ported cylinder head. A twin turbocharged Bi-Turbo version was available which made 360bhp (268kW). To further improve acceleration, the rear end gears were changed, bringing the top end speed down, but it was still a very capable high-speed tourer.

Top speed:	157 mph (251 km/h)
0–60 mph (0–95 km/h):	7.0 sec
Engine type:	In-line six
Displacement:	209 ci (3,430 cc)
Transmission:	5-speed manual
Max power:	254 bhp (189 kW) @ 6,000 rpm
Max torque:	240 lb ft (325 Nm) @ 4,000 rpm
Weight:	3,395 lb (1,543 kg)
Economy:	21 mpg (7.5 km/l)

BMW 850i

As a grander replacement for the 6-series coupe, the 1989 850i ended up bigger, heavier and more powerful. BMW designed the car to be easy to drive and virtually foolproof. It had both Automatic Stability Control and Traction Control to keep the car on the street in all situations. The former controlled the rear suspension as it incorporated a passive rear-steer system which eliminated any oversteer. The new engine for the flagship model was the same basic unit used in McLaren's F1, albeit a little de-tuned with just under half the output at 300bhp (223kW). In the 850 it was designed to be understressed, smooth and quiet. The swoopy coupe body used pillarless construction but to make up for the loss in strength, it featured longitudinal roll-over bars built into the roof. The underbody was smoothed also, helping produce the excellent 0.29 drag coefficient.

Top speed:	160 mph (256 km/h)
0–60 mph (0–95 km/h):	7.4 sec
Engine type:	V12
Displacement:	304 ci (4,988 cc)
Transmission	Six-speed manual
Max power:	300 bhp (224 kW) @ 5,200 rpm
Max torque:	335 lb ft (456 Nm) @ 4,100 rpm
Weight:	4,149 lb (1,886 kg)
Economy:	20 mpg (7.1 km/l)

BMW M3

Originally launched in 1988 as a homologation special bred for the track, the M3 developed in the 1990s with the 1993 E36 3-series. The combination of refinement, handling, plus awesome power made it immensely sellable. A MacPherson strut front and multi-link rear suspension did most of the work, but wide 17-inch (432mm) alloys and ultra-low profile tyres sharpened the car's steering without compromising ride quality. The powerplant was very high-tech, featuring twin overhead camshafts and BMW's VANOS variable valve timing to improve low-end torque whilst allowing 7,500rpm, even though the torque peak was much lower. Helping make the most of the power was a six-speed manual gearbox and traction control, but even with the latter switched off, the car remained very controllable in a slide. Few sports coupes have offered such performance and practicality.

Top speed:	140 mph (224 km/h)
0-60 mph (0-95 km/h):	5.6 sec
Engine type:	In-line six
Displacement:	195 ci (3,201 cc)
Transmission	6-speed manual
Max power:	321 bhp (239 kW) @ 7,400 rpm
Max torque:	258 lb ft (349 Nm) @ 3,250 rpm
Weight:	3,352 lb (1,523 kg)
Economy:	19.6 mpg (7 km/l)

BMW M5

With the launch of the second-generation 5-Series, BMW created a much better car with a more rigid bodyshell and excellent MacPherson strut/semi trailing arm front and rear suspension. It was a great basis on which to model the new M5 too, as all the M division had to do was lower and uprate the springs and shocks, plus fit thicker anti-roll bars, for a brilliant handling machine. Larger 8x17-inch (203x432mm) wheels at each corner allowed the fitting of 12-inch (305mm) brakes all around, which gave near-perfect brakes for the heavyweight sedan. The engine was another derived from BMW's M1 supercar, with a new forged crankshaft but the same twin-cam 24v alloy head which allowed it to rev past 7,000rpm. Post-1992 cars had 232ci (3.8 litres) and 340bhp (254kW), plus a six-speed transmission, larger brakes and 18-inch (257mm) wheels, formidable road cars, yet relaxing if required.

Top speed:	155 mph (248 km/h)
0–60 mph (0–95 km/h):	6.5 sec
Engine type:	In-line six
Displacement:	216 ci (3,535 cc)
Transmission	5-speed manual
Max power:	310 bhp (231 kW) @ 6,900 rpm
Max torque:	266 lb ft (360 Nm) @ 4,750 rpm
Weight:	3,804 lb (1,729 kg)
Economy:	16 mpg (5.7 km/l)

BMW Z3

While the Z1 roadster concept had had 8,000 cars built in 1986, it was only ever really a testbed for BMW's Z-axle arrangement. It did show, however, that people were keen for the Munich-based company to produce a roadster for the masses. Competition from the likes of Mazda and Toyota with their roadsters also meant the time was right for the 1996 Z3. Using the usual BMW layout of a front-engined, rear-drive layout, the long and sloping Z3 hood hid a 116ci (1.8-litre) engine. The car cleverly used parts from other BMWs including the front suspension from the 3-series sedan and the rear semi-trailing arm set-up from the 3-Series Compact, though both were modified for a wider track. The 24-valve engine had adjustable intake runners to promote torque at low rpm and extra bhp higher up. It also was designed to minimize friction and gave the roadster good fuel economy.

Top speed:	116 mph (185 km/h)
0–60 mph (0–95 km/h):	8.2 sec
Engine type:	In-line four
Displacement:	116 ci (1,895 cc)
Transmission	5-speed manual
Max power:	138 bhp (103 kW) @ 6,000 rpm
Max torque:	133 lb ft (180 Nm) @ 4,300 rpm
Weight:	2,732 lb (1,242 kg)
Economy:	29.4 mpg (10.5 km/l)

BMW M Coupe

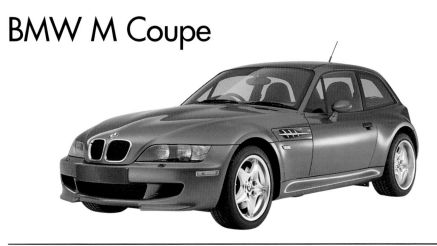

Adding a roof to an already successful Z3 roadster seemed logical, yet the almost estate-like M Coupe didn't win over everyone straight away. The proportions took some getting used to, though this was better in 'M' guise. The roof also added rigidity to the structure, making it some 2.5 times stiffer torsionally than the roadster. The effect was to sharpen up the car's responses dramatically. Understeer was built in, but with so much power it could be corrected quickly with the traction control off. The engine used twin overhead camshafts and BMW's VANOS variable valve system, and could make 321bhp (239kW) in Europe. Huge 12.4-inch (315mm) vented discs were fitted all around and inspired much confidence, as did the anti-roll bars front and rear which keep the body virtually horizontal. Inside the car was typically 'M', with figure-hugging seats, and sports wheel in leather and Alcantara.

Top speed:	139 mph (222 km/h)
0–60 mph (0–95 km/h):	5.1 sec
Engine type:	In-line six
Displacement:	192 ci (3,152 cc)
Transmission	5-speed manual
Max power:	240 bhp (179 kW) @ 6,000 rpm
Max torque:	236 lb ft (320 Nm) @ 3,800 rpm
Weight:	3,131 lb (1,423 kg)
Economy:	21 mpg (7.5 km/l)

BMW M Roadster

When BMW launched the Z3 in 1995, it came with a 140bhp (104kW) four-cylinder engine. People complained that a more powerful version wasn't available, and BMW answered their calls the following year by launching the 171ci (2.8-litre) straight-six model, then hinted at what could be with a concept M Roadster at the Geneva Motor Show, Switzerland. A year later with strong demand, the M Roadster was in production with the M3's straight-six under the hood. The BMW theory of keeping the driving and steering wheels separate continued with this model which had M3 front suspension, rear suspension from the previous 3 Series BMW and uprated springs and shocks. The double VANOS system varied both intake and exhaust timing, for greater flexibility. The car was limited to 240bhp (179kW) in the USA but the same as the M3, 321bhp (239kW), in European versions.

Top speed:	137 mph (220 km/h)
0–60 mph (0–95 km/h):	5.2 sec
Engine type:	In-line six
Displacement:	192 ci (3,152 cc)
Transmission	5-speed manual
Max power:	240 bhp (179 kW) @ 6,000 rpm
Max torque:	236 lb ft (320 Nm) @ 3,800 rpm
Weight:	3,084 lb (1,402 kg)
Economy:	27 mpg (9.6 km/l)

Borgward Isabella

Widely regarded as one of the most elegant cars ever produced, the Borgward Isabella was incredibly advanced for the 1950s. Based on the earlier Hansa model, it was offered as a saloon, estate or delivery van. In 1955, the stunning coupé model appeared, with gorgeous curves and glamorous chrome adornments. Borgwards were incredibly well-built and survival rates are good, with thriving owners clubs across the world. It had incredible noise insulation for its time, and while the engine lacked power, the car had a sporting feel thanks to excellent steering and predictable handling. The unusual 'Isabella' name came about when company boss Carl Borgward covered the badges of a prototype to disguise it from any prying eyes, using decals bearing the name of his wife! Production finished in 1962 after over 200,000 examples had been built.

Top speed:	93 mph (149 km/h)
0–60 mph (0–95 km/h):	16.0 sec
Engine type:	in-line four
Displacement:	91 ci (1,493 cc)
Transmission:	4-speed manual
Max power:	82 bhp (61 kW) at 5,200 rpm
Max torque:	84 lb ft (113 Nm) at 3,000 rpm
Weight:	2,320 lb (1,044 kg)
Economy:	33 mpg (11.8 km/l)

Boyd Smoothster (1995)

Boyd Coddington's name became synonymous with high-tech, high-buck hot rodding during the 1980s and this continued into the 1990s while his projects grew increasingly wild. His aim was to build hot rods which used classic looks but with a modern twist, and the majority of the machines his company made went out to win trophies and garner the Coddington name more recognition. The Smoothster was designed to win the prestigious 'America's Most Beautiful Roadster' award and did so in 1995. It featured hand-made sheet aluminium bodywork over a custom steel frame with one-off billet aluminium A-arms at either end for fully independent suspension. The Corvette engine is untouched except for a rework of its looks but is powerful in stock trim. The 17-inch (432mm) and 18-inch (457mm) wheels' six-spoke pattern is replicated in the twin tailpipes. The roof is a removable Carson-style top.

Top speed:	122 mph (195 km/h)
0–60 mph (0–96 km/h):	6.0 sec
Engine type:	V8
Displacement:	350 ci (5,735 cc)
Transmission	4-speed auto
Max power:	300 bhp (224 kW) @ 5,000 rpm
Max torque:	330 lb ft (447 Nm) @ 2,400 rpm
Weight:	N/A
Economy:	17 mpg (6.02 km/l)

Bugatti Royale

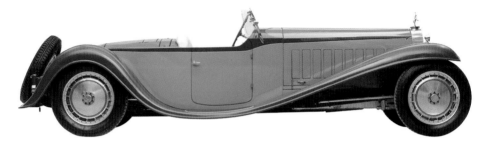

When it appeared in 1931, the Bugatti Royale was touted as the world's best car. It was also the world's biggest and most expensive offering, measuring 235in (6m) in length and powered by a massive 12,763cc (779ci) Straight Eight engine. The car was one of motoring's most spectacular failures. Designed for royalty, it proved to be so expensive that not even the stupidly rich could afford to own one, while the cable-operated brakes, incredibly vague steering, massive bulk and awkward gear linkage meant it was incredibly unpleasant to drive. Only six were built over two years, and although regarded as something of a lame duck in automotive terms, its rarity means it is highly collectable, with one example famously selling for $10 million at auction, making it once again the most expensive car in the world...

Top speed:	117 mph (187 km/h)
0–60 mph (0–95 km/h):	n/a
Engine type:	in-line eight
Displacement:	779ci (12,763cc)
Transmission:	3-speed manual
Max power:	275 bhp (204 kW) at 3,000 rpm
Max torque:	n/a
Weight:	6,999 lb (3,149 kg)
Economy:	10 mpg (3.6 km/l)

Bugatti EB110

When the global economy boomed in the late 1980s, there was a supercar revolution. Every wealthy businessman, celebrity and sports star, it seemed, hankered after a 200mph machine that would deliver awesome acceleration and tenacious grip. The attempt to revive the Bugatti name, albeit in Italy rather than the marque's native France, was a brave and ultimately foolish move, for while the EB110 was awe-inspiring, dramatically styled and equipped with a fantastic quad-turbo V12 engine, it was so long in gestation that the first deliveries weren't made until 1992. That was enough time for the global recession to hit hard, and the firm's once-packed order book was suddenly full of cancellations. An SS model, stripped down for racing, was also built. Only a handful of the 212mph (340km/h) machines were built before the project dried up in 1995 when Bugatti went bankrupt.

Top speed:	212 mph (340 km/h)
0–60 mph (0–95 km/h):	4.5 sec
Engine type:	V12
Displacement:	214ci (3,500cc)
Transmission:	6-speed manual
Max power:	553 bhp (411 kW) at 8,000 rpm
Max torque:	451 lb ft (734 Nm) at 3,750 rpm
Weight:	3,453 lb (1,554 kg)
Economy:	13 mpg (4.7 km/l)

Buick Roadmaster (1949)

Buick started to make cars again as soon as World War II was over in 1945. Their cars changed a little in style, going long and wider in looks thanks to subtle grille changes and new trim. The Roadmaster model first appeared in 1945 and was restyled for 1949 with the front fender tops extending all the way to the top of the rear fenders, thus finally ditching the sloping fender look which dated cars back to the 1930s. The looks were a big success with the public and Buick sales increased by 100,000. The Roadmaster kept a similar suspension set-up to the pre-war cars, with a separate chassis, double wishbone independent front suspension and a live axle rear on leaf springs. The big advance was Buick's Dynaflow auto gearbox, which was the first to use a torque converter. This sophisticated fluid coupling magnified the torque produced by the engine, making the Roadmaster smooth and powerful.

Top speed:	100 mph (160 km/h)
0–60 mph (0–96 km/h):	17.1 sec
Engine type:	In-line eight
Displacement:	320 ci (5,243 cc)
Transmission	2-speed auto
Max power:	150 bhp (112 kW) @ 3,600 rpm
Max torque:	260 lb ft (352 Nm) @ 2,400 rpm
Weight:	4,370 lb (1,986 kg)
Economy:	14 mpg (4.95 km/l)

Buick Skylark (1954)

In 1954 Buick celebrated 50 years in car production with the introduction of the Skylark. Designed by Harley Earl, the car was built to be the top-level Buick and thus featured much chrome trim on its custom coachbuilt body, plus a wraparound windshield. The interior was luxurious and had such features as power steering, brakes, four-way adjustable front seat and a power convertible top, all as standard equipment. It was also fitted with a 'Selectronic' radio and 'Easy Eye' tinted glass. Underneath, the car was a Roadmaster and featured that car's double wishbone front with telescopic shocks, while the rear still had leaf springs and lever-arm shocks. It all made for a smooth, relaxing drive which the powerful engine and Dynaflow transmission only further enhanced. The Skylark was quick for its day, though most correctly labelled it as a fast cruiser rather than sportscar.

Top speed:	105 mph (168 km/h)
0–60 mph (0–96 km/h):	11.5 sec
Engine type:	V8
Displacement:	322 ci (5,276 cc)
Transmission	2-speed auto
Max power:	200 bhp (149 kW) @ 4,100 rpm
Max torque:	N/A
Weight:	4,260 lb (1,936 kg)
Economy:	14 mpg (4.95 km/l)

Buick Limited (1958)

Like many companies of the era, Buick decided bigger was better for 1958 and they added the lengthened Limited to their range. The car had such innovative extras as air suspension for an ultra smooth ride, plus alloy brake drums to speed heat dispersal and hence create better braking. Also new was the Flight-Pitch Dynaflow, a version of Buick's Dynaflow, which had three rather than two turbines inside to give a smoother transition through the gears. What all this actually created was an overly soft ride which would pitch the car over in corners, and an unresponsive gearbox. The brakes were the saving grace. This car was most about showing off Buick style, however, and nowhere was this more evident than on the over-fussy rear end, which had an overhang of over 60 inches or 5ft (1.5 m). Despite this, rear leg-room was atrocious. The car lasted until 1959.

Top speed:	110 mph (176 km/h)
0–60 mph (0–96 km/h):	11.2 sec
Engine type:	V8
Displacement:	364 ci (5,964 cc)
Transmission:	3–speed auto
Max power:	300 bhp (224 kW) @ 4,600 rpm
Max torque:	400 lb ft (542 Nm) @ 3,200 rpm
Weight:	4,691 lb (2,132 kg)
Economy:	13 mpg (4.60 km/l)

Buick Riviera (1963)

Combining power and luxury, the 1963 Riviera was one of Buick's landmark cars. It was the company's first true luxury coupe and reflected styling supremo Bill Mitchell's ideals of having a clean, European-looking car. The grille, as an example, was styled on Ferrari's 250GT, while inside the long centre console was very similar to Ferrari's finest too. Buick used many parts from the corporate parts bin for the Riviera's underpinnings, with a separate chassis, wishbone suspension up front, and a live axle on coil springs at the rear. The ride was very soft and the steering over-light, but in those days that's exactly what luxury meant. It was having all the comfort of a big car in something relatively small, compared to a Cadillac or Lincoln, that made the Riviera popular. It was also quick for a top-brand machine, thanks to the Wildcat 445 engine (named after the torque figure).

Top speed:	125 mph (200 km/h)
0–60 mph (0–96 km/h):	8.0 sec
Engine type:	V8
Displacement:	401 ci (6,571 cc)
Transmission	2-speed auto
Max power:	325 bhp (242 kW) @ 4,400 rpm
Max torque:	445 lb ft (603 Nm) @ 2,800 rpm
Weight:	4,367 lb (1,985 kg)
Economy:	12 mpg (4.24 km/l)

Buick GS 400

Buick loaded its GS model with luxuries, but also gave it a powerful engine so it could hold its own amongst the street-fighter muscle cars of 1969. The drive was leisurely and the handling would turn to understeer when pushed, but in a straight line, it was incredible. Its 400ci (6.6-litre) 'Nailhead' engine is a bored and stroked version of the 340. The 400 got 11:1 compression ratio, a four-barrel carb, low-restriction exhaust and cold-air hood induction which was claimed to an 8 per cent increase in power. An uprated GM Turbo-Hydramatic three-speed auto was the transmission, and further back was a Positraction limited-slip differential to help put the power down through skinny bias-ply tyres. The fastback coupe was the most body style, though the convertible has remained the most desirable, as just 1,776 were made. In 1970, the GS 400 was replaced by the GS 455.

Top speed:	125 mph (200 km/h)
0–60 mph (0–95 km/h):	5.8 sec
Engine type:	V8
Displacement:	400 ci (6,555 cc)
Transmission	3-speed auto
Max power:	345 bhp (257 kW) @ 4,800 rpm
Max torque:	440 lb ft (595 Nm) @ 3,200 rpm
Weight:	3,594 lb (1,633 kg)
Economy:	14 mpg (5 km/l)

Buick Riviera (1969)

Rarely are Buicks used as customized cars, as their luxury street-fighter status has often meant they belong to muscle-car enthusiasts. In the right hands, however, they can be made to look good in any style, and this smoothed-out Riviera is a prime example. Externally the body has gone through a 'shave' which means all the superfluous trim and badging has been removed and the resulting holes filled in. To complement the style, concentric ring smooth hubcaps have been fitted, which blend well with the stock front and rear deep fenders. The suspension is all coil spring and even in stock form they're firm, but this owner has taken more coils out of the springs which has stiffened up the ride still further. The interior is an immaculate mix of white leather tuck 'n' roll and the stock dash equipment, plus some custom-fit stereo equipment.

Top speed:	125 mph (200 km/h)
0–60 mph (0–96 km/h):	7.2 sec
Engine type:	V8
Displacement:	430 ci (7,046 cc)
Transmission	3-speed auto
Max power:	360 bhp (268 kW) @ 5,000 rpm
Max torque:	475 lb ft (644 Nm) @ 3,200 rpm
Weight:	4,199 lb (1,908 kg)
Economy:	7 mpg (2.48 km/l)

Buick GSX

While the mid-sized GS 455 was enough for some, for others it was too sedate, so Buick launched the fearsome 1970 GSX. This car had all the power of the regular GS 455, but had improved suspension and more dynamic looks, with Magnum 500 wheels, spoilers, scoops and stripes. The suspension used independent wishbones at the front and coil springs out back (all uprated), but anti-roll bars at both ends improved cornering while 11-inch (279mm) discs and finned rear drums upgraded the brakes. While the 455ci (7.5-litre) was the biggest engine Buick produced, and standard in the base GSX, the majority of buyers went for the Stage 1 option, which had a four-barrel Quadrajet carb, high-lift camshaft, larger valves and a 10.5:1 compression ratio. With a true rating of 400bhp (298kW) and massive torque of over 500lb ft (677Nm), it was one of the most powerful in the muscle-car era.

Top speed:	123 mph (197 km/h)
0–60 mph (0–95 km/h):	5.5 sec
Engine type:	V8
Displacement:	455 ci (7,456 cc)
Transmission:	4-speed manual
Max power:	360 bhp (268 kW) @ 4,600 rpm
Max torque:	510 lb ft (690 Nm) @ 2,800 rpm
Weight:	3,561 lb (1,618 kg)
Economy:	7.1 mpg (2.5 km/l)

Buick Riviera Gran Sport

Designed by Jerry Hirshberg, the 1971 Riviera broke away from Buick's conservative look which had been associated with their previous cars. It was bigger and heavier than previous models, but the dramatic styling which brought the car to a point at eight ends, more prominent at the rear, led to the car being nicknamed the 'boat tail Buick'. It rode on a separate perimeter chassis, with an independent wishbone front and live axle rear supported on coil springs. The Gran Sport package meant stiffer springs, revised shock valving, and a thick front anti-roll bar, With fuel at just 30 cents a gallon, Buick had no qualms putting in their 455ci (7.5-litre) big-block engine, which with its long stroke made a lot of torque and the car more of a luxury cruiser than straight-line performer. The car lived for just two years before being re-styled, then dropped altogether.

Top speed:	120 mph (192 km/h)
0–60 mph (0–95 km/h):	8.1 sec
Engine type:	V8
Displacement:	455 ci (7,456 cc)
Transmission	3-speed auto
Max power:	330 bhp (246 kW) @ 4,600 rpm
Max torque:	455 lb ft (616 Nm) @ 2,800 rpm
Weight:	4,325 lb (1,965 kg)
Economy:	8 mpg (2.8 km/l)

Buick GNX

Onlookers could be fooled into thinking the Buick GNX was just another US coupe-styled car without a performance bias. That's without knowing it had help from ASC/McLaren in developing its turbocharged V6 engine, which put out a lot of horsepower and even bigger surge of torque. Initially, the car started life in 1978 as a Buick Regal with turbo V6 producing just 150hp (112kW). Four years later just 215 Grand Nationals (the 'GN' in the name) made it on the street and by 1984 power was up to 200bhp (149kW). Revised engine management and an intercooler pushed output to 235bhp (175kW) for 1986, then a year later came the association with McLaren and push to 276bhp (206kW) with huge torque. Although just 547 made it in this guise, the GNX was worth finding. It had modified uprated suspension for better handling, and a Panhard rod to increase cornering capability.

Top speed:	124 mph (198 km/h)
0–60 mph (0–95 km/h):	5.5 sec
Engine type:	V6
Displacement:	231 ci (3,785 cc)
Transmission	4-speed auto
Max power:	276 bhp (206 kW) @ 4,400 rpm
Max torque:	360 lb ft (487 Nm) @ 3,000 rpm
Weight:	3,545 lb (1,611 kg)
Economy:	23 mpg (8.2 km/l)

Buick T-Type (1987)

Buick built its T-Type through the mid-1980s and it was forerunner to the GNX. It was a tuner-friendly car and got a reputation for being able to blow away the eight-cylinder cars as soon as its turbo started to whistle and the boost came on strong. The T-Type shown has taken the forced induction to a whole new level, featuring a Ken Duttweiler race engine with variable boost for anything between 10-24psi. The gearbox is a specially prepared GM Turbo-Hydramatic, while the rear axle is an aftermarket Lenco unit located on three spherical-joint arms as per NASCAR racers. The chassis is made from tubular chrome-moly steel, so is light but extremely rigid, just what this car needs, as it can accelerate to 200mph (322km/h) in just 44 seconds. The windscreen has support bars for extra strength at high speeds, while the brakes are 13-inch (330mm) vented units all around.

Top speed:	226 mph (361 km/h)
0–60 mph (0–96 km/h):	2.8 sec
Engine type:	V6
Displacement:	260 ci (4,260 cc)
Transmission:	3-speed auto
Max power:	967 bhp (721 kW) @ 6,500 rpm
Max torque:	877 lb ft (1,189 Nm) @ 5,200 rpm
Weight:	3,200 lb (1,454 kg)
Economy:	6 mpg (2.12 km/l)

Cadillac Eldorado (1953)

The first Eldorado came from Cadillac in 1953 and it was an expensive option over the regular Series 62 range, costing some $3,600 more. Just 532 were built, so in 1954 the company dropped the price to $4,438, just $300 above the regular range, and sales went up dramatically to over 2,000. The car was the epitome of luxury and featured such revolutionary touches as the wraparound screen which became an industry standard in the 1950s. It also had a signal-seeking radio, special cut down doors, wire wheels, white sidewall tyres, leather and cloth upholstery, fog lamps and a metal tonneau cover to fit over the roof when it was electrically retracted. The engine was the first new post-war V8 on the market and it was an excellent one. It weighed 200lb (107kg) less than the former unit, had 'slipper' pistons and a shorter stroke, plus a higher compression.

Top speed:	116 mph (186 km/h)
0–60 mph (0–96 km/h):	12.6 sec
Engine type:	V8
Displacement:	331 ci (5,424 cc)
Transmission	3-speed auto
Max power:	210 bhp (157 kW) @ 4,150 rpm
Max torque:	330 lb ft (447 Nm) @ 2,700 rpm
Weight:	4,799 lb (2,181 kg)
Economy:	14 mpg (4.95 km/l)

Cadillac Eldorado Brougham (1957)

Making its mark as the most expensive Cadillac of the 1950s, the Eldorado Brougham featured every conceivable extra, and then some. Each car was hand built, and it was incredibly smooth and quiet to ride in thanks to the airbag suspension and precise automatic transmission. The car used the now familiar panoramic windshields front and rear, but unusually returned to suicide-style opening doors for the rear. Cadillac made sure the chassis was immensely strong to allow both side doors to top open without a central pillar. There were 44 interior and exterior colour options, but the car came standard with toys such as electric memory seats, cruise control, air-conditioning, and power windows, brakes and steering. The extras weighed down the car considerably hence, despite the power, the Brougham was sufficiently fast, as opposed to rapid.

Top speed:	110 mph (176 km/h)
0–60 mph (0–96 km/h):	11.4 sec
Engine type:	V8
Displacement:	365 ci (5,981 cc)
Transmission	3-speed auto
Max power:	325 bhp (242 kW) @ 4,800 rpm
Max torque:	435 lb ft (590 Nm) @ 3,400 rpm
Weight:	5,315 lb (2,415 kg)
Economy:	10 mpg (3.54 km/l)

Cadillac Series 62

General Motors needed a response to Chrysler's growing fins on the 1950s cars, and they had famous Stylist Harley Earl apply his ideas to a new Cadillac model, called the Series 62. Earl took much of his influence from the aero industry, and it showed. Huge tail fins, the biggest to appear on any car ever, stood to a point and featured bullet tail light lenses, while the front fender and grille looked like a reflection of itself, with four shotgun-style lenses, the upper two of which automatically came on at dusk and dipped from high to low beam when they detected oncoming traffic. The car used coil springs and telescopic shocks, but the top Eldorado models could be ordered with air suspension. The all-cast iron big block was enlarged for 1959 and came in two states of tune, either a 325bhp (242kW) single carb version, or the 345bhp (257kW) triple carb unit.

Top speed:	121 mph (194 km/h)
0–60 mph (0–95 km/h):	11.0 sec
Engine type:	V8
Displacement:	390 ci (6,390 cc)
Transmission	3-speed auto
Max power:	325 bhp (242 kW) @ 4,800 rpm
Max torque:	435 lb ft (589 Nm) @ 3,400 rpm
Weight:	4,885 lb (2,220 kg)
Economy:	13 mpg (4.6 km/l)

Cadillac Allanté (1993)

The 1987–1993 Allanté was certainly no ordinary Cadillac. For a start, it was styled by Italian deign house Pininfarina, and while it used a modified Eldorado platform, the all-start suspension was much tweaked in order to make the car feel more European. Sales were slow for the first few years, and so GM made changes to try and improve the situation, including more power and active suspension, but the most significant model came in 1993 with the fitting of the incredible 32v Northstar V8 in the front-wheel drive configuration. This engine was so advanced it could run for 100,000 miles (160,000km) without servicing. It worked well in conjunction with a four-speed automatic which was also computer-managed and could retard the engine's timing slightly before each gear change to smooth out the shifts. Vented discs all around and 16-inch (406mm) wheels ensured great handling too.

Top speed:	145 mph (232 km/h)
0–60 mph (0–96 km/h):	7.0 sec
Engine type:	V8
Displacement:	279 ci (4,571 cc)
Transmission	4-speed auto
Max power:	290 bhp (216 kW) @ 5,600 rpm
Max torque:	290 lb ft (393 Nm) @ 4,400 rpm
Weight:	3,720 lb (1,690 kg)
Economy:	17 mpg (6.02 km/l)

Cadillac Catera (1998)

Import cars are big competition for American manufacturers and Cadillac decided in 1996 that the best way to fight them was to have one of its own. So it started using an Opel model sold in Europe as the Omega, and named it the Catera. The only differences visually were the front and rear light clusters, which went full width on the rear and at the front were separated by a grille more akin to previous Cadillacs. The suspension was fully independent and had struts up front plus a strut and multi-link rear for exceptional ride quality and handling – enough to rival BMW, Mercedes, and Lexus. The engine was a compact 183ci (3-litre) V6 with 24 valves, twin overhead camshafts and three-stage intake runner lengths to boost torque production throughout the rev range. Powerful braking is available, thanks to vented and ABS-assisted discs all around. The Catera remains in production.

Top speed:	125 mph (200 km/h)
0–60 mph (0–96 km/h):	8.5 sec
Engine type:	V6
Displacement:	180 ci (2,962 cc)
Transmission	4-speed auto
Max power:	200 bhp (149 kW) @ 6,000 rpm
Max torque:	192 lb ft (260 Nm) @ 3,600 rpm
Weight:	3,800 lb (1,727 kg)
Economy:	22 mpg (7.79 km/l)

Cadillac STS (1998)

The Cadillacs of the 1980s had suffered dreadfully from old age and hence the company lost many sales to the likes of BMW and Mercedes. This continued through to 1992 until Cadillac completely revamped their line-up and included a new STS. This won Automobile magazine's 'Car of the Year' in 1992, but it didn't end there as Cadillac worried the competition more with the introduction of its high-tech Northstar V8 in 1993. From 1997 a new STS (Seville Touring Sedan) arrived, and it was by far the best yet, with the company so confident they even built them in right-hand-drive form to sell in Europe. The suspension used MacPherson struts and a multi-link rear, with variable shocks. The interior was fully loaded even in basic trim, while the engine could run 100,000 miles (160,000km) between tune-ups and could limp home 60 miles (96km) without coolant.

Top speed:	155 mph (248 km/h)
0–60 mph (0–96 km/h):	6.8 sec
Engine type:	V8
Displacement:	279 ci (4,571 cc)
Transmission	4-speed auto
Max power:	300 bhp (224 kW) @ 6,000 rpm
Max torque:	295 lb ft (400 Nm) @ 4,400 rpm
Weight:	4,010 lb (1,822 kg)
Economy:	26 mpg (9.20 km/l)

Callaway Corvette Speedster

Reeves Callaway's fitting of twin turbos to an Alfa Romeo GTV6 impressed
Chevrolet bosses. With his Alfa boasting an output of 230bhp (172kW), well up
on the standard car, he was asked to do the same to a Corvette. Three years later
the Callaway 'Sledgehammer' appeared, an 880bhp (656kW) supercar with the
body re-designed by French-Canadian stylist, Paul Deutschman. The Speedster's
debut at the Los Angeles Auto Show in 1991 led to 50 orders. Underneath the
dramatic low body, with 7 inches (178mm) chopped out of the stock Corvette's
screen, was adjustable coilover suspension at each corner, plus uprated
Callaway/Brembo brakes using vented discs and four-piston callipers. The engine
was stripped and fitted with an upgraded crankshaft and new pistons to allow the
fitting of twin RotoMaster turbos with intercooling. Callaway continues his
modified Corvette business today.

Top speed:	185 mph (296 km/h)
0–60 mph (0–95 km/h):	4.5 sec
Engine type:	V8
Displacement:	350 ci (5,700 cc)
Transmission	6-speed manual
Max power:	420 bhp (313 kW) @ 4,250 rpm
Max torque:	562 lb ft (761 Nm) @ 2,500 rpm
Weight:	3,200 lb (1,455 kg)
Economy:	10.4 mpg (3.7 km/l)

Callaway Camaro C8 (1994)

Callaway's Corvettes had already established his name as top in the high performance league during the early 1990s, but in 1994 turned his attention to the new Camaro and produced the C8. This was based on the stock Camaro but featured many aftermarket upgrades already available, plus many designed by Callaway themselves. The chassis used a strut brace across the engine to stiffen the front end and a subframe connectors to make the unitary structure more rigid. Eibach springs and Koni shocks at each corner stiffened the ride and enabled 0.94g on the skid pad, while the vented disc brakes came from Brembo and were 13-inch (330mm) at the front and 11-inch (279mm) at the rear. The bodykit was designed by Paul Deutschman, and providing the performance to back the looks was a stroked small-block Chevy with special Callaway induction and electronics.

Top speed:	172 mph (275 km/h)
0-60 mph (0–96 km/h):	4.7 sec
Engine type:	V8
Displacement:	383 ci (6,276 cc)
Transmission	6-speed manual
Max power:	404 bhp (301 kW) @ 5,750 rpm
Max torque:	412 lb ft (558 Nm) @ 4,750 rpm
Weight:	3,373 lb (1,533 kg)
Economy:	17 mpg (6.02 km/l)

Caterham Seven JPE

The Super 7 version of Caterham's lightweight roadster steadily developed through the 1970s and 1980s, but in 1992 the Surrey, UK-based company pulled out all the stops with their limited edition Seven JPE. The car used a tubular steel spaceframe chassis with much triangulation to create a rigid structure. Double wishbones up front and a de Dion rear with lower A-frame was used as per other Sevens, while steering was quick with a rack and pinion that needed two turns lock to lock. The highly tuned Vauxhall 122ci (2-litre) 16v engine, developed with the help of F1 driver Jonathan Palmer, hence the 'JP' in the title ('E' for Evolution), used Weber fuel injection, and each motor was built at Swindon Racing Engines. The car held the world record for 0–60mph (0–95km/h) for some time, and could do the dash and brake back to a standstill again before a Ferrari F40 hit 60mph (95km/h).

Top speed:	147 mph (235 km/h)
0–60 mph (0–95 km/h):	3.7 sec
Engine type:	In-line four
Displacement:	122 ci (1,998 cc)
Transmission:	5-speed manual
Max power:	250 bhp (186 kW)@ 7,750 rpm
Max torque:	186 lb ft (252 Nm) @ 6,250 rpm
Weight:	1,169 lb (531 kg)
Economy:	20 mpg (7.1 km/l)

Caterham Super 7 HPC

Much the same as Caterham's other models in the chassis and body, the Super 7 HPC differed in that it used a Vauxhall engine for the first time, having used mostly Ford and Rover powerplants prior to the HPC's launch in 1992. The Surrey, England based company utilized their strong steel spaceframe chassis under the HPC, with built-in roll-over bar that also serves to stiffen the rear end. The all-independent suspension used a double A-arm front set-up and de Dion rear axle, and while there were vented discs all around, they weren't huge because the car was so lightweight. Alloy 7x 16-inch (178x406mm) rims with Goodyear Eagle tyres provided all the road-contact the car needed; it took an awful lot to unstick it in corners. Power came from GM's British arm Vauxhall, the 122ci (2-litre) 16v being torquey and with twin Weber sidedraught carburettors to rev easily to 7,500rpm.

Top speed:	126 mph (202 km/h)
0–60 mph (0–95 km/h):	5.4 sec
Engine type:	In-line four
Displacement:	122 ci (1,998 cc)
Transmission	5-speed manual
Max power:	175 bhp (130 kW) @ 6,000 rpm
Max torque:	155 lb ft (210 Nm) @ 4,800 rpm
Weight:	1,385 lb (630 kg)
Economy:	19.5 mpg (6.9 km/l)

Caterham 21

It was like a Seven with clothes on, and was the Surrey, UK-based manufacturer's attempt at a more civilized version of the roadster, without losing any of the driving thrill of the 'naked' Seven. The composite body hid a tubular steel spaceframe just like the Seven's, the only difference being increased front track width to match the rear. Adjustable slim-line front wishbones with a coil-over shock arrangement, plus de Dion rear with A-frame, kept handling responsive and to the weight goal of two-thirds of a ton. The convertible has a sparse but comfortable interior, but there was no doubt about the intentions of this car, with Rover's highly acclaimed K-series unit up front. It was available in basic 97ci (1.6-litre) 118bhp (88kW) form right up to a 110ci (1.8-litre) 190bhp (141kW) VHPD (Very High Performance Derivative) version, the 'slower' doing 6.7 seconds in the 60mph dash.

Top speed:	127 mph (203 km/h)
0–60 mph (0–95 km/h):	6.7 sec
Engine type:	In-line four
Displacement:	97 ci (1,588 cc)
Transmission	6-speed manual
Max power:	136 bhp (102 kW) @ 7,000 rpm
Max torque:	115 lb ft (155 Nm) @ 5,000 rpm
Weight:	1,466 lb (666 kg)
Economy:	23.5 mpg (8.3 km/l)

Checker A11 (1980)

For 30 years the Checker cab patrolled the streets of Manhattan, and for more than four decades it's been shown in nearly every bit of TV and movie footage about New York. Checker started producing cabs back in 1956 and they were liked because of their rugged build quality, large interior and basic functionality. The A11 made its debut in 1963 and came in either a 120-inch (3.05m) or 129-inch (3.28m) wheelbase with a ultra-strong steel chassis with X-brace. Wishbones and stiff coils up front plus uprated leaf springs out back kept the suspension simple, and while most cars had drum brakes only, later versions did get front discs. In the 1950s the standard engine was a 226ci (3,703cc) straight six, but later the Chevy small-block was chosen, often set up to run on propane. Huge fenders with overriders kept cars and pedestrians at bay, while the rear had room for eight passengers.

Top speed:	98 mph (157 km/h)
0–60 mph (0–96 km/h):	15.5 sec
Engine type:	V8
Displacement:	305 ci (4,998 cc)
Transmission	3-speed auto
Max power:	155 bhp (116 kW) @ 3,800 rpm
Max torque:	250 lb ft (339 Nm) @ 2,400 rpm
Weight:	3,830 lb (1,740 kg)
Economy:	15 mpg (5.31 km/l)

Chevrolet Independence (1931)

While Ford sold more than twice as many cars as Chevy, the exclusivity is what has drawn many hot rodders to their early cars. However, this hot rod couldn't be more far removed from the original Independence, which came with a 50bhp (37kW) motor which made just over 50mph (80km/h) possible. This car has a chopped five-window body channelled over the lightweight tube-frame chassis to get the car as close to the ground as possible. The front end has a drop beam connected via four locating bars and a transverse leaf spring, while the rear consists of a 9-inch (229mm) Ford live axle, again located by four adjustable bars. The 'Rat' motor is from a late 1960s Chevelle, being the big-block Chevy reworked to accept a Weiand supercharger with intercooler for more power. Made for acceleration, this car does the quarter-mile in 9.9 seconds at nearly 140mph (224km/h).

Top speed:	170 mph (272 km/h)
0–60 mph (0–96 km/h):	4.5 sec
Engine type:	V8
Displacement:	460 ci (7,538 cc)
Transmission:	2–speed auto
Max power:	900 bhp (67 kW) @ 6,400 rpm
Max torque:	710 lb ft (963 Nm) @ 3,800 rpm
Weight:	2,850 lb (1,295 kg)
Economy:	4 mpg (1.4 km/l)

Chevrolet Coupe (1938)

Towards the end of the 1930s Chevrolet excelled in making simple yet rugged cars for the masses, often outnumbering Ford in sales. Their cars became very popular with the hot-rodding fraternity who used them and started off the trend in 'fat fendered' rods which continued with cars built in the late 1940s. Such cars could take major suspension changes and wider tyres without a great deal of bodywork modification and, with their wide engine bays, handled motor transplants with ease too. This car has been fitted with a Generation V big-block Chevy under the hood and to put all the torque down the rear's been equipped with a pair of 18.5-inch (470mm) wide tyres. A Mustang II front suspension clip has been installed along with airbag springs to alter the ride height whilst giving supreme comfort, and at the back a live axle is located with four links and coilover dampers.

Top speed:	143 mph (229 km/h)
0–60 mph (0–96 km/h):	5.1 sec
Engine type:	V8
Displacement:	454 ci (7,439 cc)
Transmission	3-speed auto
Max power:	410 bhp (306 kW) @ 6,000 rpm
Max torque:	520 lb ft (705 Nm) @ 3,400 rpm
Weight:	2,980 lb (1,354 kg)
Economy:	8 mpg (2.83 km/l)

Chevrolet Coupe (1940)

When Chevrolet launched their new model in 1940 it was significant. It was their first car to use both plastics and stainless steel, and, interestingly, while being very basic underneath, famous racing driver Juan Manual Fangio managed to win the 6,000-mile (9654km) Gran Primo Internacional Del Norte race in Argentina, South America in a Business Coupe just like this. Chevrolets often come second in popularity to Ford when creating street rods, but not in this case. This version has had a separate chassis built based on the original rails, with independent A-arm front and Jaguar independent rear suspension. The brakes are large discs all around with powerful four-pot callipers. The engine is a Corvette small-block Chevy with three two-barrel carburettors, which uses the centre carb on light throttle then all three on full throttle. It has all-electric Corvette seats.

Top speed:	125 mph (201 km/h)
0–60 mph (0–95 km/h):	6.8 sec
Engine type:	V8
Displacement:	327 ci (5,358 cc)
Transmission	4-speed auto
Max power:	300 bhp (223 kW) @ 5,000 rpm
Max torque:	321 lb ft (434 Nm) @ 3,200 rpm
Weight:	2,900 lb (1,318 kg)
Economy:	14.7 mpg (5.25 km/l)

Chevrolet Fleetmaster (1948)

Post-war Chevys were often regarded as too bulbous and weighty to make decent hot rods out of, but that all changed with the trend for 'fat fendered' cars among the custom and cruising fans. With naturally rounded lines, the cars could be further smoothed by de-badging and de-trimming, thus making them fuss-free externally, and very striking cars. This car not only has the smoothed lines, but its body has been channelled over the chassis for a low ride height, which is further enhanced on the Mustang II independent wishbone front end by 2-inch (50mm) drop spindles that effectively bring wheels up inside the arch without changing suspension geometry. The rear end is a basic live axle with leaf springs, built to be tough and durable to take the power from the Tri-Power (triple carburettors) small-block Chevy V8 with performance heads and a low restriction exhaust.

Top speed:	139 mph (222 km/h)
0–60 mph (0–96 km/h):	6.8 sec
Engine type:	V8
Displacement:	350 ci (5,735 cc)
Transmission	3-speed auto
Max power:	325 bhp (242 kW) @ 5,500 rpm
Max torque:	340 lb ft (461 Nm) @ 3,500 rpm
Weight:	3,450 lb (1,568 kg)
Economy:	14 mpg (4.95 km/l)

Chevrolet Sedan Delivery (1952)

Chevrolet first officially recognized its car-based Sedan Delivery models as separate to their other purpose-built trucks in 1934 by giving them different ID codes. However, they were built six years prior to that and remained very popular through to the late 1950s/early 1960s, after which the El Camino took over along with bigger trucks. The Sedan Delivery was a great concept for its time, however, because it combined the comfort and driveability of a regular production Sedan with the practicality of a delivery van. They also offered great promotion potential with their slab sides which were often adorned with signwriting and company decals. This model looks original but has a few tweaks to improve it, including dual carbs and a free-flowing exhaust, plus wider rims and radials, and finally a custom interior with two seats, where they left the factory with just one for the driver.

Top speed:	92 mph (147 km/h)
0–60 mph (0–96 km/h):	14.0 sec
Engine type:	In-line six
Displacement:	217 ci (3,555 cc)
Transmission	3-speed manual
Max power:	110 bhp (82 kW) @ 3,400 rpm
Max torque:	187 lb ft (253 Nm) @ 1,700 rpm
Weight:	3,100 lb (1,409 kg)
Economy:	16 mpg (5.66 km/l)

Chevrolet Corvette (1953–1955)

The Corvette didn't make a great start sales-wise, but GM persevered. It debuted at the 1953 GM Motorama Show, and production began later that year, all cars being white. In 1954 several more colours were available plus the car had an increase in power. The Corvette was the world's first production car to be made out of glass-fibre and it was a daring move. Underneath it used a separate steel chassis with an X-brace which added stiffness along with the one-piece floor moulding. Also new in the Corvette were the leaf springs mounted outside the chassis rails. The straight-six engine came from the sedan range, and under the name 'Blue Flame Special' it used a high-lift cam, higher compression ratio, modified head and double valve springs to cope with increased rpm use. The car was almost shelved in 1954, and it was only the new small-block V8 engine that saved it.

Top speed:	107 mph (172 km/h)
0–60 mph (0–95 km/h):	11.0 sec
Engine type:	In-line six
Displacement:	235 ci (3,850 cc)
Transmission:	2-speed auto
Max power:	150 bhp (112 kW) @ 4,200 rpm
Max torque:	223 lb ft (302 Nm) @ 2,400 rpm
Weight:	2,851 lb (1,295 kg)
Economy:	16 mpg (5.7 km/l)

Chevrolet Nomad (1956)

The Nomad was the top-of-the-range Chevy available from 1955 to 1957. The hottest news in 1955 was the use of the all-new small-block V8 which, displacing 265ci (4.3-litre), turned the sedans and station wagons into some of the best performers of their day. The Nomad was different to other station wagons because it was a two-door body with lifting tailgate, but its was sportingly handsome. The original car used leaf springs at the rear and double wishbones at the front, and pushed out just 162bhp (121kW) from its V8. This car has gone someway further, using 1986 Corvette front and rear suspension plus a lowered ride height for excellent handling, while the old 265 has been replaced by a fully-balanced 358ci (5.8-litre) small-block Chevy with ported heads and a B&M supercharger. So good are the Nomad's lines, little has changed except custom paint and Boyds alloys.

Top speed:	131 mph (210 km/h)
0–60 mph (0–95 km/h):	5.5 sec
Engine type:	V8
Displacement:	358 ci (5,866 cc)
Transmission:	3-speed auto
Max power:	400 bhp (298 kW) @ 4,800 rpm
Max torque:	420 lb ft (568 Nm) @ 3,000 rpm
Weight:	3,352 lb (1,523 kg)
Economy:	8.4 mpg (3 km/l)

Chevrolet Corvette (1956–1962)

Introduced in 1956 in V8 form, the Corvette established Chevrolet as kings of the US automotive world with a range of cars to suit every taste and pocket. By 1958 the car had been re-styled more aggressively and was both wider and longer. The famous small-block Chevy engine, which started out at 265ci (4.5 litres) V8, grew to 283ci (4.6 litres) by 1958, and by 1962 it was bored and stroked to 327ci (5.4 litres). The significance of this V8 engine can't be underestimated as, in fuel injected form at least, it made the Corvette one of the most powerful sportscars in the world and certainly one of the quickest at the time. Unfortunately the brakes and handling didn't match, though the steering was precise enough to catch the sudden oversteer the Corvette suffered from when pushed. But the 1956–1962 car was more about style, being inspired by fighter planes of the time.

Top speed:	135 mph (217 km/h)
0–60 mph (0–95 km/h):	6.1 sec
Engine type:	V8
Displacement:	327 ci (5,385 cc)
Transmission	4-speed manual
Max power:	360 bhp (268 kW) @ 6,000 rpm
Max torque:	352 lb ft (476 Nm) @ 4,000 rpm
Weight:	2,942 lb (1,337 kg)
Economy:	12.4 mpg (4.4 km/l)

Chevrolet 3100 Stepside (1957)

What made Chevrolet's trucks of the 1950s so liked in later decades was the ease at which they took modifications. The huge engine bays swallowed a small-block V8 with ease and in fact could take a big-block without major work. Being of wide track meant they could also handle suspension swaps from larger sedans without the need to narrow either axles or front crossmembers. The scope has produced numerous reworked examples, but many stick with the truck's original utilitarian lines as they appear aggressive in factory form. This truck has gone through the mildest of changes, featuring a tuned small-block V8 with Tri-Power three carb set-up, and uprated brakes with front discs to cope with the performance. Apart from that and the modern radials on alloy rims, the truck is just exceptionally clean and straight, with superb chrome work.

Top speed:	115 mph (184 km/h)
0–60 mph (0–96 km/h):	7.2 sec
Engine type:	V8
Displacement:	350 ci (5,735 cc)
Transmission	3-speed auto
Max power:	330 bhp (246 kW) @ 5,200 rpm
Max torque:	360 lb ft (488 Nm) @ 3,400 rpm
Weight:	3,230 lb (1,468 kg)
Economy:	14 mpg (4.95 km/l)

Chevrolet Bel Air (1957)

Stylist Harley Earl was responsible for the 1957 Chevy, and he created a car which became an American icon. His philosophy was to make cars lower, wider and longer, but he still showed aeroplane influence at this time, with the large rear fins, hood fins and large side spears. The grille looked like a huge, gaping mouth sucking in air for the engine, though that sat back some way from the front. Perhaps the most famous V8 of all time, the small-block Chevy, was used under the hood, having grown in size by then to 283ci (4.6-litre) from the original 265ci (4.3-litre). It gave the Bel Air exceptional performance, and even the handling was ahead of the competition, despite basic underpinnings of a double-wishbone front and leaf sprung live rear axle. While the Bel Air had many options, one popular one was the continental kit which extended the rear fender and re-located the licence plate.

Top speed:	115 mph (184 km/h)
0–60 mph (0–95 km/h):	8.5 sec
Engine type:	V8
Displacement:	283 ci (4,637 cc)
Transmission	3-speed manual
Max power:	220 bhp (164 kW) @ 4,800 rpm
Max torque:	270 lb ft (366 Nm) @ 2,800 rpm
Weight:	3,409 lb (1,550 kg)
Economy:	20 mpg (7.1 km/l)

Chevrolet Bel Air Modified

Because of its iconic nature and easy tuneability, the 1957 Chevy was modified from the day it was produced. However, a tell-tale sign of Harley Earl's timeless design is that few people chose to heavily modify the bodywork, instead concentrating on making the car go, stop and corner better. This car retains the original chassis, albeit restored, but has new suspension arms and 2-inch (51mm) drop spindles, as well as lowering springs to get the nose down. Custom semi-elliptical leaf springs drop the rear to match while lowering the centre of gravity to aid handling. Powering the car is still the job of a small-block Chevy, though it's heavily modified with a B&M Roots-type supercharger. To help put the power down, a narrowed 9-inch (228mm) Ford axle with Posi-traction limited-slip differential sits at the rear, along with 13-inch (330mm) wide Mickey Thompson street/strip tyres.

Top speed:	147 mph (235 km/h)
0–60 mph (0—95 km/h):	3.9 sec
Engine type:	V8
Displacement:	350 ci (5,735 cc)
Transmission	3-speed auto
Max power:	420 bhp (313 kW) @ 5,400 rpm
Max torque:	435 lb ft (589 Nm) @ 2,500 rpm
Weight:	3,197 lb (1,453 kg)
Economy:	9.4 mpg (3.3 km/l)

Chevrolet Corvette (1957)

Almost shelved in 1955, the Corvette fortunately had the Chevrolet sedan come to it rescue which gave it a new lease of life thanks to the new small-block V8 engine. At first it came in 265ci (4.5 litres) form, though had grown to 283ci (4.6 litres) by 1957. This put it among the best-selling models that year, and while the motor was powerful, the best option was the Zora Arkus Duntov-inspired 'Ramjet' fuel injection. This was expensive, and just 1,040 were sold, but it did make the '57 Corvette the quickest sportscar in the world, with an almost unheard of 0–60mph (0–96km/h) time that neither Ford nor the big cats from Jaguar could come anywhere close to. The suspension was basic, and on the whietwall-equipped skinny bias ply tyres, the car demanded driver attention, though for straight line speed the Corvette was king.

Top speed:	132 mph (211 km/h)
0–60 mph (0–96 km/h):	5.7 sec
Engine type:	V8
Displacement:	283 ci (4,637 cc)
Transmission	3-speed manual
Max power:	283 bhp (211 kW) @ 6,200 rpm
Max torque:	270 lb ft (366 Nm) @ 3,600 rpm
Weight:	2,730 lb (1,240 kg)
Economy:	13 mpg (4.60 km/l)

Chevrolet Impala (1958)

Following on from the successful 'Tri-Chevys' of 1955–1957 was tough but Chevrolet did a fine job with the 1958 Impala. It was the first they'd used the name on any cars in their range, though it was a new model supplementing the regular Bel Air, Biscayne and Delray variants. They wanted a lower look for 1958 and this required a new chassis of X-frame design with the main rails joined in the middle. Because of the lack of connection to the body sides, more mounting points were needed to the body elsewhere, and this improved structural rigidity a lot. The car ran a new W-Series engine initially designed for light truck duty. It was relatively compact and made 250bhp (186kW), though if fitted with the triple carb option could muster 315bhp (234kW). Also optional was air suspension with four rubber bellows replacing the sprigs and running off a self-levelling compressor. which was self levelling.

Top speed:	115 mph (184 km/h)
0–60 mph (0–95 km/h):	10.5 sec
Engine type:	V8
Displacement:	348 ci (5,702 cc)
Transmission	3-speed auto
Max power:	250 bhp (186 kW) @ 4,400 rpm
Max torque:	355 lb ft (454 Nm) @ 2,800 rpm
Weight:	3,459 lb (1,572 kg)
Economy:	14 mpg (5 km/l)

Chevrolet Impala modified (1958)

The 1958 Impala was the last of Chevrolet's 'tri-Chevys' because of the 1955 to 1958 cars all looking very similar and being an almost identical size. All three were favourites for modifying as they could be ordered with the small-block V8 as standard, and if they had the base straight-six, the larger engine could easily be found second-hand and slotted in. What made the 1958 model most famous was a custom version in the movie *American Graffiti*, driven by then actor but now famous movie director, Ron Howard. The car shown is typical of the 1960s customs, with the original chrome, a new tube grille, scallop paint work, reversed steel wheels, triple 1959 Cadillac tail lights and a tuck 'n' roll interior. The powerplant is a stroked small-block Chevy with triple carbs which helps the car to 14-second quarter-miles. The Impala gets its low ride through adjustable hydraulic suspension.

Top speed:	102 mph (163 km/h)
0–60 mph (0–96 km/h):	6.5 sec
Engine type:	V8
Displacement:	383 ci (6,276 cc)
Transmission	3-speed auto
Max power:	430 bhp (321 kW) @ 6,700 rpm
Max torque:	420 lb ft (570 Nm) @ 3,400 rpm
Weight:	3,447 lb (1,566 kg)
Economy:	9 mpg (3.19 km/l)

Chevrolet Corvette modified (1959)

Corvettes were fast cars for their day; in fact, most would be fast among modern sportscars today, if a little behind in the technology to harness the power. But being quick cars as standard didn't mean they weren't subject to modification, in fact, because of the performance-biased hardware from the factory, it made many people keener to upgrade theirs, so it was faster than their neighbour's. This 1959 example uses one of Chevrolet's most famous engines of the early 1960s, the 409 from the larger Impala. This one has been bored out, tuned with a higher compression ratio, and fitted with dual four-barrel Carter carbs. An aftermarket Richmond gearbox hands the power back to a live axle, as the Corvette didn't go independent at the rear until 1963. The car uses a custom tube chassis cleverly mated to the stock front suspension, while the rear has a four-bar link.

Top speed:	164 mph (262 km/h)
0–60 mph (0–96 km/h):	4.6 sec
Engine type:	V8
Displacement:	416 ci (6,816 cc)
Transmission:	6-speed manual
Max power:	454 bhp (338 kW) @ 5,500 rpm
Max torque:	460 lb ft (624 Nm) @ 5,500 rpm
Weight:	2,620 lb (1,190 kg)
Economy:	11 mpg (3.89 km/l)

Chevrolet El Camino (1959)

What did you get if you mixed a car with a truck back in the 1950s? Well, usually a compromise of both, but it wasn't as simple as that with the El Camino. It was launched by Chevrolet in response to Ford's car-based Ranchero and was beautifully styled inside and out, so it felt more like the glamorous cars of the era. Yet it had a huge loading bed, which meant that it found favour with many image-conscious small businesses. The car was based on the station wagon but had obvious traits straight from the sedans too, with the huge fins, cat eye tail lights, and headlamp eyebrows. Underneath the live axle had extra location with both a Panhard rod and torque arm, therefore reducing wheel hop while accelerating. And the car could do that in abundance, thanks to the top-option 348ci (5.7-litre) V8, which put it ahead of many performance sedans of the time.

Top speed:	131 mph (210 km/h)
0–60 mph (0–96 km/h):	8.7 sec
Engine type:	V8
Displacement:	348 ci (5,702 cc)
Transmission	3-speed auto
Max power:	315 bhp (235 kW) @ 5,600 rpm
Max torque:	357 lb ft (484 Nm) @ 3,600 rpm
Weight:	3,881 lb (1,764 kg)
Economy:	11.8 mpg (4.17 km/l)

Chevrolet Impala (1959)

Chevrolet's top-of-the-range Impala had everything in 1959. The outrageous fins, plenty of horsepower and luxurious extras. It didn't matter so much about the handling of the car to designers - the Impala was more about style so it only had a basic separate chassis with double wishbones up front and a coil sprung live rear axle. It was available with a number of powerplants, from a straight-six right up to the 348ci (5.7-litre). Stylists worked hard to get the car long and low and lose the earlier Chevys' upright stance, then gave owners an options list with which to personalise their vehicles. The car shown came with every one it seems, having side skirts, spot lights, continental kit, fender guards, remote trunk release, cruise control, air-conditioning and power everything. Inside it can carry six and due to its custom–friendly nature, it's been the model of choice for many lowrider fans.

Top speed:	134 mph (214 km/h)
0–60 mph (0–96 km/h):	9.0 sec
Engine type:	V8
Displacement:	348 ci (5,702 cc)
Transmission	3-speed auto
Max power:	315 bhp (235 kW) @ 5,600 rpm
Max torque:	357 lb ft (484 Nm) @ 3,600 rpm
Weight:	3,649 lb (1,658 kg)
Economy:	11.8 mpg (4.17 km/l)

Chevrolet Impala (1960)

The Impala was Chevrolet's top-of-the-range model in 1959, and it had everything. Huge fins, wild styling, plenty of horsepower and luxury fittings galore. It wasn't about handling, more about comfort, so it ran a basic separate chassis with double wishbones up front and a coil sprung live rear axle. It was offered with a choice of engines from a straight-six right up to the 348ci (5.7 litre) this car is equipped with. Designers concentrated on making it long and low, and gave the buyer a huge options list with which to 'customize' their vehicle. This particular car has side skirts, spot lights, a continental kit, fender guards, remote trunk release, cruise control, air-conditioning and power-assisted everything. Inside it can carry six with comfort. Due to its custom nature, it has become a firm favourite with lowrider fans in more recent times.

Top speed:	144 mph (230 km/h)
0–60 mph (0–95 km/h):	4.8 sec
Engine type:	V8
Displacement:	468 ci (7,669 cc)
Transmission	3-speed auto
Max power:	525 bhp (391 kW) @ 6,200 rpm
Max torque:	520 lb ft (704 Nm) @ 4,200 rpm
Weight:	3,250 lb (1,477 kg)
Economy:	6 mpg (2.1 km/l)

Chevrolet Corvette (1961)

Introduced in 1955 in V8 form, the Corvette established Chevrolet as kings of the US automotive world with a range of cars to suit every taste and pocket. By 1958 the car had been restyled more aggressively, and was both wider and longer. The famous small-block Chevy engine, which started out at 265ci (4.5 litres) V8, grew to 283ci (4.6 litres) by 1958 and by 1962 it was bored and stroked to 327ci (5.4 litres). The significance of this V8 engine can't be underestimated as, in fuel injected form at least, it made the Corvette one of the most powerful sportscars in the world and certainly one of the quickest at the time. Unfortunately the brakes and handling didn't match, though the steering was precise enough to catch the sudden oversteer the Corvette suffered from when pushed. But the 1956–1962 car was more about style, being inspired by fighter planes of the time.

Top speed:	135 mph (216 km/h)
0–60 mph (0–96 km/h):	6.1 sec
Engine type:	V8
Displacement:	327 ci (5,358 cc)
Transmission	4-speed manual
Max power:	360 bhp (268 kW) @ 6,000 rpm
Max torque:	352 lb ft (477 Nm) @ 4,000 rpm
Weight:	2,942 lb (1,337 kg)
Economy:	12.4 mpg (4.39 km/l)

Chevrolet Bel Air 409

Everything about the 1962 Bel Air looked plain, but to drive it was far different. Chevrolet brought it out as the horsepower wars were hotting up in the early 1960s, fitting the 409ci (6.7-litre) big-block V8 and creating a car which could chirp the tyres in every gear. In 1962 the engine was rated at 380bhp (283kW), but with twin four-barrel carburettors this went to 409bhp (305kW). Though the 409 could be ordered in any body style, most chose the coupe because of its 'bubble-top' looks and light weight. More pounds could be shed by ordering aluminium front panels from the factory; in fact Chevy made 12 cars like this which were aimed squarely at drag racers. Inside, the car was sparse as most buyers were interested only in speed, though there was a small steering column-mounted 7,000rpm rev counter. The car was so good it won the NHRA S/S (Super Stock) drag-racing championship in 1962.

Top speed:	115 mph (184 km/h)
0–60 mph (0–95 km/h):	7.3 sec
Engine type:	V8
Displacement:	409 ci (6,702 cc)
Transmission	4-speed manual
Max power:	380 bhp (283 kW) @ 6,000 rpm
Max torque:	420 lb ft (569 Nm) @ 3,200 rpm
Weight:	3,480 lb (1,582 kg)
Economy:	14 mpg (5 km/l)

Chevrolet Impala SS (1962)

Lowriding's origins can be traced back to the 1950s when the customizing craze was going full swing. Car modifiers would take their machines and lower them as far as possible for maximum visual impact. While amongst the regular family cars, these lowered rides looked aggressive and ultra cool, but they had one problem: their height. The cars couldn't be driven over anything without scraping the underneath of the car. Inventive modifiers used the hydraulic rams off of commercial vehicles to help them raise and lower their cars as required, thus the current craze of hydraulic cars began. Due to availability, bargain price and their good looks when dropped to the ground, the Chevy Impalas became very popular. This one has a full custom paint job, deep buttoned velour interior and hydraulic rams at each corner with pumps for each chromed and mounted in the trunk.

Top speed:	107 mph (171 km/h)
0–60 mph (0–96 km/h):	12.1 sec
Engine type:	V8
Displacement:	283 ci (4,637 cc)
Transmission	3-speed auto
Max power:	170 bhp (127 kW) @ 4,200 rpm
Max torque:	270 lb ft (366 Nm) @ 2,800 rpm
Weight:	3,512 lb (1,596 kg)
Economy:	15 mpg (5.31 km/l)

Chevrolet Corvette Sting Ray (1963)

Using a chassis from the cancelled Corvette SS racing programme, GM Chief stylist Bill Mitchell and designer Larry Shinoda styled their own body, called it the Stingray, then campaigned it with their own money. It was to be the shape that defined the 1963 second-generation Corvette, right down to the split rear window which Mitchell fought hard to keep. The Sting Ray came in both hardtop or open top form, and was the first Corvette to use fully independent suspension which dramatically improved the handling, allowing it to compete with the Jaguar XKE race cars. The rear used a single transverse leaf spring which ran either side of the differential, which itself could be ordered with anything from 3.08:1 to 4.56:1 gearing. The base engine was the 327ci (5.3-litre), but potential racers could order the 'Fuelie' fuel injected 360bhp (268kW) with four-speed manual and Posi rear.

Top speed:	118 mph (189 km/h)
0–60 mph (0–95 km/h):	6.1 sec
Engine type:	V8
Displacement:	327 ci (5,358 cc)
Transmission	4-speed manual
Max power:	300 bhp (223 kW) @ 5,000 rpm
Max torque:	360 lb ft (487 Nm) @ 3,200 rpm
Weight:	3,160 lb (1,436 kg)
Economy:	18 mpg (6.4 km/l)

Chevy Corvette Sting Ray ('63–'67)

The Corvette has been called 'America's favourite sportscar' and for good reason: it works as a road car, a fast GT tourer, a streets/strip racer and a circuit car. The Sting Ray which came along in 1963 made the car formidable around the world, taking on the likes of Jaguar and Ferrari and, in many cases, being successful. It was developed from a one-off race car originally built by Bill Mitchell and styled by Larry Shinoda, and by 1966 the car had developed into a formidable machine. The chassis was a steel ladder frame design with independent suspension front and rear, and the car had vented disc brakes all around. The engine was set well back in the frame to give near-perfect 50:50 weight distribution, making it handle well. The 427ci (6.9-litre) big-block was the biggest engine offered in the Corvette, the L88 version the most powerful at 435bhp (324kW).

Top speed:	135 mph (216 km/h)
0–60 mph (0–96 km/h):	5.6 sec
Engine type:	V8
Displacement:	427 ci (6,997 cc)
Transmission	4-speed manual
Max power:	435 bhp (324 kW) @ 6,200 rpm
Max torque:	460 lb ft (623 Nm) @ 4,000 rpm
Weight:	3,150 lb (1,431 kg)
Economy:	10.8 mpg (3.82 km/l)

Corvette BP Racer (1965)

Chevrolet launched its radical new Corvette in 1962, based on the Sting Ray race car. The road cars had a huge number of performance options, and it is this, plus the car's very quick pace, which made many successful race machines. This roadster is typical of the breed, with the original frame reinforced with a multi-point roll cage that stiffens up the structure and helps to make the suspension work better. The springs and shocks have all been uprated to the sort of standard that would usually rattle fillings loose on the road, though they make this roadster into the ultimate corner carver. This car uses the highest factory-rated engine, the 327ci (5.4 litre) 'Fuelie', so called because it had Rochester mechanical fuel injection. It also had specially designed aluminium cylinders heads, 11:1 compression, and a modified distributor to promote power.

Top speed:	148 mph (237 km/h)
0–60 mph (0–96 km/h):	5.4 sec
Engine type:	V8
Displacement:	327 ci (5,358 cc)
Transmission	4-speed manual
Max power:	375 bhp (280 kW) @ 6,000 rpm
Max torque:	352 lb ft (477 Nm) @ 4,000 rpm
Weight:	3,150 lb (1,431 kg)
Economy:	12 mpg (4.24 km/l)

Chevrolet II SS

With plain styling, the Chevy II was more often regarded as a leisurely old people's car. That all changed when Chevrolet installed their L79 Corvette 350ci (5.7-litre) V8 into the 1966 SS model. Having a lightweight body, the SS could easily mix it up with the best muscle cars, though looked more sedate than any with just the badges giving it away. Underneath, it relied on drum brakes which could get frightening given the performance which was on tap, and wheel hop was a problem under acceleration because of the simple leaf spring rear end. The transmission to have was the close-ratio four-speed manual which could get it easily into the 14-second range on the quarter mile, though the auto wasn't far behind. There was a base L-30 275bhp (205kW) engine too, which had double the production run of the L-29, though the latter is more collectable.

Top speed:	123 mph (197 km/h)
0–60 mph (0–95 km/h):	6.5 sec
Engine type:	V8
Displacement:	327 ci (5,358 cc)
Transmission	4-speed manual
Max power:	350 bhp (261 kW) @ 5,800 rpm
Max torque:	360 lb ft (487 Nm) @ 3,600 rpm
Weight:	3,140 lb (1,427 kg)
Economy:	14 mpg (5 km/l)

Chevrolet Chevelle SS396 (1966)

Launched in response to the Pontiac GTO and Oldsmobile 4-4-2, the Chevelle SS396 quickly gained a formidable reputation. GM had agreed to cap its cars to 400ci (6.6 litres) or under, hence the SS396 which featured the Mark IV L78 big-block, a detuned version of the engine available in the 1965 Corvette. The unit had 11:1 compression, a steel crank high-lift long duration camshaft for high-rpm use, plus an aluminium high-rise intake manifold which also responded best at high engine speeds. In order to best put down the power, the rear axle was located on four bars and used coil springs and telescopic dampers, while the front had wishbones and an anti-roll bar. While steel wheels were the standard with bias-ply tyres, Torque-Thrust D rims from American Racing were dealer options. This has them with modern radial tyres for optimum handling, without sacrificing looks.

Top speed:	130 mph (208 km/h)
0–60 mph (0–96 km/h):	6.0 sec
Engine type:	V8
Displacement:	396 ci (6,489 cc)
Transmission	4-speed manual
Max power:	375 bhp (280 kW) @ 5,600 rpm
Max torque:	415 lb ft (562 Nm) @ 3,600 rpm
Weight:	3,700 lb (1,681 kg)
Economy:	13 mpg (4.60 km/l)

Chevrolet Corvair (1966)

While being cutting edge, the first Corvair had a nasty trait which gained it a bad reputation. Its swing-axle suspension at the rear made it revolutionary, but with the rear-mounted engine over the top of it, the outside wheel would fold under the car in corners, and in some instances, the car rolled. The car had received full independent suspension in '65 and from then on the problem was solved, making following cars fine-handlers. The engine was good too, being an all-aluminium air-cooled flat six which, in turbocharged form as in the Corsa model shown, could produce exceptional performance for a compact car. The multi-dial interior and high-back seats also made the Corsa a sporty model, and Chevrolet thought they had a winner, but the damage had been done with earlier models, and production was ended in 1969, having seen 1,659,012 models produced in 10 years.

Top speed:	115 mph (184 km/h)
0–60 mph (0–96 km/h):	10.8 sec
Engine type:	Flat six
Displacement:	164 ci (2,687 cc)
Transmission	4-speed manual
Max power:	180 bhp (134 kW) @ 4,000 rpm
Max torque:	232 lb ft (314 Nm) @ 3,200 rpm
Weight:	2,720 lb (1,236 kg)
Economy:	28 mpg (9.91 km/l)

Chevrolet Suburban (1966)

Launched in 1935, the Suburban is one of Chevy's best-loved name tags, and is still in production today. It has always been based on a truck chassis, but as the owner of this vehicle wanted something different, he decided to use the front and rear axles off a 1980 GMC Jimmy, for four-wheel drive. Up front a powerful small-block Chevy provides all the power needed for either off-roading or towing, though it's something of a road performer too, with a sub-11 second time to 60mph (96km/h). To adjust the height, a set of Airlift shocks are used at each corner, but the biggest changes are inside, with a full custom interior, supportive buckets eats, digital gauges mounted inside the original housings, plus air-conditioning and a powerful sound system. It all adds up to a vehicle which can accomplish virtually everything a late-model Suburban can, but in the style of a classic body.

Top speed:	114 mph (182 km/h)
0–60 mph (0–96 km/h):	10.4 sec
Engine type:	V8
Displacement:	350 ci (5,735 cc)
Transmission:	4-speed auto
Max power:	300 bhp (224 kW) @ 4,800 rpm
Max torque:	380 lb ft (515 Nm) @ 3,200 rpm
Weight:	3,850 lb (1,750 kg)
Economy:	14 mpg (4.95 km/l)

Corvette Sting Ray 427 (1967)

Hitting the market at just over $5,000, the '67 Corvette Sting Ray was a per-formance sensation. While in 1965 the car had been available with the 396ci big-block Chevy, the 427 ci (6,997 cc) took power and torque up and made the Sting Ray a serious rival to the Shelby Cobra 427 which used Ford's big–block, though the 'Vette was less expensive. Production was just shy of 23,000 for the '67 model year, which could be an indication of buyers taking the handsome split-window shape while they could get it, because the following year the car restyled to mixed reviews. The chassis still featured Zora Arkus Duntov's excellent independent rear suspension, but in order to cope with the extra weight and power, the 427 also received stiffer suspension, a heavy-duty clutch, larger radiator and fan, and dealers recommended everyone take the four-wheel brake discs option for the obvious reason.

Top speed:	141 mph (226 km/h)
0–60 mph (0–96 km/h):	5.5 sec
Engine type:	V8
Displacement:	427 ci (6,997 cc)
Transmission	4-speed manual
Max power:	435 bhp (324kW) @ 5,800 rpm
Max torque:	460 lb ft (624 Nm) @ 4,000 rpm
Weight:	3,000 lb (1,363 kg)
Economy:	12 mpg (4.25 km/l)

Chevrolet Impala SS427

Chevrolet marketed their new-for-1967 Impala 427 with the slogan 'For the man who'd buy a sports car if it had this much room'. The theory was good, and by dropping in the big-block engine from the Corvette, the result was impressive. The engine had been released the year before and from the outset the famous 'Rat' motor was designed to produce big numbers. Staggered valves in the heads created better flow and power (at the cost of size and weight), while the torque was staggering which made hauling along the Impala easy. The Impala used a wider front track than early 1960s models and, because of the 1967 fastback coupe shape, the bodyshell was required to be very strong, which also helped handling. The SS also had superior rear-axle location with four, rather than three, links, making it one of the best-handling large muscle cars. The SS model was retired in 1968.

Top speed:	132 mph (211 km/h)
0–60 mph (0–95 km/h):	7.1 sec
Engine type:	V8
Displacement:	454 ci (7,439 cc)
Transmission	3-speed auto
Max power:	360 bhp (269 kW) @ 4,400 rpm
Max torque:	500 lb ft (677 Nm) @ 3,200 rpm
Weight:	3,860 lb (1,755 kg)
Economy:	11.5 mpg (4.1 km/l)

Chevrolet Camaro Pro Street (1968)

While muscle cars were indeed fast for their day and indeed still are, in the fastest accelerating motorsport, they look pretty tame. But as soon as the 1960s cars made it out of the showroom, they were put on to drag strips, then stripped and tuned for speed. During the late 1970s the cars took cues from the Pro Stocks classes, which used a stock bodyshell with huge drag tyres fitted underneath to get traction. It developed further, and in the late 1980s and 1990s, these street cars started turning in times that a Top Fuel dragster would have been proud of two decades earlier. This Camaro is typical of the most recent street-racing machines, with a full tube chassis lightweight front and rear racing suspension, 21-inch (533mm) wide slicks on the rear and a huge horsepower engine barely useable on the street. The Jerico gearbox has a lever per gear to aid rapid full-throttle changes.

Top speed:	175 mph (280 km/h)
0–60 mph (0–96 km/h):	2.6 sec
Engine type:	V8
Displacement:	540 ci (8,848 cc)
Transmission:	4-speed clutchless manual
Max power:	735 bhp (548 kW) @ 6,200 rpm
Max torque:	695 lb ft (942 Nm) @ 4,000 rpm
Weight:	3,674 lb (1,670 kg)
Economy:	4 mpg (1.42 km/l)

Chevrolet Camaro RS/SS (1968)

The SS badge donated a performance package on the Camaro, while the RS was a luxury package. Together, they made a formidable machine, and in 396ci (6.4-litre) form, as in this example, it was about as good as the Camaro could get. The 1968 model had changed little in the looks from the first version, but had styling differences such as the loss of the window vents in favour of GM's new Astro ventilation system, plus hidden headlights in the front grille. Mechanically it had staggered shocks and multi-leaf rear springs to control wheel hop. Ordering the SS option gave your car heavy-duty suspension, a 285bhp (213kW) 350ci (5.7-litre) V8, a nose striped and hood emblems. The 396ci (6.4-litre) big-block V8 was a separate option. Also a good idea were the 7x14 inch (178x356mm) rims which aided traction. The 325bhp (242kW) output was just one of three options with the 396.

Top speed:	130 mph (208 km/h)
0–60 mph (0–96 km/h):	6.6 sec
Engine type:	V8
Displacement:	396 ci (6,489 cc)
Transmission	3-speed auto
Max power:	325 bhp (242 kW) @ 4,800 rpm
Max torque:	410 lb ft (556 Nm) @ 3,200 rpm
Weight:	3,860 lb (1,754 kg)
Economy:	12 mpg (4.25 km/l)

Chevrolet Camaro ZL1

This car represented the zenith of Chevy's muscle cars. It's one of the most powerful Camaros ever, and also the most exclusive, with a production numbering just 69. In the 1960s Chevrolet supported the Automotive Manufacturers Association's ban by using over 400ci (6.9-litre) engines only in Corvettes or its full-size cars. However, one of Chevrolet's employees, Vince Piggins, found a loophole in the ban and created the ZL1. The car started as an SS396 model, with F41 uprated suspension, front discs, a cowl induction hood and exclusive engine unlike anything else Chevrolet had. It was an all-aluminium 427ci (7.2-litre) V8 which weighed the same as a small-block, hence the handling remained very good. However, the awesome power meant the car could run 11-second quarter-miles with racing tyres. Collectors have paid anything from $150,000 to $250,000 for a ZL1.

Top speed:	125 mph (201 km/h)
0–60 mph (0–95 km/h):	5.3 sec
Engine type:	V8
Displacement:	427 ci (6,997 cc)
Transmission:	4-speed manual
Max power:	430 bhp (321 kW) @ 5,200 rpm
Max torque:	450 lb ft (609 Nm) @ 4,400 rpm
Weight:	3,300 lb (1,500 kg)
Economy:	7 mpg (2.5 km/l)

Chevrolet Camaro Z28 (1968)

General Motors designed the Camaro to compete with Ford's Mustang, but with the likes of the Shelbys around, GM needed more power in their car. Also, in order to race in the Trams Am series, GM had to build 1,000 road models, though at the end of 1968 the new Z28 had gone well past 7,000 sales. The car needed a high-rpm race-type engine with less than 305ci (5 litres) so Chevrolet combined their 4-inch (102mm) bore 327 block with a short-stroke 3-inch (76mm) forged crank, similar to the one in their 283. With a high compression of 11:1, large valve heads and high-lift cam, it revved well, and though rated at 290bhp (216kW), output was closer to 350bhp (261kW). Handling was improved by quickening the steering, fitting harder brake-linings, stiffening the rear leaf springs, and uprating shocks. The car had a three-speed auto but the Muncie four-speed manual was often fitted.

Top speed:	123 mph (197 km/h)
0–60 mph (0–95 km/h):	6.5 sec
Engine type:	V8
Displacement:	302 ci (4,948 cc)
Transmission	4-speed manual
Max power:	290 bhp (216 kW) @ 5,800 rpm
Max torque:	290 lb ft (393 Nm) @ 4,200 rpm
Weight:	3,528 lb (1,604 kg)
Economy:	15.7 mpg (5.6 km/l)

Chevrolet Camaro Z28 Racer (1968)

The 1967 Z28 track car had been fairly unsuccessful, so the following year it received changes in the hands of various teams, but none were more famous for their race victory than the Roger Penske organization. Their Sunaco-backed car was fitted stiffer springs, Koni shocks and a rear anti-roll bar which gave the car more neutral handling. The rear had multi-leaf springs, and a Panhard rod was also fitted for maximum location of the 12-bolt live axle. To save weight, the body was acid-dipped and also given extra rigidity with more tubes in the multi-point roll cage. The steering was given a higher ratio for better response and under the nose an air dam was fitted to redirect air and minimize front end lift. The engine's displacement, actually 302.4ci (4,955cc), could be revved through to 7,000rpm, thanks to 11.5:1 compression, tubular headers and a Holley four-barrel carb.

Top speed:	140 mph (224 km/h)
0–60 mph (0–96 km/h):	5.5 sec
Engine type:	V8
Displacement:	302.4 ci (4,955 cc)
Transmission	4-speed manual
Max power:	402 bhp (299 kW) @ 6,800 rpm
Max torque:	340 lb ft (461 Nm) @ 5,500 rpm
Weight:	2,875 lb (1,306 kg)
Economy:	10 mpg (3.54 km/l)

Chevrolet Chevelle Pro Street (1968)

The Chevelle was restyled for 1968, becoming shorter and sportier, yet retaining its muscular status. While it may never have been as popular as the Camaro, it used a similar coupe shape and therefore had the necessary wide haunches suitable for the Pro Street treatment. This meant the biggest tyres out back, and here the owner has fitted Mickey Thompson racing slicks with over 3ft (0.91m) of contact patch across their width. At the front are the complete opposite skinny rims and tyres for minimum weight and thus the best weight transfer on to the rear treads. Horsepower is what it's all about in Pro Street, and this mainly strip-racing car has a massive big-block engine which is aided by the nitrous oxide injection for an extra 500bhp (373kW) on top of the standard 832bhp (620kW). A Lenco clutchless transmission makes gear-shifting as fast, as the five levers can be pulled back.

Top speed:	188 mph (300 km/h)
0–60 mph (0–96 km/h):	2.0 sec
Engine type:	V8
Displacement:	632 ci (10,356 cc)
Transmission	5-speed clutchless manual
Max power:	870 bhp (649 kW) @ 7,000 rpm
Max torque:	720 lb ft (976 Nm) @ 4,400 rpm
Weight:	3,420 lb (1,554 kg)
Economy:	2 mpg (0.71 km/l)

Chevrolet Impala SS427 (1968)

The new-for-1967 Impala 427 was marketed with the slogan 'For the man who'd buy a sports car if it had this much room'. By slotting in the big-block engine from the Corvette, the result was impressive. The engine had been released the year before and from the outset the 'Rat' motor was engineered to produce much power. Staggered valves in the heads created better flow (at the cost of size and weight), while the impressive torque made hauling along the Impala easy. The new car used a wider front track than early 1960s Chevrolets and, because of the fastback coupe shape, the bodyshell was required to be very strong, which aided handling. The SS also had superior rear axle location with four rather than three links, making it one of the best-handling large muscle cars of the era. The SS427 reverted to an option package in 1968, then was retired the following year.

Top speed:	130 mph (208 km/h)
0-60 mph (0–96 km/h):	6.0 sec
Engine type:	V8
Displacement:	400 ci (6,554 cc)
Transmission	4-speed manual
Max power:	360 bhp (268 kW) @ 5,000 rpm
Max torque:	440 lb ft (596 Nm) @ 3,600 rpm
Weight:	3,197 lb (1,453 kg)
Economy:	10 mpg (3.54 km/l)

Chevrolet Blazer (1969)

L ong at the forefront of US 4x4s, the Blazer was one of the first of what is now known as an SUV (Sport Utility Vehicle). It has become an icon and its name is still used by GM. The K5-code vehicle started out in 1969, offered by Chevrolet as a roomy on/off road vehicle with a 120bhp (89kW) base engine or 307ci (5-litre) and 350ci (5.7-litre) V8. It was utilitarian in design, but made a formidable off-roader. Because it was stiffly sprung to cope with any terrain, on the road it tended to bounce around on anything but smooth roads, but it could cruise effortlessly at 70mph (113km/h), so was ideal for US roads. The Blazer's chassis was separate and very strong, and it mounted the engine well back for perfect 50:50 weight distribution. The 350ci (5,735cc) V8 was the most popular engine choice and it was driven through an automatic with two-speed transfer case with high and low ratios.

Top speed:	98 mph (157 km/h)
0–60 mph (0–96 km/h):	15.0 sec
Engine type:	V8
Displacement:	350 ci (5,735 cc)
Transmission:	3-speed auto
Max power:	165 bhp (123 kW) @ 3,800 rpm
Max torque:	255 lb ft (345 Nm) @ 2,800 rpm
Weight:	5,157 lb (2,344 kg)
Economy:	8.7 mpg (3.08 km/l)

Chevrolet Camaro Pace Car (1969)

When the first Camaro appeared in 1967 it was rolled out to pace the famous Indianapolis 500, and two years later it was back once again in convertible form to do the same. The limited edition – just 3,675 were made – was available by ticking the Z11 option which, priced at $37, got you the racing stripes and door decals. To make a replica pace car you also had to tick the SS package, which meant a cowl induction hood and rear spoiler, plus order the hidden headlight RS grille. The actual machine which paced the event had a 375bhp (280kW) 396ci (6,489cc) V8, but in the interests of driveability, most of the replicas came with small-block 350ci (5,735cc) V8s, which still thumped out plenty of power. Chevy Rallye wheels at 7 inches (178mm) wide improved handling and a Posi-traction live rear axle ensured maximum grip from a standing start.

Top speed:	124 mph (198 km/h)
0–60 mph (0–96 km/h):	6.8 sec
Engine type:	V8
Displacement:	350 ci (5,735 cc)
Transmission	3-speed auto
Max power:	300 bhp (224 kW) @ 4,800 rpm
Max torque:	380 lb ft (515 Nm) @ 3,200 rpm
Weight:	3,395 lb (1,543 kg)
Economy:	15 mpg (5.31 km/l)

Chevrolet Camaro Z28 (1969)

For 1969 the Camaro got all-new sheet metal with more aggressive styling. In Z28
form it was designed to compete against the Mustang in the Transmission-Am
racing series, and it even stole two championships from Ford's pony car in the late
1960s. What made it most legendary, however, was the road-going versions, which
were barely tamed race cars. The chassis got uprated springs and shocks, while the
rear live axle also had staggered positioning on the shocks to help control wheel
hop, which earlier Z28s had suffered from badly. Four-wheel disc brakes were an
option too and were straight from the Corvette. From the same car were the Rallye
steel rims with 6 inches (152mm) of width to improve handling. The engine was a
short stroke 302ci (4.9-litre) so could rev very well, though it was best over
3,000rpm for manners. This car has the rare dual carb option for more power.

Top speed:	132 mph (211 km/h)
0–60 mph (0–96 km/h):	6.9 sec
Engine type:	V8
Displacement:	302 ci (4,948 cc)
Transmission	4-speed manual
Max power:	290 bhp (216 kW) @ 5,800 rpm
Max torque:	310 lb ft @ 4,200 rpm (420 Nm)
Weight:	3,050 lb (1,386 kg)
Economy:	13 mpg (4.60 km/l)

Chevrolet Corvette Stingray (1969)

The Corvette underwent a controversial restyle in 1968, and while the press reviews were mixed, the public voted with their wallets and bought 28,566 in one year. Over 15,000 of those were built with the big-block 427ci (6.9-litre) engine which shows just how performance-hungry buyers were. Even the lowest-powered 427, code L36, made 390bhp (291kW), then came the L68 with 400bhp (298kW), the L71 with 435bhp (324kW), and the over-the-top engine was the L88 with an underrated figure of 430bhp (321kW) though output was closer to 500bhp (373kW). Underneath the car was virtually the same as previous models, with an independent front and rear and disc brakes all around. This car has the mandatory four-speed Muncie 22 close-ratio gearbox which is required to take the torque and spread the power well, and with the right driver, the car could do low-13-second quarter miles.

Top speed:	135 mph (216 km/h)
0–60 mph (0–96 km/h):	5.5 sec
Engine type:	V8
Displacement:	427ci (6,997 cc)
Transmission	4-speed manual
Max power:	435 bhp (324kW) @ 5,600 rpm
Max torque:	460 lb ft (623 Nm) @ 4,000 rpm
Weight:	3,145 lb (1,429 kg)
Economy:	10 mpg (3.54 km/l)

Chevrolet Yenko Chevelle

Don Yenko was better known for his highly-tuned Camaros, but during 1969 he also turned his hand to the Chevelle, the result being an incredible street racer. He removed the 375bhp (280kW) 390ci (6.6-litre) big-block engine and replaced it with a 427ci (7.2-litre). To cope with the straight-line performance the car was fitted with disc brakes as standard, plus a Muncie four-speed manual, or GM TH400 if you preferred an auto. At the rear end the car also came with a strengthened GM 12-bolt live axle with 4.10:1 gearing as standard for maximum acceleration. It used heavy-duty suspension with coil springs at the rear and independent A-arms up front. Externally the cars were identified with 'Yenko SC' (Super Car) logos and black stripes, but even so, you rarely saw them on the street, as just 99 were built in 1969, being replaced by the Yenko Chevelle SS454 in 1970.

Top speed:	110 mph (176 km/h)
0–60 mph (0–95 km/h):	5.7 sec
Engine type:	V8
Displacement:	427 ci (6,997 cc)
Transmission	3-speed auto
Max power:	450 bhp (335 kW) @5,000 rpm
Max torque:	460 lb ft (623 Nm) @ 4,000 rpm
Weight:	3,800 lb (1,727 kg)
Economy:	8 mpg (2.8 km/l)

Chevrolet Camaro SS396 (1970)

The redesign of the Camaro came early in 1970 so these models are often referred to as the 70 1/2 Camaros. It was an instant hit on the streets, especially when Chevy announced the performance version, top of which was the SS396. The engine was actually 402ci (6.6 litres) through an increase in bore size, even though GM badged it still as a 396. Two states of tune were available, in the L-34 with 350bhp (261kW) or L-78 with 375bhp (280kW), and while the 350 version came with 10.25:1 compression and a Rochester four-barrel carb, the 385 went higher still on compression, adding an aluminium intake and a Holley four-barrel. Underneath, the extras included a heavy-duty F41 suspension package with front and rear anti-roll bars, a 12-bolt rear axle with choice of ratios and 7x14-inch (178x356mm) wheels. Cars ordered with the four-speed Muncie gearbox also got a Hurst shifter.

Top speed:	128 mph (205 km/h)
0–60 mph (0–96 km/h):	6.2 sec
Engine type:	V8
Displacement:	402 ci (6,587 cc)
Transmission	4-speed manual
Max power:	375 bhp (280 kW) @ 5,600 rpm
Max torque:	415 lb ft (562 Nm) @ 3,200 rpm
Weight:	3,550 lb (1,613 kg)
Economy:	14 mpg (4.96 km/l)

Chevrolet Chevelle SS454 (1970)

At the height of the muscle-car wars, Chevrolet played its trump card with the launch of the LS-6 454 V8. At the same time, GM lifted its displacement on mid-sized cars which meant that they could be finally fitted with engines over 400ci (6.5-litres). The result was the Chevelle SS454. The car was basic underneath with coil springs all around, but the SS package included the F41 suspension which had stiffer front springs to cope with the big-block's weight. Maganum 500 wheels were fitted to every SS Chevelle but even being wide, fitted with Polyglas tyres barely provided traction. The engine had high compression pistons, rectangular port heads and solid lifters so could rev well for a big engine. It received high-pressure air while on the move through a vacuum-operated flap on the cowl induction. Just 4,475 SS454s made it out of the factory, but all were 13-second quarter-mile cars.

Top speed:	125 mph (200 km/h)
0–60 mph (0–96 km/h):	6.1 sec
Engine type:	V8
Displacement:	454 ci (7,439 cc)
Transmission	4-speed manual
Max power:	450 bhp (336 kW) @ 5,600 rpm
Max torque:	500 lb ft (678 Nm) @ 3,600 rpm
Weight:	4,000 lb (1,818 kg)
Economy:	12.5 mpg (4.43 km/l)

Chevrolet El Camino SS454

Many muscle cars are remembered because they represent the pinnacle of the model, and the 1970–only El Camino SS454 is no different. The El Camino had seen a break of four years earlier in the 1960s, but was back by 1964 with a 396ci (6.5-litre) top engine option. It went through a major facelift in 1968 with softer, more rounded lines but still the 396ci (6.5 litre) remained. In 1970 the El Camino followed the line of the Chevelle SS by being available with the 454ci (7.4-litre) big-block 'Rat' V8. The engine came in two different versions, the mild one being the LS5 with 10.25:1 compression and 360bhp (268kW), while the wild one was the LS6 with forged aluminium pistons, a special cam, forged steel crank and rods and 11.5:1 compression for 450bhp (336kW). With a Positraction live axle and very little rear weight, the back wheels would easily light up under provocation.

Top speed:	130 mph (208 km/h)
0–60 mph (0–95 km/h):	7.0 sec
Engine type:	V8
Displacement:	454 ci (7,439 cc)
Transmission	3-speed auto
Max power:	360 bhp (268 kW) @ 4,400 rpm
Max torque:	500 lb ft (677 Nm) @ 3,200 rpm
Weight:	4,270 lb (1,941 kg)
Economy:	14 mpg (5 km/l)

Chevrolet Monte Carlo 454 (1970)

The Monte Carlo was supposed to be luxurious more than sporty, and it was built on the Chevelle platform but used a slightly longer wheelbase. It had extra rubber mounts fitted between the body and chassis to reduce vibration from the street, plus extra sound-deadening inside. The option RPO Z20 made you the SS454 model, and that incorporated the largest big-block Chevy had on offer, the infamous 'Rat'. The long stroke of the LS-5 motor produced the torque, giving the car endless power through the rev range. The following year's version of the same engine, coded LS-6, produced even more power with 450bhp (335kW). Underneath the car ran with the Chevelle's wishbone front and coil-sprung rear suspension, with an Automatic Level Control system and on-board air compressor to control ride height. Inside it featured soft vinyl bucket seats and a simulated walnut burr dash.

Top speed:	132 mph (211 km/h)
0–60 mph (0–96 km/h):	7.1 sec
Engine type:	V8
Displacement:	454 ci (7,439 cc)
Transmission	3-speed auto
Max power:	360 bhp (268 kW) @ 4,400 rpm
Max torque:	500 lb ft (678 Nm) @ 3,200 rpm
Weight:	3,860 lb (1,754 kg)
Economy:	11.5 mpg (4.07 km/l)

Chevrolet Camaro RS/SS (1971)

Camaros have always been modified, and when the new 1970 1/2 model was introduced, it addressed some of the former models' shortcomings so improved the breed and potential still further. Many styles have developed over time, but one that has been popular in the 1990s and into the 21st century is Pro Touring. This uses classic muscle-car bodies but with all the handling and finesse of a modern-day supercar. Upgraded road/race suspension, massive Baer Claw disc brakes, and large rims with modern wide and low-profile rubber are fitted on this Camaro. Inside there are modern bucket race seats, harnesses and also a modern sound system. Usually Pro Touring cars run at least five but sometimes six-speed gearboxes, but this owner has opted for a high-tech four-speed overdrive gearbox with ratchet-style shifter which provides minimal shifter movement for each gear change.

Top speed:	143 mph (229 km/h)
0–60 mph (0–96 km/h):	5.4 sec
Engine type:	V8
Displacement:	400 ci (6,554 cc)
Transmission	4-speed auto
Max power:	425 bhp (317 kW) @ 4,800 rpm
Max torque:	330 lb ft (447 Nm) @ 3,000 rpm
Weight:	3,320 lb (1,509 kg)
Economy:	17 mpg (6.02 km/l)

Chevrolet C10 (1973)

In 1973, Chevrolet's light trucks were radically altered for a much smoother and modern appearance. The roof rails went in favour of doors which opened into the roof, and curved side glass was fitted. Along the waist line of the car was a sculpted curve, which gave the truck a wide feel. With their huge engine bays and brutish looks, the 1973 C10s soon became favourites for modification. This vehicle has had the ride height reduced with lowering springs at the front and block between the leafs and axle at the rear to effectively raise the axle up to the bodywork, thus lowering the rear. Also fitted were modern wheels and tyres to further enhanced handling. Under the hood the truck was fitted with a 1970 454ci (7.4-litre) Corvette big-block and with high-flow heads plus a high-lift cam, it has been known to cover the quarter-mile in 15 seconds.

Top speed:	122 mph (195 km/h)
0–60 mph (0–95 km/h):	7.8 sec
Engine type:	V8
Displacement:	454 ci (7,439 cc)
Transmission	3-speed auto
Max power:	425 bhp (317 kW) @ 6,200 rpm
Max torque:	500 lb ft (677 Nm) @ 3,400 rpm
Weight:	4,045 lb (1,838 kg)
Economy:	7 mpg (2.5 km/l)

Chevrolet Nova SS (1973)

For 1968 the Nova filled out considerably, more towards an intermediate car. It also looked much more like many of the muscle cars of the time thanks to its fastback styling. Though the car was available with a big-block V8, by 1973 when this car was produced only the small-block V8 was on the option list. The Novas make great drag cars as they have much room under the hood for big engines and the owner of this car has chosen to install a 454ci (7.4-litre) big-block, bored out to 468ci (7.6 litres) and fully balanced. It has an Iskendarian high-lift cam, rare L88 manifold and a high-flow four-barrel Holley carburettor. Regular 454s are only rated at 450bhp (335kW), so it's no surprise this one will do the quarter-mile in 12.5 seconds. It uses the stock suspension, albeit lowered, with a pair of traction bars at the rear to help launch the car off the line.

Top speed:	144 mph (230 km/h)
0–60 mph (0–95 km/h):	4.8 sec
Engine type:	V8
Displacement:	468 ci (7,669 cc)
Transmission	3-speed auto
Max power:	525 bhp (391 kW) @ 6,200 rpm
Max torque:	520 lb ft (704 Nm) @ 4,200 rpm
Weight:	3,250 lb (1,477 kg)
Economy:	6 mpg (2.1 km/l)

Chevrolet Camaro modified (1978)

Camaros have seen modifications to make them faster, handle better, more luxurious, into glitzy show winners, and they've even been turned into automotive art pieces in museums. But the majority of them are still used to go down the drag strip very fast and this 1978 example does exactly that. It's been modified in a Pro Street style, meaning the larger race wheels are all sitting under the stock bodywork, but there's drag-racing suspension front and rear to keep weight down and help the car react to get the best possible traction off the startline. It can cover the quarter in just 9.8 seconds at a speed of over 140mph (225km/h), but is something of a crowd pleaser too, because it has exhaust headers facing upwards that have special fuel injectors and spark plugs in each pipe to shoot flames skywards. The front sits low, courtesy of adjustable airbag springs.

Top speed:	165 mph (264 km/h)
0–60 mph (0–96 km/h):	3.8 sec
Engine type:	V8
Displacement:	468 ci (7,669 cc)
Transmission	3-speed auto
Max power:	540 bhp (403 kW) @ 6,800 rpm
Max torque:	510 lb ft (692 Nm) @ 4,200 rpm
Weight:	N/A
Economy:	7 mpg (2.48 km/l)

Chevrolet Corvette Pace Car (1978)

The Corvette was 25 years old in 1978, and to celebrate a limited edition Silver Anniversary model was produced. This car was also chosen to pace the 62nd Indianapolis and more than 6,000 replica cars were built and sold through select dealers. While the styling was all new, the chassis was carried over but the new car got the FE7 Gymkhana package which included heavy-duty front and rear shocks, fatter front and rear anti-roll bars, and higher rated springs. Front and rear discs were power assisted and all the chassis upgrades gave the Corvette tremendous grip and handling. Standard fitment was the L82 high-performance 350ci (5,735cc), with greater power than in other 'Vettes thanks to high-lift camshaft, special heads with bigger valves, and forged pistons. Induction comprised a four-barrel carb and dual snorkel air cleaner, while the dual exhaust was larger, for more flow.

Top speed:	125 mph (200 km/h)
0–60 mph (0–96 km/h):	8.2 sec
Engine type:	V8
Displacement:	350 ci (5,735 cc)
Transmission	3-speed auto
Max power:	220 bhp (164 kW) @ 5,200 rpm
Max torque:	260 lb ft (352 Nm) @ 3,600 rpm
Weight:	3,401 lb (1,545 kg)
Economy:	16 mpg (5.66 km/l)

Chevrolet Monte Carlo (1979)

For the lowrider scene, the Monte Carlo is one of the most chosen cars to modify. Its suspension is ideal, being double wishbone front and a live axle rear supported on coil springs, to use hydraulic rams in place of the coils and shocks, therefore giving a fully moving set-up capable of doing any number of lowrider tricks. Yet even within the lowrider movement, fragmentation of styles has occurred and the cars which move now have their own competitions, while the show finish machines dual it out in huge halls where they can be displayed to maximum effect. Cars such as this show machine rarely get driven; inside it features an immaculate crushed-velour interior with no dash but a 6-inch (152mm) TV screen in the centre console. The interior extends into the trunk and externally there's a meticulously detailed flake paint with pinstriping and murals.

Top speed:	118 mph (189 km/h)
0–60 mph (0–96 km/h):	9.4 sec
Engine type:	V8
Displacement:	305 ci (4,998 cc)
Transmission:	3-speed auto
Max power:	120 bhp (89 kW) @ 3,800 rpm
Max torque:	240 lb ft (596 Nm) @ 2,400 rpm
Weight:	3,169 lb (1,440 kg)
Economy:	15 mpg (5.31 km/l)

Chevrolet Corvette (1982)

By 1982 the Corvette was at the end of its third-generation guise which had started back in the late 1960s. Despite tweaks over time and a mild facelift with moulded fenders in 1980, a redesign was well overdue, but Chevrolet engineers wanted this 'Vette to go out with a bang so they produced the 'Collector Edition'. It came with silver paint and clot, silver leather door trim, a lift-up rear window, bronze T-tops, plus tasteful finned aluminium wheels measuring 8x15 inches (203x381mm) and fitted with 255/60 Goodyear Eagle tyres. The only engine available was at least very good, featuring Cross Fire fuel injection and computer-controlled engine management for great power, plus over 20mpg (7.08km/l)) at steady highway speeds. The Corvette handled like a true sportscar thanks to full independent suspension, but inside was the most civilized ride yet in the model.

Top speed:	125 mph (200 km/h)
0-60 mph (0–96 km/h):	8.0 sec
Engine type:	V8
Displacement:	350 ci (5,735 cc)
Transmission	3-speed auto
Max power:	200 bhp (149 kW) @ 4,200 rpm
Max torque:	285 lb ft (386 Nm) @ 2,800 rpm
Weight:	3,425 lb (1,556 kg)
Economy:	20 mpg (7.08 km/l)

Chevrolet S10 pick-up (1984)

During the 1980s many imported trucks started to arrive in the US and were being snapped up as reliable, cheap work vehicles. Chevrolet responded by releasing the S10 and it soon became a best seller and a favourite with customizers. They started a trend known as minitrucks, where the pick-ups lost their utilitarian roots in favour of smooth street style and more radical modifications for performance and handling. This truck gets its lowered ride through drop spindles at the front and lowering blocks out back, but retains the stock springs as they're stiff as standard. The exterior mods feature a cowl induction hood, front and rear valance extensions, bullet tail lights and graphics. Billet aluminium wheels with low -profile radials help it corner with the best factory hot rod pick-ups, while the Vortech V6 engine is strong at low rpm and ideal for cruising.

Top speed:	108 mph (172 km/h)
0–60 mph (0–96 km/h):	11.2 sec
Engine type:	V6
Displacement:	262 ci (4,300 cc)
Transmission	4–speed auto
Max power:	160 bhp (119 kW) @ 4,000 rpm
Max torque:	230 lb ft (312 Nm) @ 2,800 rpm
Weight:	3,140 lb (1,427 kg)
Economy:	21 mpg (7.43 km/l)

Chevy MC SS Aerocoupe (1987)

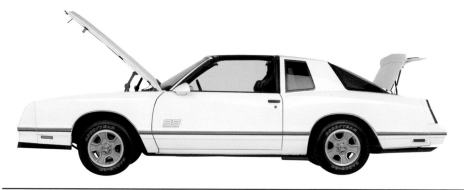

Performance started to make a welcome return to many American vehicles in the mid-1980s, and this saw the rebirth of the SS range on Chevrolet's Monte Carlos. The Aerocoupe had been designed and released in 1986 to compete with Ford's Thunderbird on the NASCAR tracks. Just 200 were built that year but it was well known the fastback style rear window and sloping nose could give the Monte Carlo a few extra mph on the top speed, much needed in NASCAR. More than 6,000 were built in 1987 and featured a separate chassis with stiffer springs, a larger front anti-roll bar, gas shocks and 7x15-inch (224x381mm) forged alloy rims with 225/60 tyres rated to 150mph (241km/h). The small-block engine got a hotter camshaft, new cylinder heads and intake, and an electronically controlled Rochester four-barrel carburettor. Monte Carlos outnumbered the Aerocoupe; 125,000 were produced.

Top speed:	130 mph (208 km/h)
0–60 mph (0–96 km/h):	8.2 sec
Engine type:	V8
Displacement:	305 ci (4,998 cc)
Transmission:	4-speed auto
Max power:	190 bhp (142 kW) @ 4,800 rpm
Max torque:	240 lb ft (325 Nm) @ 3,200 rpm
Weight:	3,526 lb (1,602 kg)
Economy:	18 mpg (6.37 km/l)

Chevrolet 454SS

With fuel concerns diminishing in the mid-1980s, manufacturers began to produce more powerful cars again and with America's pick-up obsession, a new market was soon born: the muscle truck. Chevrolet, having long been a maker of pick-ups, was one of the first to get a grip on the market with their 1989 454 C1500 truck, which had been re-styled just a year before, so looked bang up to date. Underneath the SS454 was still very trucklike, with a strong ladder frame chassis and carlike double wishbone suspension, but a leaf spring rear. All spring rates were uprated and Bilstein shocks took place of the stock ones. Also modified was the steering, with quicker gearing to help the handling. The 454ci (7.4-litre) came from the standard C/K 3/4 and 1-ton pick-ups, and with its long stroke was designed for low rpm torque delivery. Rear end 4.10:1 gears were good for rapid acceleration.

Top speed:	120 mph (193km/h)
0–60 mph (0–95 km/h):	7.2 sec
Engine type:	V8
Displacement:	454 ci (7,440 cc)
Transmission	4-speed auto
Max power:	255 bhp (190 kW) @ 4,000 rpm
Max torque:	405 lb ft (548 Nm) @ 2,400 rpm
Weight:	4,535 lb (2,061 kg)
Economy:	10 mpg (3.5 km/l)

Chevrolet Corvette ZR1

Easily the most technologically advanced engine ever put in a Corvette, the LT5 was only part of the ZR1 package. The car entered production in 1990 after much hype, and immediately looked different, thanks to the wide rear bodywork, to allow fitting of 11x17-inch (276x432mm) alloys with 315/35 tyres. Lotus designed the engine and based it on Chevy's small-block V8, but started with an aluminium-alloy block. Completely new heads used two-cams-per-bank operating four valves per cylinder. The induction used two ports and injectors per cylinder and only one of each operated below 3,500rpm. Above this with the throttle floored the other port and injector would open up and allow the full 405bhp (302kW) on later models to be unleashed. Other high-tech gadgetry included the suspension on which the driver could select a setting: Touring, Sport or Performance.

Top speed:	180 mph (288 km/h)
0–60 mph (0–95 km/h):	5.0 sec
Engine type:	V8
Displacement:	350 ci (5,735 cc)
Transmission	6-speed manual
Max power:	405 bhp (302 kW) @ 5,800 rpm
Max torque:	371 lb ft (502 Nm) @ 4,800 rpm
Weight:	3,519 lb (1,600 kg)
Economy:	14.7 mpg (5.2 km/l)

Chevrolet Camaro Z28 (1992)

The third-generation Camaro came in 1982 and lasted for 10 years, growing in power during that period and having many of the traits which made the Camaro popular from its launch in 1967. As always, the Z28 was the performance option, and in 1992, the 25th anniversary of the model, the car got a Heritage appearance package in either red, white or black, and continued the use of bolt-on spoilers and side skirt to modernize its appearance. The live rear axle had a limited-slip differential and 3.42:1 gears, and was located on longitudinal links plus a Panhard rod for improved cornering. The 305ci (5-litre) V8 had electronic Tuned Port fuel injection with an individual runner for each cylinder, and Chevrolet made the car into more of a driver's machine by fitting a 5-speed manual gearbox as standard. Production cars could do 14-second quarter-miles.

Top speed:	137 mph (219 km/h)
0–60 mph (0--95 km/h):	6.5 sec
Engine type:	V8
Displacement:	305 ci (4,998 cc)
Transmission	5-speed manual
Max power:	235 bhp (175 kW) @ 4,400 rpm
Max torque:	300 lb ft (406 Nm) @ 3,200 rpm
Weight:	3,105 lb (1,411 kg)
Economy:	13.8 mpg (4.9 km/l)

Chevrolet Caprice modified (1992)

The Caprice, which was first launched 1990, had ultra-smooth styling and lent itself well to customizing. Being a practical car, too, and coming with a V8 as standard meant it soon got the attention of hot rodders. Station-wagon versions often got used as aftermarket manufacturers' show vehicles come parts haulers, and this is one has been built along those lines but has gone a step forward and backward at the same time. This Caprice features styling touches from a 1957 Chevy Nomad, including the rear three-quarter panels and tail lights, side trim, hood spears and a classic set of polished American Racing Torque-Thrust rims on 275/50 Pirelli tyres. The interior continues on a 1950s theme with red and white tuck 'n' roll, but has rearward-facing back seats to best utilize the huge rear space. Power comes from Throttle Body fuel-injected small-block Chevy V8.

Top speed:	120 mph (192 km/h)
0–60 mph (0–96 km/h):	9.8 sec
Engine type:	V8
Displacement:	350 ci (5,735 cc)
Transmission	4-speed auto
Max power:	180 bhp (134 kW) @ 4,000 rpm
Max torque:	300 lb ft (406 Nm) @ 2,400 rpm
Weight:	4,120 lb (1,872 kg)
Economy:	18 mpg (6.37 km/l)

Dale Earnhardt's Chevy Lumina

The late Dale Earnhardt, known as 'The Intimidator', had long been a Chevrolet NASCAR driver and started with the Lumina in 1992. That turned out to be a dismal year for the team, so Chevy doubled its efforts for 1993 and was rewarded with the Winston Cup Championship. The Lumina, like all NASCARs, had to run the same shape as the street car, but underneath there was nothing of the stock sedan. A full metal spaceframe filled the inside, with trailing arms and Panhard rod locating the live rear axle. At the front it used adjustable double wishbones and huge anti-roll bar. The car used different springs rates and tyre sizes because of travelling around to the left constantly. The small-block Chevy with a compression ratio of 13:1 had a carburettor restriction plate to even out competition and to keep weight to 3,500lb (1587kg), Kevlar body panels and Lexan windows were used.

Top speed:	200 mph (320 km/h)
0–60 mph (0–95 km/h):	3.5 sec
Engine type:	V8
Displacement:	358 ci (5,866 cc)
Transmission	4-speed manual
Max power:	680 bhp (507 kW) @ 7,000 rpm
Max torque:	N/A
Weight:	3,500 lb (1,590 kg)
Economy:	N/A

Chevrolet Suburban (1993)

All Suburbans from Chevrolet have been massive, and over time (they've been in production for nearly 40 years) they have gradually taken on more luxury and style and now represent one of the best SUVs (Sport Utility Vehicle) in a packed and ever-growing market. While they offer a great deal as standard, as always for some people it's not enough, and this example show just how well the vehicles receives modifications. The car has gone through massive lowering, being some 3.5 inches (89mm) down at the front, but a huge 5 inches (127mm) lower at the rear. This helps handling, as do the 8x17-inch (203x432mm) billets with 255/50 tyres. But it's inside where most changes have occurred: power leather seats, a 56-piece Bahia Rosewood overlay set, and huge in-car entertainment system with TV, VCR and video game player. Power is via full-dressed computer-managed small-block Chevy.

Top speed:	98 mph (157 km/h)
0–60 mph (0–96 km/h):	11.2 sec
Engine type:	V8
Displacement:	350 ci (5,735 cc)
Transmission:	4–speed auto
Max power:	210 bhp (157 kW) @ 4,000 rpm
Max torque:	300 lb ft (406 Nm) @ 2,800 rpm
Weight:	4,675 lb (2,125 kg)
Economy:	14.4 mpg (5.10 km/l)

Chevrolet Corvette modified (1994)

The Corvettes through all its generations has always been a tuner's dream. A lightweight bodyshell, powerful V8 and (from the late 1960s) fully independent suspension, means all the right ingredients are there in stock form. As the car went into the 1990s, it increasingly became high-tech, but so did the aftermarket with it, hence instead of a carburettor or ignition upgrade, the engines of the generation-four cars got chipped instead, meaning their engine management was improved for more performance. This example has received not just an engine chip, but Chevy's own Performance Handling Package and a set of 1996 Corvette 17-inch (432mm) alloys. An upgraded exhaust releases more power and makes this Corvette into a more finely tuned driver's car which can do the quarter-mile in low-13-second times and pull 0.9 lateral g. The bodywork has a subtle, but effective, trunk spoiler.

Top speed:	158 mph (252 km/h)
0–60 mph (0–96 km/h):	5.0 sec
Engine type:	V8
Displacement:	350 ci (5,735 cc)
Transmission	4-speed auto
Max power:	330 bhp (246 kW) @ 5,500 rpm
Max torque:	340 lb ft (461 Nm) @ 4,000 rpm
Weight:	3,504 lb (1,592 kg)
Economy:	14 mpg (4.96 km/l)

Chevrolet Corvette Grand Sport

With a fifth-generation Corvette about to be launched, Chevrolet had to send off the previous car in style, thus the 1996 Grand Sport was conceived. It harked back to the 1960s' Grand Sport race cars which had success in the SCCA circuit series, with a striped paint scheme and many upgrades. The suspension used thicker anti-roll bars, firmer springs and shocks to create more sure-footed handling. Larger 315/35 tyres at the rear were fitted to cope with the extra power and, to get these on, special arch extensions were needed. The 405bhp (302kW) LT-5 engine would have been ideal, had it not been dropped by Chevrolet the previous year. Hence, they used the 350ci (5.7-litre) LT-4 and added modified pistons, large valves, modified cylinder heads, a hot cam and roller rockers. Behind it a ZF six-speed manual transmission was deemed necessary, and it suited the new engine perfectly.

Top speed:	168 mph (269 km/h)
0–60 mph (0–95 km/h):	4.7 sec
Engine type:	V8
Displacement:	350 ci (5,735 cc)
Transmission	6-speed manual
Max power:	330 bhp (246 kW) @ 5,800 rpm
Max torque:	340 lb ft (460 Nm) @ 4,500 rpm
Weight:	3,298 lb (1,499 kg)
Economy:	21 mpg (7.5 km/l)

Chevrolet Impala SS (1996)

Debuted as a concept in 1993, the Impala SS received an excellent response from the US public, so GM gave it the green light for production soon after. It hit the showroom floors in 1996 and proved that modern technology could produce a better muscle car. It may have only run the small-block 350ci (5.7-litre) V8, but thanks to multi-point fuel injection, engine management and excellent torque, the de-tuned Corvette motor could propel the Impala to sub-7 second 0–60mph (0–95 km/h) times and an impressive top speed, while returning 21mpg (7.5km/l). The car was no lightweight at just under two tons, yet it could be thrown around, thanks to thicker anti-roll bars, stiffer springs and de Carbon shocks. Heavy-duty police front spindles and huge 12-inch (305mm) disc brakes all around helped the inspiring feel. The interior was fully loaded; the car was way ahead of its ancestors in the luxury stakes.

Top speed:	140 mph (224 km/h)
0–60 mph (0–95 km/h):	6.6 sec
Engine type:	V8
Displacement:	350 ci (5,735 cc)
Transmission	4-speed auto
Max power:	260 bhp (194 kW) @ 5,000 rpm
Max torque:	330 lb ft (447 Nm) @ 3,200 rpm
Weight:	4,230 lb (1,923 kg)
Economy:	21 mpg (7.5 km/l)

Chevrolet Camaro Z28 (1997)

By 1993 it was the turn of the fourth-generation Camaro to carry the torch for the long-lived muscle car. Chevrolet gave the buyer a lot of bang-for-the-buck with an original sale price of under $20,000. While still featuring monocoque construction with chassis subframes at each end, the Z28 did use gas shocks all around and a torque arm, plus Panhard rod at the rear to locate the live axle very well. The small-block Chevy under the hood was the very same which had appeared for years in the Chevrolet line-up, though in this LT1 guise it was somewhat modernized with multi-point fuel injection, aluminium heads, roller cam, 10.4:1 compression and an Optispark ignition system. Best of all, the car came with a six-speed manual to exploit all the available power. To keep the Z28 lightweight, all bar the rear fenders, hood and roof were plastic.

Top speed:	155 mph (248 km/h)
0–60 mph (0–95 km/h):	6.1 sec
Engine type:	V8
Displacement:	350 ci (5,735 cc)
Transmission:	6-speed manual
Max power:	275 bhp (205 kW) @ 5,000 rpm
Max torque:	325 lb ft (440 Nm) @ 2,400 rpm
Weight:	3,475 lb (1,580 kg)
Economy:	19 mpg (6.78 km/l)

Chevrolet Corvette C5

With a presence on the US scene for nearly 50 years, the Corvette has the longest production run of any supercar, the 1997 C5 being the fifth generation. An all-new small-block V8 engine called the LS1 was designed for the C5, and it returned to pushrods. With new cylinder heads, a composite induction system, electronic fuel injection plus electronic throttle control, the motor revved in an instant like a race car and was strong throughout the range. Having a glass-fibre body and magnesium wheels, the Corvette stayed relatively lightweight. The floor was balsa wood sandwiched between steel sheets to help stiffen the structure, while the steel chassis had a few tricks up its sleeve, with alloy suspension arms and a composite monoleaf rear spring. The gearbox was part of the transaxle at the rear, thus distributing the weight evenly and making the handling superb.

Top speed:	175 mph (281 km/h)
0–60 mph (0–95 km/h):	4.7 sec
Engine type:	V8
Displacement:	347 ci (5,686 cc)
Transmission	6-speed manual
Max power:	345 bhp (257 kW) @ 5,400 rpm
Max torque:	350 lb ft (474 Nm) @ 4,400 rpm
Weight:	3,220 lb (1,464 kg)
Economy:	20.2 mpg (7.2 km/l)

Chevrolet Camaro Z28 (1996)

As soon as the fourth-generation Corvette came along in 1992, it started getting modified. It mattered not that the model was high-tech, because the aftermarket just grew increasingly high-tech to cope with the changes. This Camaro uses modern touches combined with a period-type paint scheme featuring flames, just like hot rods of the 1960s. The owner has fitted 18-inch (457mm) rims with 35-series tyres for handling, while the suspension has SLA lowering springs and uprated anti-roll bar. Under the hood much work has gone on too, with a Vortech 7psi supercharger now feeding in more air and fuel through Edelbrock aluminium heads and a larger throttle body. Being a 1996 model, this also has Chevy's own tweaked exhaust for an extra 10bhp (7kW). The interior features additional boost and fuel-pressure gauges, plus white gauges and re-trimmed flame seats.

Top speed:	168 mph (269 km/h)
0–60 mph (0–96 km/h):	4.5 sec
Engine type:	V8
Displacement:	350 ci (5,735 cc)
Transmission	4-speed auto
Max power:	430 bhp (321 kW) @ 5,200 rpm
Max torque:	490 lb ft (664 Nm) @ 3,400 rpm
Weight:	3,650 lb (1,659 kg)
Economy:	14 mpg (4.96 km/l)

Chevrolet Camaro SS (1998)

The 'SS' stood for Super Sport and the name had been used some years previous to the 1998 Camaro SS. Back in 1967 the original Camaro SS got you the 295bhp (220kW) Turbo-Fire 350ci (5.7-litre) V8 engine and special SS hood, badges and stripes. In the more recent version, output didn't seem much higher, but the all new aluminium engine could scream the Camaro SS to 60mph (95km/h) in a shade over 5 seconds and down the quarter-mile in 13 seconds. The aluminium LS1 engine featured ram air on the SS to help boost power from the usual 305bhp (227kW). At the rear the live axle remained which could upset handling, but only on the worst streets. Up front it used unequal-length wishbones, and with uprated suspension plus the 9x17-inch (229x432mm) alloys and 275/40 tyres, this could pull 0.9gs on the skid pad. It is one of Chevrolet's fastest muscle cars of all time.

Top speed:	161 mph (258 km/h)
0–60 mph (0–95 km/h):	5.2 sec
Engine type:	V8
Displacement:	347 ci (5,686 cc)
Transmission	6-speed manual
Max power:	320 bhp (238 kW) @ 5,200 rpm
Max torque:	325 lb ft (440 Nm) @ 4,400 rpm
Weight:	3,593 lb (1,633 kg)
Economy:	27 mpg (9.6 km/l)

Chevrolet Corvette hardtop (1998)

Corvettes had long been available both in the T-top and convertible form, but when the C5 arrived in the late 1990s, the company decided to produce a new version which would attract the real driving enthusiasts. It offered a hardtop-only version which came without such interior accessories as air-conditioning, power seats, electric door mirrors or a sound system. It also lost weight with the fixed top, some 70lb (52kg) in fact, because adding the roof meant the car didn't need so much strengthening in other areas. The car got the Z51 package which consisted of stiffer springs, anti-roll bars and shocks, and special 17-inch (432mm) magnesium alloy rims with ultra low-profile tyres. The engine went unchanged in output, but the only option gearbox was the manual six-speed. Standard brakes were four-wheel vented discs that could stop the car from 60mph (96km/h) in just 126ft (38m).

Top speed:	168 mph (268 km/h)
0–60 mph (0–96 km/h):	5.3 sec
Engine type:	V8
Displacement:	347 ci (5,686 cc)
Transmission	6-speed manual
Max power:	345 bhp (257 kW) @ 5,600 rpm
Max torque:	350 lb ft (474 Nm) @ 4,400 rpm
Weight:	3,245 lb (1,475 kg)
Economy:	21 mpg (7.43 km/l)

Chrysler Airflow (1934)

The Airflow was the first production car to use wind-tunnel design testing, but it also had a number of other advances. The body was built in a similar way to an aircraft, with a steel beam and truss framework for the panels to mount on. It was very aerodynamic and helped a 1934 Imperial coupe model complete a flying mile of 95.6mph (154km/h) at Bonneville salt flats. The Airflow also had a unique gearbox, fitted with helical gears to make it exceptionally quiet. Later examples were fitted with hypoid rear axles and above 45mph (72km/h) when your foot was lifted off the accelerator, an overdrive gear would automatically engage. Another first was the puncture-proof tyres, which comprised Lifeguard tyres with heavy-duty tubes and a second floating tube inside that. The car was considered too radical for its time, and had poor sales, even when the front end was restyled in 1935.

Top speed:	88 mph (141 km/h)
0–60 mph (0–96 km/h):	19.5 sec
Engine type:	In-line eight
Displacement:	298 ci (4,883 cc)
Transmission:	3–speed manual
Max power:	122 bhp (91 kW) @ 3,400 rpm
Max torque:	N/A
Weight:	4,166 lb (1,893 kg)
Economy:	16 mpg (5.66 km/l)

Chrysler Town & Country (1947)

This car was so called because the coachbuilder once commented that the front end looked town, while the rear looked country. The wood was more than decoration though, because it formed part of the structure, using white ash and Honduras mahogany inserts. The car was direct competition to the Mercury Sportsman in this niche market, but had a number of advances over that car. Firstly, it used Chrysler fluid-drive semi-automatic transmission with two high and two low gears for ultra-smooth operation. It also had the power advantage with its extra displacement straight-eight which used twin carbs. The ride was also better thanks to a double wishbones front end with coils and telescopic shocks. Whilst somewhat heavier than the Mercury, the Town & Country did feel very well built, with doors that shut like a bank vault. The car continued in production for two years.

Top speed:	105 mph (168 km/h)
0–60 mph (0–96 km/h):	20.0 sec
Engine type:	In-line eight
Displacement:	324 ci (5,309 cc)
Transmission	4-speed semi-automatic
Max power:	135 bhp (101 kW) @ 3,400 rpm
Max torque:	N/A
Weight:	4,332 lb (1,969 kg)
Economy:	14 mpg (4.95 km/l)

Chrysler C-300 (1955)

The Chrysler C-300 was one of the fastest and best-handling cars on the road at the time of launch. It was also one of the first true muscle cars thanks to the now legendary Hemi engine (which had arrived in 1951). Under the hood you'd find a motor which with hemispherical combustion chambers that placed the spark plug directly in the centre of the cylinder, thus ensuring the best burn and allowing the engine to run a slightly lower compression ratio than most of its contemporaries, whilst producing more power. The 300 was based on the Windsor two-door coupe and shared some of its components with the New Yorker and Imperial. It had a wishbone front and leaf rear, but all springs and shocks were uprated, making it a fine handler. The Hemi engine showed its potential even more the following year with 340bhp (227kW) in the 300B, making it as fast as most Ferraris of the era.

Top speed:	130 mph (208 km/h)
0–60 mph (0–96 km/h):	8.9 sec
Engine type:	V8
Displacement:	331 ci (5,424 cc)
Transmission	2-speed auto
Max power:	300 bhp (224 kW) @ 5,200 rpm
Max torque:	345 lb ft (467 Nm) @ 3,200 rpm
Weight:	4,005 lb (1,820 kg)
Economy:	14 mpg (4.95 km/l)

Chrysler 300C (1957)

No other car could match the dramatic Virgil Exner styled 300C of 1957. The huge tail fins pre-dated the Series 62 Cadillac's similar examples by two years, but the car wasn't all about style, because it also performed so amazingly that Chrysler had to tame the car down for drivers. They deliberately gave the throttle a stepped action so that the pedal had to be forcefully depressed for all eight carburettors mouths to open, thus unleashing full power. When it did the car leapt into action and made it easily one of the fastest production four-seaters in the USA. Other developments included torsion bar suspension which continued on Chrysler group cars well into the 1980s, and the Torqueflite transmission with push-button gear selection on the dashboard. To pull the car down, huge brake drums were fitted and the fronts had cooling vents fed from intakes just below the headlamps.

Top speed:	149 mph (238 km/h)
0-60 mph (0–96 km/h):	8.3 sec
Engine type:	V8
Displacement:	392 ci (6,423 cc)
Transmission	3-speed auto
Max power:	375 bhp (280 kW) @ 5,200 rpm
Max torque:	435 lb ft (590 Nm) @ 3,600 rpm
Weight:	4,389 lb (1,995 kg)
Economy:	10 mpg (3.54 km/l)

Chrysler 300G (1961)

Continuing the well respected 'letter' cars from Chrysler which had started with the 1955 C-300, the 300G was a muscle car with much to offer. On getting in, you could swivel the front seats, which was a first, then once inside you had push-button transmission and stylish aluminium dashboard, plus optional air-conditioning, electric mirrors, and a self-seeking Music Master radio. Stiffer suspension was fitted underneath to make the heavyweight a much better-handling car than its predecessors, and a tough Dana rear axle was fitted to cope with the massive power. New was Chrysler's 'Cross Ram' intake manifold, which put the dual four-barrel carbs either side of the Max Wedge V8 motor, with very long intake runners. It worked for torque production, nearing the magic 500lb ft (677Nm) mark and making the 'G' extremely quick off the line. Just 337 were built as convertibles.

Top speed:	130 mph (208 km/h)
0–60 mph (0–96 km/h):	8.4 sec
Engine type:	V8
Displacement:	413 ci (6,767 cc)
Transmission	3-speed auto
Max power:	305 bhp (227 kW) @ 5,000 rpm
Max torque:	495 lb ft (671 Nm) @ 2,800 rpm
Weight:	4,315 lb (1,961 kg)
Economy:	12 mpg (4.24 km/l)

Chrysler Turbine (1963)

While Chrysler weren't the inventors of the gas-turbine engine, they were its greatest exponents, and started by fitting one to a Plymouth Belvedere as early as 1955, developing a seventh-generation engine even in the late 1970s, which was fitted in a 1977 Dodge Aspen. The advantages with the turbine were that it could run on all kinds of fuel, including diesel and kerosene, its huge torque was available from zero rpm, it could rev to very high speeds (up to nearly 45,000rpm) very quietly, and it warmed up instantaneously. Unfortunately, it boasted little power, did precious little miles per gallon, and was heavy. For evaluation, Chrysler gave 45 gas-turbine cars to member of the public to try out, but of the 55 built, in total 46 were destroyed simply to avoid paying import duty on the Italian-built cars. Just 9 machines remain, in museums and private collections, across America.

Top speed:	115 mph (184 km/h)
0–60 mph (0–96 km/h):	10.0 sec
Engine type:	Gas-turbine
Displacement:	N/A
Transmission	3-speed auto
Max power:	130 bhp (97 kW) @ 44,600 rpm
Max torque:	425 lb ft (576 Nm) at zero output
Weight:	3,900 lb (1,772 kg)
Economy:	12 mpg (4.24 km/l)

Chrysler Sebring (1998)

The Sebring's roots go back to 1995 when Chrysler released the Cirrus and Stratus sedans to replace their ageing A-body cars. A year on they went one further by replacing their Le Baron top-selling drop-top with the new Sebring. While the sheet metal was all-new, the Sebring convertible's chassis and suspension came from the Cirrus and Stratus, which meant unitary construction and double wishbones up front plus a complex rear wishbone arrangement with trailing arms. The convertible got uprated springs and shocks plus 6.5x16-inch (165x406mm) alloys and 215/55 tyres, so the handling was top notch and made the car dynamic to drive as well as in looks. The V6 from Mitsubishi, while smooth and refined, had much weight to pull around. The car was more a cruiser than sports machine. Luxury and refinement made the Sebring America's best-selling convertible.

Top speed:	122 mph (195 km/h)
0–60 mph (0–96 km/h):	10.2 sec
Engine type:	V6
Displacement:	152 ci (2,490 cc)
Transmission	4-speed auto
Max power:	168 bhp (125 kW) @ 5,800 rpm
Max torque:	170 lb ft (230 Nm) @ 4,350 rpm
Weight:	3,382 lb (1,537 kg)
Economy:	23 mpg (8.14 km/l)

Chrysler 300M (1999)

T he 300M pays homage to the great 'letter cars' from Chrysler of the 1950s and 1960s. Cars like the 300C and 300G were amazing luxury sedans which also had huge power, and the 300M replicates those, while providing unsurpassed ride quality. More of a sports sedan than cruiser, the M had handling package option designed for it, which meant its cornering ability was higher than any of its competitors'; up to 0.83 lateral g in fact. As it was destined to be sold internationally, the design used typical 'cab-forward' styling which meant interior space was excellent; the other effect was to push the wheel out to each corner, which aided handling. The suspension was struts all around, which further enhanced the driver appeal. The original letter cars had a Hemi engine and the new one at least used the same design of engine internally, but with two cylinders less.

Top speed:	118 mph (188 km/h)
0–60 mph (0–96 km/h):	7.7 sec
Engine type:	V6
Displacement:	215 ci (3,523 cc)
Transmission	4-speed auto
Max power:	253 bhp (189 kW) @ 6,400 rpm
Max torque:	255 lb ft (345 Nm) @ 3,950 rpm
Weight:	3,567 lb (1,621 kg)
Economy:	23 mpg (8.14 km/l)

Citroën Traction Avant

Citroën was known for building revolutionary cars, and it was the Traction Avant that earned the company its visionary reputation. The name literally translates as 'forward traction', and celebrates the fact the Traction Avant was the first car to go into mass production with front-wheel-drive in 1934. But the running gear wasn't the only piece of technical wizardry, for the Traction Avant was also one of the first unitary construction cars, meaning it didn't use a separate chassis, and Citroën once famously pushed one off a cliff to demonstrate how strong the shell was. Other novelties included air-cushioned engine mounts and radial tyres. The Avant was amazingly agile to drive, and it would be up to 30 years before other manufacturers caught up. The car remained in production throughout World War II and production only finished in 1957.

Top speed:	71 mph (114 km/h)
0–60 mph (0–95 km/h):	16.4 sec
Engine type:	in-line four
Displacement:	114 ci (1,911 cc)
Transmission:	3-speed manual
Max power:	56 bhp (42 kW) at 4,250 rpm
Max torque:	90 lb ft (122 Nm) at 2,000 rpm
Weight:	2,549 lb (1,147 kg)
Economy:	21 mpg (7.5 km/l)

Citroën 2CV

As a design brief, creating a car that would carry a basket of eggs across a ploughed field without breaking was more than a little odd. But that was Citroën design chief Pierre Boulanger's brief when it came to designing the 2CV. The result was a rather quirky little car that looked like an umbrella on wheels, but was incredibly tough, mechanically simple and fitted the original brief perfectly. The 2CV's ability to cross a rutted field meant it had incredible suspension travel, and that made for some rather entertaining handling characteristics. The body would lean massively in corners, but thanks to front wheel drive and light weight, it had incredible grip. Citroën was so confident in the 2CV's abilities that it offered the prize of a brand new car to the first person who rolled one on to its roof – and well over half a century later, the prize still hasn't been claimed.

Top speed:	41 mph (66 km/h)
0–60 mph (0–95 km/h):	n/a
Engine type:	flat-twin
Displacement:	23 ci (375 cc)
Transmission:	4-speed manual
Max power:	9 bhp (7 kW) at 3,500 rpm
Max torque:	16 lb ft (22 Nm) at 1,800 rpm
Weight:	1,100 lb (495 kg)
Economy:	63 mpg (22.4 km/l)

Citroën DS

Some cars exhibit pure brilliance that brings so many new things to the industry, they become benchmarks by which others are judged. That's certainly true of the Citroën DS. Launched at the Paris Motor Show in 1955, the DS was light years ahead of its rivals in terms of technological development. The unusual bodywork wasn't just about making a style statement, for it was the most aerodynamic machine on the road in its day. Couple to that unique hydropneumatic suspension, which gave the car a wonderful ride quality, headlamps that swivelled with the steering to see round corners, inboard disc brakes and a plastic roof to keep weight to a minimum, and it's easy to see why the DS is regarded as one of the most important cars of all time. Citroën even offered a station wagon version, known as the ID.

Top speed:	95 mph (152 km/h)
0–60 mph (0–95 km/h):	18.4 sec
Engine type:	in-line four
Displacement:	114 ci (1,911 cc)
Transmission:	5-speed manual
Max power:	63 bhp (47 kW) at 4,500 rpm
Max torque:	105 lb ft (142 Nm) at 3,500 rpm
Weight:	2,575 lb (1158 kg)
Economy:	24 mpg (8.6 km/l)

Citroën GS

The GS replaced Citroën's ugly-duckling Ami range, and was an object of beauty by comparison. Neatly proportioned and well-packaged, it was one of the finest family saloons of its day. And in true Citroën style, it completely defied convention. Underneath, it used a similar hydropneumatic suspension set-up to the bigger DS, while engines were all air-cooled and horizontally opposed. Four-wheel disc brakes, an adjustable ride height and a stiff monocoque shell made for excellent roadholding. Estate versions debuted in 1972, followed by a hatchback in 1980. But by far the quirkiest variant of the GS was the 1973–75 Birotor, which used a twin rotary engine similar to those used by NSU and Mazda. They were exceptionally smooth to drive, but reliability was poor and Citroën ended up buying back most examples and destroying them to avoid expensive warranty claims!

Top speed:	90 mph (144 km/h)
0–60 mph (0–95 km/h):	18.0 sec
Engine type:	flat-four
Displacement:	62 ci (1,015 cc)
Transmission:	4-speed manual
Max power:	56 bhp (42 kW) at 6,500 rpm
Max torque:	64 lb ft (87 Nm) at 3,250 rpm
Weight:	2,197 lb (989 kg)
Economy:	44 mpg (15.8 km/l)

Citroën SM

Citroën of France took over Italian firm Maserati in 1969 and provided much-needed financial support. It also requested of Maserati that they supply the engine and transmissions for a new, rather self-indulgent Citroën supercar, the SM. Many of the SM's parts underneath were from the Citroën DS model to keep costs down, parts such as the hydro-pneumatic suspension and ultra-sensitive four wheel-disc brakes. The V6 was produced by Maserati chopping two cylinders off their 183ci (3-litre) V8 and taking it out to 163ci (2.6 litres), though later versions had 183ci (3 litres). The gearbox was fitted in front of the engine to allow the engine to sit back as far as possible in the chassis for better weight-distribution. In 1971 Citroën put four cars into the Morocco Rally and gained first, third and fourth places. Peugeot bought Citroën in 1974, and the following year the SM finished.

Top speed:	142 mph (227 km/h)
0–60 mph (0–95 km/h):	8.5 sec
Engine type:	V6
Displacement:	163 ci (2,670 cc)
Transmission	5-speed manual
Max power:	178 bhp (133 kW) @ 5,500 rpm
Max torque:	171 lb ft (232 Nm) @ 4,000 rpm
Weight:	3,197 lb (1,453 kg)
Economy:	12.4 mpg (4.4 km/l)

Citroën CX Turbo

Replacing the DS was never going to be an easy task, especially as it was still ahead of most of its rivals after a 19-year production run. But Citroën wanted to prove it could still innovate, and the CX that replaced it in 1974 was the motoring equivalent of the Millennium Falcon from *Star Wars*. With a slippery body for ultimate aerodynamics and a distinctive wedge-shaped profile, the CX was dramatic to look at. But it was even more of an adventure to drive. The steering had a direct linkage and centred itself when stationary, giving surprising and sharp responses, while the merest prod of the brake pedal would bring the car screeching to a halt. Then there was the suspension. Using Citroën's patented hydraulics, the car would sit on its belly when parked and took almost a minute to rise into action after the engine had been fired up. Brave drivers could even choose a turbocharged version, which could top 125mph!

Top speed:	126 mph (202 km/h)
0–60 mph (0–95 km/h):	8.6 sec
Engine type:	in-line four
Displacement:	151 ci (2,473 cc)
Transmission:	5-speed manual
Max power:	168 bhp (125 kW) at 5,000 rpm
Max torque:	217 lb ft (294 Nm) at 3,250 rpm
Weight:	3,107 lb (1,398 kg)
Economy:	26 mpg (9.3 km/l)

Citroën Visa

The Citroën Visa Chrono was one of the more unusual rally cars of the 1980s. Based on the Visa hatchback – a basic little car that was intended to replace the 2CV, but in actual fact was withdrawn before it's predecessor due to the latter's lasting success – the Chrono was ideal for forest and loose surface rallies. Part of its success was due to a highly flexible 1.4-litre engine, that could be tuned to deliver over 130bhp. But its main advantage over its rivals was in its handling – the Visa had a superb ride and was incredibly stable on rough and loose surfaces such as gravel, while front-wheel-drive and positive steering meant it had excellent chassis balance. The Visa also had a lightweight shell, and this advantage was enhanced further in the rally car model by the use of fibreglass body panels in place of the original steel items.

Top speed:	101 mph (162 km/h)
0–60 mph (0–95 km/h):	7.2 sec
Engine type:	in-line four
Displacement:	88 ci (1,434 cc)
Transmission:	5-speed manual
Max power:	134 bhp (100 kW) at 7,200 rpm
Max torque:	108 lb ft (147 Nm) at 5,500 rpm
Weight:	1,653 lb (744 kg)
Economy:	22 mpg (7.9 km/l)

Continental Mark II (1956)

Lincoln was Ford's premium brand, but oddly the name wasn't used on the Continental Mark II, despite it being built by the company. The car was Ford's attempt at outdoing Cadillac and oozed opulence everywhere. Inside it was swathed in Scottish leather and it had classy separate gauges, electric everything and just one optional extra: air-conditioning. The car was tailor made, with the body's trail fitted to the 'cow belly' chassis (it dropped down between each end) before being painted, sanded and polished by hand. Also, the engines were hand picked off the production line to ensure the best possible performance from each car. Once finished, all went through a 12-mile (19km) road test followed by an in-depth inspection with tuning where necessary. Ford is reputed to have lost $1,000 on each one sold, even though they were priced at $9,695, some $2,300 more than a Cadillac.

Top speed:	112 mph (179 km/h)
0–60 mph (0–96 km/h):	10.5 sec
Engine type:	V8
Displacement:	368 ci (6,030 cc)
Transmission	3-speed auto
Max power:	285 bhp (213 kW) @ 4,800 rpm
Max torque:	401 lb ft (543 Nm) @ 2,800 rpm
Weight:	4,825 lb (2,193 kg)
Economy:	12 mpg (4.24 km/l)

Cord L-29 (1930)

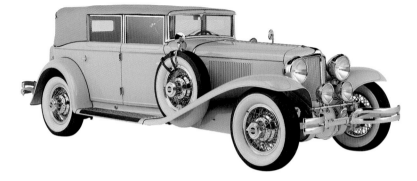

Spoilt by arriving just a day before the USA's famous stock market crash in 1930, the Cord L-29 was nonetheless extremely stylish. It was put together by the Auburn Automobile Company and named after the firm's president, E.L Cord. It was revolutionary in that it used front-wheel drive with a de Dion axle mounted under the grille, and the massive straight-eight engine had an alloy head and was set back in the chassis for good weight-distribution. Because of the drive configuration, chief design engineer John Oswald was able to style the L-29 very long and low, which made it look sleek against its contemporaries. Because of the market crash, the car sold poorly, so its price was slashed to help boost sales. Even so, the car was finished by 1931but it had done well in the Europe Concours d' Elegance shows, and paved the way for the most coveted of all Cords, the 812.

Top speed:	78 mph (125 km/h)
0–60 mph (0–96 km/h):	24.0 sec
Engine type:	in-line eight
Displacement:	299 ci (4,899 cc)
Transmission:	3–speed manual
Max power:	115 bhp (86 kW) @ 3,350 rpm
Max torque:	N/A
Weight:	4,710 lb (2,140 kg)
Economy:	12 mpg (4.2 km/l)

Cosworth Vega

The Cosworth Vega was ahead of its time and had it appeared five years later it may well have had better sales. Chevrolet brought out the compact sedan/coupe in 1970 to battle with imports. It came with a top engine option of the 110bhp (82kW), 140ci (2.3-litre) four-cylinder, which was criticized as being coarse. In 1973 Chevy had Cosworth develop the fastest Vega yet to enhance its sporty-yet-economical nature, vital in the fuel conscious mid-1970s. Cosworth used the alloy block but with a shorter stroke for 122ci (2-litre), then added an alloy twin-cam 16v head. Special pistons and electronic fuel injection saw output at 130bhp (97kW) initially, though production versions actually only managed 110bhp (82kW), due to lower compression. Uprated suspension, quicker steering and low axle gears of 3.73:1 in 1975 helped acceleration; 6x13-inch (152x330mm) alloys aided handling.

Top speed:	112 mph (180 km/h)
0–60 mph (0–95 km/h):	12.3 sec
Engine type:	In-line four
Displacement:	122 ci (1,998 cc)
Transmission	4-speed manual
Max power:	110 bhp (82 kW) @ 5,600 rpm
Max torque:	107 lb ft (145 Nm) @ 4,800 rpm
Weight:	2,639 lb (1,200 kg)
Economy:	19.6 mpg (7 km/l)

Daimler Majestic Major

The Majestic Major was the first Daimler to appear after Jaguar took over the company in 1960, and was the most prestigious car in the company's model range. The bodywork looked identical to the standard six-cylinder Majestic, except for its larger tail and slightly different front grille. But underneath the old-fashioned coachwork, the Daimler had a well-kept secret. Power was provided by a fabulous alloy-head V8 engine displacing 4,561cc and putting out a remarkable 220bhp – quite something for a car of its era. The Majestic Major could sprint from 0–60mph quicker than most contemporary sports cars in 10.3 seconds, and could comfortably cruise at 120mph, yet inside it has the trimmings of a Victorian smoking parlour, decked with wood veneer and leather. Production continued until 1968 with almost 1200 examples manufactured.

Top speed:	120 mph (192 km/h)
0–60 mph (0–95 km/h):	10.3 sec
Engine type:	V8
Displacement:	278 ci (4,561 cc)
Transmission:	3-speed auto
Max power:	220 bhp (164 kW) at 5,500 rpm
Max torque:	283 lb ft (384 Nm) at 3,200 rpm
Weight:	4,228 lb (1,902 kg)
Economy:	15 mpg (5.35 km/l)

Daimler DS420

Beloved of the United Kingdom's royal family, politicians and even local dignitaries, the DS420 became the archetypal British limousine. Based on an extended Jaguar 420G platform, the DS420 was launched in 1968, although its ornate chromework, old-fashioned interior and no-nonsense, slab-sided panels recall a much earlier era. Inside, the car was incredibly well appointed, with three rows of seats, lots of wood and leather and the option of sterling silver on the door handles and window winding handles. But the comfort was very much levelled at rear seat passengers. The chauffeur's compartment at the front was cramped and uncomfortable, while driving the DS420 could be tricky due to its enormous length and width. Continued demand from the government kept the DS420 in production until 1992!

Top speed:	115 mph (184 km/h)
0–60 mph (0–95 km/h):	13.6 sec
Engine type:	in-line six
Displacement:	258 ci (4,235 cc)
Transmission:	3-speed auto
Max power:	177 bhp (132 kW) at 4,500 rpm
Max torque:	222 lb ft (301 Nm) at 2,500 rpm
Weight:	4,702 lb (2,116 kg)
Economy:	12 mpg (4.3 km/l)

Datsun Fairlady

It was the 1961 Datsun Fairlady which started Japan's foray into the worldwide sportscar market. Its lightweight bodyshell coupled with a buzzy 122ci (2-litre) four-cylinder engine competed with British sportscars and had the MG beat on performance, if not character. The car used a separate box-section chassis, with double wishbone front suspension and a leaf sprung live rear axle on radius arms. While the car started out with drums brakes and 71bhp (53kW), by 1967 it had disc brakes up front, which offered superb stopping power. By then the Fairlady also had a new 2-litre OHC engine with 135bhp (101kW). It went through a five-speed all-syncromesh gearbox, which was leagues ahead of its rivals' transmissions. The Fairlady name was later used on Japan's limited edition version of the 240Z with 122ci (2-litre) straight six engine and excellent all-round independent suspension.

Top speed:	114 mph (182 km/h)
0–60 mph (0–95 km/h):	10.2 sec
Engine type:	In-line four
Displacement:	121 ci (1,982 cc)
Transmission	5-speed manual
Max power:	135 bhp (101 kW) @ 6,000 rpm
Max torque:	145 lb ft (196 Nm) @ 4,000 rpm
Weight:	2,115 lb (961 kg)
Economy:	26 mpg (9.2 km/l)

Datsun B-510

Datsun was little aware of the little racer it was producing when it turned out the new B-510 (known as Bluebird outside the USA) in 1967. They equipped the lightweight car well, giving it MacPherson front struts and an independent rear with trailing arms so it could really be thrown into bends with confidence. It came with a 97ci (1.5-litre) single SU-carb engine as standard and made 90bhp (67kW), but it was very useable, with little weight to carry around. This particular 510 has had a six-point cage and strut brace fitted to stiffen the chassis considerably, and the interior has been stripped in favour of aluminium panels and a single bucket seat. The engine sports twin Mikuni carbs, flat top pistons for higher compression, a gas-flowed head and high-lift cam. Vented discs, adjustable suspension and wide alloys help complete it as a street and track racer.

Top speed:	111 mph (178 km/h)
0–60 mph (0–95 km/h):	7.6 sec
Engine type:	In-line four
Displacement:	97 ci (1,595 cc)
Transmission	4-speed manual
Max power:	150 bhp (112 kW) @ 5,600 rpm
Max torque:	156 lb ft (211 Nm) @ 3,600 rpm
Weight:	2,130 lb (968 kg)
Economy:	20 mpg (7.1 km/l)

Datsun 240Z

Aimed directly at the American market, the 1969 Datsun 240Z had the looks, the handling thanks to independent suspension all around, a powerful free-revving engine plus a build quality which few could match for the money. It offered a monocoque design chassis/body, and whereas most cars of the era were still using leaf springs, the 240Z had struts all around, making it outstanding in corners. The straight-six engine was based on the Bluebird four-cylinder and was exceptionally strong, giving out plenty of power and torque while returning good economy and reliability that would see it go past 150,000 miles (241,350km) if properly serviced. Although having just two seats, it was practical with the hatchback rear. It also had a very high build quality which way surpassed anything else at its $3,526 price. The car sold over 150,000 models in 4 years.

Top speed:	125 mph (200 km/h)
0–60 mph (0–95 km/h):	8.7 sec
Engine type:	In-line six
Displacement:	146 ci (2,393 cc)
Transmission	5-speed manual
Max power:	150 bhp (112 kW) @ 6,000 rpm
Max torque:	148 lb ft (200 Nm) @ 4,400 rpm
Weight:	2,355 lb (1070 kg)
Economy:	25 mpg (8.9 km/l)

Datsun 280 ZX Turbo

While the original 1969 240Z was simple and effective, Datsun tried to make it more refined in later years. It gained weight which meant it wasn't quite as nimble and lost power. Physically it felt bigger too, but throughout the Z and ZX's history, all models offered much scope for tuning. This particular car was put together in Essex, UK, and starting with a 1979 model the owner has increased the intercooled turbocharger's boost and re-mapped the fuelling and timing for a power increase which allows 14.0 sec quarter-mile times. It uses adjustable shocks, motorsport springs, urethane bushes, uprated anti-roll bars and 9-inch/11-inch (229/279mm) alloys to maximize cornering potential, plus four-piston callipers on larger vented discs up front to increase braking power. Externally it features the IMSA arches from the ZX-R homologation special, only available in the USA.

Top speed:	144 mph (230 km/h)
0–60 mph (0–95km/h):	6.0 sec
Engine type:	In-line six
Displacement:	168 ci (2,753 cc)
Transmission:	5-speed manual
Max power:	260 bhp (194 kW) @ 5,800 rpm
Max torque:	295 lb ft (399 Nm) @ 3,000 rpm
Weight:	2,850 lb (1,295 kg)
Economy:	20 mpg (7.1 km/l)

DeLorean DMC

Founder John DeLorean, former Pontiac chief engineer and the man responsible for the GTO muscle car, started his company in 1974, though production of the DMC didn't begin until 1981 in Belfast, Ireland, in a factory paid for by the British Government. The startling body, actually brushed stainless steel over glass-fibre, made the car look exotic, but it was let down by the bought-in all-alloy V6 jointly developed by Peugeot, Renault and Volvo. The motor was never developed as a sporty performer and even though it later used Renault Alpine A 310 and A610 in turbocharged form, DeLorean never got that far, making only one prototype twin-turbo car which, ironically, worked very well. A lack of sales caused the company to close just one year after production had started, still with 2,000 cars unsold which were – years later – snapped up by collectors.

Top speed:	125 mph (200 km/h)
0–60 mph (0–95 km/h):	9.6 sec
Engine type:	V6
Displacement:	174 ci (2,850 cc)
Transmission:	5-speed manual
Max power:	145 bhp (108 kW) @ 5,500 rpm
Max torque:	162 lb ft (219 Nm) @ 2,750 rpm
Weight:	2,840 lb (1,290 kg)
Economy:	16.8 mpg (6 km/l)

DeSoto Fireflite (1955)

Being part of Chrysler, DeSoto got the technology from the parent company as soon as it was available. Hence, as early as the Fireflite had received the Hemi engine, which made it an incredible performer. A sign of how these new engines were is the fact that this customized version still uses its original 'Firedome' powerplant. Despite its near 2-ton weight, it can cover the quarter-mile in 16 seconds, helped by a custom performance exhaust. However, its real intention is as a cruiser, and for that reason it has lowered coils on the independent double wishbone front end and lowering blocks at the rear, which put the axle close to the body. While externally the car features little in the way of bodywork – aside from the obvious two-tone bright paint and pinstriping – inside it's been treated to a full tuck 'n' roll re-trim, which is indicative of 1950s customs.

Top speed:	118 mph (189 km/h)
0–60 mph (0–96 km/h):	8.2 sec
Engine type:	V8
Displacement:	331 ci (5,424 cc)
Transmission	3-speed auto
Max power:	255 bhp (190 kW) @ 5,200 rpm
Max torque:	340 lb ft (461 Nm) @ 2,800 rpm
Weight:	3,930 lb (1,786 kg)
Economy:	12 mpg (4.24 km/l)

DeSoto Pacesetter (1956)

Representing clean, stylish and classic-styled cars, DeSoto's were among the top models available on the market during the mid–1950s. They were almost amongst the most powerful cars available in the world, thanks to their version of Chrysler Hemi engine under the hood. Despite looking like a luxurious but sedate convertible, the Pacesetter nonetheless lived up to its name by being very rapid. In fact, one paced the Indy 500 in 1956, and all production cars paid homage to the race by having chequered flag badges on the rear fenders. While underneath it used the standard double wishbone front and leaf spring rear, it was inside where the Pacesetter was radically different, thanks to a split dash with twin pods and multiple gauges. It proved very quick against the competition, having a whole 100bhp (74kW) more than the V8 1957 Chevy, as an example.

Top speed:	115 mph (184 km/h)
0–60 mph (0–96 km/h):	10.2 sec
Engine type:	V8
Displacement:	341 ci (5,587 cc)
Transmission	2-speed auto
Max power:	320 bhp (239 kW) @ 5,200 rpm
Max torque:	365 lb ft (495 Nm) @ 2,800 rpm
Weight:	3,870 lb (1,759 kg)
Economy:	14 mpg (4.95 km/l)

De Tomaso Mangusta

Designed to challenge Ferrari in the late 1960s, the Mangusta was Argentine
Alexjandro de Tomaso's first volume production car, with mid-mounted Ford
V8 mated to a ZF transmission. More technically advanced than the later Pantera,
the Mangusta used folded and welded sheet steel to make a box-section central
backbone. The over-light front end used double wishbone suspension but couldn't
quite get the grip the car needed, while the rear used a reversed lower wishbone,
single transverse link plus twin radius arms per side. The wheels were magnesium
to keep weight down, but the Mangusta wasn't a great handling machine. It was,
however, quick in a straight line thanks to the Ford V8 which was also used in
Mustangs, the Shelby GT350 and AC Cobras. It was the latter the Mangusta aimed
for, as its name meant 'Mongoose', the animal which ate Cobras.

Top speed:	130 mph (208 km/h)
0–60 mph (0–95 km/h):	6.3 sec
Engine type:	V8
Displacement:	302 ci (4,950 cc)
Transmission	5-speed manual
Max power:	230 bhp (171 kW) @ 4,800 rpm
Max torque:	310 lb ft (419 Nm) @ 2,800 rpm
Weight:	2,915 lb (1,325 kg)
Economy:	13 mpg (4.6 km/l)

De Tomaso Pantera

Thanks to Ford's funds, the Pantera saw light of day in 1969, and while Alexjandro de Tomaso owned the rights to sell it in Europe, Ford retained them in the USA. Unlike the Mangusta before it, the Pantera used a steel monocoque structure because it was to be sold through Ford dealerships and thus needed to be high volume, hence fast, in production. Double wishbones were mounted at each corner and remained for the car's life, as did Ford power. In 1982 the updated GT5 was launched, with wheel arch extensions allowing 10-inch (254mm) and 13-inch (330mm) wide wheels and massive Pirelli tyres, for better cornering. The mid-mounted Cleveland V8 (named after the plant where it was built) offered much scope in tuning, as did the later 5.0 HO V8, which had twin turbochargers bolted and mustered over 180mph (289km/h) in the Gandini-styled 450 of 1990.

Top speed:	165 mph (264 km/h)
0–60 mph (0–95km/h):	5.6 sec
Engine type:	V8
Displacement:	351 ci (5,763 cc)
Transmission	5-speed manual
Max power:	350 bhp (261 kW) @ 6,000 rpm
Max torque:	333 lb ft (451 Nm) @ 3,800 rpm
Weight:	3,219 lb (1,463 kg)
Economy:	13.1 mpg (4.6 km/l)

Dodge A100 (1965)

F ord and GM virtually dominated the truck market in the 1960s, and while their trucks have long been modified, it takes a little more work to modify a Dodge pick-up. The A100 was ideal for the modification, however, as it featured an optional 273ci (4.5-litre) V8 small-block for 1965. This rev-happy engine made an ideal candidate for tuning, as this example shows. The added benefit was the motor being mounted well behind the front wheels, which improved weight-distribution even though this truck can still light up the rears at a touch of the throttle. The truck features the original suspension, albeit lowered, and Cragar chromed five-spoke rims with modern radials to improve both traction and handling. While intended mostly for work use as standard, this updated example has a reworked interior with full Sony sound system and custom-built console, plus leather seats.

Top speed:	115 mph (184 km/h)
0-60 mph (0–96 km/h):	8.4 sec
Engine type:	V8
Displacement:	273 ci (4,473 cc)
Transmission	3-speed manual
Max power:	235 bhp (175 kW) @ 5,200 rpm
Max torque:	280 lb ft (380 Nm) @ 4,000 rpm
Weight:	3,010 lb (1,368 kg)
Economy:	17 mpg (6.01 km/l)

Dodge Charger (1966)

Creating a sensation when it arrived in 1966, the first-generation Charger used fastback styling, which was quickly becoming popular. It also had engine options from 318ci (5.2-litre) right up to the legendary 426 Hemi, making it suitable for many pockets. The car was based on the new-for-1965 intermediate B-body chassis which it shared with the Coronet, and as such used Chrysler's ever-present torsion bar front end with a conventional leaf spring rear. Hemi-powered Chargers such as the model shown got stiffer front torsion bars and an anti-roll bar in an effort to handle the extra weight up front. The Hemi came at an extra cost of $900, but it combined incredible power with reasonable driveability. Power was put down through either a 3-speed Torqueflite automatic or 4-speed manual. This Charger was the car that thrust Dodge into the spotlight for the rest of that decade.

Top speed:	134 mph (214 km/h)
0–60 mph (0–96 km/h):	5.3 sec
Engine type:	V8
Displacement:	426 ci (6,980 cc)
Transmission:	4-speed manual
Max power:	425 bhp (317 kW) @ 5,000 rpm
Max torque:	490 lb ft (664 Nm) @ 4,000 rpm
Weight:	3,990 lb (1,813 kg)
Economy:	9 mpg (3.18 km/l)

Dodge Charger modified (1966)

The 1966 Charger was successful, but rarely did it get modified. For one thing, its production of just 37,344 models has made it far less easy to track one down, compared to the later restyled 1968 model. However, early versions like this can get more attention when given the right treatment. This one's torsion bar front suspension has been lowered one spline, and the rear springs have been reshaped for a 2- and 1.5-inch (50- and 38-mm) drop respectively. The stock engine has long gone, and now in its place sits a 1978 Dodge Ram truck 360ci (5.9-litre), which has been upgraded with Mopar parts (Plymouth, Dodge and Chrysler's performance arm), including a high-lift camshaft, four-barrel carburettor and an Edelbrock. The wheels used are 17-inch (432mm) Center Line billets, with 215/45s and 255/45 BF Goodrich Comp ZR radials to maximize the handling ability.

Top speed:	135 mph (216 km/h)
0–60 mph (0–96 km/h):	8.0 sec
Engine type:	V8
Displacement:	360 ci (5,899 cc)
Transmission	3-speed auto
Max power:	365 bhp (272 kW) @ 4,700 rpm
Max torque:	400 lb ft (542 Nm) @ 2,800 rpm
Weight:	3,900 lb (1,772 kg)
Economy:	14 mpg (4.95 km/l)

Dodge Charger modified (1968)

The Charger was one of the biggest two-door coupes ever built, but its size didn't mean it was slow. Its most popular big-block engine option for 1968 wasn't the Hemi but the 440ci (7.2-litre), which gave plenty of power plus good street manners. Because of the handsome lines and muscular 'Coke bottle' styling, the Chargers of 1968 and 1969 rarely see major modification. Items like the door sculpted 'vents', concealed headlamps and Ferrari-like double tail lamps make it a favourite for muscle-car fans even in stock form, and knowing that they have the full support of Chrysler's Mopar performance division for spares makes all the difference. The amount of money they are worth now also makes it sensible to keep mods to a minimum. The owner of this vehicle has made minor changes to the engine for extra power, and the car runs in the 13s in the trim used on the street.

Top speed:	140 mph (224 km/h)
0–60 mph (0–96 km/h):	7.5 sec
Engine type:	V8
Displacement:	440 ci (7,210 cc)
Transmission	3-speed auto
Max power:	400 bhp (298 kW) @ 4,800 rpm
Max torque:	4,100 lb ft (556 Nm) @ 3,600 rpm
Weight:	3,574 lb (1,624 kg)
Economy:	10.7 mpg (3.79 km/l)

Dodge Hurst Hemi Dart

Manufacturers used drag racing to display their products in the 1960s. The 1968 Hurst Hemi Dart was very successful in the NHRA Super Stock class, with no vehicle coming close. Hurst Performance and Chrysler built the 72 cars as stripped-out racers. They had the radio, heater, rear seats, sound-deadening and windows winders removed, had the battery mounted in the trunk and came in flat grey primer ready for racing paint schemes. The front fenders and hood were glass-fibre, while the steel doors and fenders were acid-dipped to thin them, and thus lose more weight. Bigger rear arches were fitted to cater for the large slick tyres and a Dana axle was fitted with 4.88:1 race gears. With 12.5:1 compression, a forged crank, solid lifter cam and twin Holley four-barrel carbs, the engine was highly tuned and was eventually rated at a more truthful 500bhp (373kW) by the NHRA.

Top speed:	140 mph (224 km/h)
0–60 mph (0–95 km/h):	3.6 sec
Engine type:	V8
Displacement:	426 ci (6,980 cc)
Transmission	4-speed manual
Max power:	425 bhp (317 kW) @ 6,000 rpm
Max torque:	480 lb ft (650 Nm) @ 4,600 rpm
Weight:	3,000 lb (1,361kg)
Economy:	6 mpg (2.1 km/l)

Dodge Charger 500 (1969)

Ford were having it all their own way on the super speedways of NASCAR in the late 1960s, so Chrysler fought back with the launch of their Charger 500. Most notable about the bodywork was the flush grille where previously there had been sunken headlamps. Dodge found the flush look helped significantly with aerodynamics so the rear window was also mounted as such. Underneath, the 500 had a unitary body/chassis with torsion bar front end and anti-roll bar, while the rear was conventional leaf springs. Disc brakes came as standard at 11 inches (280mm) diameter and were needed with the big-block powerplants. The two options were the 375bhp (280kW) 440ci (7.2-litre) Magnum engine or the Hemi which was rated at 425bhp (317kW), even though it was closer to 500bhp (373kW) in reality. The 500s won 15 races in 1969, but alas, Ford's victories numbered 30.

Top speed:	138 mph (220 km/h)
0-60 mph (0–96 km/h):	6.1 sec
Engine type:	V8
Displacement:	426 ci (6,980 cc)
Transmission	4-speed manual
Max power:	425 bhp (317 kW) @ 5,000 rpm
Max torque:	490 lb ft (664 Nm) @ 4,000 rpm
Weight:	4,100 lb (1,863 kg)
Economy:	8 mpg (2.83 km/l)

Dodge Charger Daytona (1969)

To qualify for NASCAR racing, Dodge had to build a certain number of Charger Daytonas for the street. They looked extremely radical for the time; in fact, they were too radical for most and many even had their wings and spoilers removed to be sold as regular Chargers, just to get them off the showroom floor. The Chargers were some 200lb (91kg) lighter than their Plymouth Superbird cousins, hence were fastest away from a standing start. Their aerodynamic aids didn't really come into effect until over 100mph (169km/h), which made them more visual aids than helpful in the real sense, but the visual part is something which sells the car well on the second-hand market today. The engines it used were either the 440ci (7.2-litre) Magnum or Street Hemi, a detuned version of the race engine with hydraulic lifters to quieten it down and, ultimately, limit its rpm potential.

Top speed:	135 mph (216 km/h)
0–60 mph (0–96 km/h):	5.0 sec
Engine type:	V8
Displacement:	426 ci (6,997 cc)
Transmission	4-speed manual
Max power:	425 bhp (317 kW) @ 5,600 rpm
Max torque:	490 lb ft (664 Nm) @ 4,000 rpm
Weight:	3,671 lb (1,668 kg)
Economy:	11 mpg (3.89 km/l)

Dodge Dart GTS (1969)

Dodge first introduced the compact Dart in 1963 and, far from being a performance model, it came that year with a six-cylinder engine only. But as the mid-60s turned to the late-'60s the Dart developed much like the rest of the Dodge line–up, hence it got a small-block V8 in '64, though with just 180 bhp (134 kW) performance was brisk rather than exciting. It was certainly a long way from the larger, hemi cars which had 425 bhp (316 kW) under their hoods. Even so, the Dart grew in popularity and had increasingly bigger displacement engines. By 1969 the top sport model was the GTS, which came with the company's new 340 ci (5571 cc) small-block, firmer shocks, 'Rallye' uprated springs, Red Tread wider tyres and bumble bee stripes over the trunk and sides. Optional on the engine was the 'Six Pack' consisting of three two-barrel carburettors which gave 15bhp (11kW increase in power.

Top speed:	118 mph (189 km/h)
0–60 mph (0–96 km/h):	6.8 sec
Engine type:	V8
Displacement:	340 ci (5,571 cc)
Transmission	4-speed manual
Max power:	290 bhp (216 kW) @ 5,200 rpm
Max torque:	360 lb ft (624 Nm) @ 3,800 rpm
Weight:	3,097 lb (1,407 kg)
Economy:	15 mpg (5.31 km/l)

Dodge Super Bee (1969)

Chrysler wanted to stay ahead in the muscle-car wars, and that prompted the creation of the Super Bee in 1969. Basically a bare-bones Coronet, the new Dodge was achieved by stuffing their 440ci (7.2 litres) into the lightest intermediate bodyshell available. The power came through additions such as a free-flow dual exhaust, but mostly it was down to the 'Six Pack' carburettor system. This consisted of three two-barrel Holley carbs, on which the centre one would work at part throttle, then all three at full throttle, feeding more fuel in and unleashing the full power which could propel the car down the quarter-mile in under 14 seconds. The car also handled reasonably well, thanks to heavy-duty torsion bar front suspension. The Super Bee came with a tough Dana axle with 4.1:1 gearing as standard, plus black steel wheels to show its bare-bones nature.

Top speed:	130 mph (208 km/h)
0–60 mph (0–95 km/h):	6.0 sec
Engine type:	V8
Displacement:	440 ci (7,210 cc)
Transmission	4-speed manual
Max power:	390 bhp (291 kW) @ 4,700 rpm
Max torque:	490 lb ft (663 Nm) @ 3,200 rpm
Weight:	4,100 lb (1,863 kg)
Economy:	7 mpg (2.5 km/l)

Dodge Challenger R/T SE

With the muscle-car era at its height in the late 1960s, Dodge finally got its own pony car in 1970. Aptly named the Challenger, it came with a huge list of options, including 12 engines. In Dodge tradition, the R/T (Street/Track) package was the high-performance model. The base engine option was a 335bhp (250kW) 383ci (6.3-litre) V8, but the car could be ordered with the mighty 426ci (7-litre) Street Hemi or 440ci (7.2-litre) V8s, which gave out 425bhp (316kW) and 375bhp (279kW) respectively. It was built on Chrysler's new E-body platform, sharing its firewall and front subframe with the bigger B-body cars like the Charger. The new model also used Chrysler's proven torsion bar front suspension with beefed up anti-roll bar, though the rear had leaf springs on a live axle, the latter requiring the Sure-Grip limited-slip differential option to put all the torque to the ground.

Top speed:	128 mph (205 km/h)
0–60 mph (0–95 km/h):	7.2 sec
Engine type:	V8
Displacement:	440 ci (7,210 cc)
Transmission	4-speed manual
Max power:	390 bhp (449 kW) @ 4,700 rpm
Max torque:	490 lb ft (663 Nm) @ 3,200 rpm
Weight:	3,437 lb (1,562 kg)
Economy:	9 mpg (3.2 km/l)

Dodge Challenger T/A (1970)

Dodge jumped in headfirst to the SCCA's Trans Am racer series with its aptly named Challenger, as it was going up against the likes of Ford's Mustang and Chevrolet's Camaro. It was built for just one year and featured a spec sheet that would get any gasoline head revved up. The car stuck with a small-block engine, thus keeping weight down and handling at the optimum, thanks to better balance. The suspension was uprated torsion bar at the front and a live axle rear on leaf springs, while discs came standard on the front. The engine came from the art Swinger and, though advertised at 290bhp (216kW) output, was well over 300bhp (223kW). To reinforce the racing theme a four-speed was fitted, with an auto optional. Also, to aid traction, bigger rear tyres were fitted than at the front, and this was the first Detroit muscle car to have such a set-up.

Top speed:	125 mph (200 km/h)
0–60 mph (0–96 km/h):	5.8 sec
Engine type:	V8
Displacement:	340 ci (5,571 cc)
Transmission	3-speed auto
Max power:	290 bhp (216 kW) @ 5,000 rpm
Max torque:	345 lb ft (467 Nm) @ 3,200 rpm
Weight:	3,650 lb (1,659 kg)
Economy:	12 mpg (4.25 km/l)

Dodge Coronet R/T (1970)

Dodge introduced its Coronet to the public in 1967 and with sales of over 10,000, people appreciated its complete high-performance package. By 1970 the Coronet R/T (Road and Track) was not so popular, but it remained a good combination for the street or strip-racing enthusiast. In base form it used the 440ci (7.2-litre) Wedge engine, so called because of the shape of the combustion chambers. This was a more reliable and easier to maintain engine than the famed 'Hemi' which was optional. Even in base form, the 440ci had 375bhp (279kW) with a single carb, or 390bhp (291kW) with the 'Six Pack' carb option. A torsion bar front and live axle rear, as per most in the Chrysler group, kept it smooth. In 1970 the car was barely afloat in a sea of beautiful and powerful cars (ironically, many from the Chrysler stable), and its sales dropped to 2,615. Of those only 13 had the Hemi.

Top speed:	123 mph (197 km/h)
0–60 mph (0–95 km/h):	6.6 sec
Engine type:	V8
Displacement:	440 ci (7,210 cc)
Transmission	3-speed auto
Max power:	375 bhp (279 kW) @ 4,600 rpm
Max torque:	480 lb ft (650 Nm) @ 3,200 rpm
Weight:	3,546 lb (1,612kg)
Economy:	10.6 mpg (3.78 km/l)

Dodge Charger Daytona

Debuted in 1969, the Dodge Charger Daytonas started NASCAR by impressing everyone with lap speeds just under 200mph (322km/h). A Charger won that debut race and through the season Daytonas won another 21 times. The following year, the Daytonas were joined by their similar stablemates, the Plymouth Superbirds, but 1971 was to be both their last year, as a ruling on their rear spoiler meant a reduction of engine size by a quarter, hence they couldn't be competitive. The NASCARs from this era were still relatively stock, hence the Dayonta used torsion bar front and leaf spring rear suspension, all uprated. However, the doors were welded shut to increase body stiffness, and inside a full roll cage was added for safety. The legendary Hemi engines under the hood were raised in compression to 13.3:1 and used single plane racing manifolds with a single carburettor.

Top speed:	200 mph (320 km/h)
0–60 mph (0–95 km/h):	4.3 sec
Engine type:	V8
Displacement:	426 ci (6,980 cc)
Transmission:	4-speed manual
Max power:	556 bhp (415 kW) @ 6,000 rpm
Max torque:	497 lb ft (673 Nm) @ 5,400 rpm
Weight:	3,100 lb (1,409 kg)
Economy:	N/A

Dodge Charger R/T (1971)

In 1971 the Charger, which had set the standards for full-sized sedan muscle-car performance, got a restyle. The front end was wider and had a one-piece fender for better crash protection, and this was matched at the rear where there was also a sharper roofline slope. The car was virtually unchanged on the chassis, still with torsion bars at the front and multi-leaf rear springs on the Dana 60-equipped rear axle. The 440ci (7.2-litre) Magnum engine was a racer's dream, with an ultra-strong crankshaft and connecting rods, plus a rigid cast-iron block. It also had high flow cylinder heads and an effective intake manifold with triple two-barrel carbs (the famous 'Six Pack'), so it's easy to see how the cars were so effective in NHRA Super Stock drag-racing class. Just 3,118 R/Ts were built in 1971, and only 63 had the extra option of the legendary Hemi.

Top speed:	125 mph (200 km/h)
0–60 mph (0–96 km/h):	6.0 sec
Engine type:	V8
Displacement:	440 ci (7,210 cc)
Transmission	4-speed manual
Max power:	385 bhp (287 kW) @ 4,800 rpm
Max torque:	490 lb ft (664 Nm) @ 3,200 rpm
Weight:	3,785 lb (1,720 kg)
Economy:	12 mpg (4.25 km/l)

Dodge Li'l Red Express (1979)

Based on the Adventurer 150 pick-up, the Li'l Red Express Truck was Dodge's attempt at a factory custom pick-up, and it was a very successful one. It uses the truck's standard and very strong separate chassis with a 360ci (5,899cc) V8 mounted up front for extraordinary pulling power, in fact the engine made this one of the fastest production vehicles in Detroit in 1979. It used a police-spec build, with high-lift camshaft, large four-barrel 850cfm, windage tray to help the crankshaft rev free of oil, plus a high-flow air filter and chrome dress-up items. The suspension was uprated with stiffer shocks for improved handling, while the brakes got power assistance to help bring down the speed. While in 1978 the truck had seen just 2,188 buyers, but the following year this more than doubled to 5,118, with the only change that year being the quad headlights.

Top speed:	118 mph (189 km/h)
0–60 mph (0–96 km/h):	6.6 sec
Engine type:	V8
Displacement:	360 ci (5,899 cc)
Transmission	3-speed auto
Max power:	225 bhp (168 kW) @ 3,800 rpm
Max torque:	295 lb ft (400 Nm) @ 3,200 rpm
Weight:	3,855 lb (1,752 kg)
Economy:	14 mpg (4.96 km/l)

Dodge Stealth R/T Turbo

Although badged a Dodge, the 1990 Stealth was a re-bodied Mitsubishi 3000GT, though was a superb driver's machine. It was built on the same assembly line in Japan and uses the same chassis, engine, transmission and suspension. The latter is MacPherson struts all around with trailing arms at the rear and anti-roll bars at each end. The engine had a iron block with extra ribs for strength, while the dual-overhead cam 24v heads were aluminium alloy. In base form the engine had 164bhp (122kW), while in R/T guise it managed 222bhp (165kW). The best was the R/T Turbo, which had twin Mitsubishi TD04 turbos with intercoolers to add 10psi boost for 300bhp (223kW). Hi-tech additions were four-wheel drive and four-wheel steer, a front spoiler which lowered at 50mph (80km/h) to re-direct airflow around the car, and a rear spoiler to increase downforce.

Top speed:	151 mph (243 km/h)
0–60 mph (0–95 km/h):	5.3 sec
Engine type:	V6
Displacement:	181 ci (2,966 cc)
Transmission	5-speed manual
Max power:	300 bhp (224 kW) @ 6,000 rpm
Max torque:	307 lb ft (415 Nm) @ 2,500 rpm
Weight:	3,803 lb (1,729 kg)
Economy:	18 mpg (6.4 km/l)

Dodge Spirit R/T (1991)

The first Sprit came about in 1988 as a replacement for the ageing Aries compact, but unlike the Aries, came only as a four-door sedan. It looked like any other sedan around at the time, but Dodge turned up the wick when they debuted the limited edition R/T late in 1990. It used the engine which had been developed throughout the 1980s and which had already seen duty in the Omni GLH-S and Shelby Charger GLH, this being a 134ci (2.2-litre) turbocharged engine with twin balancer shafts to keep vibration to a minimum. Through an intercooler and with twin overhead camshaft, its output was enough to beat many of the original muscle cars on the quarter-mile, but the Spirit still had the practicality of a four-door sedan. Inside the driver's car they continued with sporty bucket seats and a Getrag five-speed manual shift. Just 1,300 models were made in the one year.

Top speed:	130 mph (208 km/h)
0-60 mph (0–96 km/h):	6.9 sec
Engine type:	In-line four
Displacement:	135 ci (2,212 cc)
Transmission	5-speed manual
Max power:	224 bhp (167 kW) @ 6,000 rpm
Max torque:	217 lb ft (294 Nm) @ 2,800 rpm
Weight:	3,060 lb (1,390 kg)
Economy:	25 mpg (8.85 km/l)

Dodge Viper R/T 1992

Shown as a concept at the Detroit international Auto Show in 1989, the Viper received such an overwhelming response from the public that it couldn't fail to go into production. It was designed as a modern-day version of the 1960's 427 Cobra, with remarkably similar traits. The engine was up front and was full of torque, being the biggest production engine in the world. It sat in a tubular steel chassis which also housed independent wishbone suspension front and back. The car used rear-wheel drive, and torque was sent back via a specially designed Borg Warner gearbox, which had a lockout shift mechanism to go from first gear straight to fourth at light throttle. The motor could even pull from as little as 500rpm, or 35 mph (56 km/h) in sixth gear. The body was reinforced glass-fibre to help lightweight and the brakes were 13-inch (330mm) Brembo discs and calipers, giving immense stopping power.

Top speed:	162 mph (260 km/h)
0–60 mph (0–95 km/h):	5.4 sec
Engine type:	V10
Displacement:	488 ci (7,998 cc)
Transmission	6–speed manual
Max power:	400 bhp (298 kW) @ 4,600 rpm
Max torque:	488 lb ft (662 Nm) @ 3,600 rpm
Weight:	3,477 lb (1,580 kg)
Economy:	12 mpg (4.25 km/l)

Dodge Ram

The new Ram from Dodge came along in 1994 and made the outgoing model look very dated. The new truck's bold styling with raised hood and low-down headlights was popular; it also became the look for Dodge's later Sport Utility Vehicle, the Dakota. The range-topping Ram used a cast-iron version of the Dodge Viper's V10 engine, and it's the biggest motor available in a production pick-up. With a relatively low 8.6:1 compression ratio it has been designed to be more of a torquey low rpm unit, though still runs the sequential fuel injection. The truck used a ladder-type chassis separate to the body and the standard suspension consists of double wishbones at the front plus a live axle rear on leaf springs, which was basic but very functional and heavy duty. Four-wheel drive was an option, and with the tremendous torque, there was little the V10 Ram couldn't do.

Top speed:	113 mph (180 km/h)
0–60 mph (0–95 km/h):	7.5 sec
Engine type:	V10
Displacement:	488 ci (7,996 cc)
Transmission	4-speed auto
Max power:	300 bhp (224 kW) @ 4,000 rpm
Max torque:	440 lb ft (595 Nm) @ 2,800 rpm
Weight:	5,383 lb (2,446 kg)
Economy:	13.6 mpg (4.8 km/l)

Dodge Viper GTS

Chrysler debuted the first concept Viper in 1989 at the Detroit Motor Show. It was very well received. Two years later a production Viper RT/10 paced the Indy 500 and by 1992 the car was on sale, with buyers lining up. A year later, Chrysler did the same again by debuting a coupe concept of the Viper, and again it hit the spot with potential buyers. The first GTS coupe appeared in 1996 and addressed some of the roadster's shortcomings. It had a roof for a start, and every body panel was new. Virtually new was the engine, with so many components changed for the GTS. Power was up, naturally, but cleverly the weight was down by over 40lb (18kg) due to composite bodywork and all-aluminium suspension. It was surprisingly practical, thanks to the rear hatch/window and generous trunk space. Massive 335/35x17 radials helped put down the enormous torque through rear-wheel drive.

Top speed:	179 mph (286 km/h)
0–60 mph (0–95 km/h):	4.7 sec
Engine type:	V10
Displacement:	488 ci (7,996 cc)
Transmission	6-speed manual
Max power:	450 bhp (336 kW) @ 5,200 rpm
Max torque:	490 lb ft (663 Nm) @ 3,700 rpm
Weight:	3,384 lb (1,538 kg)
Economy:	24 mpg (8.5 km/l)

Dodge Viper GTS-R

It was logical for Chrysler to turn the GTS into a race machine and they debuted the GTS-R in 1995. In 1997 two cars entered the GT2 class in World Sportscar Racing and came first and second at the Le Mans 24 Hours in France. The GTS-R even took the World GT2 Championship overall, a first for an American production model. Despite looking very similar to the road car, the R version had many changes. The engine sat further back to aid weight-distribution and was full balanced and given 12:1 compression along with stronger forged steel connecting rods for high rpm use. A dry sump oiling system helped maintain oil pressure under hard cornering. The chassis was strengthened and fitted with spherical joints on the suspension to ensure maximum response. Panels were swapped for lightweight carbon-fibre versions, and the low bodywork was deepened to aid air flow.

Top speed:	203 mph (324.8 km/h)
0–60 mph (0–95 km/h):	3.1 sec
Engine type:	V10
Displacement:	488 ci (7,996 cc)
Transmission	6-speed manual
Max power:	650 bhp (484 kW) @ 6,000 rpm
Max torque:	650 lb ft (880 Nm) @ 5,000 rpm
Weight:	2,750 lb (1,250 kg)
Economy:	N/A

Dodge Durango

Although based on the Dakota truck chassis, the 1997 Durango didn't display truck-like handling. The frame was stiffened before being put into duty under the four-wheel drive, but kept the Dakota-style suspension with double wishbones acting on a torsion bar spring up front and a live axle rear hanging on leaf springs. The 4x4 intentions were obvious through the ride height, and while a driver had low or high ratio full-time 4WD available, they could select rear drive only to save fuel while on the highway. Three engine options were available, the 238ci (3.9-litre) V6, the better 318ci (5.2-litre) V8, or the top-of-the-range 360ci (5.9-litre) which gave exceptional performance for the big and heavy Sport Utility Vehicle. Vented 11-inch (279mm) discs could handle the pace, cruising high speed across country, or descending a 3:1incline. Inside it could seat eight comfortably.

Top speed:	115 mph (184 km/h)
0–60 mph (0–95 km/h):	8.7 sec
Engine type:	V8
Displacement:	360 ci (5,898 cc)
Transmission	4-speed auto
Max power:	250 bhp (186 kW) @ 4,000 rpm
Max torque:	335 lb ft (454 Nm) @ 3,200 rpm
Weight:	5,050 lb (2,295 kg)
Economy:	15 mpg (5.3 km/l)

Duesenberg Model J (1929)

While Rolls Royce garnered much praise for luxury motoring in Britain, it was Duesenberg who were top of the pile in the USA, though their machines were recognized and respected throughout Europe. The Model J was more than just a luxury car, as Duesenberg intended it to be a sporting drive for keen drivers. The engine was mighty, being a straight-eight cylinder with twin overhead camshafts and four valves per cylinder, plus a mercury-filled crank damper which kept it smooth running while being incredibly powerful. The suspension was developed too and the company invented the phrase about its Duesenberg taking curves 'as though on rails'. For those people with the money to buy one but who got bored with the performance, there was always a supercharger kit which could boost power up to 320bhp (238kW), which filmstar Gary Cooper did to his SSJ roadster.

Top speed:	116 mph (186 km/h)
0–60 mph (0–96 km/h):	11.0 sec
Engine type:	In-line eight
Displacement:	420 ci (6,882 cc)
Transmission:	3–speed manual
Max power:	265 bhp (198 kW) @ 4,250 rpm
Max torque:	N/A
Weight:	4,895 lb (2,225 kg)
Economy:	9.4 mpg (3.3 km/l)

Duesenberg SJ (1932)

Like most luxury and expensive machines of the time, the Duesenberg SJ came only as a rolling chassis to which the customer would add their choice of coachbuilt body. Fred Deusenberg pushed for quality and durability and the frame consisted of strong 8-inch (203mm) deep rails with vacuum-assisted four-wheel brakes with aluminium brake shoes and a variable effort dash lever for dry to icy roads. Aluminium was, in fact, used where possible because at 20ft (6m) long the car needed as many weight-saving measures as it could get. The engine was the most powerful in production in the world at the time and made the supercharged version of the SJ one of the fastest road cars available. In 1935 A.B. Jenkins averaged 135mph (216km/h) on a 24-hour Bonneville run and clocked a 160mph (258km/h) top speed. Sadly Duesenberg never knew, as he died driving one of his SJs in 1932.

Top speed:	130 mph (208 km/h)
0–60 mph (0–96 km/h):	8.5 sec
Engine type:	In-line eight
Displacement:	420 ci (6,882 cc)
Transmission	3–speed manual
Max power:	320 bhp (239 kW) @ 4,200 rpm
Max torque:	425 lb ft (576 Nm) @ 2,400 rpm
Weight:	5,000 lb (2,272 kg)
Economy:	10 mpg (3.54 km/l)

Edsel Bermuda (1958)

While the Edsel was long regarded as a flop – embarrassing for parent company Ford, as the brand was named after Henry Ford's only son – its unique looks have ensured its collectability. And the rarer a model is, the more collectable it becomes, which is why the Bermuda is probably one of the most sought-after in the range. When it arrived, the Bermuda was available in either six- or nine-seater configuration, the latter costing just $57 more for the extra seats. The car truly was a family vehicle, with such convenient extras as Tele Touch auto transmission, where the gear-selection buttons were in a circular pattern in the centre of the steering wheel, and air-conditioning, power windows, and even power lubrication, which greased all the steering and front suspension points at the touch of a button. The car was a very smooth drive and had plenty of power for long hauls too.

Top speed:	108 mph (173 km/h)
0-60 mph (0–96 km/h):	11.8 sec
Engine type:	V8
Displacement:	361 ci (5,915 cc)
Transmission	3-speed auto
Max power:	303 bhp (226 kW) @ 4,600 rpm
Max torque:	400 lb ft (542 Nm) @ 2,600 rpm
Weight:	3,853 lb (1,751 kg)
Economy:	18 mpg (6.37 km/l)

Edsel Citation (1958)

Hurried into production, the Edsel was beset by production problems and quality control. But it wasn't all bad. Once the problems had been overcome it represented a premium brand with a lot going for it, Unfortunately by then most buyers had turned to other cars! What the Citation offered was power everything including the hood and front bench seat. Unusual extras inside included the 'cyclops' style rotating speedo placed centrally in the dash, and the station-seeking radio. Underneath there was nothing radical with wishbones and leaf springs front and rear, though the powerplant was extremely torquey to make the Edsel quite a performer for its day. With hindsight it's easy to see that the car was doomed from the very start, and it now represents one of the biggest flops in motoring history. Which, ironically, is also what makes it highly collectable.

Top speed:	105 mph (168 km/h)
0–60 mph (0–96 km/h):	9.7 sec
Engine type:	V8
Displacement:	410 ci (6,718 cc)
Transmission	3-speed auto
Max power:	345 bhp (257 kW) @ 4,600 rpm
Max torque:	475 lb ft (644 Nm) @ 2,900 rpm
Weight:	4,311 lb (1,959 kg)
Economy:	10 mpg (3.54 km/l)

Ferrari 250 GT SWB

The 1959 250 GT SWB was a shorter version of the 250 GT, the SWB standing for Short Wheelbase Berniletta. This was to improve the car's agility for racing, and it worked. A year after its launch, British driver Stirling Moss took a SWB to victory at the Tourist Trophy race at Goodwood, England, and another SWB won the Tour of France. The car used a tubular steel chassis and, unusually, a live axle instead of de Dion rear. In conjunction with the double wishbone front with anti-roll bar, the set-up was very effective. To save weight there were plastic side windows and all-alloy panels for the racing cars, with the Lusso street versions having less use of alloy. Disc brakes were another first for Ferrari and vents in the nose section kept them cool. The engine had its spark plugs moved so the mechanics could access them easier, plus many eventually used six twin choke carbs.

Top speed:	140 mph (224 km/h)
0–60 mph (0–95 km/h):	6.7 sec
Engine type:	V12
Displacement:	180 ci (2,953 cc)
Transmission	4-speed manual
Max power:	280 bhp (209 kW) @ 7,000 rpm
Max torque:	203 lb ft (275 Nm) @ 5,500 rpm
Weight:	2,805 lb (1,275 kg)
Economy:	13.8 mpg (4.9 km/l)

Ferrari 275 GTB

Launched at the Paris Motor Show, France, in 1964, the 275 GTB was the most advanced Ferrari of the time. Underneath it used the traditional tubular chassis design, but instead of a live axle of de Dion rear, as used in previous Ferraris, it had double wishbones and coil springs at the rear, making it a fully independent suspension car. Also out back was a five-speed transaxle, which evened out weight-distribution very well, making the car beautifully balanced and better, many reckon, than the mighty Daytona. The front-mounted V12 was a development of the 1947 Ferrari 166 engine, but by this time it was using four camshafts and six twin-choke carburettors on the 275 GTB/4, as pictured here. Four wheel disc brakes were standard and the wheels were Campagnolo alloys, though the ultra-rare 275 GTB/C (competizione) wore Borrani wire wheels.

Top speed:	165 mph (264 km/h)
0–60 mph (0–95 km/h):	7.0 sec
Engine type:	V12
Displacement:	200 ci (3,286 cc)
Transmission	5-speed manual
Max power:	300 bhp (224 kW) @ 8,000 rpm
Max torque:	202 lb ft (274 Nm) @ 5,500 rpm
Weight:	2,426 lb (1,102 kg)
Economy:	14.7 mpg (5.25 km/l)

Ferrari Dino 246 GT

Though the earlier 1967–1968 Dino 206 styled by Pininfarina (never badged a Ferrari) had all the right ingredients of a howling V6, 5-speed gearbox and fully independent suspension, it didn't have its bugs ironed out, so the 1969 Ferrari 246GT was a better car. The Dino was advanced in that it ran the V6 mid-mounted and transverse, and because it was the first switch by Ferrari to rack and pinion steering. It used a tubular chassis with double wishbones all around, but while the first Dino had an alloy body, the 246 GT used steel so was slightly heavier. Early cars had just 121ci (1,998cc) displacement in the all-alloy engine derived from Ferrari's 97ci (1.6-litre) F2 motor, but in 1969 the blocks were made in cast iron by Fiat and given a longer stroke and larger bore. Brilliant handling and an engine which would rev past its 7,800rpm redline ensured the Dino became a collector's car.

Top speed:	148 mph (237 km/h)
0–60 mph (0–95 km/h):	7.3 sec
Engine type:	V6
Displacement:	148 ci (2,418 cc)
Transmission	5-speed manual
Max power:	195 bhp (145 kW) @ 5,000 rpm
Max torque:	166 lb ft (224 Nm) @ 5,500 rpm
Weight:	2,611 lb (1,187 kg)
Economy:	22 mpg (7.8 km/l)

Ferrari Daytona

This was the last and greatest of all the front-engined, rear-wheel drive two-seater Ferrari's and some purists regard it as one of the best Ferraris of all time. The Daytona, model name 365GTB/4, oozed style with its Pininfarina body with long hood that hid a quad-cam V12 fed by six Weber carburettors. To balance out the huge engine, the gearbox was mounted at the rear in the transaxle, giving near perfect 52:48 weight distribution. As with many Ferraris of the era, the Daytona used double wishbone suspension and anti-roll bars both ends, and had vented discs to cope with the enormous speed it was capable of. The chassis was a multi-tube affair hidden by a steel body but with alloy doors, hood and trunk lid. For 1970 this was the fastest car in the world; in fact, it remained that way for years, because 100mph (160km/h) could arrive in under 13 seconds.

Top speed:	174 mph (278 km/h)
0–60 mph (0–95 km/h):	5.6 sec
Engine type:	V12
Displacement:	268 ci (4,390 cc)
Transmission	5-speed manual
Max power:	352 bhp (262 kW) @ 7,500 rpm
Max torque:	330 lb ft (447 Nm) @ 5,500 rpm
Weight:	3,530 lb (1,604 kg)
Economy:	11.8 mpg (4.2 km/l)

Ferrari 512 BB Le Mans

When Ferrari withdrew from its sportscar racing programme in the early 1970s to concentrate on Formula One, it left a huge gap. To compensate, the North American Racing Team developed its own competition machine, based on the 512 BB (Berlinetta Boxer). They changed the front bodywork and incorporated more powerful lights for night racing, plus used hood vents to cool the radiator and side vents to air the rear-mounted 12-cylinder horizontally opposed engine. The chassis was very similar to the street car as required by racing regs, being tubular and using double wishbones front and rear, but using much bigger brake discs to cope with the endurance racing. The all-alloy flat 12 engine was based on the 183ci (3-litre) F1 engine from 1970, but strengthened and fitted with dry sump lubrication and mechanical fuel injection, which could be tuned up to 600bhp (804kW).

Top speed:	203 mph (324.8 km/h)
0–60 mph (0–95 km/h):	3.6 sec
Engine type:	Flat 12
Displacement:	302 ci (4,942 cc)
Transmission	5-speed manual
Max power:	480 bhp (358 kW) @ 7,400 rpm
Max torque:	N/A
Weight:	2,161 lb (982 kg)
Economy:	N/A

Ferrari Boxer

The 1973 Boxer was the result of direct competition from Lamborghini with their V12 Miura and the soon-to-be-debuted Countach. Ferrari used all their knowledge from Formula One to mount their horizontally opposed 12-cylinder engine behind the driver, and the result was one of the all-time Ferrari greats. The car used a hefty steel frame with twin wishbones and anti-roll bars front and rear, plus coil-over-shocks units all around but doubled up at the rear because of the extra weight. The brakes were 11-inch (279mm) discs sat behind magnesium alloy rims. Because of the length of the flat 12 engine, the gearbox had to be mounted underneath, which meant the motor was rather higher than ideal. Ferrari kept it light as possible by using Silumin alloy for the block. It also had two camshafts per side and four Weber carbs, replaced in 1981 by Bosch fuel injection.

Top speed:	165 mph (264 km/h)
0–60 mph (0–95 km/h):	6.4 sec
Engine type:	Flat 12
Displacement:	302 ci (4,942 cc)
Transmission	5-speed manual
Max power:	360 bhp (268 kW) @ 6,200 rpm
Max torque:	333 lb ft (451 Nm) @ 4,600 rpm
Weight:	3,427 lb (1,558 kg)
Economy:	13 mpg (4.6 km/l)

Ferrari 308

Probably one of the most famous Ferraris due to the amount produced (over 6,000), the 308 was also one of the most stylish from the Modena, Italy, factory. Launched in 1975 and designed to replace the V6 Dino, the 308 was to continue on the small-engined theme but it ended up a V8 and mid-engined, with the motor transversely mounted. It used the same Dino suspension and this made it a real purist's Ferrari, with plenty of potential in acceleration, deceleration and handling. The quad-cam V8 (with belt driven cams against previous Ferraris' chain drive) all-alloy and initially using multi carburettors, changed to fuel injection in 1981. Basic square-section chassis was as per Ferrari tradition, as was the double wishbone suspension which made for very nimble handling. The body was initially made in glass-fibre but this changed in 1977, when all panels became steel.

Top speed:	145 mph (232 km/h)
0–60 mph (0–95 km/h):	7.3 sec
Engine type:	V8
Displacement:	178 ci (2,927 cc)
Transmission	5-speed manual
Max power:	205 bhp (153 kW) @ 7,000 rpm
Max torque:	181 lb ft (245 Nm) @ 5,000 rpm
Weight:	3,305 lb (1,502 kg)
Economy:	16.8 mpg (6 km/l)

Ferrari 308 GT4

This was the first car from Ferrari which tried the 2+2 seating arrangement and it was unusual aside from this as Bertone styled it, instead of mainstay Pininfarina. The sharp-edged lines and out-of-proportion roof because of the extra seating required made it unconventional and disliked by many Ferrari purists. The other first was the use of a V8 which Ferrari mid-mounted for the handling benefits. Cleverly they also managed to package the gearbox below the engine to make the drive train short and therefore give extra room for the rear passengers. The chassis was a carry-over from the Dino, being fully independent with wishbones and using four-wheel vented disc brakes. The V8 was a close relative of the 268ci (4.4-litre) V12 which powered the 365 GTB, sharing its stroke and bore. Its block and heads were aluminium and it had quad cams and Weber carburettors.

Top speed:	154 mph (246 km/h)
0–60 mph (0–95 km/h):	6.9 sec
Engine type:	V8
Displacement:	178 ci (2,926 cc)
Transmission	5-speed manual
Max power:	250 bhp (186 kW) @ 7,700 rpm
Max torque:	210 lb ft (284 Nm) @ 5,000 rpm
Weight:	3,235 lb (1,470 kg)
Economy:	20 mpg (7.1 km/l)

Ferrari Testarossa

Meaning 'redhead' because of its red-coloured valve covers on the Flat 12, the
Testarossa was Ferrari's supercar for the 1980s. It was launched at the 1984
Paris Motor Show to to mixed reviews because of the ostentatious side vents and
massively wide rear just shy of 6.5ft (2m). The vents led to fan-assisted radiators
either side, while the width was needed to house the engine, which was a
progression of the 512 Berniletta Boxer engine from the 1970s. The Testarossa used
a tubular steel frame with double wishbones front and rear, all covered in
aluminium body panels. The transmission was mounted under the engine which
meant more interior space. As Ferrari put it, 'The cockpit: a living room at 190
mph.' Testers said while the Testarossa was tricky to get into, once there, it exuded
Ferrari and always seemed to have more power to offer.

Top speed:	170 mph (272 km/h)
0–60 mph (0–95 km/h):	5.4 sec
Engine type:	Flat 12
Displacement:	302 ci (4,942 cc)
Transmission	5-speed manual
Max power:	390 bhp (291 kW) @ 6,300 rpm
Max torque:	360 lb ft (487 Nm) @ 4,500 rpm
Weight:	3,675 lb (1,670 kg)
Economy:	14 mpg (5 km/l)

Ferrari F40

The F40 stole the limelight for Ferrari in 1987, the 40th anniversary of Enzo Ferrari's first car. It re-established their stand as top exotic car producer and gave the new models an edge which earlier 1980s cars had lacked. It was a race car for the street and indeed was developed on the track using a GTO Evoluzione as a testbed. The bonded composite panels were made of woven carbon-fibre and either Kevlar or Nomex, all of which were glued into place to save weight. As an example, each door weighed less than 3.5lb (1.6kg). Underneath the body there was a tubular steel spaceframe to which the engine was attached. The mid-mounted V8 for each F40 was handbuilt by Ferrari craftsmen, and twin turbos upped power. A transaxle provided drive and at each corner double wishbones and coilover shocks made the race car suspension very firm around town, but perfect over 100mph (160km/h).

Top speed:	201 mph (322 km/h)
0–60 mph (0–95 km/h):	4.2 sec
Engine type:	V8
Displacement:	179 ci (2,936 cc)
Transmission	5-speed manual
Max power:	478 bhp (356 kW) @ 7,000 rpm
Max torque:	423 lb ft (572 Nm) @ 4,000 rpm
Weight:	2,425 lb (1,102 kg)
Economy:	24 mpg (8.5 km/l)

Ferrari 355

Ferrari replaced the 348 with the 355 and created such a beautiful supercar that customers all but stopped buying their 12-cylinder Testarossa. The 355 was easier than any Ferrari before to drive and had such creature comforts as the latest in in-car entertainment plus air-conditioning as standard. Further developed than the previous 348 was the engine, which used five valves per cylinder and from a comparably small output of just under 213ci (3.5 litres) managed to put out 375bhp (279kW) at over 8,000rpm. The 355 used a similar chassis to the 348, being sheet and tubular steel forming a central stress-bearing unit with subframe at either end for the double wishbone suspension. It was far more dynamic to drive than the 348, however, and had an aerodynamically designed undertray to eliminate lift at high speed. Magnesium alloy wheels kept the weight under 3,000lb (1,360kg).

Top speed:	183 mph (293 km/h)
0–60 mph (0–95 km/h):	4.7 sec
Engine type:	V8
Displacement:	213 ci (3,496 cc)
Transmission:	6-speed manual
Max power:	375 bhp (279 kW) @ 8,250 rpm
Max torque:	268 lb ft (363 Nm) @ 6,000 rpm
Weight:	2,977 lb (1,353 kg)
Economy:	18.1 mpg (6.4 km/l)

Ferrari 360 Modena

As a replacement for the 355, the new 360 Modena not only had to look exquisite, it had to be quicker and more nimble in the handling. Pininfarina styled the body and through thousands of hours wind-tunnel testing came up with a shape that instantly shouted 'Ferrari'. But it was clever too, in that without a spoiler front or rear, it had more downforce at 70mph (113km/h) than the previous 355 had at top speed. The functional undertray helped this immensely. The 360 was the first Ferrari of all-aluminium construction, making it 131lb (59kg) lighter than the 355. Through adaptive damping, the ride quality was kept very good too, despite a set-up biased towards handling. The V8 engine was all new, with 40 valves, titanium con-rods and two cams per bank. It had one of the world's highest specific outputs of 111bhp (82kW) per litre.

Top speed:	185 mph (296 km/h)
0–60 mph (0–95 km/h):	4.5 sec
Engine type:	V8
Displacement:	219 ci (3,586 cc)
Transmission	6-speed semi-automatic
Max power:	394 bhp (294 kW) @ 8,500 rpm
Max torque:	275 lb ft (372 Nm) @ 4,750 rpm
Weight:	3,065 lb (1,393 kg)
Economy:	16 mpg (5.7 km/l)

Ferrari 550 Marenello

The 550 Marenello, named after Ferrari's home town, was another stunning Pininfarina styling job. Launched in 1996, it replaced the ageing 512 TR, itself little more than a re-styled Testarossa. Unusually, Ferrari put a front-mounted V12 in the 550, the first time since the Daytona of 1974. Although an all-new car, the Maranello had roots in the 1992 456GT and shared the same layout of double wishbones all around. To distribute the weight evenly, the gearbox was at the rear, while the engine and heads were aluminium to help reduce weight. It featured four camshafts, four-valves-per-cylinder and variable geometry intake and exhaust systems to make the most of power throughout the rev range. Incredibly, it met all emissions standards worldwide, though some felt it was over-silenced in order to meet noise regulations, hence that Ferrari wail was muted.

Top speed:	199 mph (318 km/h)
0–60 mph (0–95 km/h):	4.4 sec
Engine type:	V12
Displacement:	334 ci (5,474 cc)
Transmission	6-speed manual
Max power:	485 bhp (362 kW) @ 7,000 rpm
Max torque:	398 lb ft (539 Nm) @ 5,000 rpm
Weight:	3,726 lb (1,697 kg)
Economy:	11.8 mpg (4.2 km/l)

Ferrari F50

Celebrating their 50th anniversary, Ferrari produced the F50 in 1997. The idea was to make it like a Formula One car for the street, even though it would be far more civilized. Built with such items as a progressive clutch to ensure you didn't stall pulling away from a standstill, plus a precise gearchange and handling slightly biased towards understeer, it was very user-friendly. A strictly functional interior plus carbon-fibre monocoque chassis kept weight to a minimum. Double wishbones and inboard pushrod-operated springs took care of the suspension, and there was also adaptive damping to suit varying conditions. The engine was an F1 unit stroked to increase displacement, though remaining rev-happy to 8,700rpm. Race engine extras included dry sump lubrication, titanium connecting rods and five valves per cylinder operated by four camshafts.

Top speed:	202 mph (323 km/h)
0–60 mph (0–95 km/h):	3.7 sec
Engine type:	V12
Displacement:	287 ci (4,698 cc)
Transmission	6-speed manual
Max power:	513 bhp (382 kW) @ 8,000 rpm
Max torque:	347 lb ft (470 Nm) @ 6,500 rpm
Weight:	3,080 lb (1,400 kg)
Economy:	12 mpg (4.2 km/l)

Fiat Dino

The Dino was a well-produced joint effort by Ferrari, who needed a large company to produce its Formula 2 V6 engine and Fiat, who wanted an open-top sportscar with real credibility. The result was excellent, a high performance car with independent suspension for a great handling. The Pininfarina-styled convertible appeared first at the Turin Motor Show, Italy in 1964, while the Bertone-designed coupe came three years later. Fiat's Dino shared the Ferrari Dino's engine and gearbox, and early versions used a live rear axle, though this was changed in 1969 to an independent suspension with struts and semi-trailing arms. However, the convertible was 12 inches (305mm) shorter than the later coupe, which made it more nimble, despite the rear end handicap. While the Dino was never available in the USA, all were left-hand drive, so many have since found their way there.

Top speed:	130 mph (208 km/h)
0–60 mph (0–95 km/h):	7.7 sec
Engine type:	V6
Displacement:	147 ci (2,418 cc)
Transmission	5-speed manual
Max power:	180 bhp (134 kW) @ 6,600 rpm
Max torque:	159 lb ft (215 Nm) @ 4,600 rpm
Weight:	2,579 lb (1,172 kg)
Economy:	18 mpg (6.4 km/l)

Fiat 500

If you went to any Italian city in the 1960s, then nine out of every ten cars on the road was a Fiat 500. Such was the success of the baby Fiat that almost 3.5 million were made between 1957 and 1977, ranging from stripped-out basic town cars to the massively entertaining, race-tuned Abarth. Although the 500 could only muster 59mph (95km/h) flat-out, it could be driven incredibly quickly as the wonderful steering and incredible grip meant you didn't have to slow down for corners. Its tiny air-cooled twin-cylinder engine was incredibly basic, but had the advantage of being mounted adrift of the rear axle, meaning it could be swapped over in less than half an hour by a skilled mechanic. Its low price and running costs made it an ideal first car for many. It remains popular today and there are numerous clubs devoted to this bewitching little car.

Top speed:	59 mph (95 km/h)
0–60 mph (0–95 km/h):	n/a
Engine type:	in-line twin
Displacement:	30ci (499cc)
Transmission:	4-speed manual
Max power:	18 bhp (13 kW) at 4,600 rpm
Max torque:	22 lb ft (29 Nm) at 3,000 rpm
Weight:	1,036 lb (466 kg)
Economy:	46 mpg (16.4 km/l)

Fiat 600 Multipla

If you think French manufacturer Renault created the people carrier with the launch of the Espace, then it's time to think again. The idea of creating a car for carrying large families and building it on the platform of a small family car was very much that of Fiat, which used the architecture of the rear-engined 600 saloon to create the truly unique Multipla. The 600 Multipla was a rather odd-looking beast and was more aerodynamic going backwards than it was going forwards, but that didn't stop it capturing the hearts of European buyers, who eagerly snapped up over 160,000 examples between 1956 and 1966. One model could turn its bench seats into a bed, while the taxi version had only one seat up front alongside a luggage space. Handling was unusual – with the engine and drive wheels at the back and a long, narrow cabin, its behaviour could be unpredictable from the driver's seat, especially on wet roads.

Top speed:	66 mph (106 km/h)
0–60 mph (0–95 km/h):	54.0 sec
Engine type:	in-line four
Displacement:	39 ci (633 cc)
Transmission:	4-speed manual
Max power:	29 bhp (22 kW)
Max torque:	29 lb ft (39 Nm) at 2,800 rpm
Weight:	1,624 lb (1,209 kg)
Economy:	40 mpg (14.2 km/l)

Fiat 124 Spider Abarth

The Abarth tuning company was in financial trouble in 1971, so Fiat stepped in and took them over as part of their return to rallying. The 124 was soon conceived as the car with which that return would be made, and between the two companies a very capable machine was created in the Abarth Rallye. While the chassis remained the same, a switch from live axle to fully independent rear, with MacPherson struts and trailing arms, was made which vastly improved the car in corners. Also helping was a spherical joint front anti-roll bar which resisted body roll better. The 107ci (1,756cc) four-cylinder engine was taken from the Fiat 132 and had few changes, though each was balanced and blueprinted to ensure maximum output and reliability. Twin Weber carburettors and high compression pistons helped output, which was 200bhp (149kW) for competition versions.

Top speed:	118 mph (189 km/h)
0–60 mph (0–95 km/h):	7.5 sec
Engine type:	In-line four
Displacement:	107 ci (1,756 cc)
Transmission	5-speed manual
Max power:	128 bhp (95 kW) @ 6,200 rpm
Max torque:	117 lb ft (158 Nm) @ 5,200 rpm
Weight:	2,070 lb (941 kg)
Economy:	27 mpg (9.6 km/l)

Fiat 130 Coupé

With styling by Pininfarina and an engine by Ferrari, the Fiat 130 Coupé was always going to make it into the history books. But it was more than just the sum of its parts – the elegant, pin-sharp styling was matched by a chassis that could easily handle the power, even though it was based on the underpinnings of Fiat's humble 130 saloon. It was technologically advanced, too, with fully-independent suspension all round and ventilated disc brakes. Although the engine was identical to that of the Ferrari Dino, the 130 Coupé was never that fast thanks to its not inconsiderable weight, but it was swift enough, and with styling that turned heads on every street corner it deserves to be recognised as one of the most influential and desirable cars of its era. Production lasted from 1971 to 1975, with some 4600 examples being manufactured.

Top speed:	118 mph (189 km/h)
0–60 mph (0–95 km/h):	10 sec
Engine type:	V6
Displacement:	197 ci (3,235 cc)
Transmission:	3-speed auto
Max power:	165 bhp (123 kW) at 5,600 rpm
Max torque:	185 lb ft (251 Nm) at 3,400 rpm
Weight:	3,528 lb (1,587 kg)
Economy:	19 mpg (6.8 km/l)

Fiat 850 Spider

Small sports cars have always been a Fiat speciality, and in the case of the 850 Spider it's easy to see why. Its pretty Bertone-penned bodywork concealed a tiny rear-mounted 817cc four-cylinder engine, making it cheap to buy and run. And although the powerplant might not deliver masses of power, the 850's finely-balanced chassis, light and agile steering and responsive gearbox make it an absolute pleasure to drive. The engine revs cleanly to 6,600rpm, giving the car a far more sporting charcter than its performance figures would suggest, while the tail-happy chassis gave handling charcteristics of a true thoroughbred sports car. The Spider's only real downfall came from its build quality – Fiat used cheap metal during its manufacture, and subsequently rust was always a problem for any owner. A Sports Spider was also produced with a 903cc engine.

Top speed:	84 mph (136 km/h)
0–60 mph (0–95 km/h):	20.0 sec
Engine type:	in-line four
Displacement:	50 ci (817 cc)
Transmission:	4-speed manual
Max power:	52 bhp (39 kW) at 6,200 rpm
Max torque:	46 lb ft (62 Nm) at 4,000 rpm
Weight:	1,640 lb (738 kg)
Economy:	35 mpg (12.5 km/l)

Fiat Coupé

Fiat's mid-1990s entry to the growing coupé market was nothing if not dramatic. Launched in 1996, the striking two-door had individual styling and amazing performance. Designed by Chris Bangle, who later went on to introduce a new and controversial design language at BMW, the Coupé's lines built by Pininfarina were a melee of sharp angles and curves, with a distinctive wedge-shaped profile. It may have caused a stir, but the little Fiat looked fantastic. And under the bonnet, a two-litre 20-valve five-cylinder engine offered excellent performance, especially in turbo form. The turbocharged model had enormous reserves of torque and breathtaking power delivery, but the handling could catch out unskilled drivers at the limit. Production has now ceased but the car remains sought after and there are a number of driver's clubs worldwide.

Top speed:	155 mph (250 km/h)
0–60 mph (0–95 km/h):	6.5sec
Engine type:	in-line five
Displacement:	122 ci (1,998 cc)
Transmission:	five-speed manual
Max power:	220 bhp (163 kW) at 5,750 rpm
Max torque:	228 lb ft (309 Nm) at 2,500 rpm
Weight:	2,966 lb (1,334 kg)
Economy:	23.5 mpg (8.4 km/l)

Ford Model T (1918)

The Model T is arguably one of the most famous of all American cars, and therefore has a place in everyone's heart. Hot rodders have taken to it since the 1920s, stripping the car from its already basic specification to make it lighter and therefore turning it into more of a racer. Though at first the cars received tuned versions of the standard four cylinder 183ci (3-litre) motors, by 1932 the Flathead V8 was in production, and it wasn't long before that found its way into the stripped Model Ts, which were then raced on the dry lakes of southern California. The T Bucket, as shown here, came about in the 1960s as a development of the stripped-out cars, though by then more often than not they had Chevy's small-block, and strong rear axles with huge tyres to get maximum straight-line performance. The skinny front wheels were purely to keep it lightweight.

Top speed:	115 mph (184 km/h)
0–60 mph (0–96 km/h):	5.2 sec
Engine type:	V8
Displacement:	350 ci (5,735 cc)
Transmission	4–speed auto
Max power:	250 bhp (186 kW) @ 5,000 rpm
Max torque:	328 lb ft (444 Nm) @ 3,200 rpm
Weight:	2,198 lb (999 kg)
Economy:	18.1 mpg (6.4 km/l)

Ford Model A (1928)

After sales of over 15 million cars, the Model T made way for the Model A in 1928. While the previous car had done well, it was dated in technology by the late 1920s, but the A more than made up for it with new-found refinement and an all-new engine. In fact it had double the power of the Model T and the extra torque was because of a longer stroke crankshaft. Another development was the use of battery-fed ignition. Further changes occurred in the chassis, which had four-wheel brakes against the two rears which had featured on T, plus higher effort steering and 19-inch (482mm) wheels in place of the 21-inchers (533mm) to give a lower ride height and more suspension travel. By 1929, two million Model As had been produced, but in 1931 sales dropped due to competition from Chevy and the Great Depression. There were also rumours of a new V8 Ford for 1932.

Top speed:	65 mph (104 km/h)
0–60 mph (0–96 km/h):	32.0 sec
Engine type:	In-line four
Displacement:	201 ci (3,293 cc)
Transmission	3–speed manual
Max power:	40 bhp (30 kW) @ 2,200 rpm
Max torque:	128 lb ft (173 Nm) @ 1,000 rpm
Weight:	2,212 lb (1,005 kg)
Economy:	18 mpg (6.4 km/l)

Ford Model A Pick-up (1929)

Like most early Fords, the Model A was subject to much modification but still remained in the shadow of the 1932 Ford, which could naturally take a V8 engine as it had a Flathead eight-cylinder as standard. The A could just about take one at a squeeze, though many hot rodders used the 1932's chassis with the lighter A body on it to make their hot rods. This particular car uses a virtually stock Model A pick-up body mounted on a separate chassis based on the dimensions of the original frame. At the front, this car uses a beam axle which is similar to the original set-up, but which has kick-ups either side of the beam in order to allow the body to sit lower. The engine is a mildly tuned version of Ford's much later Windsor small-block V8 engine, and the power is handled by a 9-inch (227mm) live axle, which is of similar vintage to the motor.

Top speed:	129 mph (206 km/h)
0–60 mph (0–96 km/h):	5.3 sec
Engine type:	V8
Displacement:	351 ci (5,751 cc)
Transmission:	4–speed auto
Max power:	304 bhp (227 kW) @ 4,900 rpm
Max torque:	380 lb ft (515 Nm) @ 3,200 rpm
Weight:	2,470 lb (1,122 kg)
Economy:	13.8 mpg (4.88 km/l)

Ford Hi-Boy 1932 Roadster

The term 'hot rod', to many people involved with such cars, can mean only one car: the 1932 Ford roadster. These cars have been the backbone of the rodding scene for over 60 years, the trend for them beginning as early as the late 1930s. Back then, young guys were picking them up very cheaply, stripping everything but the essentials off of them, then racing their cars on the street or, in the case of Southern California where the movement began, on the dry lake beds which were both flat and vast. While the hot-rod movement has grown to incorporate all manner of cars, the 1932 roadster remains. This one is typical of the cars built in the 1960s, with split wishbone front radius arms, a beam front axle, live axle rear and a small-block up front, though in this case it's Ford. Period touches include the wide steel rims and fenderless body which saved weight.

Top speed:	120 mph (192 km/h)
0-60 mph (0–95 km/h):	6.0 sec
Engine type:	V8
Displacement:	302 ci (4,948 cc)
Transmission:	3-speed manual
Max power:	250 bhp (186 kW) @ 4,500 rpm
Max torque:	275 lb ft (372 Nm) @ 3,000 rpm
Weight:	2,250 lb (1,022 kg)
Economy:	15 mpg (5.3 km/l)

Ford Model 18 Coupe (1932)

The line 'You gonna go after him John', is from the immortal film *American Graffiti*, where John Milner (played by Paul LeMat) is asked whether he's going to chase the tuned 1955 Chevy of Bob Falfa (a young Harrison Ford). The two square up in the final scene, with Milner in this five-window coupe hot rod. Set in 1962, the film centres around one night in a southern Californian town. Milner paroles the main cruise in his 'Deuce coupe' powered by a 1966 327ci (5.3-litre) Corvette engine with 'Fuelie' (fuel injection) heads and a Man-a-Fre quad carb manifold. The car used a Chevy sedan rear axle with a transverse leaf spring and ladder bars for optimum traction, while the front used the original beam axle but kicked-up either end to lower the nose of the car. The wheels were reversed versions of what was available on larger Chevy sedans, but chromed here for show.

Top speed:	125 mph (200 km/h)
0–60 mph (0–96 km/h):	6.2 sec
Engine type:	V8
Displacement:	327 ci (5,358 cc)
Transmission	4–speed manual
Max power:	370 bhp (283 kW) @ 6,000 rpm
Max torque:	380 lb ft (515 Nm) @ 3,800 rpm
Weight:	2,680 lb (1,218 kg)
Economy:	15 mpg (5.3 km/l)

Ford Roadster (1932)

Hot rodding became huge throughout the 1950s and '60s, and never really stopped even into the 1990s. What it did as time went on is used new technology and it seemedd like as soon as a new engine was debuted, within months one had found its way into a hot rod. However, in a turn against the high-tech cars, some owners built their cars using the parts they grew up with, which began a trend to a new style called 'nostalgia' cars. This example shows the style well, using a Nailhead Buick engine (because of the small vertical intake valves) to provide much torque. A drop beam axle with four bar location and transverse leaf spring support the front, while out back a 9-inch (229mm) Ford live axle rear is situated on coilovers and a four-bar racing set-up. In a further nod towards the rods and aeroplanes of the 1950s, this owner has painted flames on the side of his car.

Top speed:	120 mph (192 km/h)
0–60 mph (0–96 km/h):	5.8 sec
Engine type:	V8
Displacement:	401 ci (6,571 cc)
Transmission:	4–speed auto
Max power:	410 bhp (305 kW) @ 4,400 rpm
Max torque:	445 lb ft (603 Nm) @ 2,800 rpm
Weight:	2,338 lb (1,062 kg)
Economy:	7 mpg (2.5 km/l)

Ford Coupe 1934

The 1934 Ford was one of the first from the blue oval company to get away from the overly square look which had dated cars back to the look of a horse-drawn carriage. The shapely, swept-back grille and flowing fenders quickly gained many fans and because all 1934 models came with a V8, the cars were also popular to tune up and thus came into the world of hot rodders. Like all cars of the era, the 1934 used a separate steel chassis and these still figure in many hot rodders' re-builds today. This car in fact retains the beam front axle too, though with telescopic dampers. At the rear it's much more high-tech with the use of a Corvette independent suspension. This hot rod has a very period appearance with many accessories of the era attached to the body. It goes like a modern supercar, however, thanks to a tuned small-block Chevy which has been bored out to 358ci (5,866cc).

Top speed:	127 mph (203 km/h)
0-60 mph (0–95 km/h):	8.7 sec
Engine type:	V8
Displacement:	358 ci (5,866 cc)
Transmission	4-speed manual
Max power:	330 bhp (264 kW) @ 5,500 rpm
Max torque:	339 lb ft (459 Nm) @ 3,400 rpm
Weight:	2,403 lb (1,092 kg)
Economy:	13.8 mpg (4.9 km/l)

Ford Model 830 Pick-up (1935)

Pick-ups have always been a part of the American way of life, and this extends to hot rods. Their lightweight bodies and utilitarian looks go against the grain but that's part of their attraction. They also came with strong chassis and uprated suspension so could take a lot of modifying without major component renewal. Saying that, for the ultimate in style and performance, you have to build any car from the ground up, and that means completely new underpinnings. This pick-up uses a custom steel separate chassis with a Mustang II independent wishbone front end and live axle rear with semi-elliptical springs and traction bars. The engine is the hot rodder's favourite, a small-block Chevy giving mid-14 second potential on the quarter-mile. In typical street rod fashion, this pick-up features a custom interior with leather and air-conditioning for the ultimate in cruising.

Top speed:	110 mph (176 km/h)
0–60 mph (0–96 km/h):	6.4 sec
Engine type:	V8
Displacement:	350 ci (5,735 cc)
Transmission	3-speed auto
Max power:	320 bhp (238 kW) @ 5,400 rpm
Max torque:	360 lb ft (488 Nm) @ 3,800 rpm
Weight:	3,280 lb (1,491 kg)
Economy:	15 mpg (5.31 km/l)

Ford Roadster (1936)

By 1936 cars from Ford had started to swell in size and each new year brought a model with great advances in both technology and design. But every example was well liked by the public, who flocked to Ford like no other manufacturer as they offered cheap yet good-quality transport. As the street rodding industry saw a revival in the 1980s, many firms went into the reproduction of early Ford bodies as they were becoming so difficult to find in good-condition steel. Offering them in glass-fibre which wouldn't rot and was lightweight seemed perfect for the majority of builders who wanted to construct their own cars from kit form at home. This car uses one such body on a vintage shaped chassis but with extra strength. The front and rear suspension are beam and live axle respectively, while power comes from a basic tune small-block Chevy which can still pull the car to quick speeds.

Top speed:	120 mph (192 km/h)
0–60 mph (0–96 km/h):	6.9 sec
Engine type:	V8
Displacement:	350 ci (5,735 cc)
Transmission	4-speed auto
Max power:	250 bhp (186 kW) @ 4,800 rpm
Max torque:	320 lb ft (434 Nm) @ 3,200 rpm
Weight:	2,350 lb (1,068 kg)
Economy:	13 mpg (4.60 km/l)

Ford Deluxe V8 (1939)

Often regarded as Ford's finest pre-war cars, the 1939–1940 V8s had up-to-the-minute styling and plenty of power, thanks to the latest developments of the V8 Flathead engine. In this car's case, the optional 85bhp (63kW) motor was up 20bhp (15kW) thanks to a new intake manifold and carburettor. Underneath, the car used a similar chassis to that which had been developed for the 1934 model year, with an X-braced twin rail design. The suspension it used went even further back in time, being almost identical to the Model T's set-up of a beam front and live rear axle supported on transverse leaf springs, but then Henry Ford always did believe in keeping his cars simple and therefore cheap. New for 1939 were four-wheel hydraulic brakes, which made the Fords much safer and more reassuring to drive. By the later 1930s the popular airflow look was evident on Ford's designs.

Top speed:	87 mph (139 km/h)
0–60 mph (0–96 km/h):	17.4 sec
Engine type:	V8
Displacement:	221 ci (3,621 cc)
Transmission	3-speed manual
Max power:	85 bhp (63 kW) @ 3,800 rpm
Max torque:	155lb ft (210 Nm) @ 2,200 rpm
Weight:	2,898 lb (1,317 kg)
Economy:	18 mpg (6.37 km/l)

Ford Model 81A (1938)

Ford were the first company to introduce a V8 in a mass production car in the early 1930s, and they continued thanks to massive public demand. By 1938 the engines were standard across the board, but other manufacturers were using them too and in particular Chevy, who regularly overtook Ford in sales. To compensate, Ford split its models into two distinctly different version, the Deluxe and Standard. This car is the Deluxe, shown by the grille splitting into two distinct arcs at the top, whereas the Standard had a vertical top. Little remains of the standard car underneath, except for a strengthened version of the stock chassis. A Mustang II wishbone suspension clip is fitted at the front, while the rear uses leaf spring on a live axle. Its Chevy V8 has received the mildest of tune-ups but still has plenty of power to make this a boulevard bruiser.

Top speed:	122 mph (195 km/h)
0–60 mph (0–96 km/h):	6.1 sec
Engine type:	V8
Displacement:	350 ci (5,735 cc)
Transmission	4-speed auto
Max power:	345 bhp (257 kW) @ 5,600 rpm
Max torque:	360 lb ft (488 Nm) @ 4,000 rpm
Weight:	2,350 lb (1,068 kg)
Economy:	14 mpg (4.95 km/l)

Ford Coupe (1940)

While still using the separate fender design which had evolved from the 1920s and 1930s, the 1940 Ford coupe had rounded lines which dictated how cars were to appear in the next decade. The car, while once proving affordable and simple transportation for many Americans, went on to be a hot rodders' favourite, as its Flathead V8 could be easily tuned. As V8 engines developed and more became available cheaply, so hot rodders fitted older cars with increasingly powerful engines, the small-block Chevy being a favourite. This car uses the basic rails strengthened to take Mustang II front suspension and a 9-inch (229mm) Ford live rear axle on leaf springs. The small-block has been treated to a high-lift camshaft, re-worked heads, a dual plane intake manifold plus Holley four-barrel carb, so it can run the quarter in 14 seconds while giving cruising comfort for four.

Top speed:	123 mph (197 km/h)
0–60 mph (0–95 km/h):	6.4 sec
Engine type:	V8
Displacement:	350 ci (5,735 cc)
Transmission	3-speed auto
Max power:	345 bhp (257 kW) @ 5,600 rpm
Max torque:	360 lb ft (487 Nm) @ 4,000 rpm
Weight:	2,769 lb (1,259 kg)
Economy:	15 mpg (5.3 km/l)

Ford F1 (1948)

Being one of the most popular workhorses of the time, the F1 had many fans as it was tough, reliable and could be ordered with the optional 239ci (3.9-litre) Flathead V8. The F1 was Ford's first new production vehicle following the war, and it had increased room over pre-war models, plus greater refinement, something that truck lovers were to demand more of in later models. As the trucks were built rugged in the first place, this one has needed little to cope with the extra power provided by a small-block Ford V8. A 9-inch (229mm) Ford rear axle puts down the torque well, but apart from that, just the gearbox has changed, with all fitting where they're supposed to without major modification. The original suspension remains, with lowering blocks on the front leaf springs to get the nose 'in the weeds' and the rear having the axle put above the leaf springs, instead of below, as standard.

Top speed:	105 mph (168 km/h)
0–60 mph (0–96 km/h):	8.7 sec
Engine type:	V8
Displacement:	351 ci (5,751 cc)
Transmission	3-speed auto
Max power:	275 bhp (205 kW) @ 4,800 rpm
Max torque:	380 lb ft (515 Nm) @ 3,400 rpm
Weight:	3,120 lb (1,418 kg)
Economy:	15 mpg (5.31 km/l)

Ford Custom Tudor (1950)

Known as one of the toughest on and off road races in the world, the Carrera Panamericana, has long been run and in the early 1950s Ford entered carssimilar to this one. The Tudor sedan was lightweight and rugged, and with a Flathead V8, which had proved reliable and durable, the car was ideal for the nlong distance event. Five decades later the same cars are still proving tough contenders, though this version has far more packed in than the original race machines. It has a similar chassis layout but is strengthened with a six-point roll cage. There are double wishbones up front and leaf springs at the rear, uprated and supplemented by anti-roll bars front and rear plus a Watts linkage on the beefy 9-inch (229mm) Ford axle. The Flathead has been bored out and stroked for extra displacement and power, and the gearbox is the ultra-tough Borg Warner T10 'Toploader'.

Top speed:	110 mph (176 km/h)
0–60 mph (0–96 km/h):	10.1 sec
Engine type:	V8
Displacement:	290 ci (4,752 cc)
Transmission	4-speed manual
Max power:	226 bhp (168 kW) @ 4,000 rpm
Max torque:	240 lb ft (325 Nm) @ 2,600 rpm
Weight:	3,112 lb (1,414 kg)
Economy:	15 mpg (5.31 km/l)

Ford Woody

Woodys were always regarded as the family station wagon with a country feel, until surfers found them useful for their long boards. They became firm favourites with both surfers and hot rodders, who had lifestyles that were very alike with a disregard to conforming to the norm. Most surf wagons were kept stock mechanically but just lowered and sometimes fitted with custom wheels. This 1950 Ford has taken the Woody to another level with late-model Mustang independent front suspension and a narrowed 9-inch (228mm) Ford axle located on a four-bar set-up. The power comes via a supercharged small-block Chevy with massive torque, and to put the power down the owner has fitted 13-inch (330mm) wide Mickey Thompson Pro Street Radials at the rear. The rear seat has been removed, but the interior features air-conditioning and a multi-speaker sound system.

Top speed:	147 mph (235 km/h)
0–60 mph (0–95 km/h):	4.7 sec
Engine type:	V8
Displacement:	406 ci (6,653 cc)
Transmission	4-speed auto
Max power:	410 bhp (305 kW) @ 5,100 rpm
Max torque:	450 lb ft (609 Nm) @ 3,100 rpm
Weight:	3,402 lb (1,546 kg)
Economy:	16.7 mpg (5.9 km/l)

Ford Crestline Sunliner (1952)

Customising was always an art in which individual touches shone through. It's beauty was that virtually any body style could be chosen, though true customising started in the 1950s so that's where many people choose their base material from. The Ford Crestline Sunliner from '52 wasn't chosen as often as the early post–war Fords, but even so it lent itself well to the treatment as the general body shape was very similar to the new–for–'49 model. This car has a host of extras, and in customising the right type of extras are essential – things like upmarket hubcaps, whitewall tyres, grille teeth made from bumper overriders, A-pillar spotlamps and flames to give a real hot rod feel. The accessories inside are just as important, with fluffy dice hanging from the rear view mirror for luck, plus a tweaked dash with peaked switches. This car has also had a roof chop.

Top speed:	112 mph (179 km/h)
0–60 mph (0–96 km/h):	10.5 sec
Engine type:	V8
Displacement:	302 ci (4,948 cc)
Transmission	3-speed auto
Max power:	150 bhp (112 kW) @ 4,200 rpm
Max torque:	240 lb ft (325 Nm) @ 4,500 rpm
Weight:	3,415 lb (1,552 kg)
Economy:	16 mpg (5.66 km/l)

Ford Courier Custom Delivery (1955)

The 1955 Courier struck an ideal balance between luxury and practicality for small storekeepers and salesmen. It was restyled for the same year and looked sleeker and more purposeful than its previous incarnation, plus it had the new 272ci (4.4-litre) Y-block V8 with 162bhp (121kW) to replace the ageing Flathead. Years later the same vehicles offer the same practicality even as customs, though they're not favoured as much as two-door sedans because of their weight and heavy proportions. That didn't bother the owner of this vehicle, who has changed it by adding Camaro front wishbone suspension, a Ford 9-inch (229mm) rear on leaf springs, and Chevy engine with supercharger. Like many custom, the body has been fully smoothed and uses a remote key fob for entry to the doors and rear tailgate. Inside the rear is fitted with custom tweed upholstery.

Top speed:	128 mph (205 km/h)
0–60 mph (0–96 km/h):	6.3 sec
Engine type:	V8
Displacement:	350 ci (5,735 cc)
Transmission	3-speed auto
Max power:	365 bhp (272 kW) @ 5,800 rpm
Max torque:	410 lb ft (556 Nm) @ 3,600 rpm
Weight:	3,210 lb (1,459 kg)
Economy:	12 mpg (4.24 km/l)

Ford Thunderbird (1955)

The Thunderbird appeared a year after the Corvette and was direct competition. Ford's new two-seater had the same layout of a separate chassis with live rear axle on leaf springs, but with one important difference: it had a V8. The 265ci (4.3-litre) engine gave the performance people expected and a year later, a larger, 312ci (5.1-litre) unit was available. The T-bird had other advanced features such as power brakes and steering, making it a better car to drive. The car came with a glass-fibre bolt-on hardtop, but had the option of a folding convertible roof for an extra $290. At first the T-Bird carried its spare wheel above the rear fender, but Ford extended the rear for 1957, which meant it could be carried in the trunk. The extra weight put into the rear of the car also helped ride quality. Most desirable is the rare 300bhp (225kW) supercharged 1957 F-Bird, of which just 211 were made.

Top speed:	122 mph (195 km/h)
0–60 mph (0–95 km/h):	9.5 sec
Engine type:	V8
Displacement:	292 ci (4,785 cc)
Transmission	3-speed manual
Max power:	212 bhp (158 kW) @ 4,400 rpm
Max torque:	297 lb ft (402 Nm) @ 2,700 rpm
Weight:	3,050 lb (1,386 kg)
Economy:	13 mpg (4.6 km/l)

Ford F-100 (1956)

As far as classic trucks are concerned, the F-100 rates among the top models in most people's eyes. Its brutish styling won it fans right away, plus it was one of the most powerful, and therefore fastest, trucks in its day. It quickly achieved cult status in later years, because it was one of the best-looking Stepside trucks to be produced, and also one of the last, as the Fleetside styling was introduced just two years later (with the sides flush with the cab). This custom version uses suspension kits front and rear to lower the truck as far as it can practically go, but doesn't use modern trickery anywhere else. The engine is a tuned version of the Ford Y-block from the 1950s with triple two-barrel carbs, and the truck still drives through a three-speed manual transmission which makes performance lively. In order to stop it, the owner has fitted power disc brakes.

Top speed:	110 mph (176 km/h)
0–60 mph (0–96 km/h):	8.1 sec
Engine type:	V8
Displacement:	296 ci (4,850 cc)
Transmission	3-speed manual
Max power:	300 bhp (224 kW) @ 4,500 rpm
Max torque:	270 lb ft (366 Nm) @ 2,300 rpm
Weight:	3,175 lb (1,443 kg)
Economy:	14 mpg (4.95 km/l)

Ford Fairlane Crown Victoria (1956)

Show cars had long used transparent roof sections to display their interior s and give the cars a light, airy feel, but few cars made it into production with such novelties. The Crown Victoria was different though, and used a similar Plexiglas section to the 1954 Ford Skyliner. It was a great idea for making the car feel less claustrophobic, but buyers were never really convinced enough and they preferred the safer option of the regular hardtop coupe. The underpinnings used a perimeter chassis with conventional suspension, consisting of double wishbones up front and leaf springs at the rear, all dampened by telescopic shock absorbers, thus making the ride very smooth. The engine was powerful, coming straight from the Thunderbird and giving plenty of straight line power low down in the rev range. Poor sales again in 1956 ensured the end of the Crown Victoria.

Top speed:	107 mph (171 km/h)
0–60 mph (0–96 km/h):	12.2 sec
Engine type:	V8
Displacement:	312 ci (5,112 cc)
Transmission	3-speed auto
Max power:	225 bhp (168 KW) @ 4,600 rpm
Max torque:	317 lb ft (430 Nm) @ 2,600 rpm
Weight:	3,299 lb (1,499 kg)
Economy:	15 mpg (5.31 km/l)

Ford Fairlane (1957)

Widely regard as one of the most stylish cars of the time, the 1957 Ford didn't excel in ostentatious chrome and fins like other manufacturers, though neither did it abstain completely. It had little wing peaks at the rear highlighted with chrome trim which ran along the side to break up the bodywork. The headlamps were peaked, like many other models of the era, but the grille and fender were surprisingly plain, and the fuss-free appearance made the car look both wider and lower. This car features much of the original running gear, though the suspension has been lowered by fitting shorted coils in the front and axle blocks at the rear, and at each corner there now sits low-profile tyres on new 15-inch (381mm) chrome wheels to improve handling. The engine is the top option 1957 Thunderbird engine, but with an extra 10bhp (7kW) out through a better exhaust.

Top speed:	120 mph (192 km/h)
0–60 mph (0–96 km/h):	10.2 sec
Engine type:	V8
Displacement:	312 ci (5,112 cc)
Transmission	3-speed auto
Max power:	255 bhp (190 kW) @ 4,600 rpm
Max torque:	354 lb ft (480 Nm) @ 2,800 rpm
Weight:	3,400 lb (1,545 kg)
Economy:	12.4 mpg (4.38 km/l)

Ford Thunderbird (1957)

The Thunderbird appeared a year after the Corvette and was direct competition. Ford's new two-seater had the same simple layout of a separate chassis with live rear axle on leaf springs, but with the important difference of a V8 up front. The 265ci (4.3-litre) engine gave the performance people expected, and a year later a larger, 312ci (5.1-litre) unit became available. The T-bird also had other advanced features such as power brakes and steering, making them better cars to drive. The car came with a glass-fibre bolt-on hardtop, but had the option of a convertible roof for an extra $290. At first the T-Bird carried its spare wheel above the fender, but Ford extended the rear for 1957, which meant it could be carried in the trunk. The extra weight put into the rear of the car also helped ride quality. This was the best-selling of all early Thunderbirds.

Top speed:	122 mph (195 km/h)
0–60 mph (0–96 km/h):	9.5 sec
Engine type:	V8
Displacement:	292 ci (4,785 cc)
Transmission:	3-speed manual
Max power:	212 bhp (158 kW) @ 4,400 rpm
Max torque:	297 lb ft (402 Nm) @ 2,700 rpm
Weight:	3,050 lb (1,386 kg)
Economy:	13 mpg (4.60 km/l)

Ford Thunderbird Phase I/II (1957)

Most desirable of all Thunderbirds was the rare 300bhp (223kW) supercharged 1957 F-Bird, of which just 208 were made. The car came about through Ford wanting to compete in a flying-mile competition at Daytona Beach, Florida. NASCAR ran the event and stipulated that in order to compete, the car must be homologated, so Ford made the necessary amount of 200 and fitted each one with a Paxton-McCulloch centrifugal supercharger which gave an extra 75bhp (56kW) and 40lb ft (54Nm) torque, enough to propel the car to a flying mile of 93.312mph (150.13km/h), beating the record held by a Duntov Corvette. The car went through very few changes other then the addition of a blower, but because of its rarity, an unrestored clean model can now command a price upwards of $60,000. Few are left, but Ford fans who grew up at the time of the two-seater Thunderbirds pay for good examples.

Top speed:	130 mph (208 km/h)
0–60 mph (0–96 km/h):	9.2 sec
Engine type:	V8
Displacement:	312 ci (5,112 cc)
Transmission	3-speed manual
Max power:	300 bhp (224 kW) @ 4,800 rpm
Max torque:	336 lb ft (455 Nm) @ 3,400 rpm
Weight:	3,145 lb (1,429 kg)
Economy:	15 mpg (5.31 km/l)

Ford Fairlane modified (1958)

While 1958 isn't considered a landmark year for cars out of Detroit, Ford were at least top of what was out there. Their cars had stylish lines and seemed blend all the trends of the time together the best. Their Fairlane hardtop coupes had pillarless styling, glitzy yet stylish front and rear ends, and looked very well proportioned. In recent decades, when people have become tired of seeing the same Chevys getting modified, they've turned straight to Ford as they offer striking potential for customizing. This example uses little more than 2-inch (50mm) drop spindles at the front and 3-inch (76mm) lowering blocks at the rear, but its effect is dramatic, along with flame paint and whitewall-equipped chromed steels. It uses Ford's underrated engine from the 1960s, the torquey 390ci (6.4-litre) big-block, which easily puts the Fairlane 500 among the early muscle machines.

Top speed:	115 mph (184 km/h)
0–60 mph (0–96 km/h):	8.4 sec
Engine type:	V8
Displacement:	390 ci (6,390 cc)
Transmission	3-speed auto
Max power:	340 bhp (254 kW) @ 5,000 rpm
Max torque:	430 lb ft (583 Nm) @ 3,200 rpm
Weight:	3,485 lb (1,584 kg)
Economy:	15 mpg (5.31 km/l)

Ford Fairlane Skyliner (1959)

Revolutionary at the time, the Skyliner offered a practical hardtop coupe plus the style of a drop top. The retractable hardtop roof was a masterpiece in engineering and required 7 electric motors, 13 switches, 10 solenoids, 8 circuit breakers and over 600ft (182m) of wiring to make it function. The car was fairly conventional underneath with a separate chassis and double wishbones up front with leaf springs at the rear, though the frame did have an X-brace to give it extra strength as the roof was not part of the structure. On the body, one of the best changes for the 1959 model year was the switch to large, round tail lights, which became a trademark feature of early 1960s Fords. Standard was the Mercury's 292ci (4.78-litre) Flathead V8, though with fuel at 20 cents a gallon, the big-blocks were favoured, and this has the 352ci (5.3-litre) Police Interceptor special.

Top speed:	112 mph (179 km/h)
0–60 mph (0–96 km/h):	10.5 sec
Engine type:	V8
Displacement:	352 ci (5,768 cc)
Transmission	3-speed auto
Max power:	300 bhp (224 kW) @ 4,600 rpm
Max torque:	381 lb ft (517 Nm) @ 2,800 rpm
Weight:	4,064 lb (1,847 kg)
Economy:	14 mpg (4.95 km/l)

Ford Thunderbird (1960)

It seems odd now that Ford changed the direction of the Thunderbird from its two-seater origins, when it was launched as direct competition to the Corvette. But sales dictate direction, and as evidence of how much the public liked the 1960 T-bird, it sold over twice as many cars as the 1958 model. Unitary construction was adopted in 1958 to make the car handle better, but it also featured a dropped floorpan to lower the ride height and, thus, the centre of gravity. Coil springs all around gave an excellent ride quality, and although the car wasn't as sporty as the original T-birds, it was quieter and more refined. This model was the top option in its year, having the Lincoln 430ci (7-litre) cast-iron engine up front, which made the car very heavy. However, it was one of the most rapid machines of its day, which was one reason it sold well in those horsepower-hungry times.

Top speed:	121 mph (194 km/h)
0–60 mph (0–96 km/h):	8.2 sec
Engine type:	V8
Displacement:	430 ci (7,046 cc)
Transmission	3-speed auto
Max power:	350 bhp (261 kW) @ 4,800 rpm
Max torque:	490 lb ft (664 Nm) @ 3,100 rpm
Weight:	4,381 lb (1,991 kg)
Economy:	15.7 mpg (5.55 km/l)

Ford Galaxie Starliner (1961)

This Galaxie hot rod carries the now legendary SOHC Ford engine which was developed in order to compete with Chrysler's Hemi-engined NASCAR racers. It made an impressive 675bhp (503kW) on Ford dyno, but it was outlawed immediately because it was too good. The engines did make it on several factory-sponsored A/FX drag racers, which subsequently won their class in 1965. Even so, it never made it into a production car, though some de-tuned engines were sold over the counter. One of those made its way into this modified Galaxie, which has had to have the hood reshaped to fit the induction system. Elsewhere the car features stiffer front suspension to cope with the weight, plus there's a Top Loader gearbox and 4.30:1 geared rear end with Detroit Locker differential. Quarter-miles zip by in just 13 seconds for this Starliner, but it looks like a period factory racer.

Top speed:	130 mph (208 km/h)
0–60 mph (0–96 km/h):	5.4 sec
Engine type:	V8
Displacement:	427 ci (6,997 cc)
Transmission	4-speed manual
Max power:	625 bhp (466 kW) @ 7,000 rpm
Max torque:	515 lb ft (698 Nm) @ 3,800 rpm
Weight:	3,660 lb (1,663 kg)
Economy:	7 mpg (2.47 km/l)

Ford Galaxie Sunliner (1961)

Wider than any other Ford produced in the 1960s, the 1961 Galaxie range was huge in every respect. The Sunliner topped the range and was over 79 inches (2m) wide. It ran nothing radical on the separate chassis, but it did use ideas developed during NASCAR racing to transform the suspension and handling of the car. The body has a minor facelift for this use with a concave grille and stylish single side crease which developed into horizontal fins at the rear. There was a detachable hardtop roof available for the Sunliner, but most opted for the electric folding top. Even in base form the Sunliner had a 300bhp (224kW) V8, but buyers could opt for the Police Interceptor tune which had 401bhp (299kW) and pushed the car under seven seconds in the 0–60mph (0–96km/h) sprint. In the rapidly changing motor world of the early 1960s, the new car lasted but a year before getting a redesign.

Top speed:	122 mph (195 km/h)
0–60 mph (0–96 km/h):	9.5 sec
Engine type:	V8
Displacement:	390 ci (6,390 cc)
Transmission	3-speed auto
Max power:	300 bhp (224kW) @ 4,600 rpm
Max torque:	427 lb ft (579 Nm) @ 2,800 rpm
Weight:	3,792 lb (1,723 kg)
Economy:	12 mpg (4.24 km/l)

Ford Thunderbird (1962)

The square lines were abandoned for 1961 in the third-generation Thunderbird, but the car remained as popular as ever, with over 73,000 built in that year alone. The new cigar shape was powered by just the one engine option: the 390 ci (6.4- litre) big-block. It was a heavy engine, but by now the Thunderbird wasn't so much a sportscar as a luxury cruiser. For that same reason, it was softly sprung and hence didn't corner very well, though it was better than initial impressions would lead you to believe, and once at a reasonable speed, the handling turned more neutral. The styling has turned this era T-bird into a classic, and cars like the Sports Roadster shown remain much in demand, partly because of the enclosed tonneau rear. Also available that year was the Coupe, Landau and convertible. The car was restyled in 1964.

Top speed:	118 mph (188 km/h)
0–60 mph (0–96 km/h):	9.3 sec
Engine type:	V8
Displacement:	390 ci (6,390 cc)
Transmission	3-speed auto
Max power:	300 bhp (224 kW) @ 4,600 rpm
Max torque:	427 lb ft (579 Nm) @ 2,800 rpm
Weight:	4,471 lb (2,032 kg)
Economy:	10 mpg (3.54 km/l)

Ford Falcon Racer (1963)

This Ford Falcon actually uses very little in the way of Ford parts. While it looks like a hardtop coupe, it is actually a convertible body and has had the roof from another Falcon welded on. All that remains of the steel body is the roof, rear three-quarters and doors, while the rest are glass-fibre moulded items in order to save weight. For the same reason, and for improved safety, the glass has also made way for Lexan, reinforced plastic. The frame has been built to the NHRA's (National Hot Rod Association) drag-racing standards for the class of Super Gas, to which the cars run an index of 9.90 seconds on the quarter-mile. The chassis is tubular steel and the front and rear suspension uses lightweight coilover damper units with tubular locating arms. The engine is based on a Ford 460ci (7.5-litre) big-block, but with a stroker crankshaft and a race-spec build.

Top speed:	160 mph (256 km/h)
0–60 mph (0–96 km/h):	2.8 sec
Engine type:	V8
Displacement:	500 ci (8,193 cc)
Transmission	2-speed auto
Max power:	710 bhp (529 kW) @ 7,000 rpm
Max torque:	685 lb ft (929 Nm) @ 5,200 rpm
Weight:	2,015 lb (916 kg)
Economy:	6 mpg (2.12 km/l)

Ford Galaxie 500XL (1963)

The slogan 'Win on Sunday, sell on Monday' was boasted by Ford as they heated up the competition in NASCAR, the Galaxie XL being their star machine. The XL stood for 'extra light' and the trunk lid, doors, hood and front fenders were all moulded in glass-fibre, while the fenders were made in aluminium. Even the rest of the body panels were made from lighter-gauge steel, all of which helped save 700lb (318kg) in weight. The front suspension was kept as double wishbone, while the rear was a live axle with semi-elliptical springs and telescopic shocks, In order to get the best acceleration, 4.56:1 gears were fitted in the axle. The engine was built for racing with a 12.2 compression high-lift cam and dual Holley four-barrel carbs. Inside, the car used low back van seats, while all sound-deadening plus the heater, radio and clock had been removed to further reduce weight.

Top speed:	115 mph (184 km/h)
0–60 mph (0–96 km/h):	4.7 sec
Engine type:	V8
Displacement:	427ci (6,997 cc)
Transmission	4-speed manual
Max power:	425 bhp (317 kW) @ 6,000 rpm
Max torque:	480 lb ft (650 Nm) @ 3,700 rpm
Weight:	3,772 lb (1,714 kg)
Economy:	6 mpg (2.12 km/l)

Ford Fairlane Thunderbolt (1964)

After getting beat by Pontiac and Chrysler in the NHRA's Super Stock class of 1963, Ford went all out for the following season and created the Thunderbolt. It didn't pretend to be anything but a full-blown drag machine, available through Ford only to racers. To fit the huge 427 engine, an outside company, Dearborn Steel Tubing, had to widen the shock towers, plus move the A-arm pivot point out by an inch. The car's high beam headlights were replaced with air intakes to feed the engine, and simple steel wheels were fitted as many got replaced by lightweight racing alloys. The leaf sprung rear end had a torque arm locating the axle to help launch the car, and the battery was mounted in the trunk for improved weight distribution. The body featured lightweight glass-fibre panels where possible, but it was the race-tuned engine which helped push the car to 11.7-second quarters.

Top speed:	130 mph (208 km/h)
0–60 mph (0–96 km/h):	4.7 sec
Engine type:	V8
Displacement:	427 ci (6,997 cc)
Transmission	4-speed manual
Max power:	425 bhp (317 kW) @ 6,000 rpm
Max torque:	480 lb ft (650 Nm) @ 3,700 rpm
Weight:	3,225 lb (1,465 kg)
Economy:	7 mpg (2.47 km/l)

Ford Falcon GT (racer)

The successful start of the Falcon in 1960 led Ford to develop the car further in the following years. Although over 410,000 cars had sold the previous year, in 1961 they produced a Falcon Sprint model with a V8, then in 1962 they sent race-prepared cars to Europe for use in rallying events. In 1964 the car was re-styled with squarer, neater lines, though it faced tough competition from in-house with the new Mustang which, ironically, was a Falcon underneath. This race Falcon is today used in historic circuit competition. It uses lowered and stiffened suspension and in order to lose weight, its hood, trunk, and front fenders have been moulded in glass-fibre. The engine is a High Performance V8, which means it has a slightly increase compression ratio, higher-lift camshaft and free-flowing exhaust. It works through the brutally strong Borg Warner T10 'Top Loader' gearbox.

Top speed:	135 mph (216 km/h)
0–60 mph (0–95 km/h):	6.4 sec
Engine type:	V8
Displacement:	289 ci (4,735 cc)
Transmission	4-speed manual
Max power:	271 bhp (202 kW) @ 6,000 rpm
Max torque:	312 lb ft (422 Nm) @ 3,400 rpm
Weight:	2,811 lb (1,278 kg)
Economy:	12.4 mpg (4.4 km/l)

Ford Lotus Cortina

It was Ford's Walter Hayes who in 1963 persuaded Lotus boss Colin Chapman to produce a limited run of Cortinas with Lotus engines. The intention was to produce 1,000 cars, but its popularity saw three times that amount made. In 1964 Jim Clark won the British Saloon Car Championship and in 1965 Sir John Whitmore won the European Saloon Car Championship. Looking fairly plain externally apart from the green stripes, the Lotus Cortinas sat lower and the front MacPherson struts had new uprated springs and shocks, while at the rear the leaf springs were removed and replaced by an A-frame arrangement plus radius arms and coil-over-shock units. The standard 1500 Ford bottom end was used along with a twin-cam head and twin Webers. A great car to drive fast, the Lotus Cortinas now command high prices and are still used in historic racing.

Top speed:	106 mph (170 km/h)
0–60 mph (0–95 km/h):	9.9 sec
Engine type:	In-line four
Displacement:	95 ci (1,558 cc)
Transmission	4-speed manual
Max power:	105 bhp (78 kW) @ 5,500 rpm
Max torque:	108 lb ft (146 Nm) @ 4,000 rpm
Weight:	2,038 lb (926 kg)
Economy:	28 mpg (10 km/l)

Ford GT40

Ford attempted to buy Ferrari in 1963, and when they failed, it was all-out war on the race track. Ford joined with Lola to turn the Lola GT into the prototype Ford GT, then in 1964 came out with the GT40, so called because it stood just 40 inches (1016mm) high. They weren't very successful and failed to finish in any races. But with huge resources the programme continued with Carroll Shelby at the helm, and in 1965 production of the road-going GT40 started for homologation plus a GT40 won its first race. In 1966 three GT40s fitted with 427 big-block engines took Le Mans with a 1-2-3 win, beating Ferrari. After this the cars used the smaller 289ci (4.7-litre) V8s, but were just as successful. They had a sheet steel semi-monocoque with separate subframes for the rear engine and gearbox, and very deep sills (where the fuel cells were housed) meant the whole structure was extremely stiff.

Top speed:	165 mph (264 km/h)
0–60 mph (0–95 km/h):	5.5 sec
Engine type:	V8
Displacement:	289 ci (4,735 cc)
Transmission	4-speed manual
Max power:	306 bhp (229 kW) @ 6,000 rpm
Max torque:	328 lb ft (444 Nm) @ 4,200 rpm
Weight:	2,200 lb (1,000 kg)
Economy:	14.7 mpg (5.25 km/l)

Ford Falcon Ranchero (1965)

Ford introduced the Ranchero as 'America's lowest price pick-up' in 1960, priced at just $1,882. It was based on the Falcon platform and power came from a 144ci (2.6-litre), 90bhp (67kW) engine, though its saloon counterpart was fitted with a V8 and hence the ranchero could swallow one with ease. This made them popular with modifiers, who liked the lightweight, no-frills approach that could get them very quick cars for relatively little money. This example uses a 302ci (4.9-litre) V8 tuned with aftermarket intake, heads and camshaft from Edelbrock, plus a free-flowing dual exhaust. As the Ranchero shares its underpinnings with the Mustang, the owner of this car has used 1969 Mustang front disc s and traction bars. The rims are aftermarket alloys in 8x15 (203x381mm) and 10x15-inch (251x381mm) with BF Goodrich tyres, giving improved handling and better traction.

Top speed:	120 mph (192 km/h)
0–60 mph (0–96 km/h):	7.4 sec
Engine type:	V8
Displacement:	302 ci (4,948 cc)
Transmission	4-speed manual
Max power:	200 bhp (149 kW) @ 4,400 rpm
Max torque:	285 lb ft (386 Nm) @ 3,200 rpm
Weight:	2,820 lb (1,281 kg)
Economy:	16 mpg (5.66 km/l)

Ford Mustang GT (1965)

With massive sales in its first year, Ford pushed the Mustang further by bringing out the performance GT 2+2 in 1965. It used a fastback roofline to gain extra rear space, and had sporty touches such as the louvers on the rear pillars. As costs had to be kept down, little was done to the stock chassis which had a double wishbone front and leaf spring rear. A special handling package did come with the GT however, which included heavy duty springs and shocks plus quicker 22:1 ratio steering, Standard for the GT also were fade-resistant front disc brakes. Although three transmissions were available, the one to have was the four-speed Borg Warner 'Top Loader', while the engine to order was the 'K-code' which had 10.5:1 compression, four-barrel carb, solid lifter camshaft and high-flow air filter. Testers christened the K-code car 'a four-passenger Cobra'.

Top speed:	123 mph (197 km/h)
0–60 mph (0–95 km/h):	7.3 sec
Engine type:	V8
Displacement:	289 ci (4,735 cc)
Transmission	4-speed manual
Max power:	271 bhp (202 kW) @ 6,000 rpm
Max torque:	312 lb ft (422 Nm) @ 3,400 rpm
Weight:	3,100 lb (1,409 kg)
Economy:	15 mpg (5.35 km/l)

Ford Galaxie 500

Like many muscle cars, the 1966 Galaxie 500 used the simple formula of a massive engine up front driving the rear wheels. It had stacked headlamps, all new suspension and the emphasis was more on comfort, despite obviously being a muscle machine. The A-arm suspension was very good and went on to be used in NASCAR competition, while at the rear coil springs and control arms replaced the former leaf spring set-up. It all added up to a refined ride but the big-block up front could soon change that. Up to 1965 the biggest engine in the Galaxie had been the 427ci (6.9 litres), but the 428ci (7-litre), also part of the FE range of big-block Fords, was built mainly to produce torque. It was a more streetable engine than the 427 engine, but still had plenty of power and incredible torque at low rpm. Inside, being a top-of-the-range car, the 500 featured leather seats and wood trim.

Top speed:	105 mph (168 km/h)
0–60 mph (0–95 km/h):	8.2 sec
Engine type:	V8
Displacement:	428 ci (7,013 cc)
Transmission	3-speed auto
Max power:	345 bhp (257 KW) @ 4,600 rpm
Max torque:	462 lb ft (626 Nm) @ 2,800 rpm
Weight:	4,059 lb (1,845 kg)
Economy:	9 mpg 93.2 km/l)

Ford Mustang (1966)

Such huge popularity has produced an equally massive aftermarket for the Mustang, so owners can pick from a large range of components to produce very individual cars when they choose to modify them. The owner of this coupe example has left nothing untouched, although the looks tell you exactly what the car is. What's obvious from the outside is the 17-inch (432mm) diameter wheels and billet grilles front and rear, the latter of which houses 900 LEDs for the tail lights. Inside the car has leather and billet aluminium which is matched in the trunk too, where the battery and stereo equipment is mounted. The suspension has been upgraded to Mustang II on the front and to a 9-inch (229mm) Ford rear axle on stiffened leaf springs out back. The motor is a late-model Mustang 32 Modular V8, with Kenne Bell supercharger and multipoint fuel injection.

Top speed:	141 mph (226 km/h)
0–60 mph (0–96 km/h):	4.3 sec
Engine type:	V8
Displacement:	281 ci (4,604 cc)
Transmission	3-speed auto
Max power:	392 bhp (292 kW) @ 5,800 rpm
Max torque:	405 lb ft (549 Nm) @ 4,500 rpm
Weight:	3,358 lb (1,526 kg)
Economy:	12 mpg (4.24 km/l)

Ford Fairlane 427

It was right in the middle of the fierce muscle-car wars that Ford launched the Fairlane 427. They widened the shock towers in the engine bay and fitted larger front coil springs in order to cope with both the size and weight of the 427, which basically was a de-tuned race engine. The output was a 'mere' 410bhp (305kW) with single carburettor, but on the Fairlane most came with twin carbs and, therefore, 425bhp (317kW). The body and chassis were unitary and the car could be ordered with a handling package which consisted of longer leaf springs on the live rear axle, front disc brakes and larger 15-inch (381mm) wheels fitted with blackwall tyres. Only one gearbox, Borg-Warner's 'Top Loader' T10, could handle the engine's torque, so every Fairlane 427 got one. Being a thinly disguised race car meant potential purchasers had to be carefully screened by dealers.

Top speed:	121 mph (194 km/h)
0-60 mph (0–95 km/h):	6.0 sec
Engine type:	V8
Displacement:	427 ci (6,997 cc)
Transmission	4-speed manual
Max power:	425 bhp (317 kW) @ 6,000 rpm
Max torque:	480 lb ft (650 Nm) @ 3,700 rpm
Weight:	4,100 lb (1,863 kg)
Economy:	16 mpg (5.7 km/l)

Ford Galaxie 500 (1968)

During the 1960s the Galaxie turned from a muscle car into something more subtle and formal, though it remained a good seller for Ford. The car had lost its ground-breaking lines in favour of the fastback style, which was fast becoming the norm later that decade, though Dodge and Plymouth had the edge on shape. This custom version has taken the stock look and colour-coded everything to help bring the shape up to date, also helped by the addition of modern billet alloy rims with low-profile tyres. Three-inch drop spindles have been fitted to lower the front, while the rear does the same through lowering blocks between the leaf springs and live axle. The body has been seam welded to make it torsionally stiffer, and to take advantage of the extra handling available, there's a modified 390ci (6.3-litre) big-block engine with new headers, an Edelbrock intake and a bigger carb.

Top speed:	110 mph (176 km/h)
0-60 mph (0–96 km/h):	7.9 sec
Engine type:	V8
Displacement:	390 ci (6,390 cc)
Transmission:	3-speed auto
Max power:	365 bhp (272 kW) @ 5,800 rpm
Max torque:	370 lb ft (501 Nm) @ 3,400 rpm
Weight:	3,554 lb (1,615 kg)
Economy:	12 mpg (4.25 km/l)

Ford Mustang GT/CS (1968)

The Mustang was extremely popular during its first few years of production, but competition from other manufacturers saw a drop in sales for 1968, so Ford released a number of limited-edition models to rectify the situation. The GT/SC was one, and it stood for Grand Turismo California Special. As a GT, it got heavy-duty springs and shocks, dual exhaust with special double protruding tips (for this year only) and a thicker front anti-roll bar. The CA part of the deal added special side scoops, Shelby-style rear lights, a plain grille and special emblems all over. Under the hood of this special was the mighty 390ci (6.3-litre) big-block, which had huge torque throughout the rev range. It could easily accelerate the car to 14-second quarter-mile times in stock form, but it was most impressive on the street once the Goodyear Polyglas bias-ply tyres had found grip.

Top speed:	120 mph (192 km/h)
0–60 mph (0–96 km/h):	7.5 sec
Engine type:	V8
Displacement:	390 ci (6,390 cc)
Transmission	3-speed auto
Max power:	280 bhp (209 kW) @ 4,400 rpm
Max torque:	403 lb ft (546 Nm) @ 2,600 rpm
Weight:	3,635 lb (1,652 kg)
Economy:	14 mpg (4.96 km/l)

Ford Mustang Boss 302 (1969)

While the Boss 302 was a rare machine that went to driving enthusiasts or, more often, racers, enough made it into the hands of modifiers, and the car provided a great base on which to start work. The owner of this Boss has further lowered the suspension with different coil springs up front and reverse-eye leaf springs at the rear. Relocated arms ensure correct geometry on the front double wishbones, as this car is made to handle and has virtually zero body roll through corners, thanks to the anti-roll bars front and rear. The 302 engine has been fitted with the race-type injection stacks that poke through the hood, for extended rpm use through the Borg Warner T10 manual gearbox and 4.11:1 geared Ford 9-inch (229mm) rear end. Magnesium rims at 8 inches (203mm) wide with modern Goodyear 225/50ZR15 low-profile tyres complete the style.

Top speed:	149 mph (238 km/h)
0–60 mph (0–96 km/h):	4.8 sec
Engine type:	V8
Displacement:	302 ci (4,948 cc)
Transmission	4-speed manual
Max power:	400 bhp (298 kW) @ 6,500 rpm
Max torque:	343 lb ft (465 Nm) @ 4,300 rpm
Weight:	3,209 lb (1,458 kg)
Economy:	18 mpg (6.37 km/l)

Ford Mustang Mach 1 (1969)

The Mach 1 sat between the mighty Boss 429 and the highly strung 302, and with the great 428 Cobra Jet engine, it was just what many Mustang fans were waiting for. The Cobra Jet motor had a strong bottom end, which made it ideal for performance use, and in 1969 it came in three states of tune, the Drag Pack being the top version, with the Super Cobra Jet engine. Inside, the Mach 1 had specially designed instruments heavily set into the dash, plus a split dash top and high-backed bucket seats. Externally the style was more evident with a Shaker hood that attached an intake directly to the engine-top through the hood, thus you could see the engine 'shaking' as it idled. The spring and shock rates were firmed up, and the rear shocks were staggered either side of the axle to reduce wheel hop which was prevalent on high-bhp Mustangs.

Top speed:	121 mph (194 km/h)
0–60 mph (0–96 km/h):	5.3 sec
Engine type:	V8
Displacement:	428 ci (7,013 cc)
Transmission	3-speed auto
Max power:	335 bhp (250 kW) @ 5,200 rpm
Max torque:	440 lb ft (596 Nm) @ 3,400 rpm
Weight:	3,420 lb (1,554 kg)
Economy:	20 mpg (7.08 km/l)

Ford Torino Talladega

In 1969 NASCAR Ford and Chrysler battled it out. In response to the dominating Dodge Charger 500, Ford came up with the Torino Talladega which cleaned up in its first year with 30 victories. Based on the Fairlane Torino which had appeared in 1968, the Talladega had the same monocoque chassis. The suspension used a double wishbone front and a leaf spring rear, though the back had staggered shocks to counter wheel hop. All Talladegas came with the 428ci (7-litre) Cobra Jet big-block V8 engine, rated at 335bhp (250kW); for insurance output was closer to 450bhp (335kW). It had 10.6:1 compression, a steel crank, stronger con rods and a 735cfm Holley carb. The suspension used stiffer springs and shocks plus a thicker anti-roll bar up front. At the rear a Traction Lok diff and 3.25:1 gears were stock. For better aerodynamics a tapered nose was stretched by 5 inches (127mm).

Top speed:	130 mph (208 km/h)
0–60 mph (0–95 km/h):	5.8 sec
Engine type:	V8
Displacement:	428 ci (7,013 cc)
Transmission	3-speed auto
Max power:	335 bhp (250 kW) @ 5,200 rpm
Max torque:	440 lb ft (595 Nm) @ 3,400 rpm
Weight:	3,536 lb (1,607 kg)
Economy:	14 mpg (5 km/l)

Ford Escort RS1600

Looking like one of the ordinary Escorts, the RS1600 certainly didn't shout about its potential the way modern rally winners do, though it was very successful. Ford had used the 1968 Escort Twin Cam to replace the Lotus Cortinas and a competition version of the car won the Finland 1000 Lakes Rally that year and the following two seasons. In 1970 Ford homologated a Cosworth-engined, 16-valve version of the regular Escort, using the Twin Cam's reinforced bodyshell, negative camber plates on the strut front suspension, plus lowered and uprated rear leaf springs. Larger 5.5x13-inch (139x330mm) steel rims were fitted, though many were changed for Minilite magnesium rims. The engine was based on the cast-iron Cortina block, but with alloy head, twin camshafts, 16 valves and 10:1 compression. Twin Weber carbs and an oil cooler re-located the battery in the trunk.

Top speed:	114 mph (182 km/h)
0–60 mph (0–95 km/h):	8.3 sec
Engine type:	In-line four
Displacement:	98 ci (1,601 cc)
Transmission:	4-speed manual
Max power:	120 bhp (89 kW) @ 6,500 rpm
Max torque:	112 lb ft (152 Nm) @ 4,000 rpm
Weight:	1,965 lb (893 kg)
Economy:	20 mpg (7.1 km/l)

Ford Torino Cobra (1970)

While the new-for-1970 Torino GT was a good muscle car, the Cobra was the bare-knuckle fighter version. It was based on said sporty GT, but instead of the small-block, it featured a 429ci (7-litre) big-block but it wasn't the Boss 429, even though it made a lot of power, thanks to 11.3:1 compression, upgraded heads, a high-lift cam and high-flow Holley carburettor. If the Drag Pack was ordered the engine received solid lifter cam, oil cooler, forged pistons, a four-bolt main cap block, and an even larger carb for 375bhp (280kW) and a lot more durability in racing. To cope with the power the Cobra could be ordered with either a Traction Lok limited-slip differential with 3.91:1 gears, or for more serious racers there was the harsher, more noisy Detroit Locker with 4.30:1 gearing for best acceleration. The Shaker hood scoop even had a ram air system for more power on the move.

Top speed:	118 mph (189 km/h)
0–60 mph (0–96 km/h):	5.9 sec
Engine type:	V8
Displacement:	429 ci (7,030 cc)
Transmission	4-speed manual
Max power:	370 bhp (276 kW) @ 5,400 rpm
Max torque:	450 lb ft (610 Nm) @ 3,400 rpm
Weight:	4,000 lb (1,818 kg)
Economy:	12 mpg (4.25 km/l)

Ford Falcon GT HO Phase III

The Australian Ford Falcon came out in 1967. It was based on the XR four-door sedan, but out went the straight-six in favour of a 289ci (4.7-litre) V8, and in went buckets seats and a four-speed manual. By 1971 the car reached its high-point with the 351ci (5.8-litre), 300bhp (231kW) XT-sedan based Falcon GT HO, the latter letter standing for 'Handling Option'. The Phase II was born to win Australia's famous 'Bathurst 500' race, so had front and rear anti-roll bars, stiffened springs, front discs, enlarged rear drum brake and a lower ride height. Under the hood there was the famous Cleveland 351ci (5.75-litre) engine which had more performance through better balancing, free-flowing heads, a solid-lifter camshaft and 780cfm carburettor. In this lightweight car it made the performance shattering. The Falcon GTs were known as 'Super Roos' and had logos on each front wing.

Top speed:	144 mph (230 km/h)
0–60 mph (0–95 km/h):	5.7 sec
Engine type:	V8
Displacement:	351 ci (5,751 cc)
Transmission:	4-speed manual
Max power:	300 bhp (223 kW) @ 5,400 rpm
Max torque:	380 lb ft (314 Nm) @ 3,400 rpm
Weight:	2,748 lb (1,249 kg)
Economy:	14 mpg (5 km/l)

Ford Mustang Boss 351 (1971)

The Boss Mustang was based on a the new-for-1971 fastback design model, or 'SportsRoof' as Ford called it. It superseded the Boss 302 and 429 versions and, though bigger, was both quicker and equally good in cornering. The suspension remained conventional with coil sprung wishbones and a thick anti-roll bar at the front, plus a leaf spring rear with staggered shocks to prevent wheel hop. The Boss got stiffer suspension, however, and continued the previous model's stiffer spindles and reinforced shock towers for improved durability under hard cornering. The brakes were better too with 11.3-inch (287mm) vented discs at the front that could stop the car from 80mph (129km/h) in 250ft (76.2m). Optional 7x15-inch (178x381mm) Magnum wheels also improve the Boss. Inside, the dash had a wraparound feel with instruments in the centre console and a large, T-handle shifter.

Top speed:	116 mph (186 km/h)
0-60 mph (0–96 km/h):	5.8 sec
Engine type:	V8
Displacement:	351 ci (5,751 cc)
Transmission	4-speed manual
Max power:	330 bhp (246 kW) @ 5,400 rpm
Max torque:	370 lb ft (502 Nm) @ 4,000 rpm
Weight:	3,550 lb (1,613 kg)
Economy:	12 mpg (4.25 km/l)

Ford Grand Torino Sport (1972)

The redesigned Torino became a single model series in 1972 split into just two options:the base and Grand Torino. While not as sharp-looking as their previous incarnations, they had the trademark muscle-car swept-back roofline and the classic formula of a V8 engine mounted up front and driving the rear wheels. This modified version has received a 351ci (5.75-litre) Cleveland V8, now displacing 357ci (5.8 litres) thanks to a rebore. Fitted are high compression pistons, modified heads, a high-lift cam, roller rockers (for increased rpm use) and electronic ignition. The car has received changes in the suspension, too, with lowered springs and uprated shocks. Along with modern radial tyres on wide Magnum 500 optional rims, they make the Torino far better than the standard car at taking corners. Inside it sports a multi-gauge dash and a modern sound system.

Top speed:	130 mph (208 km/h)
0–60 mph (0–96 km/h):	7.2 sec
Engine type:	V8
Displacement:	357 ci (5,850 cc)
Transmission	3-speed auto
Max power:	340 bhp (254 kW) @ 6,200 rpm
Max torque:	360 lb ft (488 Nm) @ 4,200 rpm
Weight:	3,496 lb (1,589 kg)
Economy:	14 mpg (4.96 km/l)

Ford Mustang Mach 1

The 1973 Mach 1 was the biggest of all Mustangs, and a long way from the sporty car intention of the early Mustang design. Not only was it larger (due to complaints about cramped passenger space in the early cars), it was also heavier and plusher, though it handled well, due to the competition suspension which included heavy-duty front and rear springs, front and rear anti-roll bars and re-valved shocks. Coming in 1973, the car was strangled by emissions and as such the 302ci (5-litre) engine offered a fraction of the performance available in 1969 with the very first Mach 1. But you could opt for the 351ci (5.8-litre) engine with a four-barrel carburettor if you wanted to hot things up a little. The 1973 Mach 1's stylish fastback lines and comfortable ride made it a hit, and over 35,000 cars were produced, which was good, considering the fuel crisis hitting gas-guzzler sales.

Top speed:	110 mph (176 km/h)
0–60 mph (0–95 km/h):	10.4 sec
Engine type:	V8
Displacement:	302 ci (4,948 cc)
Transmission	3-speed auto
Max power:	136 bhp (101 kW) @ 4,200 rpm
Max torque:	232 lb ft (314 Nm) @ 2,200 rpm
Weight:	3,090 lb (1,404 kg)
Economy:	14 mpg (5 km/l)

Ford Mustang Boss 429

When Ford wanted to use a new engine in NASCAR, to qualify it was required to build 500 production cars. Instead of putting their new 429ci (7.2-litre) into the mid-sized Torinos which they were racing, they decided to shoehorn it into the Mustang. The 429 motor was unlike any other Ford motor, being much wider in the cylinder head, thanks to its semi-'Hemi' combustion chamber design. It meant the Mustang strut towers had to be widened and the battery moved to the trunk. The Boss used a the 'Top Loader' close-ratio, four-speed manual transmission because the autos couldn't handle the power. Modified suspension comprised uprated springs, anti-roll bar and re-valved shocks. The Boss 429 was the most expensive non-Shelby Mustang ever to be produced, but nonetheless the 428 Cobra Jet version was the fun on the street.

Top speed:	118 mph (189 km/h)
0–60 mph (0–95 km/h):	6.8 sec
Engine type:	V8
Displacement:	429 ci (7,030 cc)
Transmission	4-speed manual
Max power:	375 bhp (279 kW) @ 5,200 rpm
Max torque:	450 lb ft (609 Nm) @ 3,400 rpm
Weight:	3,870 lb (1,760 kg)
Economy:	13.8 mpg (4.9 km/l)

Ford Escort RS2000

Ford was famous for its rally cars of the 1970s, and its RS2000 was the most prominent and successful European rally car of the era, and soon became a performance road car. It shared the basic mechanicals of other MkII Escorts, with MacPherson struts at the front and a live axle rear on leaf springs. Although lowered and uprated, little else was done to the suspension. Externally it was a different matter, with a small trunk spoiler, matt black fenders and grille, a sloping nose cone with spoiler and quad lights, and the classic Ford RS four-spoke alloys. The engine was a derivative of the American 'Pinto' unit, and was called such. Although used in other Fords, the RS got a slightly increased compression ratio and free-flowing exhaust so was more powerful. Inside it used Recaro seats with fishnet headrests and had a short-throw shifter which made gear-changing a blast.

Top speed:	108 mph (173 km/h)
0–60 mph (0–95 km/h):	8.7 sec
Engine type:	In-line four
Displacement:	122 ci (1,993 cc)
Transmission	4-speed manual
Max power:	110 bhp (74 kW) @ 5,500 rpm
Max torque:	119 lb ft (161 Nm) @ 4,000 rpm
Weight:	2,035 lb (925 kg)
Economy:	25 mpg (8.9 km/l)

Ford Mustang (1980s)

With the arrival of the 'Fox' Mustang in 1979, Ford had built themselves a winner and sold over a million cars up to 1993. Because of sheer amount of 1979–1993 cars, a massive aftermarket worth billions of dollars was established, and modifications go from the likes of a high-flow air filter to blown 700bhp (522kW) road cars which can cover the quarter-mile in under 10 seconds. This particular car is a wild road machine, fitted with fender extensions to fit the 10-inch (254mm) and 13-inch (330mm) wide wheels, a new nose section, huge rear wing to aid downforce and some good engine mods to boost the powerful V8. A larger throttle body to allow more air in, plus a high lift camshaft and free-flow exhaust help this car to run in 13.4 seconds on the quarter-mile. Saleen Racecraft suspension has been fitted also, both lowering and uprating the handling.

Top speed:	150 mph (240 km/h)
0–60 mph (0–95 km/h):	5.2 sec
Engine type:	V8
Displacement:	306 ci (5,014 cc)
Transmission	5-speed manual
Max power:	370 bhp (276 kW)@ 4,800 rpm
Max torque:	300 lb ft (406 Nm) @ 3,000 rpm
Weight:	3,560 lb (1,618 kg)
Economy:	17 mpg (6 km/l)

Ford Mustang SVO

Putting a four-cylinder engine and pushing it as a high-performance model gave Ford a hard time in 1984. They were just reacting to higher fuel prices and the demand for smaller-engined cars, using the 'Fox' platform from regular Mustangs and fitting an uprated version of their 140ci (2.3-litre) engine. The four-cylinder came in 88bhp (65kW) form as standard, but the addition of a turbo gave it 143bhp (107kW). This wasn't enough to ensure good sales, however, so power was upped for 1985 1/2 cars onwards to 175bhp (130kW) with 15psi boost. In 1986 it was the best for power and handling, thanks to the lightweight engine. A stiffer front anti-roll bar, rear anti-roll bar, uprated springs, and adjustable Koni shocks made cornering very rapid, while four-wheel disc brakes brought the stopping power up to scratch. Cheaper fuel brought the V8 back, and the SVO was no more after 1986.

Top speed:	140 mph (224 km/h)
0–60 mph (0–95 km/h):	6.7 sec
Engine type:	In-line four
Displacement:	140 ci (2,294 cc)
Transmission	5-speed manual
Max power:	205 bhp (153 kW) @ 5,000 rpm
Max torque:	240 lb ft (325 Nm) @ 3,000 rpm
Weight:	3,036 lb (1,380 kg)
Economy:	25 mpg (8.9 km/l)

Ford RS200

A midst the fury of 600bhp (447kW) Group B rally cars, Ford needed a serious competitor, so launched the 1984 RS200, 'RS' standing for Rallye Sport, while the number simply meant the amount produced. A year later, the factory's RS won the first rally event it entered, then came third in the World Rally Championship. In 1986, following horrific crashes in Portugese Rally in which spectators were killed, Group B rally cars were banned, but the RS200s continued to be used in motorsport and on the road. The RS used a mid-mounted four-cylinder with the transmission in the front axle. It used a built-in roll cage tied into large tubular subframes. The engine was the ultimate development of Cosworth's BD (belt-driven camshaft) all-alloy motor, with Garrett turbocharger, four valves per cylinder and dry sump lubrication. Road versions had 250bhp (185kW), competition 700bhp (522kW).

Top speed:	140 mph (224 km/h)
0–60 mph (0–95 km/h):	6.1 sec
Engine type:	In-line four
Displacement:	110 ci (1,803 cc)
Transmission	5-speed manual
Max power:	250 bhp (185 kW) @ 6,500 rpm
Max torque:	215 lb ft (291 Nm) @ 4,000 rpm
Weight:	2,607 lb (1,185 kg)
Economy:	16 mpg (5.7 km/l)

Ford Sierra Cosworth RS 500

When Ford debuted its new jelly mould Sierra in 1982, it was a radical design, a long way from the boxy Cortina it'd replaced. Yet few people envisaged it being a high-performance machine capable of taking on supercars. Ford did produce the V6-equipped XR4i in 1983 and even though it showed potential in the Sierra chassis, it wasn't radically quick. The 1985 RS Cosworth was, however, very fast, and Ford wanted to race it so needed to homologate the car. They produced the RS500, made exactly 500 and added many performance extras. A large rear spoiler with extra raised lip increased downforce at speed, while the rear end driveshafts and bearings were uprated to cope and the four vented discs given an anti-lock system. The engine used a thicker casting block, forged internal parts and a larger turbo which gave out 9psi as stock but 22psi in competition for 570bhp (425kW).

Top speed:	154 mph (246 km/h)
0–60 mph (0–95 km/h):	6.1 sec
Engine type:	In-line four
Displacement:	122 ci (1,993 cc)
Transmission	5-speed manual
Max power:	224 bhp (167 kW) @ 6,000 rpm
Max torque:	205 lb ft (277 Nm) @ 3,500 rpm
Weight:	2,734 lb (1,243 kg)
Economy:	20 mpg (7.1 km/l)

Ford Mustang 5.0 LX

Few cars can claim to have made such an impact on the United States during the 1980s as the 1987–1993 5.0L Mustang. For a cheap price it gave enthusiasts a powerful V8 engine, enough luxury and good handling, and because of this was a big hit. In base 'LX' form, the car came without the range-topping GT's bodykit, hence it weighed less and was quicker. Various magazines testing the car in the USA had the Borg Warner T5 manual five-speed versions running low-14-second quarter-miles, surpassing many higher powered muscle cars of the 1960s and early 1970s. Certainly it was vastly superior in handling, thanks to progressive rate springs and a 'Quadra-shock' horizontal shocks at either side of the axle to prevent wheel hop and increase traction. The LX was so quick in standard form that even the US police chose it for high-speed patrol work.

Top speed:	138 mph (221 km/h)
0–60 mph (0–95 km/h):	6.2 sec
Engine type:	V8
Displacement:	302 ci (4,948 cc)
Transmission	5-speed manual
Max power:	225 bhp (167 KW) @ 4,400 rpm
Max torque:	300 lb ft (406 Nm) @ 3,000 rpm
Weight:	3,145 lb (1,429 kg)
Economy:	22 mpg (7.8 km/l)

Ford Mustang GT (1987)

When the 'Fox' Mustang debuted in 1979, the public quickly warmed to it, and Ford knew they'd got themselves a winner. In fact they sold over a million up to 1993. The sheer amount on the road meant an aftermarket for performance parts quickly grew, and modifications go from the likes of a high-flow air filter to blown 700bhp (522kW) road cars which can cover the quarter-mile in under 10 seconds. This particular car is a heavily altered road machine, having been fitted with IMSA-style fender bulges to fit the 10-inch (250mm) and 13-inch (330mm) wide wheels, a new nose section, huge rear wing to aid downforce and some good engine mods to boost the already powerful V8. A larger throttle body to allow more air in plus a performance camshaft and free-flow exhaust help this car to run in 13.4 seconds on the quarter. Racecraft uprated suspension lowers the car and improves handling.

Top speed:	150 mph (240 km/h)
0–60 mph (0–96 km/h):	5.2 sec
Engine type:	V8
Displacement:	306 ci (5,014 cc)
Transmission	5-speed manual
Max power:	370 bhp (276 kW) @ 4,800 rpm
Max torque:	300 lb ft (406 Nm) @ 3,000 rpm
Weight:	3,560 lb (1,618 kg)
Economy:	17 mpg (6.02 km/l)

Ford T-bird Turbo Coupe (1987)

Ford's Thunderbird looked very dated and a way too conservative to be successful in the early 1980s. However, Ford was quick to realize it needed a change, so a restyle was in order for 1983. The new look was dramatic and it stirred up much interest again. The car looked dynamic and modern, but even so, in the rapidly changing 1980s, by 1987 it need a facelift. While the car's profile didn't change, it did get significant upgrades with flush-fitting lights and side glass, plus all new sheet metal. Ford also introduced two sporty versions: the 5.0L V8 and the Turbo Coupe. The latter used the former Mustang SVO unit, a turbo four-cylinder engine with intercooler, forged pistons and an oil cooler. Riding on the well-established Fox platform, it used upgraded suspension and 16-inch (406mm) rims. Through its Borg Warner T5 the car could attain 15-second quarter-miles.

Top speed:	137 mph (219 km/h)
0–60 mph (0–96 km/h):	7.1 sec
Engine type:	In-line four
Displacement:	140 ci (2,300 cc)
Transmission	5-speed manual
Max power:	190 bhp (142 kW) @ 4,600 rpm
Max torque:	180 lb ft (244 Nm) @ 3,600 rpm
Weight:	3,380 lb (1,536 kg)
Economy:	23 mpg (8.14 km/l)

Ford Escort RS Cosworth

Ford planned the Escort to take over from the Sierra in rallying as early as 1988, as they needed a smaller car to win the World Rally Championship (WRC). They gave the job of development to SVE (Special Vehicle Engineering) and Cosworth, who shortened the Sierra Cosworth 4WD sedan's floorpan and put it under the Escort shell, giving it wider arches to maintain the standard track width. Viscous couplings split the power 34:66 front /rear, giving a bias towards rear-wheel drive which proved very effective. The four-cylinder Cosworth engine was fitted with a hybrid Garrett T3/TO4B turbocharger and two stage intercooler, and to help reduce turbo lag, a Weber-Marelli multi-point electronic fuel injection system tuned the turbo to overboost slightly. While successful in various races, it took until the car's last season, 1997, for Spanish driver Carlos Sainz to bring home the WRC for Ford.

Top speed:	137 mph (219 km/h)
0-60 mph (0–95 km/h):	5.8 sec
Engine type:	In-line four
Displacement:	122 ci (1,993 cc)
Transmission	5-speed manual
Max power:	227 bhp (169 kW) @ 6,250 rpm
Max torque:	224 lb ft (303 Nm) @ 3,500 rpm
Weight:	2,811 lb (1,278 kg)
Economy:	25 mpg (8.9 km/l)

Ford Thunderbird SC (1990)

The Thunderbird SC (Super Coupe) was introduced in 1989 and won Motor Trend magazine's 'Car of the Year'. The new super sleek styling was just part of the deal, as the car sat on an all-new platform with A-arms up front and a full independent rear with pivoting axle halfshafts. The SC was a celebration of 35 years of the Thunderbird, and came with black wheel and paint. It also had beefier springs and gas shocks, plus four-wheel disc brakes which were vented at the front to aid cooling. While T-birds of the past had used four cylinders, V6s or V8s, the new car was exclusively V6 powered, and the SC used an Eaton supercharger in conjunction with sequential fuel injection to boost output. Dual tailpipes was one way of telling the SC from regular Thunderbirds, along with the 7x16-inch (178x406mm) alloys on 225/60 Goodyear Eagle tyres.

Top speed:	141 mph (226 km/h)
0–60 mph (0–96 km/h):	7.4 sec
Engine type:	V6
Displacement:	231 ci (3,600 cc)
Transmission	5-speed manual
Max power:	210 bhp (157 kW) @ 4,000 rpm
Max torque:	315 lb ft (427 Nm) @ 2,600 rpm
Weight:	3,701 lb (1,682 kg)
Economy:	17 mpg (6.02 km/l)

Ford F-150 Lightning

The F-150 Ford had been providing transport for many Americans since the 1960s. It had always used V8s but none had a performance edge. When, in 1992, the F-series truck was given a facelift, it became a best-seller for Ford, so to further enhance it they had their Special Vehicle Team (SVT) produce a hot rod version, the Lightning. SVT wanted it to drive and perform like a supercar so they re-valved the steering for better response, added lowered and stiffened springs then put 17-inch (431mm) wheels at each corner with wide, low-profile tyres. The team chose the 351ci (5.8-litre) Windsor small-block V8 and added GT40 heads, new manifolds, a Lightning-specific cam, and a custom computer from the Mustang GT. The fenders and grille were colour-coded to distinguish it and the interior fitted with buckets seats, completing it as a real driver's truck.

Top speed:	120 mph (192 km/h)
0–60 mph (0–95 km/h):	7.5 sec
Engine type:	V8
Displacement:	351 ci (5,751 cc)
Transmission	4-speed auto
Max power:	240 bhp (179 kW) @ 4,200 rpm
Max torque:	340 lb ft (460 Nm) @ 3,200 rpm
Weight:	4,378 lb (1,990 kg)
Economy:	17 mpg (6 km/l)

Ford Mustang Cobra (1993)

The Series 3 Mustang had been in production since 1979, so by 1993 was well overdue for replacement. To bow out with a bang, the Ford engineers came up with the best version of all: the Cobra. Using the 215bhp (160kW) GT as a base, a new grille, sill panel mouldings, rear valance and spoiler were made, plus the car was given 17-inch (432mm) wheels and low-profile tyres. Lowered suspension, interestingly with softer rate springs, gave the car better handling and a more civilized ride. Power was up to 235bhp (175kW) thanks to GT40 heads, a special intake, bigger throttle body, larger injectors and a revised roller camshaft. Disc brakes all around improved the braking over the standard GT, but aside from this, the car was similar. The most radical was the Cobra R, a race-only version which had luxuries removed – such as the air-con, radio, and rear seats – to save weight.

Top speed:	151 mph (242 km/h)
0–60 mph (0–95 km/h):	5.8 sec
Engine type:	V8
Displacement:	302 ci (4,948 cc)
Transmission	5-speed manual
Max power:	235 bhp (175 kW) @ 5,000 rpm
Max torque:	285 lb ft (386 Nm) @ 4,000 rpm
Weight:	3,225 lb (1,465 kg)
Economy:	21 mpg (7.5 km/l)

Ford Mustang Cobra R (1995)

Up until the introduction of the 2000 Cobra R, the 1995 model was the fastest Mustang ever. The 'R' stood for race and the Special Vehicle Team (SVT) at Ford made sure owners weren't going to lose any. Inside the car the sound-deadening was deleted, as was the radio, rear seats, rear window defrost, electric windows and air-conditioning, in an effort to save weight. The Cobra R even came with basic velour seats, as Ford realized most people would change these for race buckets. Eibach progressive rate springs and Koni adjustable shocks were fitted, and the front anti-roll bar was fattened. The engine was that from the Ford Lightning, a 351ci (5.8-litre) V8 with GT40 heads, special Cobra intake, SVO camshaft and bigger mass air meter. It put out so much torque that Ford had to fit a stronger gearbox so chose the Tremec 3550. This car ran 12-second quarter-mile times.

Top speed:	150 mph (240 km/h)
0–60 mph (0–95 km/h):	5.5 sec
Engine type:	V8
Displacement:	351 ci (5,751 cc)
Transmission	5-speed manual
Max power:	300 bhp (224 kW) @ 4,800 rpm
Max torque:	365 lb ft (494 Nm) @ 3,750 rpm
Weight:	3,325 lb (1,511 kg)
Economy:	17 mpg (6 km/l)

Ford Mustang GT (1998)

The 1998 Mustang GT was a progression of the body style which appeared in 1994, taking over from the much-loved but dated Series 3 'Fox' Mustang. Though heavier than the Series 3 due to extra stiffening in the shell structure, the car felt more solid to drive and handled far better. The real change was when the 5.0L V8 engine was replaced by the all-new 281ci (4.6-litre) 'Modular' V8 in 1996, which offered an increase in refinement at the cost of torque. By 1998 the GT was putting out 225bhp (167kW) and 285lb ft (386Nm) torque and the engine was a keen revver. It used a live axle with four locating bars and separate coil springs and shocks at the rear, while at the front MacPherson struts with lower wishbones gave a good ride and handling. To satisfy Mustang lovers, Ford added scoops on the side bodywork and vertically segmented rear lights, plus a running horse in the grille.

Top speed:	141 mph (226 km/h)
0-60 mph (0–95 km/h):	6.3 sec
Engine type:	V8
Displacement:	281 ci (4,604 cc)
Transmission	5-speed manual
Max power:	225 bhp (167 KW) @ 4,400 rpm
Max torque:	285 lb ft (386 Nm) @ 3,500 rpm
Weight:	3,462 lb (1,573 kg)
Economy:	20 mpg 97.1 km/l)

Ford Taurus SHO (1998)

The name SHO stood for Super High Output; Ford wanted this model to compete against the imports from both Europe and Japan. The drive train consisted of a V8, transversely mounted and with heads developed and built in Japan by Yamaha, as with previous SHO models. With four valves per cylinder and a balancer shaft to smooth out the dynamics, the engine was a keen revver all the way through the 7,000rpm redline. The only downside was the engine produced most of its best power above 4,500rpm, so low-speed response wasn't as good, though Ford made sure at least 80 percent of the torque was available at 2,000rpm. The suspension had a strut front and multi-link rear, with computer-controlled shock absorbers. Inside, the SHO came fully equipped with air-conditioning, cruise control, plus power windows, steering seats, mirrors and sunroof, making it a luxurious fast tourer.

Top speed:	139 mph (222 km/h)
0–60 mph (0–96 km/h):	7.8 sec
Engine type:	V8
Displacement:	208 ci (3,408 cc)
Transmission	3-speed auto
Max power:	235 bhp (175 kW) @ 6,100 rpm
Max torque:	230 lb ft (311 Nm) @ 4,800 rpm
Weight:	3,395 lb (1,543 kg)
Economy:	19 mpg (6.73 km/l)

Ford F-350 Super Duty (1999)

America's obsession with trucks means they have excellent sales figures. And with so many of the vehicles on the road, it's understandable that people want to personalize their vehicles. This Super Duty might be just a few years old but the owner has gone through the vehicle and added many modifications. To start with, the truck has received an 8-inch (203mm) lift kit allowing the body and chassis more travel, and a bolt-in cage has been added to the rear should the inevitable happen while off-road. At each corner sit huge 12x16.5-inch (305x419mm) American Egle rims with Dick Cepek 38-inch (965mm) tall tyres, giving the F-350 a baby monster truck look. The engine is Ford's immense Triton V10 which can return great economy given the size and provides incredible pulling power. Chassis hardware consist of Ford's twin Traction beams, live axles and a central viscous coupling.

Top speed:	96 mph (153 km/h)
0–60 mph (0–96 km/h):	10.2 sec
Engine type:	V10
Displacement:	415 ci (6,800 cc)
Transmission	4-speed auto
Max power:	275 bhp (205 kW) @ 4,250 rpm
Max torque:	410 lb ft (556 Nm) @ 2,650 rpm
Weight:	6,710 lb (3,050 kg)
Economy:	14 mpg (4.96 km/l)

Ginetta G4

The Walklett brothers – Ivor, Bob, Douglas and Trevor – made their first production car in 1958, and during the 1960s their cars were successful club racers. Their first G4 was sold in 1964 and was remarkably similar to this 1998 version. That first G4 used very lightweight design with a tubular space frame and independent front suspension but a live rear axle, and power came from a 92ci (1,500cc) Ford engine which could get it to 60mph (95km/h) in less than 7 sec. The modern car retained the same chassis layout and independent wishbone front, but with an independent rear wishbone set-up too. Adjustable Spax coil-over-shocks provided good tuneability at each corner. The new G4 also used a Ford engine, this time the ultra modern Zetec unit as fitted in the Focus. Available with either fuel injection or twin Weber carbs, the latter produced the quickest car.

Top speed:	130 mph (208 km/h)
0–60 mph (0–95 km/h):	5.0 sec
Engine type:	In-line four
Displacement:	110 ci (1,796 cc)
Transmission	5-speed manual
Max power:	150 bhp (113 kW) @ 6,250 rpm
Max torque:	130 lb ft (176 Nm) @ 3,700 rpm
Weight:	1,256 lb (571 kg)
Economy:	27 mpg (9.6 km/l)

GMC FC-101 Stepside (1951)

GMC introduced their new range of light-duty trucks in 1947, with smoother styling and a redesigned cab. The cab gave an extra inch headroom but, more importantly, an extra 7 inches (178mm) leg-room, which made all the difference to many buyers. It also had improved glassware, making visibility much better in this utility vehicle. Underneath it remained very much the same as the previous CC/EC series models, with solid axle front and rear supported on leaf springs, though the telescopic shocks were a big improvement for ride quality, and buyers could opt for an extra set on the rear if they carried heavy loads. The engine was given slightly more power for the 1951 model year, along with better electrics and optional twin tail lamps, and through a four-speed manual, while performance wasn't brisk, it was torquey at low rpm, which is exactly what most owners needed.

Top speed:	83 mph (132 km/h)
0–60 mph (0–96 km/h):	22.0 sec
Engine type:	In-line six
Displacement:	228 ci (3,736 cc)
Transmission	4-speed manual
Max power:	100 bhp (74 kW) @ 3,400 rpm
Max torque:	187 lb ft (253 Nm) @ 1,700 rpm
Weight:	3,275 lb (1,488 kg)
Economy:	17 mpg (6.01 km/l)

GMC Typhoon

Part of GMC's plans to move its image into the performance market started with creating the ultimate pick-up, the GMC Syclone. But a year later, with the continuing popularity of Sport Utility Vehicles, GMC followed that with the Typhoon which had room enough for five adults plus their luggage space. The Typhoon used the same underpinnings at the Syclone with a separate chassis, live rear axle and 11-inch (279mm) ABS-assisted and vented discs. The engine was from the GMC Jimmy, all cast-iron but uprated from the stock 165bhp (123kW) thanks to an intercooled turbo and re-calibrated engine management. The torque was split 35:65 front/rear with a mechanical centre differential and viscous coupling, though the live rear axle also used a limited-slip differential. A four-speed auto just about handled the torque but a strict warning sticker not to tow with the vehicle had to be put inside.

Top speed:	124 mph (198 km/h)
0–60 mph (0–95 km/h):	5.4 sec
Engine type:	V6
Displacement:	262 ci (4,293 cc)
Transmission	4-speed auto
Max power:	280 bhp (209 kW) @ 4,400 rpm
Max torque:	350 lb ft (474 Nm) @ 3,600 rpm
Weight:	3,822 lb (1,737 kg)
Economy:	25 mpg (8.9 km/l)

GMC Syclone

The Syclone was based on GMC's Sonoma truck, and while it didn't have a great deal of load space, it was exceptionally quick with a 4.9 second 0–60mph (0–95 km/h) time, which then was faster than a Ferrari 348 and even the mighty Corvette ZR-1. But it wasn't all straight-line performance for the pick-up, because with its four-wheel drive system it was also incredibly good through the bends too. GMC kept the bias towards rear-wheel drive with a 35:65 front/rear torque split, adding a limited-slip differential in the live rear axle to ensure maximum traction. They also gave the pick-up both lowered and uprated springs and shocks to further enhance the pick-up's sporting feel. The Syclone quickly built up a strong following in the USA, and while as standard they could run the quarter-mile in 14 seconds, the current record for a road Syclone stands in the 10s.

Top speed:	125 mph (200 km/h)
0–60 mph (0–95 km/h):	5.2 sec
Engine type:	V6
Displacement:	262 ci (4,293 cc)
Transmission:	4-speed auto
Max power:	280 bhp (208 kW) @ 4,400 rpm
Max torque:	350 lb ft (474 Nm) @ 3,600 rpm
Weight:	3,422 lb (1,555 kg)
Economy:	25 mpg (8.9 km/l)

Graham Hollywood (1941)

When Auburn-Cord-Duesenberg went out of the business in the late 1930s two companies battled to save the incredible Cord, and one of those was Graham-Paige. They took the front-wheel drive 810/812 and turned it into a rear-wheel drive before fitting their own restyled body called the Hollywood. They needed a new front axle to replace the driveshaft-equipped front-wheel drive set-up, so chose a simple but rather ancient (by then) beam axle on leaf springs, matched at the rear with leaf springs either end of a live axle. The ride offered was best cruising at speed, where the car was in a class of its own. The engine wasn't particularly large but with a supercharger, it did offer plenty of torque and the three-speed gearbox smoothed out its operation well. While the car seemed to offer an afterlife for the Cord, it was too costly to produce, and by late 1941 it was finished.

Top speed:	89 mph (142.4 km/h)
0–60 mph (0–96 km/h):	14.6 sec
Engine type:	In-line six
Displacement:	218 ci (3,572 cc)
Transmission	3-speed manual
Max power:	124 bhp (92 kW) @ 4,000 rpm
Max torque:	182 lb ft (247 Nm) @ 2,400 rpm
Weight:	3,240 lb (1,472 kg)
Economy:	17 mpg (6.01 km/l)

Greer-Black-Prudhomme rail (1962)

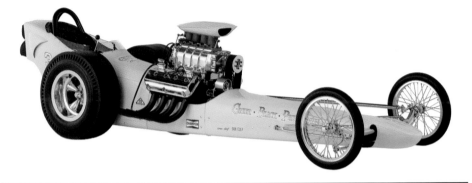

This dragster hails from a time before massive sponsorship and multi-million dollar championships. It also represents drag racing in its purest form, being a Top Fuel dragster. This class evolved from stripped-down Model T racers of the early 1930s, which were little more than a chassis and engine. As these cars developed, they grew longer wheelbases to make them more stable at speed, but retained the front engine format into the late 1960s, before switching to rear engines for safety reasons. The Greer, Black & Prudhomme car was backed by Tom Greer, the engine was by Keith Black, and the driving was handled by Don Prudhomme, who later went on to become World NHRA Top Fuel Champion. The car features a chrome-moly tubular chassis and a Chrysler Hemi with modified 6/71 GMC supercharger. It did the quarter in 7.7 seconds at 270mph (434km/h).

Top speed:	270 mph (432 km/h)
0–60 mph (0–96 km/h):	N/A
Engine type:	V8
Displacement:	398 ci (6,522 cc)
Transmission	None, direct drive to axle
Max power:	830 bhp (619 kW) @ 7,000 rpm
Max torque:	795 lb ft (1,078 Nm) @ 4,000 rpm
Weight:	N/A
Economy:	N/A

Honda Civic CRX

L ooking like a small hatchback, the CRX had more in common with the two-seater
sports coupes of the 1980s. It started with a 92ci (1.5-litre) three-valve per
cylinder unit which produced an impressive 100bhp (74kW), but the car was re-
designed in 1986 and packed a fearsome punch with its new twin-cam 16v engine
which coaxed 125bhp (93kW) from just 98ci (1.6 litres). The new CRX benefited
from a new suspension design with double wishbones all around and anti-roll bars,
though it still handled on the firm side and many regarded it as a street-legal go-
kart. Being strictly a front-engined, front-wheel drive two-seater meant that the car
was nose heavy, so it needed the rear spoiler to provide downforce. Even so, the
car's handling and steering was extremely precise and with the engine buzzing
around the 6,000rpm power peak, it was a formidable opponent cross-country.

Top speed:	121 mph (194 km/h)
0–60 mph (0–95 km/h):	8.6 sec
Engine type:	In-line four
Displacement:	97 ci (1,590 cc)
Transmission	5-speed manual
Max power:	125 bhp (93 kW) @ 6,000 rpm
Max torque:	100 lb ft (135 Nm) @ 5,000 rpm
Weight:	2,086 lb (948 kg)
Economy:	30 mpg (10.7 km/l)

Honda NSX

Aiming to build the perfect sportscar and Honda racing experience and put it all into one of the most dynamic shapes ever from Japan, the NSX challenged Ferrari for looks and Porsche for build quality but conquered all in the ease of driving. The car was very simple to use and drive very quickly. Aluminium alloys were used exclusively throughout the car, from suspension arms through the entire engine to the body. Twin wishbones front and back made the car's handling exceptional, while electric power-steering reduced the assistance as speed increased, down to nothing at high speed. The V6 engine was another marvel of Honda's V-Tech engineering with quad cams, the intake of which activated a more aggressive cam profile beyond 5,800rpm, thus not sacrificing torque. To cheat wind the underside was flat and the rear shape of the car helped reduce lift at speed.

Top speed:	162 mph (259 km/h)
0–60 mph (0–95 km/h):	5.4 sec
Engine type:	V6
Displacement:	182 ci (2,977 cc)
Transmission	5-speed manual
Max power:	274 bhp (204 kW) @ 7,000 rpm
Max torque:	210 lb ft (284 Nm) @ 5,300 rpm
Weight:	3,021 lb (1,373 kg)
Economy:	16.2 mpg (5.7 km/l)

Honda NSX Type-R

The NSX was an easy supercar to drive quickly, but what Honda wanted with its 1992 Type-R version was a more suitable track car, hence the 'R' for 'racing'. Unlike other Type-Rs, this one really was for smooth surfaces only. While little could be done to save weight on the alloy chassis and suspension components, Honda manage to lose 268lb (121kg) from the car by scrapping the air-con, underseal, stereo, and spare wheel, and replacing the stock seats and removing other non-essential items. The body had few items which hadn't already been given lightweight consideration, but Honda did change the plastic-covered steel fenders for alloy items, thus helping the car's diet. The only other change was the wheels, which were lighter, forged units, rather than cast. Engine power barely changed, though the unit was fully balanced and blueprinted to withstand racing use.

Top speed:	169 mph (270 km/h)
0–60 mph (0–95 km/h):	5.1 sec
Engine type:	V6
Displacement:	183 ci (2,997 cc)
Transmission	5-speed manual
Max power:	280 bhp (209 kW) @ 7,300 rpm
Max torque:	209 lb ft (283 Nm) @ 5,400 rpm
Weight:	2,712 lb (1,233 kg)
Economy:	18 mpg (6.4 km/l)

Honda Prelude VTi

Honda's sporty Prelude appeared in 1992 but was replaced by the sharp version here in 1996 and output was up by 7bhp (5kW) in the VTi. In Honda's racing tradition, it used double wishbone suspension all-around and managed to combine very little body roll in corners with a surprisingly supple ride. The car used electronics to give four-wheel steering which first saw light on the early Preludes; at low speed the rear wheels would turn one way to make parking easier, while at high speed the wheels turn to improve the handling and cornering. Massive ABS-assisted discs at each corner give the Prelude VTi the finest brakes in the sports coupe market. But the car wasn't all about sporty pretensions, because inside it was jam-packed with luxuries such as power sunroof, heated seats, air-conditioning, a leather wheel, cruise control and a high-power audio system.

Top speed:	142 mph (227 km/h)
0–60 mph (0–95 km/h):	6.6 sec
Engine type:	In-line four
Displacement:	132 ci (2,157 cc)
Transmission	5-speed manual
Max power:	197 bhp (147 kW) @ 7,100 rpm
Max torque:	156 lb ft (211 Nm) @ 5,250 rpm
Weight:	2,908 lb (1,322 kg)
Economy:	28 mpg (10 km/l)

Honda Accord Type R

Up until the 1990s Honda had been known for sensible family cars, but that all changed with the development of their V-Tech models which demonstrated a new performance side of the company. The 1997 Accord was re-designed as more roomy and was available with a V6 engine, but it wasn't until the following year that the fireworks really started with the launch of the Type R. This used an Accord sedan platform, but with a much stiffer body and uprated and lowered suspension on the all-round double wishbone set-up. Power came through a 134ci (2.2-litre) twin-cam 16v four-cylinder using the latest development of Honda's V-Tech system. With 11:1 compression, low friction pistons and sequential fuel injection it would rev through to 8,500rpm, and thanks to a limited-slip differential could put the power down, making it one of the best-handling front-wheel drive sedans.

Top speed:	140 mph (224 km/h)
0–60 mph (0–95 km/h):	7.1 sec
Engine type:	In-line four
Displacement:	132 ci (2,157 cc)
Transmission	5-speed manual
Max power:	209 bhp (156 kW) @ 7,200 rpm
Max torque:	158 lb ft (214 Nm) @ 6,700 rpm
Weight:	3,098 lb (1,408 kg)
Economy:	25 mpg (8.9 km/l)

Hudson Terraplane (1936)

While competing with the likes of the more mainstream Fords and Chevrolets, the Hudson Terraplane offered a number of interesting design features that put it ahead of its rivals and marked the models as rugged and reliable transport. The chassis was incredibly strong, but whereas most cars had their bodies bolted to the frame, the Terraplane had its welded at around 30 points to make the whole structure very rigid and thus the ride quality better. Also, the company favoured wider tyres than most, then ran them at a lower pressure to further enhance the ride. At the front the beam axle was located by radius arms which improved feel and gave a measure of anti-dive under hard braking. Finishing the car off were the brakes which were hydraulic; in case these failed and the pedal went to the floor, a mechanical set of brakes was activated on the rear only.

Top speed:	80 mph (128 km/h)
0–60 mph (0–96 km/h):	23.2 sec
Engine type:	In-line six
Displacement:	212 ci (3,474 cc)
Transmission:	3-speed manual
Max power:	88 bhp (65 kW) @ 3,800 rpm
Max torque:	N/A
Weight:	2,740 lb (1,245 kg)
Economy:	16 mpg (5.66 km/l)

Hudson Super Six (1949)

Hudson introduced their 'Step Down' range in the late '40s to much acclaim. They featured low-slung, sleek styling and slab sides, but were notable for other advances. They used unitary construction with the body and chassis as one, to provide better torsional control. They also had a powerful six-cylinder engine on the Super Six, which weighed less than the straight eight but still gave the car a low centre of gravity so it handled well. The cars were natural to turn into lead sleds because of their fared-in rear wheels and rounded styling. The owner of this car has 'shaved' all the trim off the bodywork, then blended in the front and rear lights plus a sun visor to make the body as smooth as possible. Under the hood lies a fuel-injected small-block Chevy, again fully smoothed, but colour-coded in white, like the full leather interior with some original and some modern digital instruments.

Top speed:	124 mph (198 km/h)
0–60 mph (0–96 km/h):	9.0 sec
Engine type:	V8
Displacement:	350 ci (5,735 cc)
Transmission	4-speed auto
Max power:	310 bhp (231 kW) @ 5,000 rpm
Max torque:	340 lb ft (461 Nm) @ 2,400 rpm
Weight:	3,554 lb (1,615 kg)
Economy:	14.7 mpg (5.2 km/l)

Hudson Hornet (1952)

The introduction of Hudson's Step Down range – which basically meant the chassis was stepped down for the main floor section so the body could be lower – made the cars great handlers because of the lower centre of gravity. While other cars would screech and understeer in corners, the Hudsons would offer handling cornering, which would turn into four-wheel drifts if pushed, thus making them far more predictable. They also had unconventional but very smooth styling so became a favourite with those wanting something different from the norm. Hudson stuck with their six-cylinder for the Hornet, enlarging it to 308ci (5 litres) to take on the V8 cars in NASCAR, which in 1953 it did, with many wins. This led to the production of the 7-X racing option engine, which featured a hotter cam, heavy duty crank, and revised cylinder head for 210bhp (157kW).

Top speed:	93 mph (149 km/h)
0–60 mph (0–96 km/h):	11.0 sec
Engine type:	In-line six
Displacement:	308 ci (5,047 cc)
Transmission	4-speed manual
Max power:	145 bhp (108 kW) @ 3,800 rpm
Max torque:	257 lb ft (348 Nm) @ 1,800 rpm
Weight:	3,600 lb (1,636 kg)
Economy:	21 mpg (7.43 km/l)

Imperial Crown (1961)

Chrysler made Imperial a marque in its own right in 1955 and aimed it squarely at the luxurious Cadillacs and Lincolns. The spectacular-looking 1957 Imperials, deigned by stylist Virgil Exner, had ideas which were continued into the early 1960s. His quad headlights continued, but this time he put them in small body coves to make the car stand out from the prevalent integrated look. The car continued the tradition of a separate chassis which helped reduce noise intrusion and vibration, important for such a luxury car. Chrysler's torsion bar suspension was also fitted up front, which was a big improvement over coil springs, to make Imperials one of the best-riding premium cars. The tooling costs of the Hemi meant a new engine was designed, called the 'Wedge Head'. Not only was this cheaper, but it also required less tune-ups and was more flexible throughout the rev range.

Top speed:	120 mph (192 km/h)
0–60 mph (0–96 km/h):	10.0 sec
Engine type:	V8
Displacement:	413 ci (6,767 cc)
Transmission	3-speed auto
Max power:	350 bhp (261 kW) @ 4,600 rpm
Max torque:	470 lb ft (637 Nm) @ 2,800 rpm
Weight:	4,790 lb (2,177 kg)
Economy:	15 mpg (5.31 km/l)

Iso Grifo

Italian millionairre Renzo Rivolta wanted a car that could rival the likes of Lamborghini and Ferrari, but couldn't find anything on the market to match. So instead, he commissioned his own. Penned by Giorgetto Guigiaro and powered by a Chevrolet Corvette V8 engine, the Grifo was the striking result. By combining Italian style with American muscle, Renzo's Iso company, which started out making refrigerators, created one of the most stunning classics of the 1960s. The Grifo had performance and handling to match its looks, while a 7.0-litre engine was introduced for 1968 giving it 170mph (264km/h) capability. Only high prices and the need for each car to be built by hand restricted production, and although only 504 examples had been built by the time that manufacture ceased in 1974, the Grifo was revered by many.

Top speed:	163 mph (264 km/h)
0–60 mph (0–95 km/h):	6.4 sec
Engine type:	V8
Displacement:	327 ci (5,359 cc)
Transmission:	5-speed manual
Max power:	350 bhp (259 kW) at 5,800 rpm
Max torque:	360 lb ft (488 Nm) at 3,600 rpm
Weight:	3,036 lb (1,366 kg)
Economy:	13.8 mpg (4.9 km/l)

Isuzu Piazza

The Piazza had all the hallmarks of a car that could have been great, but in reality it never was. It started life as an Italdesign concept car called Ace of Clubs, and in 1981 Japanese 4x4 manufacturer Isuzu decided to put it into production. Unfortunately, the concept car was built on the platform of a 1979 Opel Kadett, and Isuzu elected to stay with the same chassis for production models of the Piazza. That meant that although the car went quickly and looked stylish, the handling was atrocious. Build quality was a disaster, too, and the Piazza never really recovered from there. That's a shame, because later cars had a new chassis developed by British sports car maker Lotus and were infinitely better to drive. Although now a rare sight, the Piazza remains an interesting curiosity for fans of Japanese marques.

Top speed:	121 mph (195 km/h)
0–60 mph (0–95 km/h):	8.4 sec
Engine type:	in-line four
Displacement:	121 ci (1,996 cc)
Transmission:	5-speed manual
Max power:	150 bhp (112 kW) at 5,400 rpm
Max torque:	167 lb ft (226 Nm) at 3,000 rpm
Weight:	2810 lb (1,264 kg)
Economy:	27 mpg (9.6 km/l)

Jaguar XK120

When launched in 1948, the XK120 was an incredibly fast machine. Its six-cylinder engine was very smooth and the power almost unending, but the car remained easy to drive, thanks to a large steering wheel and progressive handling. Its styling was also very modern, with the swoopy curves and aerodynamic shape inspired by the early 1940s BMW 328 Mille Miglia racer. The 120 used wishbone front suspension with torsion bar springs, while at the rear a live axle remained on leaf springs. It was effective enough, especially on the C-Type race car, which was based on the XK120. Inside it had Jaguar comfort with full Connolly leather seats and door trims, plus a well laid-out dash with large gauges. The twin-cam straight-six was an extremely robust unit which was used up until the 1960s in XJ sedans. In the 120 it had twin SU carbs and a torque-biased power delivery.

Top speed:	121 mph (194 km/h)
0–60 mph (0–95 km/h):	11.3 sec
Engine type:	In-line six
Displacement:	210 ci (3,442 cc)
Transmission:	4-speed manual
Max power:	180 bhp (134 kW) @ 5,300 rpm
Max torque:	203 lb ft (275 Nm) @ 4,000 rpm
Weight:	3,039 lb (1,381 kg)
Economy:	13.8 mpg (4.9 km/l)

Jaguar Mk2

One of Britain's most evocative cars, the Jaguar Mk2 is an all-time classic. Beloved of bank managers and bank robbers alike, the Mk2 combined top levels of luxury with excellent performance and inspired roadholding. Not only was it a great car to drive and be driven in, but it looked stunning, too. The unique curvy body was beautiful from any angle, while the distinctive oval radiator grille established itself as a Jaguar trademark. All Mk2s were great cars to drive, but the model most cherished by enthusiasts was the 3.8-litre with manual transmission, which had performance to match the finest sports cars of the era. The Mk 2 also spawned a Daimler offshoot, following Jaguar's acquisition of its rival manufacturer in 1960. The 250 V8 had the engine from the Daimler Dart Roadster and more luxurious trim.

Top speed:	125 mph (202 km/h)
0–60 mph (0–95 km/h):	9.2 sec
Engine type:	in-line six
Displacement:	231 ci (3,781 cc)
Transmission:	4-speed manual/3-speed auto
Max power:	220 bhp (156 kW) at 5,500 rpm
Max torque:	240 lb ft (325 Nm) at 3,000 rpm
Weight:	3,400 lb (1,530 kg)
Economy:	20 mpg (7.1 km/l)

Jaguar D-Type

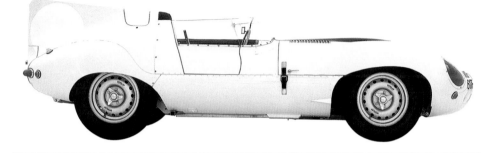

The D-Type was built with one race in mind: Le Mans, in France. But it wasn't as if Jaguar had been without success, as their XK 120C MkII, otherwise known as the C-Type, had been successful in the early 1950s and had been clocked doing 180mph (289km/h) on a closed Belgian highway. To make it as light and advanced as possible, the D-Type used a centre monocoque section with separate front subframe, where most cars were using ladder frames. There was still a live axle at the rear, but up front were double wishbones and longitudinal torsion bar springs. The engine was a version of Jaguar's famous XK unit, featuring an iron block and ally head with twin high-lift camshafts, bigger inlet valves and three twin Weber carbs. It used dry sump lubrication to remain reliable in racing. Later, fuel injection gave 304bhp (227kW). The rear fin was for high-speed stability.

Top speed:	162 mph (259 km/h)
0–60 mph (0–95 km/h):	5.4 sec
Engine type:	In-line six
Displacement:	210 ci (3,442 cc)
Transmission	4-speed manual
Max power:	250 bhp (186 kW) @ 6,000 rpm
Max torque:	242 lb ft (327 Nm) @ 4,000 rpm
Weight:	2,460 lb (1,118 kg)
Economy:	20 mpg (7.14 km/l)

Jaguar E-Type

When the E-Type was displayed at the Geneva Motor Show, Switzerland, in 1961, orders flooded into Jaguar because nothing else at the time could match it for looks, pace and performance at the $3,400 price. It used a monocoque similar to the one developed in the racing D-Type Jags, with separate steel subframes, the front carrying double wishbones and torsion bar springs, while the rear rubber mounted unit held an excellent lower wishbone/upper driveshaft arrangement with large inboard discs and two coil-cover-shocks units per side. The engine was again a development of the previously used XK straight-six, with triple SU carbs giving a very smooth and torquey power delivery that was well suited to the four-speed and long-geared final-drive gears. Testing on Britain's famous M1 motorway proved these cars were very capable of their quoted 150mph (241km/h) top speed.

Top speed:	150 mph (240 km/h)
0–60 mph (0–95 km/h):	7.3 sec
Engine type:	In-line six
Displacement:	231 ci (3,781 cc)
Transmission	4-speed manual
Max power:	265 bhp (197 kW) @ 5,500 rpm
Max torque:	260 lb ft (352 Nm) @ 4,000 rpm
Weight:	2,463 lb (1,119 kg)
Economy:	14.5 mpg (5.1 km/l)

Jaguar E-Type Lightweight

While the E-Type was based on a similar chassis to the racing D-Type, and used an even more advanced independent rear suspension, it was never designed to be a race car. However, it had encouraging results in the hands of private racers, which persuaded Jaguar to make a limited number of very special 'Lightweight' cars. The body was made in aluminium and the fenders were removed completely while other omissions included badges, trim and most of the interior. The car was based on the E-Type roadster, but used a fixed hardtop which helped with rigidity. Suspension was uprated with stiffer torsion bars and a fatter anti-roll bar up front. At the rear it had modified wishbones, lightened hub carriers and stiffer shocks. Power was upped with Lucas fuel injection and a cast-alloy block. Just 12 cars were produced, and most are still about, having a great racing history.

Top speed:	157 mph (251 km/h)
0-60 mph (0–95 km/h):	5.0 sec
Engine type:	In-line six
Displacement:	230.5 ci (3,781 cc)
Transmission	5-speed manual
Max power:	344 bhp (255 kW) @ 6,500 rpm
Max torque:	314 lb ft (424 Nm) @ 4,750 rpm
Weight:	2,220 lb (1,009 kg)
Economy:	15 mpg (5.3 km/l)

Jaguar XJ6

If 'Grace, Space and Pace' was the mantra behind Jaguar's cars, then the XJ6 had the lot. Jaguar boss William Lyons was a true car enthusiast, and the XJ6 was very much his brainchild – he even influenced the styling and engineering, and took a hands-on approach in the car's development. The XJ6 was an instant success, with stunning styling that worked from every angle, a fantastic ride quality and handling poise that could put many a sports car to shame. In 1972, a fabulous V12 engine joined the line-up and brought with it new levels of luxury, while facelifts came in 1973 and 1979. The car continued in production for 17 years and was always a strong seller, especially in the USA. Even the very latest XJ saloon, which uses bonded aluminium technology and computer wizardry, has styling that is almost a facsimile of the original XJ6, such was the perfection of its design.

Top speed:	120 mph (194 km/h)
0–60 mph (0–95 km/h):	10.1 sec
Engine type:	in-line six
Displacement:	170 ci (2,791 cc)
Transmission:	3-speed auto/4-speed manual
Max power:	180 bhp (134 kW) at 5,500 rpm
Max torque:	283 lb ft (384 Nm) at 3,750 rpm
Weight:	3,627 lb (1,632 kg)
Economy:	20 mpg (7.1 km/l)

Jaguar XJC

As great to drive and beautifully engineered as the XJ6 was, it lacked a sporting appeal that would make it sell to younger generation drivers. Jaguar realised this, and in 1975 some sportiness was added in with the introduction of the XJC. Based on the same wheelbase as the XJ6, the XJC had a sleeker two-door bodyshell and a smaller cabin. Like the XJ saloon, it came with a choice of six-cylinder or V12 engines, both of which had massive reserves of power and excellent refinement. All XJCs came with a vinyl-covered roof as standard, but although Jaguar touted this as a desirable extra, its true purpose was to disguise an unsightly seam where the roof of an XJ6 saloon had to be chopped and welded again to fit! Just over 10,000 were built between 1975 and 1978 when production ceased, making it one of the rarest production cars built by Jaguar.

Top speed:	139 mph (222km/h)
0–60 mph (0–95 km/h):	8.8 sec
Engine type:	V12
Displacement:	326 ci (5,343 cc)
Transmission:	3-speed auto
Max power:	244 bhp (180 kW) at 5,250 rpm
Max torque:	269 lb ft (364 Nm) at 4,500 rpm
Weight:	4,195 lb (1,887 kg)
Economy:	14 mpg (5.0 km/l)

Jaguar XJR-9LM

With a history of racing that hadn't been pushed properly in 30 years, Jaguar decided to get serious about endurance racing after the USA 'Group 44' team took a Jaguar back to Le Mans in 1986. Jaguar put motorsport guru Tom Walkinshaw in charge of their World Championship campaign and the following year they ran the XJR-8, winning eight rounds to take the FIA Prototype Championship with almost twice as many points as their nearest rival. In 1988 the new and agile XJR-9 debuted and won three races before entering the Le Mans 24-hour, France, in which one of the three entered won outright. The XJR-9's monocoque chassis was made in carbon-fibre and Kevlar composite and used double wishbones plus 13-inch (330mm) disc brakes all around. Part of the car's success, the mid-mounted all-alloy V12, was very reliable in competition.

Top speed:	236 mph (377 km/h)
0–60 mph (0–95 km/h):	N/A
Engine type:	V12
Displacement:	426 ci (6,995 cc)
Transmission	5-speed manual
Max power:	745 bhp (556 kW) @ 7,250 rpm
Max torque:	610 lb ft (826 Nm) @ 5,500 rpm
Weight:	2,315 lb (1,052 kg)
Economy:	N/A

Jaguar XJR-S

Being associated with luxury cars that floated along, Jaguar needed outside help when it came to pumping up their ageing XJS in 1988. They turned to Tom Walkinshaw, in charge of running Jaguar Sport. Walkinshaw set about making important tweaks here and there to put the flabby-handling XJS back on track. In the suspension revised spring pressures, re-valved shocks and new bushes made it much more taut in corners. Wider wheels and tyres took care of the rest of the driver feedback, and the steering also had its assistance reduced to improve the feel. The all-alloy V12 was pushed out to 366ci (5,997cc) in displacement from the standard 323ci (5,337) unit by increasing the stroke of the crankshaft, then in 1991 the XJR-S got a new look and a race-derived engine management system, along with revisions to the intake and exhaust. Production ended in 1995.

Top speed:	155 mph (248 km/h)
0–60 mph (0–95 km/h):	6.5 sec
Engine type:	V12
Displacement:	366 ci (5,993 cc)
Transmission	3-speed auto
Max power:	333 bhp (248 kW) @ 5,250 rpm
Max torque:	365 lb ft (494 Nm) @ 3,650 rpm
Weight:	4,023 lb (1,828 kg)
Economy:	14 mpg (5 km/l)

Jaguar XJ220

It was top Jaguar engineer Jim Randle who came up with the idea for a 542 bhp (403 kW) supercar. A Concept was built for the British Motor Show in 1988, but it wasn't until Ford took over Jaguar the following year that the go ahead for production was given. Jaguar with a V12 and four-wheel drive, the car eventually debuted at the track with a twin-turbo V6 and two-wheel drive, plus it was 9.8 inches (250mm) shorter than the concept. The Sport got the job of building it and while the concept was shown, debut car crushed the track record at the famous 14–mile (22-km) Nurburgring circuit, Germany, and reached test speeds of 213 mph (340 km/h). This resulted in a final model in 1992 which went into production, taking 12 days to make each one of the 275 built. Each one cost $400,000 and, at the time, it was the fastest production car ever.

Top speed:	218 mph (349 km/h)
0-60 mph (0–95 km/h):	3.8 sec
Engine type:	V6
Displacement:	213.5 ci (3,498 cc)
Transmission	5-speed manual
Max power:	542 bhp (403 kW) @ 7,000 rpm
Max torque:	N/A
Weight:	3,250 lb (1,477 kg)
Economy:	10 mpg (3.54 km/l)

Jaguar XKR

The all-new XK8 appeared at the Geneva Motor Show, Switzerland, in 1996, with both the coupe and convertible versions powered by the new lightweight alloy AJ-V8 244ci (4-litre) engine. In 1997 came Jag's new sedan, the XJR which used a supercharger on the same V8 for incredible performance, which overshadowed the more sporting XK8. So, for 1998 the blown V8 was installed in the coupe and called the XKR. While running the same chassis as the XK8, the XKR had re-calibrated suspension with computer-adjustable damping. The quad-cam V8 was all-alloy and the lightest V8 in its class, plus it was high-tech with variable camshaft timing. The Eaton M112 supercharger gave 28 percent more power, and to cope the XKR had 12-inch (305mm) vented discs all around with high-friction pads. The gearbox was from a Mercedes Benz to handle the increased torque.

Top speed:	155 mph (248 km/h)
0–60 mph (0–95 km/h):	5.1 sec
Engine type:	V8
Displacement:	244 ci (3,996 cc)
Transmission	5-speed auto
Max power:	370 bhp (275 kW) @ 6,150 rpm
Max torque:	387 lb ft (524 Nm) @ 3,600 rpm
Weight:	3,850 lb (1,750 kg)
Economy:	14 mpg (5 km/l)

Jaguar S Type

The original 1963 Jaguar S-Type was based on a lengthened Mk 2 platform and using much of the same frontal bodywork. The S-Type name was revived by Jaguar in 1998 for its mid-size executive model launched at the Birmingham Motor Show, which even drew styling cues from the original – the front radiator grille being the most obvious of these. Based on the Lincoln LS chassis, the car's wheelbase is actually longer than the Jaguar XJ8 and that of its main rival, the BMW 5-Series. Two engines are offered with the S-Type: a new US-built 3.0 litre V6 producing 240 bhp, and the XJ8's 4.0 litre V8, with a highly efficient Nippondenso engine management system. Despite its sporting set up, the car retains a lavish interior and smooth ride which is largely due to its 50:50 weight distribution and reworked Lincoln suspension.

Top speed:	150 mph (220 km/h)
0–60 mph (0–95 km/h):	6.6 sec
Engine type:	V8
Displacement:	244 ci (3,996 cc)
Transmission:	5-speed auto
Max power:	281 bhp (209 kW) at 6,100 rpm
Max torque:	287 lb ft (427 Nm) at 4,300 rpm
Weight:	3,770 lb (1,710 kg)
Economy:	23 mpg (9.7 km/l)

Jeep CJ-7 (1977)

Jeep were owned by the American Motor Company (AMC) in the mid-1970s, and they responded to the growth of the leisure industry by building a modern version of the military Jeep: the CJ-7. The new vehicle had a longer wheelbase and got six-cylinder power, and was also the first jeep to become available with a Turbo-Hydramatic gearbox. Hard top and soft top versions were available, but they all used the same rugged separate ladder-style frame which was almost identical to that used on the World War II Jeeps. Semi-elliptical springs were used all around on the twin-live axle set-up, with part-time four-wheel drive coming on the manual version and the Quadratrac permanent four-wheel drive being optional on both the manual and automatic. As many were used off-road, the Jeep came with a four-point roll cage, but otherwise was little changed styling-wise from the original Jeep shape.

Top speed:	73 mph (117 km/h)
0–60 mph (0–96 km/h):	11.4 sec
Engine type:	In-line six
Displacement:	232 ci (3,801 cc)
Transmission:	4-speed manual
Max power:	100 bhp (74 kW) @ 3,600 rpm
Max torque:	185 lb ft (251 Nm) @ 1,800 rpm
Weight:	3,100 lb (1,409 kg)
Economy:	17.2 mpg (6.09 km/l)

Jeep Grand Cherokee

The success and heritage of the Jeep name was something Chrysler wanted to capitalize on when they launched the Jeep Grand Cherokee in 1993. It boasted Chrysler's Uni-frame structure which was a monocoque crafted in steel and using Quadra-Coil suspension on live front and rear axles with anti-roll bars and gas-filled shocks. The Quadra-Trac 4WD was very useful, being an on-demand system with a viscous coupling centre differential with the torque split between front and rear axles, depending on surface conditions. The body was more rounded than previous Cherokees and in fact it had one of the most aerodynamic shape of any Sport Utility Vehicle. It also had short overhangs and could approach a hill of 37 degrees or leave one of 30 degrees. Best of all was the 360ci (5.9-litre) V8 which gave the Grand Cherokee more supercar-like performance on the road.

Top speed:	124 mph (198 km/h)
0–60 mph (0–95 km/h):	8.2 sec
Engine type:	V8
Displacement:	360 ci (5,899 cc)
Transmission	4-speed auto
Max power:	237 bhp (176 kW) @ 4,050 rpm
Max torque:	345 lb ft (467 Nm) @ 3,050 rpm
Weight:	4,218 lb (1,917 kg)
Economy:	13 mpg (4.6 km/l)

Jeep Wrangler (1998)

The Jeep is well known as a wartime vehicle which kept American servicemen on the move; in fact it's often referred to as the original off-roader. The car and name developed through the decades, and Chrysler bought the right to produce it in 1988, when they took bought the American Motor Company. That spurred the release of the Jeep Wrangler Renegade, with wider arch extensions and a 244ci (4-litre) straight-six. The Sahara was simply a limited edition of the same Jeep Wrangler, even though it looked slightly different, thanks to new sheet metal (all bar the doors, in fact) and round headlamps, fitted from 1996-on models. Like the original Jeep, the Sahara used a strong ladder frame underneath with front and rear live axles. The gearboxes available were a 5-speed manual or 3-speed auto, with standard low and high four-wheel drive ratios.

Top speed:	112 mph (179 km/h)
0–60 mph (0–96 km/h):	8.8 sec
Engine type:	In-line six
Displacement:	244 ci (4,000 cc)
Transmission	5-speed manual
Max power:	184 bhp (137 kW) @ 4,600 rpm
Max torque:	220 lb ft (298 Nm) @ 3,600 rpm
Weight:	3,349 lb (1,522 kg)
Economy:	12 mpg (4.25 km/l)

Jensen CV8

Richard and Alan Jensen began as coachbuilders, producing attractive bodies on various chassis available from British manufacturers, but went into production of their own cars in 1935. Their 1940s and 1950s cars were large and used some of the biggest British engines of the time, typically Austin straight-six 244ci (4-litre) units. Their range turned more sporty from 1952 with the 541, very similar in looks to this CV8 which appeared 10 years later. The slanted headlights provoked love 'em or hate 'em reactions, but what won many fans was the use of a new 360ci (5.9-litre) V8 engine from Chrysler. With the CV8 having a lightweight glass-fibre body, the motor gave tremendous performance. The chassis comprised two main large tubes which ran front to rear, with Austin-derived front wishbones and a limited-slip differential equipped live axle which hung on leaf springs.

Top speed:	136 mph (218 km/h)
0–60 mph (0–95 km/h):	6.7 sec
Engine type:	V8
Displacement:	383 ci (6,276 cc)
Transmission	3-speed auto
Max power:	330 bhp (246 kW) @ 4,800 rpm
Max torque:	425 lb ft (575 Nm) @ 3,000 rpm
Weight:	3,600 lb (1,636 kg)
Economy:	13 mpg (4.6 km/l)

Jensen Interceptor

Replacing the controversially styled CV8 in 1966, just four years after it'd been launched, the Interceptor was virtually the same car underneath. It used a steel tube chassis, four-wheel disc brakes, double wishbone front and leaf spring rear suspension, plus a Panhard rod and live rear axle. What made the difference to buyers was the Vignale-styled steel body, though it did have a downside as it was prone to bad rusting. The Chrysler powerplants remained, options being a 383ci (6.2-litre) or, from 1971 on, a 440ci (7.2-litre) which even came with the legendary Six pack triple carb set-up. Although the car went through various updates from 1969 to 1971, Jensen went out of business through loss of sales in 1976. However, a MkIV version did make it out in 1983, built by new company Jensen Parts & Service. The late 1990s also saw a revival in the Jensen name and new models.

Top speed:	137 mph (219 km/h)
0–60 mph (0–95 km/h):	6.4 sec
Engine type:	V8
Displacement:	383 ci (6,276 cc)
Transmission	3-speed auto
Max power:	330 bhp (246 kW) @ 4,600 rpm
Max torque:	450 lb ft (609 Nm) @ 2,800 rpm
Weight:	3,696 lb (1,680 kg)
Economy:	10.7 mpg (3.8 km/l)

Jowett Jupiter

It might look like an old relic today, but the Jowett Jupiter was a technological tour de force when it debuted in 1950. With a tubular spaceframe chassis and alloy panels bolted to a framework of smaller steel tubes, it employed build traits that are common in the most advanced sports cars of today. It's no surprise, then, that when the tiny British maker entered the Le Mans 24 hour race for the first time in 1950, the Jupiter went home with an emphatic class victory. Power came from the characterful flat-four engine of the Jowett Javelin saloon, meaning the Jupiter could also enjoy a lively power delivery with the added advantage of a low centre of gravity. Even today, the Jupiter is a responsive and rewarding car to drive. Production lasted for only four years. A few examples were even built with a plastic laminate body.

Top speed:	84 mph (134 km/h)
0–60 mph (0–95 km/h):	16.8 sec
Engine type:	flat-four
Displacement:	91 ci (1,485 cc)
Transmission:	4-speed manual
Max power:	60 bhp (45 kW) at 4,500 rpm
Max torque:	84 lb ft (114 Nm) at 3,000 rpm
Weight:	2,121 lb (954 kg)
Economy:	20 mpg (7.1 km/l)

Lamborghini Miura

This was the stunning machine that, in 1966, started the mid-engined trend in supercars, making Ferraris appear out of date both in technology and looks. The Miura was also the first supercar with a quad-cam V12 engine. The sensation of the Geneva Motor Show, Switzerland in 1966, the Bertone low-slung design was almost space-age in concept, and firmly put an identity on future supercars. Its massive side sills were an indication of the new chassis design, using a steel monocoque with big sills and a large centre tunnel. The engine was held in a stamped steel frame behind the occupants and featured an alloy block and heads, with classic hemispherical combustion chambers borrowed from an American design, and four camshafts even though it had only two valves per cylinder. The later, SV version had more power with 385bhp (287kW) in 1971, but the fuel crisis saw the end of the car in 1973.

Top speed:	172 mph (275 km/h)
0–60 mph (0–95 km/h):	6.9 sec
Engine type:	V12
Displacement:	240 ci (3,929 cc)
Transmission	5-speed manual
Max power:	370 bhp (276 kW) @ 7,700 rpm
Max torque:	286 lb ft (387 Nm) @ 5,500 rpm
Weight:	2,851 lb (1,296 kg)
Economy:	11.2 mpg (4 km/l)

Lamborghini Espada

Marcelo Gandini's four-seater concept car for the 1967 Geneva Motor Show, the Marzal, provided the inspiration for Lamborghini's Espada. With wide bodywork and bulky glass area, the Espada was more of a grand tourer than it was a sports car, while the unconventional looks were quick to polarize opinion – it was a car that you eiher loved or hated. Inside, there was enough room for four, but the driving position was awkward and incredibly uncomfortable, while it was impossible to see some of the instruments without straining to see beneth the rim of the steering wheel. Handling wasn't brilliant because of the car's weight, but with a 350bhp V12 powerplant under the bonnet it was still startlingly swift. Production stretched to 1217 examples manufactured between 1968 and 1978. The Series II cars had optional power steering and Series III (built from 1973) had an altered nose and improved brakes and suspension.

Top speed:	155 mph (248 km/h)
0–60 mph (0–95 km/h):	6.9 sec
Engine type:	V12
Displacement:	240 ci (3,929 cc)
Transmission:	5-speed manual
Max power:	350 bhp (261 kW) at 7,500 rpm
Max torque:	290 lb ft (393 Nm) at 5,500 rpm
Weight:	3,740 lb (1,683 kg)
Economy:	14 mpg (5.0 km/l)

Lamborghini Countach

The Bertone-styled Lamborghini Countach stunned everyone when it was launched in 1971 at the Geneva Motor Show, Switzerland. It went into production three years later and, incredibly, could reach speeds of up to 190mph (305km/h). Through the 1980s it was developed, particularly with the engine which went to four camshafts with the 'Quattrovalvole' version, for a mighty 455bhp (339kW). Though many supercars were using fuel injection by 1990, the Countach shunned this in favour of six Weber downdraught carburettors, and sounded all the better for it. Double wishbones at the front and trailing arms plus wishbones at the rear kept the cornering very flat, while massive discs with cooling ducts from the bodywork kept braking highly efficient, no matter what the speed. This is a design icon which lasted 20 years prior to the equally stunning Diablo taking over.

Top speed:	178 mph (285 km/h)
0–60 mph (0–95 km/h):	5.2 sec
Engine type:	V12
Displacement:	315 ci (5,167 cc)
Transmission	5-speed manual
Max power:	455 bhp (339 kW) @ 7,000 rpm
Max torque:	369 lb ft (499 Nm) @ 5,200 rpm
Weight:	3,188 lb (1,449 kg)
Economy:	11.8 mpg (4.2 km/l)

Lamborghini LM002

In 1977 Lamborghini hoped to be part of a US military project and produced the rear-engined Cheetah concept for the 1977 Geneva Motor Show, Switzerland. By the early 1980s, though, American company AM had won the Army contract with their cheaper Humvee. Despite this, Lamborghini pressed on with the LM002 and it was available from 1985. It used a brutally strong and complex steel spaceframe chassis with bonded aluminium panels. Independent self-levelling suspension was fitted and Kevlar-reinforced tyres were specially developed. The engine came straight from the Countach supercar, virtually unchanged except for a waterproof air intake and fuel injection. A more powerful LM004 model with Lamborghini's marine V12 put out 434lb ft (587Nm) torque. The interior was fully loaded with leather trim, air-con and power everything as standard.

Top speed:	126 mph (202 km/h)
0–60 mph (0–95 km/h):	8.5 sec
Engine type:	V12
Displacement:	315 ci (5,167 cc)
Transmission	5-speed manual
Max power:	450 bhp (336 kW) @ 6,800 rpm
Max torque:	369 lb ft (536 Nm) @ 4,500 rpm
Weight:	5,954 lb (2,706 kg)
Economy:	10.2 mpg (3.6 km/l)

Lamborghini Diablo

With the Countach looking very dated by the late 1980s, Lamborghini needed an answer to take them into the next decade. The company created a super Countach in order to evaluate parts for its new sportscar. At first the car came out with just rear-wheel drive, but in 1991 it was decided that in order to harness the full power quota which the car was to put out, it would need 4WD, so the VT version was launched. This was still heavily biased to rear-wheel drive, however, with just 27 per cent going to the front. The engine used was the same throughout, being a 60-degree V12 which was based on a design from Lamborghini's first V12 in 1963. It was all-alloy in construction and use short stroke to allow very high revving. Handling was nothing short of amazing, with double wishbones all around and a very wide track.

Top speed:	205 mph (328 km/h)
0–60 mph (0–95 km/h):	4.3 sec
Engine type:	V12
Displacement:	350 ci (5,729 cc)
Transmission	5-speed manual
Max power:	492 bhp (366 kW) @ 7,000 rpm
Max torque:	428 lb ft (579 Nm) @ 5,200 rpm
Weight:	3,475 lb (1,579 kg)
Economy:	13.1 mpg (4.6 km/l)

Lancia Beta

Sadly, the Lancia Beta is remembered for all the wrong reasons. Instead of casting a rose-tinted glance in the direction of its fine handling, versatile model range and alloy-head twin cam engines, all most people remember about the car was its propensity to rust like a tin can abandoned on a beach. Using cheap imported metal almost ruined the company, as Lancia faced thousands of warranty claims for rusty Betas from their disgruntled owners. And that's a crying shame, because for its era the Lancia was one of the best cars on the market in terms of driver appeal, with wonderfully crisp steering and all-wheel disc brakes coupled to a fantastically compliant chassis. Supercharged Volumex models are of particular interest thanks to their sports car-like performance. They have a small bump in the bonnet to accomodate the supercharger.

Top speed:	122 mph (197 km/h)
0–60 mph (0–95 km/h):	10.1 sec
Engine type:	in-line four
Displacement:	121 ci (1,995 cc)
Transmission:	5-speed manual
Max power:	135 bhp (101 kW) at 5,500 rpm
Max torque:	152 lb ft (207 Nm) at 3,000 rpm
Weight:	2,400 lb (1,080 kg)
Economy:	28 mpg (9.7 km/l)

Lancia Gamma

The Gamma was Lancia's answer to European executive cars such as the Ford Granada and Citroen CX when it was launched in 1976. A large four-door saloon with distinctive sloped rear end styling, it was billed as one of the most important cars in Lancia's history. Sadly, it wasn't to be – it might have looked stunning, but poor reliability and shocking build quality meant it never achieved its projected sales targets. The car's unusual 2.5-litre flat four engine had character and was fairly powerful, but a design flaw meant that cambelts were prone to slipping, with disastrous consequences. Rust was a problem, too. The most attractive Gamma variant was the distinctive two-door coupé, styled by Pininfarina, which went on to achieve cult status among collectors. Revised Series 2 cars became available from 1980, with numerous minor changes to the design.

Top speed:	121 mph (196 km/h)
0–60 mph (0–95 km/h):	9.9 sec
Engine type:	flat-four
Displacement:	152 ci (2,484 cc)
Transmission:	5-speed manual/3-speed auto
Max power:	140 bhp (104 kW) at 5,400 rpm
Max torque:	153 lb ft (208 Nm) at 3,000 rpm
Weight:	2,910 lb (1,309 kg)
Economy:	25 mpg (9.0 km/l)

Lancia Stratos

Italian coachbuilder Bertone can take credit for the Stratos, as it debuted the concept at the 1970 Turin Motor Show, Italy. Inspired by the first car, the Stratos HF appeared a year later at the same show, using a Ferrari V6 engine. Lancia had taken note of the car, and when in 1973 they needed 500 cars built for rally homologation, they commissioned Bertone to do the work. Later that year the Stratos took its first win at the Spanish Firestone Rally, but the real results came the following year when the homologation production was completed and the Stratos won the first of three consecutive World Rally Championships. Its success is down to how well it was built. It had a centre steel cage with rear frame holding the engine and strut suspension, while the front end had wishbones. Lancia continued using the quad-cam Dino engine, with three Weber twin-choke carbs in road form.

Top speed:	140 mph (224 km/h)
0–60 mph (0–95 km/h):	7.0 sec
Engine type:	V6
Displacement:	147 ci (2,418 cc)
Transmission	5-speed manual
Max power:	190 bhp (141 kW) @ 7,000 rpm
Max torque:	166 lb ft (224 Nm) @ 5,500 rpm
Weight:	2,161 lb (982 kg)
Economy:	16.8 mpg (6 km/l)

Lancia Thema 8.32

It might look like a mundane 1980s saloon, but the Thema 8.32 had a hidden secret. Under the bonnet, the car was equipped with a quad cam Ferrari engine – the 8 stood for V8 and the 32 referred to the number of valves. The engine was originally derived from the Ferrari 308 Quattrovalvole, but most of them were built by Ducati. With modified suspension to cope with the extra power, the 8.32 was a startling machine, with incredible performance and superb handling. But it was also luxurious, with an interior trimmed in light ash wood and leather. Among its more unusual options was a rear aerofoil that could be manually operated by the driver. Because the 8.32 was only sold in limited numbers, right-hand-drive versions were never engineered and it was never sold officially in right-hand-drive markets such as the United Kingdom.

Top speed:	140 mph (227 km/h)
0–60 mph (0–95 km/h):	6.8 sec
Engine type:	V8
Displacement:	179 ci (2,927 cc)
Transmission:	5-speed manual
Max power:	215 bhp (159 kW) at 6,750 rpm
Max torque:	210 lb ft (285 Nm)
Weight:	3,087 lb (1389 kg)
Economy:	17 mpg (6.1 km/l)

Lancia 037 Rallye

Lancia turned to Italian tuning specialists Abarth to help develop its new rally car in 1981. In a bid to take on the likes of the Audi quattro and Ford RS200, the 037 was based on the centre section of the Beta Montecarlo coupé , with an entirely new spaceframe chassis and mid-mounted supercharged 2.1-litre four cylinder engine. Although many drivers criticised the 037 for being too much of a handful to drive – like other rally cars of the period it was purely a rear wheel drive – it was ultimately a success, winning the world championship in 1983. An even more extreme Evo 2 version appeared in 1984, with a slight power increase and a larger bore and stroke. As well as the competition cars, Lancia built 200 037s for road use in order to homologate the car for competition use, and these were equally unforgiving to drive.

Top speed:	140 mph (227 km/h)
0–60 mph (0–95 km/h):	6.0 sec
Engine type:	in-line four
Displacement:	129 ci (2,111 cc)
Transmission:	5-spd manual
Max power:	325 bhp (262 kW) at 8,000 rpm
Max torque:	n/a
Weight:	2117 lb (953 kg)
Economy:	18 mpg (6.5 km/l)

Lancia Delta Integrale

Originally conceived as a homologation special for rallying, this car was first launched as the Delta HF Turbo 4x4 in 1987, but within months was badged the Integrale. It grew wide arches for fatter alloys, but retained four doors and remained practical. The road car echoed the rally car, using a permanent 4WD system with epicyclic centre differential and viscous coupling, plus Torsen limited-slip differentials. Suspension was similar front and rear with MacPherson struts and anti-roll bars. The car used a development of the 122ci (2-litre) four-cylinder engine from the Thema sedan, with a cast-iron block and alloy head. Multi-point injection and a turbo were standard, and from 1989 it was also 16v. As a combination of handling, balance and power, few cars could beat the Intergrale, and it lasted in competition until 1994, remaining as good as many of the upcoming road/rally cars.

Top speed:	137 mph (219 km/h)
0–60 mph (0–95 km/h):	5.7 sec
Engine type:	In-line four
Displacement:	122 ci (1,997 cc)
Transmission	5-speed manual
Max power:	210 bhp (157 kW) @ 5,750 rpm
Max torque:	227 lb ft (307 Nm) @ 2,500 rpm
Weight:	2,954 lb (1,342 kg)
Economy:	22 mpg (7.8 km/l)

Land Rover Series One

L and Rover made no secret of the fact that its first 4x4 was based on a Jeep – although there has been serious rivalry between the two brands ever since. At the Land Rover's inception, the Rover Car Company's chief designer, Maurice Wilks, was looking for a vehicle that could be used to remove felled trees from his Welsh holiday home, and hit on the idea of using an ex-WW2 Jeep. Then he realised tht Britain should have a utility vehicle of its own, and the Land Rover was born. With selectable four-wheel drive, leaf springs and a durable ladder-frame chassis, the earliest Land Rover was a massive success with farmers and had true go-anywhere ability. Due to a steel shortage at the time, the body was made of aluminium. The fact that the simplicity of its styling is still echoed in today's Defender proves just how right the original concept was, with over two million vehicles sold.

Top speed:	60 mph (96 km/h)
0–60 mph (0–95 km/h):	n/a
Engine type:	in-line four
Displacement:	122 ci (1,997 cc)
Transmission:	2x4-speed manual
Max power:	52 bhp (39 kW) at 4,000 rpm
Max torque:	101 lb ft (137 Nm) at 1,500 rpm
Weight:	2,968 lb (1,336 kg)
Economy:	17.5 mpg (6.2 km/l)

Land Rover Defender

The vehicle we now know as the Defender was born in 1983 as the Land Rover 90 and 110, depending on whether you chose a short or a long wheelbase. It was the first major change to the Land Rover's construction since the Series II model debuted in 1958, although even then some parts were interchangeable with earlier models. The Defender name was added in 1990, when Land Rover introduced its first direct injection diesel engine— the Tdi. For the first time since its launch, the Land Rover had the performance to match its off-road ability. The Tdi engine was updated again in 1993 with a more efficient injection system, while an all-new five-cylinder Td5 engine appeared in 1998. It may have been in production for over two decades, but the Defender remains the toughest 4x4 on the market and continues to sell well.

Top speed:	85 mph (136 km/h)
0–60 mph (0–95 km/h):	19.2 sec
Engine type:	in-line four diesel
Displacement:	152 ci (2,495 cc)
Transmission:	2x5-speed manual
Max power:	113 bhp (83 kW) at 4,000 rpm
Max torque:	195 lb ft (265 Nm) at 1,800 rpm
Weight:	4,635 lb (2,086 kg)
Economy:	26 mpg (9.2 km/l)

Lexus LS400

For a Japanese firm to challenge the likes of BMW and Mercedes for top honours in the executive class might have seemed too big a mountain to climb, but Lexus was on the ball straight away when it launched the LS400 in 1990. It might not have had the badge, but thanks to a quad-cam 250bhp (186kW) 244ci (4-litre) V8 and masses of equipment for a bargain price, it quickly gained fans. Double wishbone suspension made it an agile car given its size too, while rack and pinion steering kept it precise in corners, and an intelligent five-speed transmission gave the driver the best of both worlds, depending on their mood. Massive brake discs of 12-inches (304mm) all around with, naturally, ABS, were reassuring given the speeds the LS400 was capable of and inside the luxury of satellite navigation, a CD-Rom, sound system, leather and wood made it a very comfortable grand tourer.

Top speed:	155 mph (248 km/h)
0–60 mph (0–95 km/h):	6.3 sec
Engine type:	V8
Displacement:	242 ci (3,969 cc)
Transmission	5-speed auto
Max power:	290 bhp (216 kW) @ 6,000 rpm
Max torque:	300 lb ft (406 Nm) @ 4,000 rpm
Weight:	3,886 lb (1,766 kg)
Economy:	17 mpg (6 km/l)

Light Car Co. Rocket

With project accomplishments such as the McLaren MP4/4 F1 car and the road-going McLaren F1, designer Gordon Murray knew what a good road/race car needed. Hence, when he formed the Light Car Company with Chris Craft in 1991, the two-seater Rocket used all his ideas. Being lightweight was imperative and to achieve this the car used a multi-tube spaceframe chassis with thin but strong double A-arms at either end and coilover shock units. The engine is straight from a Yamaha FZR 1000 motorbike and sits in the rear as a stressed member, giving the chassis yet more strength. The standard sequential gearbox provides drive to twin speed axle, which makes cruising more relaxed, plus provides a reverse which isn't available on the bike gearbox. The engine used a roller bearing crank, five valves per cylinder and four Mikuni carbs, plus an 11,000rpm redline.

Top speed:	130 mph (208 km/h)
0–60 mph (0–95 km/h):	4.8 sec
Engine type:	In-line four
Displacement:	61 ci (1,002 cc)
Transmission	5-speed sequential
Max power:	143 bhp (107 kW) @ 10,500 rpm
Max torque:	77 lb ft (104 Nm) @ 8,500 rpm
Weight:	882 lb (401 kg)
Economy:	20 mpg (7.1 km/l)

Lincoln Zephyr (1939)

While the 1939 and 1940 Lincoln Zephyr looked much like the Ford designs of the same era, underneath they were significantly different. The Zepyr was the base model Lincoln and was to use a Flathead V8 like the Fords, but under the order of Henry Ford instead they had a V12 engine developed from the V8 but with a 75-degree angle. Early models suffered from overheating, warped bores and oil sludge build-up due to inadequate crankcase ventilation, but this was solved and later engines also had hydraulic lifters for quieter, more reliable, running. The Zephyr was revolutionary in that it used unitary construction as opposed to a separate chassis, but aside from that, it was basic and dated with solid axles and transverse leaf springs. What was different was the Columbia two-speed rear axle which effectively doubled the gears to six forward speeds.

Top speed:	87 mph (139 km/h)
0–60 mph (0–96 km/h):	16.0 sec
Engine type:	V8
Displacement:	267 ci (4,375 cc)
Transmission	3-speed manual
Max power:	110 bhp (82 kW) @ 3,900 rpm
Max torque:	180 lb ft (244 Nm) @ 3,500 rpm
Weight:	3,790 lb (1,722 kg)
Economy:	16 mpg (5.66 km/l)

Lincoln Capri (1954)

An all-new Lincoln was launched in 1952 and was built through '54, and it had the brand new engine to replace the dated Flathead V8. The new 317ci (5.2-litre) unit was extremely smooth, thanks to eight crankshaft counterbalances where most V8s had just six, plus it was easily tuned. The new car also had a very stiff chassis, with six crossmembers on the separate frame, making the car's new MacPherson strut suspension work well and improving the model's durability. In its inaugural year the Capri took the Carrera Panamericana in first, second, third and fourth places, then did the same the following year, but just first and second places in 1954. But the Capri boasted more than performance as it also has power-operated leather seats, power windows, power steering and brakes, and even a Hydramatic transmission. In 1956 the car was dramatically restyled; production fell by 50 percent.

Top speed:	108 mph (173 km/h)
0–60 mph (0–96 km/h):	13.4 sec
Engine type:	V8
Displacement:	317 ci (5,194 cc)
Transmission	3-speed auto
Max power:	205 bhp (153 kW) @ 4,200 rpm
Max torque:	280 lb ft (380 Nm) @ 1,800 rpm
Weight:	4,250 lb (1,931 kg)
Economy:	19 mpg (6.72 km/l)

Lincoln Continental Mk IV (1959)

Everything about the Mk IV was big. It was one of the largest cars ever to come out of Detroit, and had the biggest-capacity engine ever available in a passenger car up until the 1960s. Like the Skyline which had arrived just two years before, the Lincoln used a retractable hardtop which neatly stowed away in the trunk, but when up, the rear screen raked inwards and offered an opening window for rear-passenger ventilation. Given the ostentatious time, the Mk IV was one of the least fussy cars from Detroit, but it was immensely stylish with its wide, canted headlight grille and work-of-art fenders both ends. Suspension was conventional for the time, with wishbones and leaf springs front and rear, while the all cast-iron engine thumped out enormous torque to make the Mk IV a great cruiser and, significantly, quicker than the Cadillacs.

Top speed:	118 mph (188 km/h)
0–60 mph (0–96 km/h):	10.4 sec
Engine type:	V8
Displacement:	430 ci (7,046 cc)
Transmission	3-speed auto
Max power:	350 bhp (261 kW) @ 4,400 rpm
Max torque:	490 lb ft (664 Nm) @ 2,800 rpm
Weight:	5,192 lb (2,360 kg)
Economy:	7 mpg (2.47 km/l)

Lincoln Continental (1961)

Lincoln worked hard to make their 1961 Continental one of the best ever, and it won praise for its high construction standards. It had a new, streamlined body with slab sides and a flush-fitting grille, plus 'clap-hand' doors which opened away from each other for excellent access. It was advanced, and because of the emphasis on quality, had no concessions towards weight-saving. The huge chassis was on a 123-inch (3.12m) wheelbase and ran self-adjusting brakes, along with coil springs and leaf springs front and rear. It was inside where the innovations were, with power-assisted features such as the windows, door locks, hydraulic wipers, steering, six-way seats, plus there was air-conditioning and cruise control. The car was very subtle in its styling, too, compared to what was available just to previous years. New, small lights and conservative use of chrome made it a favourite for stately owners.

Top speed:	117 mph (187 km/h)
0–60 mph (0–96 km/h):	11.2 sec
Engine type:	V8
Displacement:	430 ci (7,046 cc)
Transmission	3-speed auto
Max power:	300 bhp (224 kW) @ 4,100 rpm
Max torque:	465 lb ft (630 Nm) @ 2,000 rpm
Weight:	5,220 lb (2,372 kg)
Economy:	12 mpg (4.24 km/l)

Lincoln Continental Mk III (1969)

Henry Ford II put his personal stamp on this design of Lincoln's luxury coupe. It was very long for a two-door coupe and in fact had the longest hood ever produced on a US car (over 6ft or 1.8m). Under it was 150lb (68kg) of sound-deadening to quieten the 460ci (7,538cc) V8, though it couldn't dampen the performance, thanks to the huge torque produced. The suspension was set deliberately soft, so the car floated in style over the worst of surfaces, while the interior wrapped the driver in leather-lined luxury and wood trim, with a distinctly stately like dash. The engine – unusually for a luxury vehicle but typical for the late 1960s – ran 10.5:1 compression and a four-barrel carburettor for tremendous performance, and the car was brought down in speed by the power-assisted 11.7-inch (280mm) front discs and huge rear drum brakes.

Top speed:	123 mph (196 km/h)
0–60 mph (0–96 km/h):	10.3 sec
Engine type:	V8
Displacement:	460 ci (7,538 cc)
Transmission	3-speed auto
Max power:	365 bhp (272 kW) @ 4,600 rpm
Max torque:	500 lb ft (678 Nm) @ 2,800 rpm
Weight:	4,475 lb (2,034 kg)
Economy:	13 mpg (4.60 km/l)

Lincoln Continental Coupe (1975)

Featuring every idea that improved luxury, the Lincoln Continental of 1975 was truly a masterpiece in high-class motoring. The chassis was separate in order to best insulate the cabin from road noise, and the springs and shocks were suitably soft to cushion the ride. The 9-inch (229mm) live axle was located by trailing arms, a torque arm and a transverse link to ensure good stability despite the wallowing ride, and 11.8-inch (300mm) vented discs were fitted at the front with optional anti-lock drums at the rear to stop the heavyweight. Externally, the styling remained conservative with classy lines, hidden headlights behind vacuum-operated panels, plus covered rear arches to emphasize the long and low appearance. Inside there was power everything and deep button velour bench seats, plus walnut veneer trim. An auxiliary fuel tank allowed an extra 100 miles (160km) of motoring.

Top speed:	118 mph (189 km/h)
0-60 mph (0–96 km/h):	10.4 sec
Engine type:	V8
Displacement:	460 ci (7,538 cc)
Transmission	3-speed auto
Max power:	215 bhp (160 kW) @ 4,000 rpm
Max torque:	338 lb ft (458 Nm) @ 2,800 rpm
Weight:	5,219 lb (2,372 kg)
Economy:	9 mpg (3.19 km/l)

Lincoln Continental Mk V (1978)

The Lincoln range had always concentrated on luxury before light weight, but in 1978 that changed with the launch of the Mk V Continental. While looking almost identical to its predecessor the Lincoln Coupe, it was almost 500lb (227kg) lighter, which made it perform and handle better. This didn't stop designers having a field day with the options list, however, as the Mk V featured every possible extra to pamper the occupants. The Diamond Jubilee edition as shown celebrated the start of the Lincoln company 60 years earlier in 1918, after Henry Martyn Leland walked out of Cadillac having disagreed with GM boss William C. Durant about wartime production. Leland named the company after the president whom he had first voted for in 1864, and over a century later the Cadillac bearing the anniversary edition displayed glitz on wheels and sold over 72,000 in total for 1978.

Top speed:	118 mph (189 km/h)
0–60 mph (0–96 km/h):	9.8 sec
Engine type:	V8
Displacement:	460 ci (7,538 cc)
Transmission	3-speed auto
Max power:	210 bhp (157 kW) @ 4,200 rpm
Max torque:	357 lb ft (484 Nm) @ 2,200 rpm
Weight:	4,567 lb (2,075 kg)
Economy:	9 mpg (3.19 km/l)

Lincoln Mk VII LSC (1990)

Marketed as a grown-up Mustang, the Lincoln LSC ran on an identical Fox platform and came with the same specification engine as the street-brawling 5.0 GT Mustang. Although somewhat heavier than the smaller car, the LSC (luxury super coupe) had tremendous pick up and the standard auto gearbox harnessed the power well. Where it was vastly superior to other cars on the same platform (such as the earlier Thunderbird and Mercury Cougar) was with its ride quality, which was super smooth, thanks to air suspension. It was still an okay handler because of fattened anti-roll bars, ABS-assisted disc brakes all around and 7x16-inch (178x406mm) alloys with Goodyear Eagle 225/60 tyres. Inside it had luxury features such as climate control, 12-way power seats, cruise control, tilt column, plus power windows, mirrors, door locks and steering. The only optional was leather seats.

Top speed:	137 mph (219 km/h)
0–60 mph (0–96 km/h):	8.0 sec
Engine type:	V8
Displacement:	302 ci (4,948 cc)
Transmission	4-speed auto
Max power:	225 bhp (168 kW) @ 4,200 rpm
Max torque:	300 lb ft (407 Nm) @ 3,000 rpm
Weight:	3,779 lb (1,717 kg)
Economy:	16 mpg (5.66 km/l)

Lincoln MkVIII

Being Ford USA's premium brand, Lincoln has always had the bias towards luxury, but the MkVIII took it to a new level. Carrying on developments made in the MkVII, the 1993 model became superior and had radically modern looks in order to take on the influx of European and Japanese cars. The new swoopy lines won many fans, as did the new all-alloy 32-valve V8 Modular engine later used in the Mustang Cobra. Coupled to the new 4R70W automatic overdrive transmission, the drive train made the MkVIII a capable performer, which could also be laid-back. Handling was very good too, the car feeling agile whilst remaining supple, thanks to air springs at each corner. To get in you had to punch in a code before the door handle would operate, but once inside you were treated to a very modern and ergonomic dash, with a full complement of toys.

Top speed:	123 mph (197 km/h)
0–60 mph (0–95 km/h):	7.0 sec
Engine type:	V8
Displacement:	281 ci (4,601 cc)
Transmission	4-speed auto
Max power:	290 bhp (216 kW) @ 5,750 rpm
Max torque:	285 lb ft (386 Nm) @ 4,500 rpm
Weight:	3,765 lb (1,711 kg)
Economy:	22 mpg (7.8 km/l)

Lincoln Navigator

The Sport Utility vehicle market has become bigger than ever in the USA in the past decade, and at the top in terms of prestige and capabilities is the Lincoln Navigator. It hit the market in 1998 and used the floorpan and running gear of the Ford Expedition, which itself could be traced back to the F-150 pick-up. However, for both comfort and adjustability, the Navigator used air springs which work in conjunction with the automatic load-levelling facility, and when off-road, the car lifts by an inch for extra clearance. Though the live axle might have seemed dated, it was well located with upper and lower trailing arms plus a Panhard rod. The engine was a larger version of the modular unit used in other Fords, called the 'Triton'. It used a single cam per bank and sequential fuel injection and was highly reliable, not needing servicing for 100,000 miles (160,000km).

Top speed:	109 mph (174 km/h)
0–60 mph (0–95 km/h):	11.4 sec
Engine type:	V8
Displacement:	330 ci (5,400 cc)
Transmission	4-speed auto
Max power:	230 bhp (171 kW) @ 4,250 rpm
Max torque:	325 lb ft (440 Nm) @ 3,000 rpm
Weight:	5,557 lb (2,526 kg)
Economy:	14.7 mpg (5.25 km/l)

Lincoln Town Car Cartier (1999)

This is a full-sized car of the old school, with an emphasis on maximum luxury and minimum driver fatigue. But it's built with modern standards and technology, hence is barely over 2 tons (2.03 tonnes) – excellent, given the specification. The Two Car had first received its more rounded lines in 1997 but underneath it continued with a double wishbone front and live axle rear. What the car did have to help ride was a Watts linkage on the back axle and air springs to smooth out the bumpiest of surfaces. The Town Car used the same engine as it had done since the early 1990s, that being the Ford Modular unit with single cam per bank, sequential multi-point fuel injection, and Ford's high-tech EEC-V engine management. It's whisper-quiet, even at speed. The Cartier edition shown means leather, and every other optional extra is fitted as standard.

Top speed:	130 mph (208 km/h)
0–60 mph (0–96 km/h):	7.9 sec
Engine type:	V8
Displacement:	281 ci (4,604 cc)
Transmission	4-speed auto
Max power:	220 bhp (164 kW) @ 4,500 rpm
Max torque:	290 lb ft (393 Nm) @ 3,500 rpm
Weight:	4,015 lb (1,825 kg)
Economy:	23 mpg (8.14 km/l)

Lister Storm

Lister were involved with Jaguar racing cars back in the 1950s, but in 1983 they were commissioned to build racing versions of the Jaguar XJS V12, which was the first step to producing its own Lister Le Mans and MkIII race cars. Company founder Laurence Pearce wanted to realize a dream of making a supercar for the road, and by 1991 enough capital had been raised to start on the Storm. The car was more function over form, with an alloy honeycomb structure forming the monocoque and carbon-fibre making up the bodywork. The engine it used was still an enlarged Jaguar V12 unit, but with twin superchargers running at 9psi boost. Pulling it down from the huge speed were 14.5 (368mm) and 12.5-inch (317mm) vented Brembo discs with alloy four-pot callipers. The suspension with tubular A-arms at front and a multi-link rear was stiff, but ideal for fast road and track use.

Top speed:	200 mph (320 km/h)
0–60 mph (0–95 km/h):	4.1 sec
Engine type:	V12
Displacement:	427 ci (6,996 cc)
Transmission	6-speed manual
Max power:	594 bhp (443 kW) @ 6,100 rpm
Max torque:	580 lb ft (785 Nm) @ 3,450 rpm
Weight:	3,169 lb (1,440 kg)
Economy:	12 mpg (4.2 km/l)

Lotus Elite

The Elite was Lotus boss Colin Chapman's first attempt at a road car, and first appeared in 1957. It was also a technical revelation, being the first car to be built with a fibreglass monocoque which helped keep its overall weight down. It used independent suspension all round, with wishbones and coils at the front, and struts at the back. That gave the Elite a firm ride but incredibly nimble handling, while the lightweight bodywork meant performance was excellent, albeit at the expense of a noisy cabin. A Special Equipment version, dubbed SE, appeared in 1960 and came with a close-ratio gearbox and increased power output, while power was increased again in 1962. Lotus sold nearly 1000 Elites before the model was replaced by the cheaper and even more entertaining Elan in 1964. The Elite was a successful racer too, with six class wins at Le Mans in six years.

Top speed:	115 mph (186 km/h)
0–60 mph (0–95 km/h):	12.5 sec
Engine type:	in-line four
Displacement:	74 ci (1,216 cc)
Transmission:	4-speed manual
Max power:	83 bhp (62 kW) at 6,100 rpm
Max torque:	75 lb ft (102 Nm) at 3,300 rpm
Weight:	1,422 lb (640 kg)
Economy:	28 mpg (10.0 km/l)

Lotus Elan (1971)

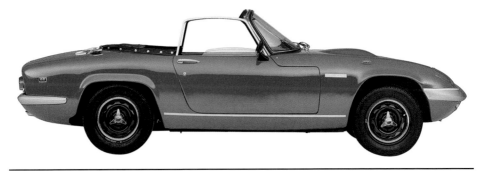

The flyweight Lotus Elan is regarded as one of the best-handling cars ever made, which is some tribute, given it was designed in the 1960s. Created by Lotus founder Colin Chapman, it used a simple backbone chassis and fitted Triumph Herald independent front suspension with Chapman's own patented struts on the independent rear. The car was supposed to use a glass-fibre monocoque, but in order to test prototypes quickly, they had a separate steel chassis. It worked so well that the Elan went into production like this, with a glass-fibre body. The engine was from the Lotus Cortinas of the time, starting out as a 85ci (1.4-litre) unit but later changing to 95ci (1.5-litre). The power was exceptional but it was the car's 1515lb (687kg) that made it so lively. In corners it didn't under- or oversteer, but tracked on a line around bends and gave huge levels of grip even on 6.4-inch (165mm) tyres.

Top speed:	118 mph (189 km/h)
0–60 mph (0–95 km/h):	7.0 sec
Engine type:	In-line four
Displacement:	95 ci (1,558 cc)
Transmission	4-speed manual
Max power:	126 bhp (94 kW) @ 6,500 rpm
Max torque:	113 lb ft (153 Nm) @ 5,500 rpm
Weight:	1,515 lb (688 kg)
Economy:	26 mpg (9.2 km/l)

Lotus Esprit V8

With the original wedge-shaped Esprit – star of the James Bond movie *For Your Eyes Only* – starting to look long in the tooth, Lotus turned to British design guru Peter Stevens to give the car a freshen up for the 1990s. The result was a rounder and more stylish offering than before, at the expense of added weight. At first, though, it still used the original 2.2-litre turbo engine, which was renowned for poor reliability and high repair costs. The Esprit got the powerplant it needed in 1996, with the introduction of a Lotus-designed 3.5-litre V8. The new engine coincided with a minor facelift, that gave the Esprit meatier wheelarches, a larger rear wing and new door handles. Performance was incredible, but the car was killed off in late 2003 because of stringent new European emissions regulations. The engines of the latest version have the signature of the engine maker etched on a steel plaque.

Top speed:	155 mph (250 km/h)
0–60 mph (0–95 km/h):	5.9 sec
Engine type:	V8
Displacement:	213 ci (3,506 cc)
Transmission:	5-speed manual
Max power:	349 bhp (260 kW) at 6,500 rpm
Max torque:	295 lb ft (400 Nm) at 4,250 rpm
Weight:	2,968 lb (1,336 kg)
Economy:	18 mpg (6.5 km/l)

Lotus Esprit Turbo

The Esprit remains one of the longest production run supercars ever. Launched in 1980, it is still being made in the 21st century, albeit in a much revised high-performance machine. Yet it is unique among supercars because it uses just four cylinders, aided by a Garrett T3 intercooled turbo. In typical Lotus fashion the Esprit used a steel backbone chassis into which the engine is mounted longitudinally directly behind the driver. Independent suspension featured throughout with double wishbones at the front and a twin transverse link at the rear. The engine was all-alloy with 16 valves and a special overboost facility to harness a full 300bhp (224kW) in short bursts. In 1996 the four-cylinder 134ci (2.2-litre) S4 was replaced by a V8 version to satisfy stringent American emissions regulations, later supplemented with a 240bhp (179kW), 122ci (2-litre) Esprit GT3.

Top speed:	162 mph (259 km/h)
0–60 mph (0–95 km/h):	4.7 sec
Engine type:	In-line four
Displacement:	133 ci (2,174 cc)
Transmission	5-speed manual
Max power:	264 bhp (197 kW) @ 6,500 rpm
Max torque:	264 lb ft (357 Nm) @ 3,900 rpm
Weight:	2,649 lb (1,204 kg)
Economy:	21 mpg (7.5 km/l)

Lotus Carlton/Omega

Mixing one of the world's top sportscar names with a mass-production manufacturer resulted in one of the most striking and fastest sedans with the 1990 Lotus Carlton. Using a standard Vauxhall Carlton GSi 3000 bodyshell, Lotus took it and re-designed the running gear, putting in a multi-link rear axle, twin tube shocks and some of the biggest brakes ever seen on a production sedan with 13-inch (330mm) and 11.8-inch (299mm) discs. For power Lotus started with the 183ci (3-litre) twin-cam straight six and fitted a longer stroke crank to produce 220ci (3.6 litres), plus new pistons for a lower compression to allow the fitting of twin Garret T25 turbos. The turbos were intercooled and helped propel the car to just shy of 180mph (290km/h), with an acceleration that left most exotic machines behind. Just 950 were produced; 510 were left-hand drive, called Lotus Omegas.

Top speed:	176 mph (282 km/h)
0–60 mph (0–95 km/h):	5.1 sec
Engine type:	In–line six
Displacement:	221 ci (3,615 cc)
Transmission	6–speed manual
Max power:	377 bhp (281 kW) @ 5,200 rpm
Max torque:	419 lb ft (567 Nm) @ 4,200 rpm
Weight:	3,640 lb (1,655 kg)
Economy:	20 mpg (7.1 km/l)

Lotus Elan (1989)

Although the concept was a sound one, the new Elan came at a bad time for Lotus. Launched in 1989 with a worldwide recession looming, the car had been built using an Isuzu drive train to help reduce costs, but people weren't convinced enough by the front-wheel drive car to let it live far beyond the lean times. Lotus had used a version of its own backbone-style chassis adapted for the new powerplant and it all worked very well. The car had amazing grip and the 98ci (1.6-litre) fuel injected engine revved freely and gave plenty of torque thanks to a water-cooled turbocharger. The body was made via Vacuum-Assisted Resin Injection using a form of glass-fibre, so was very light. A specially designed front suspension wishbone arrangement kept torque steer down to a minimum while at the rear lower wishbones and upper transverse links kept the car very flat in cornering.

Top speed:	136 mph (218 km/h)
0–60 mph (0–95 km/h):	6.5 sec
Engine type:	In-line four
Displacement:	97 ci (1,588 cc)
Transmission	5-speed manual
Max power:	165 bhp (123 kW) @ 6,600 rpm
Max torque:	148 lb ft (200 Nm) @ 4,200 rpm
Weight:	2,254 lb (1,024 kg)
Economy:	19.6 mpg (7 km/l)

Lotus Elise

Few people in the early 1990s expected the floundering UK-based Lotus to come up with such a impressive car. The company wowed everyone with the debut of the handsome Elise at the Frankfurt Motor Show, Germany in 1995, the theory behind the design being pure Lotus, in that it had to be lightweight with an emphasis on handling and performance. The stark nature of the interior helped get the Elise down to an incredibly low 1600lb (725kg). It also stayed slim by utilizing aluminium alloys wherever possible, including brake discs and uprights. The Elise team were clever in other areas too, using an extruded aluminium chassis made in sections and bonded together, as opposed to welding. Power came from Rover's compact K-series engine, again all-alloy and with remarkable output, particularly torque, from its 110ci (1.8 litres).

Top speed:	124 mph (198 km/h)
0–60 mph (0–95 km/h):	5.5 sec
Engine type:	In-line four
Displacement:	109 ci (1,796 cc)
Transmission	5-speed manual
Max power:	118 bhp (88 kW) @ 5,500 rpm
Max torque:	122 lb ft (165 Nm) @ 3,000 rpm
Weight:	1,594 lb (724 kg)
Economy:	29.4 mpg (10.5 km/l)

Marcos Mantis

Like many small car manufacturers in the early 1970s, Marcos went out of business but was revived in 1981 when founder Jem Marsh made a comeback with updated versions of his sporty coupes. Although the cars started out with four-cylinder engines, by the mid-1980s a Rover V8 was being used. As the Rover went out of production in the mid-1990s, Marcos turned to Ford for their modular V8 and the Mantis was born. The wild glass-fibre bodywork hid a strong, separate tubular steel backbone, with MacPherson struts up front and wishbones at the rear. The wheels were 17-inch (432mm) up front while the rears were taller and wider. All Mantis cars with seven-spoke alloys ran a Vortech supercharger on the Ford 32-valve modular engine which gave 450bhp (336kW). The massive hood bulge both made room for the motor and extracted hot air via vents.

Top speed:	161 mph (258 km/h)
0–60 mph (0–95 km/h):	4.8 sec
Engine type:	V8
Displacement:	281 ci (4,601 cc)
Transmission	5–speed manual
Max power:	352 bhp (262 kW) @ 6,000 rpm
Max torque:	300 lb ft (406 Nm) @ 4,800 rpm
Weight:	2,620 lb (1,191 kg)
Economy:	21 mpg (7.5 km/l)

Maserati 3500GT

An Italian muscle car, the 3500GT combined stylish lines with a highly strung and powerful straight-six engine. The car was more to be enjoyed as a grand tourer than a circuit machine for the street, as its steering wasn't very communicative. It used a tubular steel chassis consisting of two main members running the length of the car with outriggers along the sills. To the front sat a double wishbone arrangement and at the rear, leaf springs were highest tech option at the time. The engine was a twin-cam design made in alloy and was ahead of its time by using twin spark plugs fired by twin coil, plus mechanical fuel injection by Lucas. For 1958 the 3500GT was one very quick car in a straight line, beating both the Aston DB4 and Ferrari 250 Lusso. For that reason it's a highly sought after classic worth many times more than its original sale price.

Top speed:	129 mph (206 km/h)
0–60 mph (0–95 km/h):	7.5 sec
Engine type:	In-line six
Displacement:	213 ci (3,485 cc)
Transmission	4-speed manual
Max power:	230 bhp (171 kW) @ 5,500 rpm
Max torque:	224 lb ft (303 Nm) @ 4,500 rpm
Weight:	3,180 lb (1,445 kg)
Economy:	17 mpg (6 km/l)

Maserati Bora

Through financial backing from Citroen, who became the major shareholder in 1968, Maserati agreed to produce two mid-engined cars, the V6 Marek and V8 Bora. The Bora was Maserati's first to use mid-engine mounting and it created a supercar to rival the likes of Ferrari and Lamborghini. It had a semi-monocoque design with folded sheet steel front and cabin sections, while the rear had a subframe in which both the engine, gearbox and suspension were mounted. The 287ci (4.7-litre) V8 had been designed in the 1950s and used four overhead camshafts, an aluminium block and heads, and hemispherical combustion chambers for increased power. The body was steel and, despite no wind-tunnel testing, managed a drag coefficient of just 0.30, which wasn't equalled in years of car production. A long production run of 9 years saw 570 cars made.

Top speed:	160 mph (256 km/h)
0–60 mph (0–95 km/h):	6.5 sec
Engine type:	V8
Displacement:	288 ci (4,719 cc)
Transmission	5-speed manual
Max power:	310 bhp (231 kW) @ 6,000 rpm
Max torque:	325 lb ft (440 Nm) @ 4,200 rpm
Weight:	3,570 lb (1,623 kg)
Economy:	10 mpg (3.5 km/l)

Maserati Biturbo

As a former producer of supercars which had folded in 1975 and been brought out by Alejandro de Tomaso, Maserati needed a big revival come the early 1980s. It needed a mainstream car so they chose to mimic the 3-Series BMW with a new compact sedan that would have power, refinement and driver involvement. The 1981 Biturbo was the result. It used a MacPherson strut front and Chapman strut rear, and had performance extras such as a Sensi-tork limited-slip differential and four-wheel disc brakes. The aluminium V6 engine started out with 122ci (2-litre) displacement but had grown to 170ci (2.8-litres) by 1988. The twin turbos suffered from lag to start with, but this was all but gone in later models, though the oversteer was still very evident, especially in the wet. One of the car's best attributes was the steering, which was widely praised by critics.

Top speed:	128 mph (205 km/h)
0–60 mph (0–95 km/h):	7.2 sec
Engine type:	V6
Displacement:	152 ci (2,491 cc)
Transmission	5-speed manual
Max power:	185 bhp (138 kW) @ 5,500 rpm
Max torque:	208 lb ft (282 Nm) @ 3,000 rpm
Weight:	2,394 lb (1,088 kg)
Economy:	17 mpg (6 km/l)

Maserati Ghibli

Although it never achieved massive success, the 1992 Ghibli was a stunning machine. Its main competition being the BMW 3-series, it used a similar layout with a two-door coupe monocoque body and front-engined/rear-wheel drive package. MacPherson struts and semi-trailing arm rear combined with four position shocks, all thoroughly developed through Maserati's race experience, made the ride and handling inspiring. Steering through the rack and pinion was equally razor-sharp. What further enhanced the experience was an all-alloy, four-valve per cylinder short-stroke 171ci (2.8-litre) V6 which liked to be revved. Coupled with twin turbos, the Ghibli's powerplant produced stunning torque, easily enough to rival BMW's M3. This is an Italian thoroughbred from a company which has successfully produced supercars alongside sedans.

Top speed:	153 mph (245 km/h)
0–60 mph (0–95 km/h):	5.6 sec
Engine type:	V6
Displacement:	170 ci (2,790 cc)
Transmission	5-speed manual
Max power:	280 bhp (209 kW) @ 5,500 rpm
Max torque:	317 lb ft (429 Nm) @ 3,750 rpm
Weight:	2,998 lb (1,363 kg)
Economy:	24 mpg (8.5 km/l)

Mazda RX-7

After a successful Le Mans in 1991, in which Mazda came first with its 700bhp, (522kW) high-revving R26B rotary-powered car, the new RX-7 made its debut. It immediately jumped from sportscar to supercar, thanks to a design brief which stated the car had to be as light and fast as possible. While the shell was steel, the advanced double wishbone suspension was all-alloy, and components were directly bolted to the chassis without bushings for more precise handling. Alloy cross braces were used within the body, making a very stiff structure. The engine was based on the original twin rotor Wankel design, and having few moving parts meant it could rev very quickly. The key was the twin-turbo set-up, one of which started the lag-free performance, the other joining in at 4,500rpm, whereupon it would rapidly rev to its redline.

Top speed:	156 mph (250 km/h)
0–60 mph (0–95 km/h):	5.3 sec
Engine type:	Twin rotor Wankel
Displacement:	158 ci (2,616 cc)
Transmission	5-speed manual
Max power:	255 bhp (190 kW) @ 6,500 rpm
Max torque:	217 lb ft (294 Nm) @ 5,000 rpm
Weight:	2,800 lb (1,273 kg)
Economy:	13.8 mpg (4.9 km/l)

Mazda Miata

Looking like the Lotus Elan from the 1960s, the Mazda Miata (MX5 in UK) re-ignited the sportscar market single-handedly in 1989. Like the Elan, it used a very simple formula of front-engine, rear-wheel drive with tight suspension, all in a lightweight package. The car started with just 97ci (1.5 litres) and 116bhp (86kW) thanks to 16 valves and a slightly increased redline over the Mazda 323 model it came from. Underneath was a steel monocoque with engine/transmission plus rear axle subframes, and double wishbones front and rear. The rack and pinion steering was made high-geared so drivers could adjust the car's line very quickly in corners, though it needed a lot of provocation to go off line as the handling was well-balanced and neutral. The car was easy for a convertible, too, requiring just two buttons to be pressed and two levers to be folded before the roof would go down.

Top speed:	121 mph (194 km/h)
0–60 mph (0–95 km/h):	9.1 sec
Engine type:	In-line four
Displacement:	97 ci (1,598 cc)
Transmission	5-speed manual
Max power:	116 bhp (86 kW) @ 6,500 rpm
Max torque:	100 lb ft (136 Nm) @ 5,500 rpm
Weight:	2,073 lb (942 kg)
Economy:	24.8 mpg (8.8 km/l)

McLaren F1

Every McLaren F1 made lost money, such was the attention to detail and over-meticulous design from the UK-based F1 team. Just 100 were produced, going to specialist collectors around the world and having standard extras such as a complete tool kit (a 6ft/1.8m high chest), gold-plated engine bay, custom-fit McLaren F1 luggage, and full McLaren engine diagnostics anywhere in the world. The F1 was made from carbon composites with honeycomb crossbeams for an immensely strong structure. It needed every bit of strength with power that could accelerate the car to 150mph (241km/h) in 12 seconds. The undertray used venturi tunnels to create a drop in pressure, thus pulling the car towards the ground. A central driving position was ideal and the car easy to drive. At around $1,130,000 when debuted, it was the most expensive road car ever to buy new.

Top speed:	231 mph (370 km/h)
0–60 mph (0–95 km/h):	3.2 sec
Engine type:	V12
Displacement:	370 ci (6,064 cc)
Transmission	6-speed manual
Max power:	627 bhp (468 kW) @ 7,300 rpm
Max torque:	479 lb ft (649 Nm) @ 4,000 rpm
Weight:	2,245 lb (1,020 kg)
Economy:	12.4 mpg (4.4 km/l)

Mercedes 300SL

The infamous 'Gullwing' first saw light in 1952 as a race car. It used a spaceframe chassis with a network of small tubes and hence was lightweight, though the high chassis sides meant fitting conventional doors was out of the question, hence the 'Gullwing' design, which just about provided enough room to get in. While strong, the chassis was let down by the suspension fitted to it, in particular the rear which used as swing axle set-up that made for tricky handling, and the brakes which were all drums and not very efficient. The SL used a sedan engine, but with dry sump lubrication and mechanical fuel injection, which required a bulge in the hood, the other bulge being simply to balance the design. The 1957 Roadster was much better, with improved rear suspension, power disc brakes, and a less cramped interior.

Top speed:	165 mph (265 km/h)
0–60 mph (0–95 km/h):	9.0 sec
Engine type:	In-line six
Displacement:	183 ci (2,996 cc)
Transmission	4-speed manual
Max power:	240 bhp (197 kW) @ 6,100 rpm
Max torque:	216 lb ft (292 Nm) @ 4,800 rpm
Weight:	2,850 lb (1,295 kg)
Economy:	18 mpg (6.4 km/l)

Mercedes Benz 190E 2.5-16 Evo II

Mercedes put out a Cosworth tuned 190E in 1983, but in 1988 it needed to homologate a car for Group A racing and the 225bhp (167kW) 190E 2.5-16 Evo was the result. Just a year later, the Evo II came with an extra 10bhp (7kW) and this was the ultimate 190E. At the front the car used a MacPherson strut set-up, while the rear had a multi-link. The springs were lowered and the shocks uprated, but they also incorporated full adjustability and self-levelling with a sophisticated system. The bodywork was styled on the European touring cars, with extended arches covering new 8x17-inch (203x431mm) alloys. The spoilers front and rear had function, being adjustable to increase downforce. Cosworth again worked their magic on the four-cylinder 150ci (2.4-litre) engine, balancing the rotating assembly and giving it more aggressive cam timing to achieve the power.

Top speed:	156 mph (250 km/h)
0–60 mph (0–95 km/h):	6.8 sec
Engine type:	In-line four
Displacement:	150 ci (2,463 cc)
Transmission:	5-speed manual
Max power:	232 bhp (173 kW) @ 7,200 rpm
Max torque:	181 lb ft (245 Nm) @ 5,000 rpm
Weight:	2,955 lb (1,343 kg)
Economy:	20 mpg (7.1 km/l)

Mercedes Benz 500SL

The SL line started in 1952 with the 'Gullwing', but even with the launch of the fourth-generation model in 1989, the car remained a comfortable grand tourer with a quick turn of speed. The V8 500SL was the top of the line in 1989 and mixed high-tech with luxury. It used a very strong monocoque structure with MacPherson struts and a multi-link rear allied to electronically controlled shocks which had four different settings, depending on the driver's mood. If the worst happened and the car tipped over, hydraulic rams would spring a roll bar into place in one-third of a second. The power top could fold away in 30 sec, the five-way adjustable seats had the belts mounted on them, and the gearbox had standard or sport mode settings. High-tech continued in the engine, with electronic variable valve timing, which changed depending on load and speed, all the time remaining immensely smooth.

Top speed:	155 mph (248 km/h)
0–60 mph (0–95 km/h):	6.1 sec
Engine type:	V8
Displacement:	303 ci (4,973 cc)
Transmission	4-speed auto
Max power:	326 bhp (243 kW) @ 5,500 rpm
Max torque:	332 lb ft (449 Nm) @ 4,000 rpm
Weight:	4,167 lb (1,894 kg)
Economy:	13.4 mpg (4.7 km/l)

Mercedes Benz 560 SEC

This was the final guise of the W126 S-Class coupes, and Mercedes decided on using the biggest engine option available as their main rival, BMW, was rumoured to be bringing out a V12 luxury car. It was the first time the 338ci (5.6-litre) V8 had been used in anything but the flagship S-class four-door sedan, but it suited the intended luxury sport nature of the coupe very well, making it a very quick car. While the coupe ran the same suspension and drive train, its wheelbase was shortened, which made it a more nimble handler, but it retained some luxury on the rear with an optional self-levelling rear. The engine was one of Mercedes' energy concept V8s which had appeared in S-Class sedans in 1979. It featured air-swirl injection for optimum fuel atomization, fuel cut-off on the over-run, and a very low idle speed, yet in Europe could still muster 300bhp (224kW).

Top speed:	145 mph (232 km/h)
0–60 mph (0–95 km/h):	7.0 sec
Engine type:	V8
Displacement:	338 ci (5,547 cc)
Transmission	4-speed auto
Max power:	238 bhp (177 kW) @ 5,200 rpm
Max torque:	287 lb ft (388 Nm) @ 3,500 rpm
Weight:	3,858 lb (1,753 kg)
Economy:	20 mpg (7.1 km/l)

Mercedes Benz C36 AMG

L ike its big brother, the awesome E55, the C36 was equally devastating. With a launch of the C-Class in 1993 to replace the 190 model, it wasn't long before Mercedes-Benz's tuning arm, AMG, got their hands on the sedan. The company started with the very popular 195ci (3.2-litre) in-line six powering the bigger E-Class and S-Class cars. AMG increased the displacement to 220ci (3.6 litres) before installing it, thus making it the largest six-cylinder produced by Mercedes-Benz at the time. Four other areas were also modified, these being the wheels which comprised wide 17-inch (432mm) alloys and low-profile tyres, the suspension which used lowered coil springs and adjustable shocks, the discs which were increased in size and the transmission which featured sporting tweaks. The body was subtle with tell-tale wheels and twin square exhaust pipes unique to the model.

Top speed:	152 mph (243 km/h)
0–60 mph (0–95 km/h):	6.0 sec
Engine type:	In-line six
Displacement:	220 ci (3,606 cc)
Transmission	4-speed auto
Max power:	268 bhp (199 kW) @ 5,750 rpm
Max torque:	280 lb ft (379 Nm) @ 4,000 rpm
Weight:	3,458 lb (1,571 kg)
Economy:	20 mpg (7.1 km/l)

Mercedes C43 AMG

The formula for the C43 AMG seemed so simple: drop a big engine into small wagon, add sports suspension and one practical high-speed hauler was produced. But the conversion was by no means quickly carried out, and much thought went into the fitting of the V8. Being all-alloy meant the new motor was actually lighter than the cast-iron straight-six, creating a better balanced car. AMG added stiffer springs, shocks and anti-roll bars, plus 17-inch (432mm) alloys, slighter wider at the rear, to make the handling superb. Mercedes' own ESP (Electronic Stability Program) kept the traction and also had reigns on the yaw to prevent sideways slippage. AMG revised the camshafts on the engine, an oil cooler and free-flowing intake to extract a further 27bhp (20kW) and 7 lb ft (9.4Nm), making an awesome package, reaching 100mph (160km/h) in just over 15 seconds.

Top speed:	155 mph (248 km/h)
0–60 mph (0–95 km/h):	5.9 sec
Engine type:	V8
Displacement:	260 ci (4,266 cc)
Transmission	5-speed auto
Max power:	302 bhp (225 kW) @ 5,850 rpm
Max torque:	302 lb ft (409 Nm) @ 3,250 rpm
Weight:	3,448 lb (1,567 kg)
Economy:	24 mpg (8.5 km/l)

Mercedes Benz S600

Replacing the 560SEL as Mercedes' flagship model, the S600 set new standards in big sedan production. While its luxury was something many people had come to expect from the Stuttgart, Germany company, the car still had a few surprises. Items such as rain-sensitive windscreen wipers, electronic everything, including front and rear seats, sun shades and steering wheel adjustment, showed that Mercedes were at the forefront of limousine-like quality. But the S600 was marketed as being more than just a gadget machine, with adverts showing it as a performance car with a lot of driver involvement. Thanks to double wishbones at the front and a self-levelling multi-link rear, it handled very well. The brand new all-alloy 48v V12 engine was insisted on by Mercedes' marketing department, and it had massive torque through the rev range. For safety it used ASR to prevent tailslides during loss of traction.

Top speed:	155 mph (248 km/h)
0–60 mph (0–95 km/h):	6.6 sec
Engine type:	V12
Displacement:	365 ci (5,987 cc)
Transmission	5-speed auto
Max power:	389 bhp (290 kW) @ 5,300 rpm
Max torque:	420 lb ft (569 Nm) @ 3,800 rpm
Weight:	4,960 lb (2,254 kg)
Economy:	17 mpg (6 km/l)

Mercedes Benz SLK

Mercedes had never built a small, affordable sportscar prior to the 1996 SLK, but in creating the car, took on the likes of Porsche, BMW, Alfa and MG in what was fast becoming a very popular new market. The car therefore needed to be lightweight, handle well and offer a style-conscious appearance. Mercedes kept the car rigid, strong yet light by using magnesium and high-strength steel in the unitary construction. Suspension was multi-link rear and double-wishbone front, while the roof was an engineering masterpiece. In 25 seconds the handsome fixed top would turn into a complex folding arrangement that went into the trunk. With the roof down there was little wind buffeting due to excellent aerodynamics and a rear wind deflector. The 140ci (2.3-litre) four-cylinder engine received a supercharger which livened up the car, making the most of its superb chassis.

Top speed:	143 mph (229 km/h)
0–60 mph (0–95 km/h):	7.5 sec
Engine type:	In-line four
Displacement:	140 ci (2,295 cc)
Transmission	5-speed manual
Max power:	193 bhp (144 kW) @ 5,300 rpm
Max torque:	200 lb ft (271 Nm) @ 2,500 rpm
Weight:	2,922 lb (1,328 kg)
Economy:	17.3 mpg (6.1 km/l)

Mercedes Benz ML320

The ML was Mercedes' first proper 4WD, as the former G-Wagon was really just a development of the van and hence drove like one. The ML, on the other hand, was like a Mercedes saloon, thanks to a well-designed independent suspension system using coil springs all around. The 4WD set-up used Mercedes ETS with two differentials and if the system detected a loss of traction to a wheel, it would apply brake pressure and force more traction to the other three wheels. It made the car very capable off road, whilst retaining very civilized on-road ride quality. Underneath was well protected, with nothing lower than 8.5 inches (216mm) and the fuel tank, exhaust and differential protected by crossmembers on the ladder frame chassis. The V6 engine used three valves and twin spark plugs per cylinder, ensuring maximum combustion and low emissions, essential for sales in California.

Top speed:	112 mph (179 km/h)
0–60 mph (0–95 km/h):	8.9 sec
Engine type:	V6
Displacement:	195 ci (3,199 cc)
Transmission	5-speed auto
Max power:	215 bhp (160 kW) @ 5,500 rpm
Max torque:	233 lb ft (315 Nm) @ 3,000 rpm
Weight:	4,200 lb (1,909 kg)
Economy:	15.7 mpg (5.6 km/l)

Mercedes Benz E55 AMG

Few are as subtle about their performance as the AMG Mercedes sedans. The E55 looked barely different from the regular car, but massive 18-inch (457mm) rims, reduced body height and low-profile tyres meant much to those in the know. It was based on the E-Class sedan with power from a re-worked version of the 262ci (4.3-litre) V8. The car featured an advanced multi-link rear suspension with double wishbones at the front, all uprated and with lower springs. Another aid was ESP, Electronic Stability Protection, which kept the car stable in all conditions via ABS and traction control. The engine was bored and stroked for its 329ci (5,391cc) displacement and the fourth valve in each cylinder was sacrificed for an extra spark plug, ignited just after the first for compete combustion. A variable length intake manifold widened the torque curve on the V8, making it a true highway stormer.

Top speed:	155 mph (248 km/h)
0–60 mph (0–95 km/h):	5.4 sec
Engine type:	V8
Displacement:	332 ci (5,439 cc)
Transmission	5-speed auto
Max power:	354 bhp (264 kW) @ 5,500 rpm
Max torque:	391 lb ft (529 Nm) @ 3,000 rpm
Weight:	3,600 lb (1,636 kg)
Economy:	15 mpg (5.3 km/l)

Mercury Sportsman (1946)

While the Sportsman didn't pack any new technology, nor a powerful engine (as the name suggested), it did have a beautifully designed body and a ride quality which belied its ancient underpinnings. The styling was brought about by Bob Gregorie, who had to create the feel of the upmarket Lincoln Continental without the cost, so he produced wood panelling in maple and mahogany which dovetailed exquisitely throughout the rear of the car. As mentioned, underneath the car had nothing revolutionary. There was a separate steel chassis with large centre tunnel to house the torque tube (like all Mercurys of the time), while the suspension was plain old solid axle with transverse leaf springs at both ends. Even using the biggest Flathead V8 of the time, the car's performance was still leisurely, though it did have good low speed torque, and the powerplant was very reliable.

Top speed:	82 mph (131 km/h)
0–60 mph (0–96 km/h):	21.2 sec
Engine type:	V8
Displacement:	239 ci (3,916 cc)
Transmission	3-speed manual
Max power:	100 bhp (74 kW) @ 3,800 rpm
Max torque:	N/A
Weight:	3,407 lb (1,548 kg)
Economy:	16 mpg (5.66 km/l)

Mercury Montclair (1955)

While overshadowed somewhat by its older brother, the 1949–1951 Mercury, the 1955 versions also offered custom potential, thanks to factory touches like the peaked headlamps, heavily chromed grille and fared-in rear arches. While sitting low as standard, this owner has gone further by fitting Camaro double wishbone front suspension and a live rear axle from the same car. However, instead of regular coil or leaf springs, a set of airbag springs have been installed. These can be controlled by an on-board compressor to raise or lower the suspension and give the car a ground-scraping look with the convenience of smooth driving, thanks to the whole body effectively riding on air. The original engine is long gone in favour of the cheapest and most tuneable engine, Chevy's 350ci (5.7-litre) V8. Other custom touches include a tuck x'n' roll interior, chopped roof, and extra grille teeth.

Top speed:	120 mph (192 km/h)
0–60 mph (0–96 km/h):	9.3 sec
Engine type:	V8
Displacement:	350 ci (5,735 cc)
Transmission	3-speed auto
Max power:	210 bhp (157 kW) @ 4,000 rpm
Max torque:	285 lb ft (386 Nm) @ 2,800 rpm
Weight:	3,558 lb (1,617 kg)
Economy:	16 mpg (5.66 km/l)

Mercury Lead Sled

In the 1950s as hot rodding took over America, both the racing side and the street side developed. Styles started to fracture and some guys turned to improving their cars for show, more than go, hence customs became popular. The new-in-1949 Mercury was a very radical design, aerodynamic and flowing and looking almost ready-chopped with its low roof line. Within a few years it was available cheaply and hot rodders began using the Merc body so much that it quickly became synonymous with customizing. The car is referred to as lead sled because in the days before plastic bodyfiller, car re-finishers used molten lead to fill seams or trim holes, which was then shaped with body files. This particular car is typical of the late 1950s/early 1960s, with custom wheel caps, flame paint, 1954 De Soto toothed grille and rear fenders skirts. It runs a small-block Chevy for power.

Top speed:	120 mph (192 km/h)
0–60 mph (0–95 km/h):	7.8 sec
Engine type:	V8
Displacement:	350 ci (5,735 cc)
Transmission	3-speed auto
Max power:	380 bhp (283 kW) @ 5,100 rpm
Max torque:	380 lb ft (514 Nm) @ 3,200 rpm
Weight:	3,374 lb (1,533 kg)
Economy:	9 mpg (3.2 km/l)

Mercury Comet Cyclone (1965)

The Comet was seen by most to be granny's grocer-getter, but that changed when the Cyclone GT option came in 1965. The car was essentially an upmarket Ford Falcon, being stretched in the wheelbase but retaining the wishbone front end and leaf spring rear. What made it better was the revised spring and shock rates to improve handling. The engine was Ford's 289ci (4.7-litre) Falcon/Mustang V8, but in the Cyclone fitted with a higher-lift camshaft, 10.5:1 compression pistons, and a four-barrel carb. Through the Top Loader manual the car did 15-second quarters. Externally the styling took cues from Pontiac's best-selling GTO, with square ends, stacked headlights and slim roof pillars. At a cost of $346 more than the Falcon, it was only natural that the Cyclone had a plusher interior, so featured tinted glass, bucket seats, power windows and even seat belts!

Top speed:	124 mph (198 km/h)
0–60 mph (0–96 km/h):	7.4 sec
Engine type:	V8
Displacement:	289 ci (4,735 cc)
Transmission	4-speed manual
Max power:	271 bhp (202 kW) @ 6,000 rpm
Max torque:	312 lb ft (423 Nm) @ 3,400 rpm
Weight:	2,994 lb (1,360 kg)
Economy:	15 mpg (5.31 km/l)

Mercury Cougar Eliminator

Mercury launched their own pony car two years after the Mustang. Called the Cougar, it was essentially a stretched Mustang. The Eliminator came in 1969 and had an independent front with double wishbones and coils springs and a live axle rear on leaf springs, with staggered shocks to limit wheel hop under acceleration. And it could accelerate hard, no matter which engine option you had, either the Boss 302 or 428 Cobra Jet. The smaller of the two pumped out 290bhp (216kW) while the latter was conservatively rated at 335bhp (250kW) to fool the insurance companies, though it was more like 410bhp (305kW). The 428 could also be ordered with a ram air system and if the owner specified the 'Drag Pak', the car would receive an oil cooler and 4.3:1 axle gears. Owners got over-the-counter help: quadruple Weber carbs, two four-barrel carbs and race exhaust headers.

Top speed:	106 mph (170 km/h)
0–60 mph (0–95 km/h):	5.6 sec
Engine type:	V8
Displacement:	428 ci (7,013 cc)
Transmission	3-speed auto
Max power:	335 bhp (250 kW) @ 5,200 rpm
Max torque:	440 lb ft (595 Nm) @ 3,400 rpm
Weight:	3,780 lb (1,718 kg)
Economy:	6.2 mpg (2.2 km/l)

Mercury Cougar GT-E (1968)

To start with, the Cougar was more of a refined cruiser, a sort of upmarket Mustang. But just a year on in 1968 Ford went with the flow of demand and shoehorned in their 427ci (6.9-litre) big-block to create the GT-E. Inside it retained its luxury with overhead map lights, a long centre console and wood grained dash. Underneath it was beefed up with traction bars, heavy-duty suspension, Traction Lock limited-slip differential and 3.91:1 gears. The engine ran at 10.9:1 compression and had the option of two four-barrel carbs to feed its huge thirst. This made the Cougar a fearsome street racer, with 14 seconds possible at the strip once a 'super tune' of adjusting the timing and removing the air filter had been carried out. The GT-E was replaced by the Eliminator in 1969 and 1970, showing how much the public liked what Ford were doing.

Top speed:	128 mph (204 km/h)
0–60 mph (0–96 km/h):	7.0 sec
Engine type:	V8
Displacement:	427 ci (6,997 cc)
Transmission	3-speed auto
Max power:	390 bhp (291 kW) @ 5,600 rpm
Max torque:	460 lb ft (623 Nm) @ 3,200 rpm
Weight:	3,174 lb (1,442 kg)
Economy:	8 mpg (2.83 km/l)

Mercury Cyclone Spoiler (1970)

All Ford group cars were redesigned in 1970s, and this included Mercury with its Cyclone. Besides smoother lines and contours, it got a new engine, the 429ci (7-litre) big-block Ford, which packed huge torque. Mercury being a premium Ford brand meant the ride quality was very good, though the car was happier going quickly in a straight line than cornering. Underneath it used Mercury's Montego unitary platform, stretched to improve the ride on the heavy-duty coil sprung front and leaf sprung rear, with front anti-roll bar. The styling was the, by then, popular fastback muscle-car styling and a hidden light front grille with distinctive gunsight-type grille centre. Adding the Dragpack option gave a Hurst shifted four-speed plus higher rear end gearing, making the Spoiler a low-14-second quarter-mile machine. The Cyclone only lasted another year before being axed.

Top speed:	126 mph (202 km/h)
0–60 mph (0–96 km/h):	6.2 sec
Engine type:	V8
Displacement:	429 ci (7,030 cc)
Transmission	4-speed manual
Max power:	370 bhp (276 kW) @ 5,400 rpm
Max torque:	450 lb ft (610 Nm) @ 3,400 rpm
Weight:	3,773 lb (1,715 kg)
Economy:	9 mpg (3.19 km/l)

Mercury Capri 5.0L (1986)

Based on the Fox platform, the new-for-1979 Mercury Capri ran alongside its more successful Mustang stablemate during the 1980s. It was offered only as a hatchback with a bulbous back window, and came with slightly widened arches, and these less attractive points saw its sales gently decline throughout the 1980s. However, it still represented something of a performance bargain, thanks to a strong and revvy V8 with sequential fuel injection and excellent economy, plus it was at least practical, thanks to the hatchback rear. The RS package gave the car gas shocks and a pair of Quad shocks which were arranged horizontally to the rear axle to control wheel hop, plus meaty Goodyear Eagle 2125/60 tyres on 7x15-inch (244x381mm) alloy rims. With a very positive T5 Borg Warner manual gearbox, it made quite a driver's car, one which would accept all the same mods as a Mustang.

Top speed:	134 mph (214 km/h)
0–60 mph (0–96 km/h):	6.5 sec
Engine type:	V8
Displacement:	302 ci (4,948 cc)
Transmission	5-speed manual
Max power:	200 bhp (149 kW) @ 4,000 rpm
Max torque:	285 lb ft (386 Nm) @ 3,000 rpm
Weight:	3,150 lb (1,431 kg)
Economy:	23 mpg (8.14 km/l)

Mercury Cougar (1999)

First shown as the MC2 concept at the 1997 Detroit Motor Show, the Mercury Cougar got a very positive public reaction so was put into production immediately. It used the Contour sedan platform but with significantly altered springs, bushing and shocks rates to make the Cougar more sporting. The car was also lowered by 1.5 inches (38mm) to get the centre of gravity down and hence improve handling. Power came from the Ford Duratec V6, with a 60-degree V and short stroke. The block and heads are alloy and four overhead camshaft hollow to help make the powerplant very lightweight. What brought buyers back to the car was its radical styling, or, as Ford called it: 'New Edge'. Unusually, the car was known under the same name in Europe where it successfully took over from the ageing Probe and had not just a V6 but a Zetec 16v 130bhp (97kW) engine.

Top speed:	135 mph (216 km/h)
0–60 mph (0–96 km/h):	8.0 sec
Engine type:	V6
Displacement:	155 ci (2,540 cc)
Transmission	5-speed manual
Max power:	170 bhp (127 kW) @ 6,250 rpm
Max torque:	165 lb ft (224 Nm) @ 4,250 rpm
Weight:	3,065 lb (1,393 kg)
Economy:	29 mpg (10.27 km/l)

MGB GT V8

Fitting a V8 into the MGB had been tried prior to the launch of the official car by British Leyland (BL) in 1973. Many specialist tuners had completed the conversion and the ideal engine was within the BL stable, that being the Rover V8, the design of which had been bought from Buick in the 1960s. The Rover displaced just 214ci (3,499cc) and, being all-aluminium, weighed barely more than the MGB's cast-iron four-cylinder engine. This kept the MGB V8's handling very balanced, though it was obvious the set-up leaned more towards a grand tourer than out-and-out sports car. Up front the car used double wishbones with coil springs and lever arm shocks, while the rear had leaf springs on a live axle. A brake servo helped the disc front and drum rear cope with the extra speed available. All MGB GT V8s came in fastback form, and not until the 1992 MG RV8 was there a V8 in a roadster.

Top speed:	125 mph (200 km/h)
0–60 mph (0–95 km/h):	8.5 sec
Engine type:	V8
Displacement:	215 ci (3,528 cc)
Transmission	4-speed manual
Max power:	137 bhp (102 kW) @ 5,000 rpm
Max torque:	193 lb ft (261 Nm) @ 2,900 rpm
Weight:	2,387 lb (1,085 kg)
Economy:	24 mpg (8.5 km/l)

MG Metro 6R4

Just like Ford with its RS200, Austin Rover wanted the ultimate Group B World Rally Championship machine, but had to homologate 200 road-going models. The project was given to Williams Grand Prix Engineering in 1981 and by the end of 1982 they had their first mid-engined Metro with a V6 that was simply a Rover V8 minus two cylinders. Later production cars used a bespoke V6, dubbed the V6 4V because of the four valves per cylinder. While the car looked like an Austin Metro on steroids, it only used that car's body, strengthened by an integral roll cage and using MacPherson struts at each corner of the tubular chassis. The car had a full length undertray which hid three torque-splitting differentials on the four-wheel drive system. Road going cars had 250bhp (186kW), but later Evo models were up to 410bhp (335kW) while full rallycross cars could produce 600bhp (487kW).

Top speed:	140 mph (224 km/h)
0–60 mph (0–95 km/h):	4.5 sec
Engine type:	V6
Displacement:	182 ci (2,991 cc)
Transmission	5-speed manual
Max power:	250 bhp (186 kW) @ 7,000 rpm
Max torque:	225 lb ft (305 Nm) @ 6,500 rpm
Weight:	2,266 lb (1,030 kg)
Economy:	20 mpg (7.1 km/l)

MG Maestro Turbo

When Austin Rover launched the Maestro in 1983, it hardly won people's hearts. It looked dowdy and dated, but it was cheap and offered a wide range of models plus a 98ci (1.6-litre) MG version. A year on, through criticism about a lack of power considering it was a sporting brand, the MG Maestro got a 122ci (2.0-litre) engine and 115bhp (86kW), which helped sales considerably, though critics were still sceptical about the MG branding on this slightly warm hatchback. The big difference came when the Maestro Turbo was launched at the British Motor Show in 1988. With a 10psi Garrett T3 turbo bolted to the new O-Series engine, it was the quickest MG ever, remaining so until well into the 1990s. Uprated and lowered suspension, bigger brake discs and 15-inch (381mm) alloys meant it handled very well too. Just 505 cars were built, making it a collectable in the UK.

Top speed:	135 mph (216 km/h)
0–60 mph (0–95 km/h):	6.4 sec
Engine type:	In-line four
Displacement:	122 ci (1,994 cc)
Transmission	5-speed manual
Max power:	150 bhp (112 kW) @ 5,100 rpm
Max torque:	169 lb ft (229 Nm) @ 3,500 rpm
Weight:	2,460 lb (1,118 kg)
Economy:	25 mpg (8.9 km/l)

MG RV8

The 1992 MG RV8 was an attempt to re-create a classic as a celebration of the 30th anniversary of the first MGB. The bodywork looked distinctly MG, but with rounded edges, blended-in fenders and lights, which echoed all the original touches. In fact, the doors and trunk lid were identical to the old car's, as was the underneath. Still there was the front wishbone suspension and live axle suspension on leaf springs, but with Koni telescopic shocks. What brought the car alive was its 244ci (4-litre) V8 engine, taken from the Range Rover but being a development of the old Buick all-aluminium V8. The unit gave excellent torque at low rpm but couldn't keep up with other British sportscars from the likes of TVR or Marcos. Inside the RV8, again it looked familiar, but the theme was luxury with a full walnut-veneer dashboard and leather seats/panels.

Top speed:	136 mph (218 km/h)
0–60 mph (0–95 km/h):	7.0 sec
Engine type:	V8
Displacement:	240 ci (3,946 cc)
Transmission	5-speed manual
Max power:	190 bhp (142 kW) @ 4,750 rpm
Max torque:	234 lb ft (137 Nm) @ 3,200 rpm
Weight:	2,425 lb (1,102 kg)
Economy:	22 mpg (7.8 km/l)

MGF

The MG name was kept alive by Rover during the 1980s with cars like the MG
Metro and MG Maestro, though purists disregarded these as 'badge cars'. In
order to keep the MG spirit alive properly, the 1992 MG RV8 was launched, but what
MG really needed in the 1990s was a high-production, modern roadster and it came
about with the launch of the MGF in 1995. The car used a revolutionary hydro-gas
independent suspension system with gas-filled 'springs' interconnected front and
rear, and on wishbones. This gave it an amazing ride and unrivalled ride quality.
The engine, too, was advanced, being Rover's ultra light 110ci (1.8-litre) K-series
unit, with Rover's Variable Valve Control (VVC) that continuously varied the intake
cam timing. Mounting the motor midships gave the MGF incredible balance and
turned it into an enthusiastic driver's car, true to the MG spirit.

Top speed:	131 mph (210 km/h)
0–60 mph (0–95 km/h):	7.8 sec
Engine type:	In-line four
Displacement:	110 ci (1,796 cc)
Transmission	5-speed manual
Max power:	143 bhp (107 kW) @ 7,000 rpm
Max torque:	128 lb ft (173 Nm) @ 4,500 rpm
Weight:	2,471 lb (1,123 kg)
Economy:	23 mpg (8.2 km/l)

Mini Cooper

Britain had already developed a love affair with the Mini when the Cooper model debuted in 1961. Tuned by formula one constructor John Cooper, the extra power output of the sporty models made the most out of the Mini's incredible chassis. Handling was amazing, and the car soon became a hit with racers, famously winning the Monte Carlo Rally in 1964, 1965 and 1967 against bigger and much more powerful opposition. The Mini Cooper's finest hour came in 1969 with the famous British crime movie *The Italian Job*, where a trio of red, white and blue Mini Coopers were driven through the sewers of Turin in a dramatic stunt sequence. The original Cooper died in 1971, but Rover reintroduced the model name in 1990 with essentially the same car, almost 30 years after it had made its debut. The last Mini rolled off the production line in Birmigham, England, in October 2001.

Top speed:	97 mph (157 km/h)
0–60 mph (0–95 km/h):	10.9 sec
Engine type:	in-line four
Displacement:	78 ci (1,275 cc)
Transmission:	four-speed manual
Max power:	76 bhp (56 kW) at 6,000 rpm
Max torque:	79 lb ft (107 Nm) at 3,000 rpm
Weight:	1,457 lb (656 kg)
Economy:	30 mpg (10.7 km/l)

Mitsubishi Starion

The Starion was one of the first Japanese sports cars to use a turbocharger, being launched in 1982 with a 170bhp (126kW) engine. That car suffered from turbo lag, but it got better in later models and by 1989 it was all-but gone, though by then the engine had increased to 158ci (2.6 litres) in size and peak power had actually gone down, thanks to a catalytic converter being required. Even with the power drop, the 1989 model was the best Starion there had been. It also looked more aggressive, with widened arches. The neutral handling was mostly due to the good balance of 53:47 front/rear weight distribution. The car used MacPherson struts front and rear and the spring rates were set hard, so body was minimal but at the cost of a very firm ride. Out back two things helped to down power, one being wider tyres than the front with 225/50x16s, the other being a limited-slip differential.

Top speed:	135 mph (216 km/h)
0–60 mph (0–95 km/h):	8.3 sec
Engine type:	In-line four
Displacement:	156 ci (2,555 cc)
Transmission	5-speed manual
Max power:	168 bhp (125 kW) @ 5,000 rpm
Max torque:	215 lb ft (291 Nm) @ 2,500 rpm
Weight:	3,050 lb (1,386 kg)
Economy:	22 mpg (7.8 km/l)

Mitsubishi Galant VR4

The Galant which was launched in 1987 didn't look like a performance car, with its dull, boxy shape. However, in VR-4 form it was a formidable rally car, with Pentti Arikkala driving the car to victory in the British Lombard-RAC Rally. The car was packed with high-tech gadgetry in a way only Mitsubishi knew how. Its Active Four system had 4WD, four-wheel steer which would alter the rear wheel angle by up to 1.5 degrees under 32mph (51km/h), plus anti-lock brakes and all-round independent suspension with MacPherson struts up front and double wishbones at the rear. Also fitted was electronically controlled suspension, with the world's first active ride in a production car, and it used electronic valves in the shocks to limit roll in corners and pitch during acceleration or braking. The multi-valve, twin-cam engine used an intercooled turbo which in rally form could hit 290bhp (216kW).

Top speed:	135 mph (216 km/h)
0–60 mph (0–95 km/h):	6.4 sec
Engine type:	In-line four
Displacement:	122 ci (1,997 cc)
Transmission	5-speed manual
Max power:	195 bhp (145 kW) @ 6,000 rpm
Max torque:	203 lb ft (275 Nm) @ 3,000 rpm
Weight:	3,250 lb (1,477 kg)
Economy:	28 mpg (10 km/l)

Mitsubishi Lancer Evo 5

A rally car for the street was how to describe Mitsubishi's Evo 5. It was in fact a very easy car to drive very quickly cross-country, no matter what the weather. This is did with a permanent four-wheel drive biased slightly towards the rear wheels, and an Active Yaw Control to prevent sideways slippage. Excess speed was easily dealt with thanks to 12-inch (305mm) vented discs and powerful four-pot Brembo callipers at each corner. The 16-valve 122ci (2-litre) four-cylinder engine was a development of previous Evo models and featured contra-rotating balance shafts to keep the engine smooth up to the 6,500rpm redline. The turbo's massive intercooler mounted in the front grille ensured a dense supply of air, which aided the enormous power output and hit of torque. The car was good enough to give make Tommy Makinen World Rally Championship Champion three times.

Top speed:	147 mph (235 km/h)
0–60 mph (0–95 km/h):	4.7 sec
Engine type:	In-line four
Displacement:	122 ci (1,997 cc)
Transmission	5-speed manual
Max power:	276 bhp (206 kW) @ 6,500 rpm
Max torque:	274 lb ft (371 Nm) @ 3,000 rpm
Weight:	3,160 lb (1,436 kg)
Economy:	26 mpg (9.2 km/l)

Mitsubishi Eclipse Spyder GS-T

Initially only available in coupe form when it was launched in 1989, the Eclipse was built in Illinois and not Japan. It was based on the Galant running gear and featured front-wheel drive in the top GS-T model, but an outstanding 4WD system in the other range-topping model, the GSX, which was virtually unstickable in corners. It wasn't until 1996 that the roadster version became available, and without a roof it needed much strengthening. Mitsubishi did this by including a new rear deck and seat panel, thicker sills, re-designed inner arches and a reinforced windshield frame. The suspension remained, being effective from the start, thanks to a wishbone front and multi-link rear system. The engine featured an alloy head with twin overhead camshafts, four valves per cylinder, multi-point electronic fuel injection and a Garrett turbo which ran 1.0 bar (14.5 psi) boost.

Top speed:	130 mph (208 km/h)
0–60 mph (0–95 km/h):	6.4 sec
Engine type:	In-line four
Displacement:	122 ci (1,997 cc)
Transmission	5-speed manual
Max power:	210 bhp (157 kW) @ 6,000 rpm
Max torque:	214 lb ft (289 Nm) @ 3,000 rpm
Weight:	3,053 lb (1,382 kg)
Economy:	21.4 mpg (7.6 km/l)

Mitsubishi 3000GT

The 1991 3000GT was loaded with gadgets. Underneath, the chassis was a rigid steel monocoque with MacPherson struts up front and a double wishbone rear with trailing arms, and electronically adjustable shocks. There was a four-wheel steering system which could increase steering angles up to 1.5 degrees according to speed, steering wheel input and surface friction. Then there was the 4WD with viscous coupling between the front and rear wheels which incorporated a torque split transfer system to prevent loss of grip. Inside it was fully loaded, with a digital screen to control temperature. The engine was state-of-the-art, with quad cams, twin intercooled turbochargers and multi-point fuel injection. Externally, front and rear spoilers lowered and raised at 50mph (80km/h) to help aerodynamics. The only hindrance was the car's weight because of all the equipment.

Top speed:	152 mph (243 km/h)
0–60 mph (0–95 km/h):	6.0 sec
Engine type:	V6
Displacement:	181 ci (2,972 cc)
Transmission	5-speed manual
Max power:	281 bhp (209 kW) @ 6,000 rpm
Max torque:	300 lb ft (406 Nm) @ 3,000 rpm
Weight:	3,990 lb (1,814 kg)
Economy:	21 mpg (7.5 km/l)

Mitsubishi FTO

The 1995 FTO was only produced for Japan, but due to public demand and the growth of importers around the world, it was in many other countries soon after. It had an excellent combination of a revvy engine, brilliant front-wheel drive handling and a luxurious interior in a shapely coupe. The front suspension had MacPherson struts and lower wishbones while the rear was more complex with transverse upper and lower links, longitudinal links and an anti-roll bar. The brakes were very effective, being discs all around which required very little effort to pull the car's speed down rapidly. Though it came with a 110ci (1.8-litre) four-cylinder in base form, the real performer was the MIVEC (Mitsubishi Induction Valve Electronic Control) 122ci (2-litre) V6, which beyond 5,600rpm would use a more radical camshaft profile for more power up to the 8,200rpm redline.

Top speed:	140 mph (224 km/h)
0–60 mph (0–95 km/h):	7.5 sec
Engine type:	V6
Displacement:	122 ci (1,998 cc)
Transmission	5-speed manual
Max power:	200 bhp (149 kW) @ 7,500 rpm
Max torque:	148 lb ft (200 Nm) @ 4,800 rpm
Weight:	2,534 lb (1,152 kg)
Economy:	28 mpg (10 km/l)

Mitsubishi Pajero Evo

The Paris-Dakar Rally runs each year from France to Africa, across deserts and extreme rough terrain. Cars built for it need to have a rugged 4WD, loads of space for supplies, but most of all they have to be fast and reliable. Mitsubishi launched their Pajero Evo in 1997 to compete in the rally and immediately scored a 1-2-3 win, proving it wasn't a fluke by doing the same in 1998. The Pajero uses a very strong ladder frame chassis with thick crossmembers, and up front features a double wishbones independent, while at the rear a live axle sits on coil springs. The 4WD system can switch to 2WD at speeds up to 60mph (96km/h). The 215ci (3.5-litre) all-alloy engine has four valves per cylinder and uses Mitsubishi's MIVEC system which electronically changes the valve timing. The huge fenders came from the rally-winning machine and covered 10-inch (254mm) wide tyres.

Top speed:	125 mph (200 km/h)
0–60 mph (0–95 km/h):	8.0 sec
Engine type:	V6
Displacement:	213 ci (3,497 cc)
Transmission	5-speed semi-auto
Max power:	280 bhp (209 kW) @ 6,500 rpm
Max torque:	256 lb ft (347 Nm) @ 3,500 rpm
Weight:	4,370 lb (1,986 kg)
Economy:	19 mpg (6.7 km/l)

Morris Minor

The Morris Minor, Britain's dearly loved small car, had a production span of 23 years. Revolutionary when it came out, thanks to the independent torsion bar front suspension and spacious interior, it became the cheap practical motor for thousands of families and remains a popular car in the UK today. This example was built from one of the Traveller woody-type two-door estates and has kept a very stock look, though cleverly it has a 2-inch (50mm) roof chop and widened rear arches to house the bigger tyres needed. Under the hood, where there used to be a 50ci (830cc) four-cylinder, there's now a supercharged 241ci (3.9-litre) Rover all-aluminium V8, which can get the car down the quarter-mile in under 14 seconds. Inside, the car is very stock too, featuring a full original interior with just the enlarged transmission tunnel giving evidence of any change.

Top speed:	125 mph (200 km/h)
0–60 mph (0–95 km/h):	5.1 sec
Engine type:	V8
Displacement:	241 ci (3,950 cc)
Transmission	3-speed auto
Max power:	300 bhp (224 kW) @ 5,750 rpm
Max torque:	325 lb ft (440 Nm) @ 4,300 rpm
Weight:	2,400 lb (1,090 kg)
Economy:	16 mpg (5.7 km/l)

Morris 1100/1300

With the Mini enjoying incredible sales success thanks to its clever use of interior packaging and fine handling, BMC decided to enlarge the concept with the wheel-at-each-corner 1100/1300 range. The Morris 1100 debuted in 1962 and looked modern, with clean lines and surprisingly entertaining driving characteristics. It featured a transversely-mounted A-Series engine and four-speed gearbox-in-sump transmission to keep production costs to a minimum and maximise interior space, although access to the boot was hampered by a narrow loading aperture. Thanks to BMC policy of 'badge-engineering', the Morris 1100 and 1300 were also sold as Austins, MGs, Wolseleys, Rileys and Vanden Plas versions. It was replaced by the Austin-only Allegro in 1973 – a retrograde step, as its replacement was an inferior car.

Top speed:	79 mph (126 km/h)
0–60 mph (0–95 km/h):	22.2 sec
Engine type:	in-line four
Displacement:	67 ci (1,098 cc)
Transmission:	4-speed manual
Max power:	36 bhp (41 kW) at 5,100 rpm
Max torque:	60 lb ft (81 Nm) at 2,500 rpm
Weight:	1,652 lb (743 kg)
Economy:	40 mpg (14.3 km/l)

Nash Healey (1951)

Donald Healey is better known for his involvement with Austin throughout Europe, but he worked with American company Nash after a meeting with Nash-Kelvinator president George Mason aboard the *Queen Elizabeth* liner in 1949. The two found they had common ground and hatched a plan to build a Nash-Healey sportscar, which was built in the UK and shown in prototype form the following year. Racing that same year, it took a ninth at the Mille Miglia and a 4th at the Le Mans 24-hour. At first, the roadster looked unusual, with both headlights mounted in a narrow and fussy grille, but by 1951 Pininfarina had restyled the car into the style shown, making it far more handsome. The car used an Ambassador sedan motor with an aluminium cylinder head, hotter camshaft and higher compression ratio. In 1952 with revisions it received an extra 10bhp (7kW).

Top speed:	105 mph (168 km/h)
0–60 mph (0–96 km/h):	11.5 sec
Engine type:	In-line six
Displacement:	252 ci (4,140 cc)
Transmission	3-speed manual with overdrive
Max power:	135 bhp (100 kW) @ 4,000 rpm
Max torque:	230 lb ft (312 Nm) @ 2,000 rpm
Weight:	2,950 lb (1,340 kg)
Economy:	22 mpg (7.78 km/l)

Nash Metropolitan (1957)

While looking as glitzy and typically 1950s as any other American car, in fact the Metropolitan was produced for the US market in England. Its body was built by Ludlow and Fisher in Birmingham, and this was based on an Austin chassis which came from the factory just a short distance away. With its tiny four-cylinder engine, it was a long way from the powerful cruisers that were abundant on American highways, but it was quite lively, thanks to low gearing. It did at least look like an American convertible, albeit one which had shrunk in the wash, thanks to a continental kit, two-tone paint and whitewall tyres. The car could seat just two in comfort and a third at a squeeze for short journeys. Remarkably, it went over 104,000 in sales in seven years, no doubt due to its cuteness, as well as its economical engine.

Top speed:	75 mph (120 km/h)
0–60 mph (0–96 km/h):	24.1 sec
Engine type:	In-line four
Displacement:	91 ci (1,489 cc)
Transmission	3-speed manual
Max power:	52 bhp (39 kW) @ 4,500 rpm
Max torque:	69 lb ft (94 Nm) @ 2,100 rpm
Weight:	1,885 lb (856 kg)
Economy:	38 mpg (13.4 km/l)

Nissan Silvia Turbo

In the mid-1980s Nissan needed to re-create some of the magic of the 240Z, so set to work designing a compact coupe shape with plenty of punch. The Silvia Turbo was the result, and while it didn't convince many in the looks, it certainly had the power and handling. Sensibly, they kept the car rear-wheel drive which meant the engine was mounted longitudinally up front at a time when most manufacturers were switching to transverse engines and front-wheel drive applications. The independent suspension was kept simple with MacPherson struts up front and semi-trailing arms rear, with fat anti-roll bars both ends along with disc brakes, which were also vented up front. As a turbo was used, Nissan felt it unnecessary to have 16 valves, so stuck with a basic 8-valve engine which was both effective and lightweight, though it did need revving to make the power.

Top speed:	124 mph (198 km/h)
0–60 mph (0–95 km/h):	8.3 sec
Engine type:	In-line four
Displacement:	110 ci (1,809 cc)
Transmission	5-speed manual
Max power:	137 bhp (102 kW) @ 6,000 rpm
Max torque:	191 lb ft (258 Nm) @ 4,000 rpm
Weight:	2,580 lb (1,173 kg)
Economy:	23 mpg (8.2 km/l)

Nissan 300ZX Turbo

When the 300ZX's ancestor, the 240Z, was launched in 1969 it established itself as a diver's machine with plenty of torque, good handling and handsome coupe styling. Over the years that car turned into the early 1980s bloated 300ZX, which even in turbocharged form wasn't a great car. So when Nissan wanted to produce a replacement 300ZX, it started with a clean sheet. The 1990 hi-tech car had a stiffened bodyshell, double wishbone and multi-link rear suspension complemented by four-wheel steering. The engine was state-of-the-art with 24 valves, quad camshafts, variable valve-timing on the inlet cams, sequential fuel injection and direct ignition with a coil for each cylinder. Hybrid Garret T2/T25 twin turbos blew through twin intercoolers for the massive power output. The car wasn't as pure as the original 240Z, but it did provide as much driver involvement.

Top speed:	155 mph (248 km/h)
0–60 mph (0–95 km/h):	5.8 sec
Engine type:	V6
Displacement:	180 ci (2,960 cc)
Transmission	5-speed manual
Max power:	300 bhp (223 kW) @ 6,400 rpm
Max torque:	273 lb ft (369 Nm) @ 3,600 rpm
Weight:	3,485 lb (1,584 kg)
Economy:	14 mpg (5 km/l)

Nissan Sunny GTi-R

The 1980s Sunny was a typical small hatchback, so when Nissan decided they wanted to go rallying with it later that decade, it had to go through severe changes. The monocoque was strengthened to cope and Nissan gave the car a sophisticated 4WD system with a central viscous coupling and limited-slip differentials for remarkable grip. Independent MacPherson strut suspension was fitted all around with a slightly lowered ride height but only understated 14-inch (335mm) alloys. With the body also restrained (just a rear spoiler and hood vent), the GTi-R was a stealthy machine. The all-aluminium engine had twin cams, 16 valves, Bosch electronic multi-point fuel injection and an air-to-air intercooled turbo which was free of lag and gave tremendous torque. The car lasted from 1990 to 1994 and was more a spectacular road car than successful rally car.

Top speed:	134 mph (214 km/h)
0–60 mph (0–95 km/h):	6.1 sec
Engine type:	In-line four
Displacement:	122 ci (1,998 cc)
Transmission	5-speed manual
Max power:	220 bhp (164 kW) @ 6,400 rpm
Max torque:	197 lb ft (267 Nm) @ 4,800 rpm
Weight:	2,750 lb (1,250 kg)
Economy:	21 mpg (7.5 km/l)

Nissan Figaro

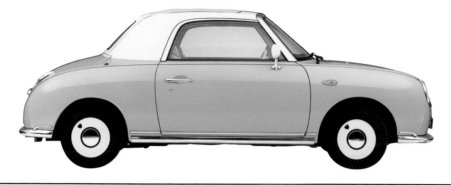

If you passed a Nissan Figaro in the street you could be forgiven for thinking it was a 1950s British sports car. And that's exactly what Nissan was trying to achieve with the model, as British classics have a cult following in Japan. Based on the platform of the Micra, the Figaro was built from 1991 onwards to a limited production of 20,000 units – and if you wanted one, you had to enter a lottery for the chance to get your name on the waiting list. By far the Figaro's cutest feature was its interior – you got chrome-rimmed dials, a smart ivory-coloured three-spoke steering wheel and lots of retro-style chrome rocker switches, while the seats were trimmed in fine quality leather. However it was a very modern car, with a reasonable 987cc engine and an automatic transmission. The sliding soft top could be stored in the boot for open-air motoring.

Top speed:	97 mph (157 km/h)
0–60 mph (0–95 km/h):	11.3 sec
Engine type:	in-line three
Displacement:	60 ci (987 cc)
Transmission:	3-speed auto
Max power:	76 bhp (57 kW) at 6,000 rpm
Max torque:	78 lb ft (106 Nm) at 4,400 rpm
Weight:	1,786 lb (804 kg)
Economy:	35 mpg (12.5 km/l)

Nissan 200SX

With the 300ZX about to end production in 1995, Nissan needed to fill the gap. The 200SX had been in production since 1988 and had steadily been growing in popularity, so they took that car and complete re-vamped it for 1994, adding more performance and improving areas where the old car had been criticized. Formerly a fastback inspired by the Porsche 944, the new car had a coupe body and was also re-styled inside to look more European. The engine was increased in size from 110 to 122ci (1.8 to 2 litres) and featured twin overhead cams, variable intake timing to increase torque at low rpm and a low-pressure turbocharger with intercooler. A MacPherson front and multi-link rear suspension set-up gave fantastic handling, more biased to driver involvement because it used rear-wheel drive. Due to low sales, the car was re-styled with a more aggressive front for 1996.

Top speed:	146 mph (234 km/h)
0–60 mph (0–95 km/h):	7.5 sec
Engine type:	In-line four
Displacement:	122 ci (1,998 cc)
Transmission	5-speed manual
Max power:	197 bhp (147 kW) @ 5,600 rpm
Max torque:	195 lb ft (264 Nm) @ 4,800 rpm
Weight:	2,789 lb (1,268 kg)
Economy:	26 mpg (9.2 km/l)

Nissan Skyline GT-R

The Skyline name goes back to 1955, but it wasn't until the launch of the first GT-R in 1989, by then the eighth-generation model, that it was noticed. By 1994 the car had developed into a street racer and used many high-tech gadgets. It had Super HICAS four-wheel steering which detected steering input, turning rate, the car's speed, the YAW rate and lateral G-forces for the best grip. The four-wheel drive system was computer-controlled for optimum traction, with sensors and a multi-plate clutch at each wheel so no wheelspin occurred. The brakes consisted of 12.8-inch (325mm) and 11.8-inch (299mm) vented discs, all ABS assisted. The engine was equally high-tech with throttle bodies for each cylinder and twin turbos. It could put out far more than was advertised and held the Nurburgring production car lap record for years, taking 8 minutes to cover 14 miles (22 km).

Top speed:	155 mph (248 km/h)
0–60 mph (0–95 km/h):	5.6 sec
Engine type:	In-line six
Displacement:	157 ci (2,568 cc)
Transmission	5-speed manual
Max power:	277 bhp (207 kW) @ 6,800 rpm
Max torque:	271 lb ft (367 Nm) @ 4,400 rpm
Weight:	3,530 lb (1,604 kg)
Economy:	15.7 mpg (5.6 km/l)

NSU Ro 80

If a car is deemed good enough to be named European car of the year, then it's guaranteed sales success, surely? Not in the case of the controversial NSU Ro80. Universally praised at launch for its incredible styling, excellent performance and superb high-speed refinement, the Ro80 was also a technical masterpiece. It was the first volume production car to use a rotary engine, which has fewer moving parts than a conventional unit and offers exceptional smoothness. But unfortunately, the engine hadn't been properly developed, and was prone to failure as the seals between the tips of the rotors and combustion chamber wore out, sometimes as early as 15,000 miles. Later cars were vastly improved in terms of reliability, but NSU's reputation was ruined and sales never recovered. A great shame, because the Ro80 was a brilliant piece of design.

Top speed:	110 mph (178 km/h)
0–60 mph (0–96 km/h):	13.4 sec
Engine type:	Twin-rotary Wankel
Displacement:	61 ci (995 cc)
Transmission:	3-speed semi-automatic
Max power:	115 bhp (86 kW) at 5,500 rpm
Max torque:	121 lb ft (164 Nm) at 4,500 rpm
Weight:	2,695 lb (1,213 kg)
Economy:	15.7 mpg (5.6 km/l)

Olds 88 Holiday Coupe (1956)

One of the best-looking cars of the decade, the Olds Holiday Hardtop Coupe had very clean lines and the popular panoramic windshield which was duplicated at the rear. The 88 model sold close to 400,000 models during 1956 and this has ensured the car's longevity and use even today, albeit often in modified form. The owner of this example has rightly chosen to avoid spoiling the car's original lines, but has made significant changes elsewhere. Modifications such as lowered and uprated suspension help to lower the centre of gravity and improve the handling dramatically, and all is not standard in the drive train either. The owner has swapped in a Rocket J-2 engine with its triple carb set-up, which provides the sort of performance you'd expect more from a modern V8 sedan. The colour is straight from a 1990's Ford Thunderbird and finishes the overall look perfectly.

Top speed:	121 mph (194 km/h)
0–60 mph (0–96 km/h):	8.7 sec
Engine type:	V8
Displacement:	371 ci (6,079 cc)
Transmission	3-speed manual
Max power:	312 bhp (233 kW) @ 4,600 rpm
Max torque:	410 lb ft (556 Nm) @ 2,800 rpm
Weight:	3,771 lb (1,714 kg)
Economy:	11.8 mpg (4.17 km/l)

Oldsmobile Super 88 (1960)

The Super 88 was Oldsmobile's factory hot rod, and over 16,000 were sold in 1960. All GM cars featured a new chassis for 1959 and the Super 88 ran an X-braced steel frame with independent front and live axle rear, all on coil springs. This custom version has been changed by adding lowered and uprated springs from a 1969 Chevy and air shocks at the rear. While the Super 88 left the factory with a torquey 394ci (6.5-litre) V8, this car's has since been replaced by a small-block Chevy for cost and ease of tuning, and the new unit is both lighter and more powerful in addition. Body modifications include the hood being extended and peaked by 2 inches (50mm), the tail lights frenched (sunken) into the body, and the side trim being shaved for a smooth look. The rims are 8 inches (203mm) wide and carry low profiles to bring the handling up to modern standards.

Top speed:	120 mph (192 km/h)
0–60 mph (0–96 km/h):	8.3 sec
Engine type:	V8
Displacement:	350 ci (5,735 cc)
Transmission	3-speed auto
Max power:	345 bhp (257 kW) @ 5,800 rpm
Max torque:	370 lb ft (502 Nm) @ 3,000 rpm
Weight:	3,860 lb (1,754 kg)
Economy:	14 mpg (4.95 km/l)

Oldsmobile Starfire (1961)

Like many cars of the time, the 1961 Oldsmobile Starfire had a bargelike feel thanks to light steering, soft suspension and wallowing ride. But this was exactly how people liked it, as they associated these attributes with quality and prestige. Yet the Starfire was intended to be sporting amongst its rivals and so had a torquey big-block engine. The chassis was stronger than most, featuring a separate frame with four steel triangulated crossmembers to promote torsional rigidity. This worked most noticeably on the convertible, which was particularly solid in construction. Dual exhaust gave away the engine's sporting prowess, which had an improved induction system and hotter camshaft, as well as the Skyrocket's four-barrel carb and high-compression pistons. Through the smooth Hydramatic gearbox, it performed extremely well, making the Starfire very quick for its size and bulk.

Top speed:	120 mph (192 km/h)
0–60 mph (0–96 km/h):	9.0 sec
Engine type:	V8
Displacement:	394 ci (6,456 cc)
Transmission	3-speed auto
Max power:	330 bhp (246 kW) @ 4,600 rpm
Max torque:	440 lb ft (596 Nm) @ 2,800 rpm
Weight:	4,305 lb (1,956 kg)
Economy:	12 mpg (4.24 km/l)

Oldsmobile 4-4-2 W-30 (1966)

Most people associate the 4-4-2 package with the later model Oldsmobiles, but it actually started life in 1964 as an option on the F-85 intermediate model. In the following year, GM limited its engines to 400ci (6.55 litres) in intermediate-sized cars, and as such, the 425 Olds engine had to be destroked to 400ci, and this motor became part of the 4-4-2 package. The F-85 for 1966 was restyled and the 4-4-2 was again available as an option. This car came about in an increased effort to promote the company's presence on the drag strip. For $279 the W-30 package gave the engine a high-lift camshaft, bigger valves and a pair of hoses that gave fresh air to the triple two-barrel Rochester carburettors. Most W-30 models in 1966 were the stripped-out two-door pillared coupes, and as 4-4-2s, featured stiffer rate springs and shocks, plus front and rear anti-roll bars.

Top speed:	130 mph (208 km/h)
0–60 mph (0–96 km/h):	6.0 sec
Engine type:	V8
Displacement:	400 ci (6,554 cc)
Transmission	4-speed manual
Max power:	360 bhp (268 kW) @ 5,000 rpm
Max torque:	440 lb ft (596 Nm) @ 3,600 rpm
Weight:	3,197 lb (1,453 kg)
Economy:	10 mpg (3.54 km/l)

Oldsmobile Tornado (1966)

Normally conservative in its car production, Oldsmobile shocked everyone with the launch of the radical Tornado in 1966. The main reason for the shock was the fact that the car was the first to use front-wheel drive in nearly 30 years, since the 1930s Cord. But the layout set the tone for GM cars for the next two decades. The engine was mounted conventionally and even had the torque converter on the rear, but from there a 2-inch (50mm) Morse chain sent drive to the transmission which went forward to the front differential. At the rear in place of the live axle was a single beam, supported on leaf springs but with four shocks, two mounted conventionally and two sitting horizontally. The layout produced an excellent handling vehicle. Top engine option was the W-34 package which gave out 400bhp (298kW), thanks to a high-lift cam and twin free-flowing exhausts.

Top speed:	124 mph (198 km/h)
0–60 mph (0–96 km/h):	9.9 sec
Engine type:	V8
Displacement:	425 ci (6,964 cc)
Transmission	3-speed auto
Max power:	385 bhp (287 kW) @ 4,800 rpm
Max torque:	475 lb ft (644 Nm) @ 3,200 rpm
Weight:	4,655 lb (2,115 kg)
Economy:	12 mpg (4.25 km/l)

Oldsmobile Hurst/Olds

In the 1960s George Hurst owned a speed shop and in 1968 one of his engineers, Jack 'Doc' Watson, built him a special Oldsmobile 4-4-2. George was so taken by the car he approached Oldsmobile with the idea of building hopped-up cars for them. The result was the Hurst/Olds, and by 1972 the cars were so revered that a convertible was chosen to pace the 56th Indy 500. The pace car was based on the W30 model which was fitted with the 455ci (7.4-litre) big-block engine. This had as much as 500lb ft (677Nm) torque in previous tune, though emissions regulations kept it down for 1972, even with the hood's functional cold-air scoops. A special Hurst shifter sat on the TurboHydramatic three-speed gearbox, which kept it lively. Uprated springs and shocks, with front and rear anti-roll bars, gave the Hurst/Olds well-balanced handling. In typical luxury, the hood was power operated.

Top speed:	132 mph (211 km/h)
0–60 mph (0–95 km/h):	6.8 sec
Engine type:	V8
Displacement:	455 ci (7,456 cc)
Transmission	3-speed auto
Max power:	300 bhp (223 kW) @ 4,700 rpm
Max torque:	410 lb ft (555 Nm) @ 3,200 rpm
Weight:	3,844 lb (1,747 kg)
Economy:	8 mpg (2.8 km/l)

Oldsmobile 4-4-2 modified (1968)

Oldsmobile's 4-4-2 cars demanded respect on the street. They made so much torque even in stock form that they could chirp the tyres in all three gears as they accelerated. But GM's self-imposed limit of 400ci (6.5 litres) on its cars in the 1960s meant that none could use over that amount of cubic inches, at a time when both Ford and Chrysler was going well over that displacement. What the owner of this hot-rodded Oldsmobile has done is get one of the 1970 455ci (7.4-litre) Rocket engines, which came about as restrictions were lifted. It's the biggest and most powerful engine Oldsmobile ever offered, and with a few special mods it makes enough power to push this near 2-ton car to 13-second quarter miles. The rest of the car is pretty much how Oldsmobile intended, with uprated anti-roll bars and stiffer springs for improved handling. Special features include a 1970 Oldsmobile dash.

Top speed:	134 mph (214 km/h)
0–60 mph (0–96 km/h):	6.2 sec
Engine type:	V8
Displacement:	455 ci (7,456 cc)
Transmission	3-speed auto
Max power:	410 bhp (306 kW) @ 5,500 rpm
Max torque:	517 lb ft (701 Nm) @ 3,500 rpm
Weight:	3,890 lb (1,768 kg)
Economy:	9.4 mpg (3.33 km/l)

Oldsmobile Cutlass Rallye 350

Back in the 1960s, insurance was turning into a headache on big-block muscle cars, so manufacturers offered alternatives with small-block engines. The Oldsmobile Rallye 350 was one of the best but was offered only in 1970. It was regular in engineering terms as it was based on the Cutlass, featuring wishbones front and coil-sprung live axle rear with upper and lower control arms. However, front and rear anti-roll bars, heavy duty springs and shocks meant good handling, and more balance, too, with less weight up front than the big-block cars. Also good was performance, with the 350ci (5.7-litre) engine producing plenty of power and impressive torque. All the Rallyes came in Sebring Yellow and featured the functional cold-air intake hood from the W30 big-block model. For 1971 the Rallye was dropped and power on the small-block Cutlass went down to 260bhp (194kW).

Top speed:	122 mph (195 km/h)
0–60 mph (0–95 km/h):	7.0 sec
Engine type:	V8
Displacement:	350 ci (5,735 cc)
Transmission	3-speed auto
Max power:	310 bhp (231 kW) @ 4,600 rpm
Max torque:	390 lb ft (528 Nm) @ 3,200 rpm
Weight:	3,574 lb (1,624 kg)
Economy:	14 mpg (5 km/l)

Oldsmobile 4-4-2 W-30 (1972)

The 1968 and 1969 4-4-2 cars had been awesome but were limited by the GM ban on any engine over 400ci (6.5 litres) in its mid-sized cars. By 1970 they'd lifted that ban and Buick were free to slot in their 455ci (7.4-litre) big-block, which made the new 4-4-2 very quick on the street. As standard, the 4-4-2 had heavy-duty springs and shocks, plus thick front and rear anti-roll bars, but the W-30 also added a glass-fibre hood with cold-air induction, a rear trunk spoiler, an increase in power, in part thanks to an aluminium intake, and 7x14 (178x356mm) Rallye wheels which gave great handling. Typical for Buick, they retained luxury inside the car, with high-backed bucket seats, tuck 'n' roll vinyl, wood veneer and power windows. Performance extras included a Muncie manual gearbox which, though a little tricky to use off the line, didn't sap so much engine power.

Top speed:	129 mph (206 km/h)
0–60 mph (0–96 km/h):	7.1 sec
Engine type:	V8
Displacement:	455 ci (7,456 cc)
Transmission	4-speed manual
Max power:	300 bhp (224 kW) @ 4,700 rpm
Max torque:	410 lb ft (556 Nm) @ 3,200 rpm
Weight:	3,828 lb (1,740 kg)
Economy:	8 mpg (2.83 km/l)

Oldsmobile Vista Cruiser (1972)

Muscle cars were predominantly two-door hardtop coupes or convertibles, but such was the list of options available with many models, that a shrewd and wealthy buyer could come up with something completely different. That's what's happened with this full-specification Oldsmobile wagon, kitted out with a full 4-4-2 W-30 package. Only three of these cars were ever built and the package options have equipped it with heavy-duty suspension, front and rear anti-roll bars, a glass-fibre hood with cold-air intake for the huge 455ci (7,456cc) engine, a Positraction limited-slip differential, and 3.73:1 gears, plus it has the practicality of a family hauler with rear massive luggage space and a roof rack. In this particular car the engine has been fully balanced and blueprinted, meaning it puts out at least the factory-rated figures, but more likely it's actually slightly higher.

Top speed:	120 mph (192 km/h)
0–60 mph (0–96 km/h):	6.5 sec
Engine type:	V8
Displacement:	455 ci (7,456 cc)
Transmission	3-speed auto
Max power:	300 bhp (224 kW) @ 4,700 rpm
Max torque:	410 lb ft (556 Nm) @ 3,200 rpm
Weight:	4,150 lb (1,886 kg)
Economy:	7 mpg (2.48 km/l)

Oldsmobile Hurst Olds (1983)

Some 15 years after the first Hurst Olds, an anniversary collaboration model was debuted. A total of 3,000 were produced and each used a tuned 307ci (5.03-litre) small-block V8, though performance was a long way from the muscle cars available first time around. The cars were based on the mid-sized Cutlass, and though somewhat smaller than the first cars, retained the front-engined rear-drive format. Upgrades to the suspension included thicker anti-roll bars, stiffer springs and shocks, quicker ratio steering, shorter gearing and 7x15-inch (178x381mm) wheels. The emphasis was more on handling than power; the small-block was tuned with Delco electronic ignition, a Rochester carb and low restriction exhaust. Power went from 140bhp (104kW) to 180bhp (134kW). Typically Hurst was the shifter; the triple Lightning Rods meant first, second, and third gears could be selected manually.

Top speed:	120 mph (192 km/h)
0–60 mph (0–96 km/h):	8.4 sec
Engine type:	V8
Displacement:	307 ci (5,030 cc)
Transmission	Hurst 4–speed auto
Max power:	180 bhp (134k kW) @ 4,000 rpm
Max torque:	245 lb ft (332 Nm) @ 3,200 rpm
Weight:	3,535 lb (1,606 kg)
Economy:	17 mpg (6.02 km/l)

Opel GT

The influence of parent company GM's Chevrolet's Corvette on Opel's first sports car was obvious. From its distinctive 'shark nose' to its curvaceous flanks, the Opel GT launched in the summer of 1968 was every inch a scaled-down Corvette. But unlike the Chevy, the GT was made from steel and the bodywork was built in France by coachbuilders Brissoneau and Lotz. Power came from a choice of four-cylinder engines: a budget 1.1-litre version or a far more popular 1.9, offering lively performance and incredibly agile handling. Over 80 per cent of cars built were shipped to the USA, where owners relished the idea of a compact Corvette, but many were subsequently shipped back to Europe, where the GT has a much stronger classic following. Production ended in August 1973 after over 100,000 cars had been sold.

Top speed:	110 mph (178 km/h)
0–60 mph (0–95 km/h):	10.1 sec
Engine type:	in-line four
Displacement:	116 ci (1,897 cc)
Transmission:	4-speed manual/3-speed auto
Max power:	102 bhp (76 kW) at 5,200 rpm
Max torque:	121 lb ft (164 Nm) at 3,600 rpm
Weight:	2,100 lb (945 kg)
Economy:	33 mpg (11.8 km/l)

Opel Manta

With Ford enjoying Europe-wide success with the massively popular Capri, GM decided it was time to answer back. Its reply came at the Paris show in 1970, in the form of the Opel Manta, which, like the Capri, was a smart two-door coupé built on the underpinnings of a humble saloon – in the Opel's case, the Ascona. Also like the Capri, the Manta had a massive choice of engines and trim, meaning finding two identical examples was nigh on impossible. Neat styling touches included a thick C-pillar and Ferrari-style round tail lamps. Fastest and most desirable was the Manta GT/E, introduced in 1973. It came with electronic Bosch fuel injection, auxiliary driving lamps, a matt black bonnet and Rostyle sports wheels. but was not available as a right-hand drive. Later models had rounder styling and a rear hatchback. Almost 500,000 were produced.

Top speed:	102 mph (163 km/h)
0–60 mph (0–95 km/h):	11.2 sec
Engine type:	in-line four
Displacement:	116 ci (1,897 cc)
Transmission:	4-speed manual/3-speed auto
Max power:	102 bhp (76 kW) at 5,200 rpm
Max torque:	121 lb ft (164 Nm) at 3,600 rpm
Weight:	2,150 lb (967 kg)
Economy:	26 mpg (9.3 km/l)

Packard 6/110 (1940)

While most luxury cars were using a V8 or, in some cases, a V12, Packard shunned these for its junior car, the 6/110, the name of which denoted six cylinders and 110bhp (82kW). Packard customers expected smooth, silent and ultra-refined engines, and the 110 still met those requirements whilst being less punchy than the V8 cars. The cars were designed to be luxurious rather than lightweight or sporting, hence most of the time a few extra pounds here or there didn't matter. However, in the case of the X-braces chassis, the crossmember was drilled to save weight. At the front the car was hi-tech for the time, as it had an independent double wishbone set-up with coil springs which gave an excellent ride quality. The rear consisted of a live axle on two longitudinal leaf springs. Other useful extras were air-conditioning, an overdrive gearbox and electrical windshield wipers.

Top speed:	75 mph (120 km/h)
0–60 mph (0–96 km/h):	20.1 sec
Engine type:	V8
Displacement:	245 ci (4,014 cc)
Transmission	3-speed manual
Max power:	100 bhp (74 kW) @ 3,600 rpm
Max torque:	195 lb ft (264 Nm) @ 4,500 rpm
Weight:	3,200 lb (1,454 kg)
Economy:	16 mpg (5.66 km/l)

Packard Caribbean (1954)

Packard were long considered a fairly conservative car manufacturer, but they wanted to change their image in the early 1950s so debuted a show car from the Henney Body Company. The following year it appeared again in show form as the Pan American, and reaction was so strong that Packard decided to go into production with a luxury convertible version, the range-topping Caribbean. The car used a fairly conventional chassis, with twin C-section rails supporting a double wishbone independent front arrangement and a leaf sprung rear axle. Even so, the 1954 had improved power from the Flathead straight-eight engine, plus body touches such as two-tone paint, partially enclosed rear wheels and new tail lights. Inside it featured a colour-coded interior and such luxuries as power steering and a power top which took just 30 seconds to lower.

Top speed:	101 mph (162 km/h)
0–60 mph (0–96 km/h):	15.8 sec
Engine type:	In-line eight
Displacement:	359 ci (5,882 cc)
Transmission	2-speed auto
Max power:	212 bhp (158 kW) @ 4,000 rpm
Max torque:	310 lb ft (420 Nm) @ 2,000 rpm
Weight:	4,400 lb (2,000 kg)
Economy:	17 mpg (6.01 km/l)

Panoz Roadster

Likened to a Shelby Cobra of modern times, the Panoz Roadster used a similar build and borrowed many components from Ford's Mustang. Head of the company Danny Panoz took over the Irish motorsports company in 1994 to create a car which offered pure thrills for driving enthusiasts. The Roadster debuted that same year. Two years later the car had developed further into the AIV (aluminium-intensive vehicle) Roadster, so called as it used aluminium in the chassis, engine and body. The original frame was conceived by racing-car engineer Frank Costin (the 'cos' in Marcos) and consisted of large-bore aluminium tubes with backbone. Race A-arm suspension came in either standard or sport form, while the 13-inch (330mm) ABS disc brakes were straight from the Mustang Cobra and provided the Panoz with astonishing braking power. The engine was Ford's 32-valve unit.

Top speed:	131 mph (210 km/h)
0–60 mph (0–95 km/h):	4.5 sec
Engine type:	V8
Displacement:	281 ci (4,604 cc)
Transmission	5-speed manual
Max power:	305 bhp (227 kW) @ 5,800 rpm
Max torque:	300 lb ft (406 Nm) @ 4,800 rpm
Weight:	2,459 lb (1,117 kg)
Economy:	19.9 mpg (7.1 km/l)

Panther Solo

The Solo was overdue, as it was to be launched in 1985, but Toyota brought out their MR2. As such, the car was delayed until 1989 when a newer, more complex chassis could be produced which incorporated 4WD. A steel floorpan was joined to front and rear subframes while the centre cockpit and bodywork was made in composite material. At the front the car used MacPherson struts, while at the rear double wishbones helped give the great cornering power. The engine was the same Cosworth unit which had been developed for the Sierra, though in the Panther it was mounted behind the driver. Up front was rack and pinion steering while brakes were 10-inch (254mm) ABS-assisted discs. The driving experience was good, but the looks weren't convincing enough and, after just 26 cars had been made, Panther gave in to the tough competition and stopped production in 1990.

Top speed:	142 mph (227 km/h)
0–60 mph (0–95 km/h):	7.0 sec
Engine type:	In-line four
Displacement:	122 ci (1,993 cc)
Transmission	5-speed manual
Max power:	204 bhp (152 kW) @ 6,000 rpm
Max torque:	198 lb ft (268 Nm) @ 4,500 rpm
Weight:	2,723 lb (1,237 kg)
Economy:	22 mpg (7.8 km/l)

Peugeot 504 Cabriolet

If the Peugeot 504 saloon was a durable, tough but ultimately quite ugly workhorse, then the Pininfarina-designed Cabriolet version was its complete opposite. Stunning to look at and rewarding to drive, the 504 Cabriolet was a massively desirable car in its day. Unusually for a car of its era, the roof could be folded completely out of sight and stored under a narrow tonneau cover behind the rear seats, while other neat touches included stylised rear light clusters and discreet Pininfarina badges on the rear flanks. Power came from a 1.8-litre fuel-injected four-cylinder engine, although this was later joined by a 2.6-litre V6 with the arrival of the Mk 2 model, which had individual square headlamps, in 1974. Production of all Cabriolet versions continued until 1983. The saloon remains in production today in Nigeria and Kenya, where the sight of 504s is commonplace.

Top speed:	111 mph (180 km/h)
0–60 mph (0–95 km/h):	12.0 sec
Engine type:	in-line four
Displacement:	120 ci (1,971 cc)
Transmission:	5-speed manual/4-speed auto
Max power:	110 bhp (82 kW) at 5,600 rpm
Max torque:	131 lb ft (178 Nm) at 3,000 rpm
Weight:	2,685 lb (1,208 kg)
Economy:	20 mpg (7.1 km/l)

Peugeot 205 T16

This was one of the infamous Group B rally contenders homologated for the road in the same vein as Ford's RS200 and MG's 6R4, but this car was the most successful rally machine, taking the constructors' championship in 1985 and 1986 and making world champions of Timo Salonnen and Juha Kankkunen. The T16 was a 205 two-door hatchback only in looks, because underneath it used a strong steel monocoque with rear tubular frame holding the transversely mounted engine and gearbox which was accessed by hinging rear bodywork. A centre differential split drive between the front and rear wheels, depending on conditions, from 25:75 to 45:55 front/rear. Double wishbones, anti-roll bars and coil-over-shocks made up the suspension. Powering the car was an all-alloy 16v engine with Bosch fuel injection, dry sump lubrication and an intercooled KKK turbo.

Top speed:	128 mph (205 km/h)
0–60 mph (0–95 km/h):	7.8 sec
Engine type:	In-line four
Displacement:	108 ci (1,775 cc)
Transmission	5-speed manual
Max power:	200 bhp (149 kW) @ 6,750 rpm
Max torque:	188 lb ft (256 Nm) @ 4,000 rpm
Weight:	2,436 lb (1,107 kg)
Economy:	23 mpg (8.2 km/l)

Peugeot 406 Coupe

A rare beauty from a major car manufacture, the 406 Coupe had many people thinking it was from Italy and not France. Therein lies the truth, as the car was styled by Italian design firm Pininfarina. The Coupe was based on the 406 sedan and the top model used the silky 183ci (3-litre) 24-valve V6. The coupe managed to combine excellent street manners and a smooth ride with both sharp steering and fabulous handling. Even with front-wheel-drive, the chassis nonetheless coped with the V6's power exceptionally well, and the car could pull the speed down just as quickly, thanks to anti-lock Brembo disc brakes. Being the flagship model in the 406 range, the Coupe also has luxurious equipment with full electrics inside including seats, a 10-speaker CD system, while externally there were moisture-sensitive wipers and seven colour options unique to the Coupe.

Top speed:	146 mph (234 km/h)
0–60 mph (0–95 km/h):	7.9 sec
Engine type:	V6
Displacement:	180 ci (2,946 cc)
Transmission	5-speed manual
Max power:	194 bhp (145 kW) @ 5,500 rpm
Max torque:	197 lb ft (266 Nm) @ 4,000 rpm
Weight:	3,274 lb (1,488 kg)
Economy:	23 mpg (8.2 km/l)

Plymouth Fury

It was Fury by name and fury by nature for the 1958 two-door from Plymouth, because while it looked like it had more style than substance, it was quicker than most in its day. Furys had always been fitted with Chrysler's biggest powerplant available since their launch in 1956, and the 1957 cars' 318ci (5.2-litre) engine disappeared after a year to be replaced by a more powerful 350ci (5.7-litre) V8. The Fury got the reputation for being Detroit's best-handling car in 1957, and this was mostly down to Chrysler's new-for-1957 'Torsion Air Ride' suspension which had longitudinal torsion bar springs up front. The design was so good it lasted through until 1980 in the Volaire. The car handled well also because it had a low centre of gravity due to the car's low stance. Styling was typical for the era, with high fins on the rear, wraparound front and rear windshields, and pillarless side windows.

Top speed:	122 mph (195 km/h)
0–60 mph (0–95 km/h):	8.0 sec
Engine type:	V8
Displacement:	350 ci (5,735 cc)
Transmission	3-speed auto
Max power:	305 bhp (227 kW) @ 5,000 rpm
Max torque:	370 lb ft (501 Nm) @ 3,600 rpm
Weight:	3,510 lb (1,595 kg)
Economy:	13 mpg (4.6 km/l)

Plymouth Fury modified (1957)

Pro Street cars were really a street offshoot of the late 1970s Pro Stock drag-racing class. Pro Stock cars had to use the standard body of a street-going car, but apart from this many alterations were allowed to make them go quicker. In reality, the standard body was the only part of the race car which made the transition from the street, the rest of the car featuring a full tubular spaceframe in lightweight steel, plus lightweight suspension and a stripped interior with aluminium panels replacing steel wherever possible. This Plymouth is typical of later Pro Street cars, where the emphasis came back to them being streetable, hence it has a stock interior and even stock front suspension, although the powerplant is anything but stock. It's a drag motor barely tamed for street use, but it can catapult this Fury down the quarter-mile in just 7.5 seconds at over 190mph (306km/h).

Top speed:	197 mph (315 km/h)
0–60 mph (0–96 km/h):	2.6 sec
Engine type:	V8
Displacement:	511 ci (8,373 cc)
Transmission	3-speed auto
Max power:	1,485 bhp (1,107 kW) @ 7,200 rpm
Max torque:	1,250 lb ft (1,695 Nm) @ 4,200 rpm
Weight:	3,520 lb (1,600 kg)
Economy:	N/A

Plymouth Savoy 426 (1963)

The early 1960s saw Chrysler, GM and Ford doing battle on both the race tracks and drag strips across America. Chrysler's 1963 weapon of choice was the Super Stock Savoy, a lightweight, race-prepped car with their most powerful engine. Chrysler cleverly did as much to make the Savoy as suitable a drag racer as possible, things like mounting the battery in the trunk to help weight-distribution, and deliberately leaving the torsion bar front suspension set in a high position to aid weight transfer to the rear wheels during acceleration. The engine was tuned to the max, with the wedge-designed chamber taking 13.5:1 compression, and massive valves allowing flow up to 7,500rpm. Dual four-barrel carbs fed the engine, and a free-flowing exhaust was designed to further improve output. The Super Stock was regularly on the winner's podium during its inaugural year.

Top speed:	125 mph (200 km/h)
0–60 mph (0–96 km/h):	5.0 sec
Engine type:	V8
Displacement:	426 ci (6,980 cc)
Transmission	3-speed auto
Max power:	425 bhp (317 kW) @ 5,600 rpm
Max torque:	470 lb ft (637 Nm) @ 4,400 rpm
Weight:	3,400 lb (1,545 kg)
Economy:	7 mpg (2.47 km/l)

Plymouth GTX 426 Hemi

In direct competition to Pontiac's GTO, Plymouth brought out the Hemi-powered GTX. More of a luxury vehicle with an awesome powerplant than out-and-out racer, the car nonetheless dominated on the track or street. The Hemi engine, which had arrived in 1964, was specially de-tuned with a new cam and lower compression (10.25:1) to make it better at low revs, but kept two four-barrel carbs. Chrysler's torsion bar front end was assisted by tubular shocks and an anti-roll bar. The brakes were heavy-duty drums, with 11-inch (279mm) front discs as options. The gearbox had its shift points altered to better suit the Hemi's power, but there was a manual available. Inside, the seats were thickly padded and the dash hinted of what could be achieved with its 150mph (241km/h) speedometer. The GTX was all about speed, because it could easily run the quarter-mile in 13 seconds (12 with racing tyres).

Top speed:	127 mph (203 km/h)
0--60 mph (0–95 km/h):	4.8 sec
Engine type:	V8
Displacement:	426 ci (6,980 cc)
Transmission	3-speed auto
Max power:	425 bhp (317 kW) @ 5,000 rpm
Max torque:	490 lb ft (663 Nm) @ 4,000 rpm
Weight:	3,535 lb (1,606 kg)
Economy:	12 mpg (4.2 km/l)

Plymouth Road Runner

When Chrysler realized muscle-car fans of the 1960s wanted a high-power, no-frills car at reasonable costs, they responded and came up with the Road Runner. The company paid Warner Bros $50,000 to use the cartoon character's name and logo on the car, and although the forecast was sales of 2,500, the Road Runner was such a success it sold 44,589. It used uprated torsion bars at the front and leaf springs on the live axle, which had 3.23:1 gears though higher ratios for better acceleration were available. The engine was the basic cast-iron big-block which had been in production since the 1950s, in this form displacing 383ci (6,276cc) but putting out tremendous torque. The heads, camshaft, and exhaust were all from the 440ci (7.2-litre) motor. Despite its size, the Road Runner in basic form was relatively lightweight and performed well, making it an instant classic.

Top speed:	130 mph (208 km/h)
0–60 mph (0–95 km/h):	6.7 sec
Engine type:	V8
Displacement:	383 ci (6,276 cc)
Transmission	3-speed auto
Max power:	335 bhp (250 kW) @ 5,200 rpm
Max torque:	425 lb ft (575 Nm) @ 3,400 rpm
Weight:	3,400 lb (1,545 kg)
Economy:	12 mpg (4.2 km/l)

Plymouth Barracuda (1967)

Chrysler's pony car was launched two weeks before Ford's Mustang in 1965, and was as good a car to drive, had as many options, but to many eyes didn't quite have the looks. The base engine was the 145bhp (108kW) slant-six 225ci (3,687cc), while the base V8 was a 273ci (4,473cc). The only other choice was the 383ci (6,276cc) which, while nowhere near the Hemi in power, still pumped out a very strong 400lb ft (542Nm) torque. In the sub-3,000lb (1,361kg) Barracuda this gave performance aplenty. It started out on Chrysler's Valiant platform to keep costs down, which meant a torsion bar front and live rear axle on leaf springs. Optional were the Sure Grip limited-slip differential, racing stripes and bucket seats. The following year options got even better with the Formula S package, which added a 4-speed manual transmission, anti-roll bars, dual exhaust and wider tyres.

Top speed:	120 mph (192 km/h)
0–60 mph (0–96 km/h):	7.0 sec
Engine type:	V8
Displacement:	383 ci (6,276 cc)
Transmission	4-speed manual
Max power:	280 bhp (209 kW) @ 4,200 rpm
Max torque:	400 lb ft (542 Nm) @ 2,400 rpm
Weight:	2,940 lb (1,336 kg)
Economy:	12 mpg (4.25 km/l)

Plymouth Duster 340

Towards the end of the 1960s, with muscle cars getting out of reach financially to many buyers, the Chrysler Corporation decided to bring in a new entry-level performance machine. It was achieved by combining the 340ci (5.6-litre) small-block engine with a lightweight, two-door version of their Valiant bodyshell. The result was the 1970 Duster 340 and although regarded as a budget racer, it could easily hold its own against bigger-engined cars. Chrysler's trusted torsion bar front suspension meant it was comfortable (and cheap to produce), and leaf springs out back held the live axle in place, the latter coming with 3.23:1 gears and optional Sure Grip limited-slip differential. The standard transmission was a three-speed manual, though a four-speed was on the option list, as was the Torqueflite automatic. Externally the car had a matt black hood with '340 Wedge' graphic.

Top speed:	120 mph (192 km/h)
0–60 mph (0–95 km/h):	6.0 sec
Engine type:	V8
Displacement:	340 ci (5,571 cc)
Transmission	3-speed auto
Max power:	275 bhp (205 kW) @ 5,000 rpm
Max torque:	340 lb ft (460 Nm) @ 3,200 rpm
Weight:	3,500 lb (1,590 kg)
Economy:	16 mpg (5.7 km/l)

Plymouth Hemi 'Cuda

This model represented one of the best of all Chrysler muscle cars, having a handsome bodystyle and the awesome Hemi V8. In standard form the car used a monocoque centre section with chassis subframes front and rear, but this particular machine has been through what is known as 'back-halving' which means the back half of the car has had its stock suspension cut out to be replaced by a drag-racing four-link and coil-over-shocks. Also, to house the 18.5-inch (470mm) wide Mickey Thompson street/strip racing tyres, the car has been fitted with aluminium 'tubs' for inner arches which means the back seat and most of the trunk space has gone. The engine here has been modified by Dick Landy Industries and output is up by around half over the standard Hemi. A four-speed manual and 4.56:1 geared rear end put it down the quarter-mile in 11 seconds.

Top speed:	137 mph (219 km/h)
0–60 mph (0–95 km/h):	4.3 sec
Engine type:	V8
Displacement:	432 ci (7,079 cc)
Transmission	3-speed auto
Max power:	620 bhp (462 kW) @ 6,500 rpm
Max torque:	655 lb ft (887 Nm) @ 5,100 rpm
Weight:	3,945 lb (1,793 kg)
Economy:	9.4 mpg (3.3 km/l)

Plymouth Road Runner (1970)

The good thing about so many muscle cars is that although nowadays they can be beaten by some modern machines, they can be made to run quicker still thanks to the healthy aftermarket. Often the performance parts available today far exceed the benefits of parts available over 30 years ago, so making more power in these old brutes is not difficult. This Road Runner has gone through an increase in compression and has been fitted with a Mopar Performance camshaft plus high-flow exhaust and electronic ignition, for an extra 65bhp (48kW) over stock. The rear end has wider alloys to fit 12-inch (305mm) wide rubber, which helps traction dramatically. The stock suspension remains, albeit lowered by one spline on the front torsion bars, but otherwise it remains very similar, so retains excellent value too. On the strip it can regularly produce low 13-second quarter miles.

Top speed:	137 mph (219 km/h)
0–60 mph (0–96 km/h):	5.0 sec
Engine type:	V8
Displacement:	440 ci (7,210 cc)
Transmission	3-speed auto
Max power:	440 bhp (328 kW) @ 5,500 rpm
Max torque:	500 lb ft (678 Nm) @ 4,000 rpm
Weight:	3,475 lb (1,579 kg)
Economy:	10.2 mpg (3.61 km/l)

Plymouth Superbird

Plymouth built the 1970 Superbird to win NASCAR. Ford had been dominating the races in the 1960s with their Talladegas and even the 1969 Dodge Daytona couldn't defeat them. So, in 1970 the 'Bird came out with better aerodynamics and enough downforce for 200mph (320km/h). Under the hood the by-then legendary 426ci (6.9-litre) Hemi was fitted. This engine was so-called because of its hemispherical combustion chambers, which meant it could use bigger valves and thus let more fuel in. The Superbird was so fast that it won 21 races and the championship in its first season but NASCAR rules to keep competition even imposed engine restrictions on cars with rear wings, and so it was banned. Plymouth had trouble selling the street versions because of its looks, so many had the nose cones and rear spoilers stripped to be sold as standard Dodge Chargers.

Top speed:	140 mph (224 km/h)
0–60 mph (0–95 km/h):	6.1 sec
Engine type:	V8
Displacement:	426 ci (6,980 cc)
Transmission	4-speed manual
Max power:	425 bhp (317 kW) @ 5,000 rpm
Max torque:	490 lb ft (663 Nm) @ 4,000 rpm
Weight:	3,841 lb (1,745 kg)
Economy:	13.8 mpg (4.9 km/l)

Plymouth 'Cuda 383

The 'Cuda was another handsome example of Chrysler's E-body cars. These shared the front end with the larger B-body models so had room for the biggest V8s on offer in the Dodge/Plymouth stable. The 1971 'Cuda 383 had, as the name suggests, a 383ci (6.3-litre) V8 which shared the block, heads, exhaust and camshaft. Only the crankshaft was different, with less stroke and displacement. Although not the quickest of muscle cars, the 'Cuda 383 nevertheless pumped out massive torque and could still turn in mid-14 second quarter-mile. The chassis was conventional Chrysler, using torsion bars up front which drag racers often raised a couple of splines to transfer weight more to the rear tyres. Stiffer springs all around improved handling and the Sure-Grip Dana axle helped traction. Because of falling demand, the 'Cuda 383 was made for just two years, then axed.

Top speed:	120 mph (192 km/h)
0–60 mph (0–95 km/h):	7.8 sec
Engine type:	V8
Displacement:	383 ci (6,276 cc)
Transmission	3-speed auto
Max power:	300 bhp (224 kW) @ 4,800 rpm
Max torque:	410 lb ft (555 Nm) @ 3,400 rpm
Weight:	3,475 lb (1,579 kg)
Economy:	12 mpg (4.2 km/l)

Plymouth Road Runner (1971)

The original road Runner in 1968 was a runaway success for Chrysler, and when the new car was designed in 1971, it continued with much the same proven options as before. Underneath, it wasn't changed at all, save for a slightly shorter wheelbase and wider track which improved handling response. Also changed was the interior with a much-improved layout of the dash, pistol grip shifter and high back seats which offered better support. The base engine was the 383ci (6.2-litre), but this particular car was fitted with the famous Street Hemi from the factory. Just 55 Road runners made it out of the factory with this engine and for this year the valves got hydraulic lifters in place of slid ones, which made maintenance easier and the engine quieter. This motor, through the standard-issue four speed Muncie gearbox, could push the Road Runner deep into 13-second quarter-mile times.

Top speed:	125 mph (200 km/h)
0–60 mph (0–96 km/h):	5.7 sec
Engine type:	V8
Displacement:	426 ci (6,980 cc)
Transmission	4-speed manual
Max power:	425 bhp (317 kW) @ 4,700 rpm
Max torque:	490 lb ft (664 Nm) @ 3,200 rpm
Weight:	3,640 lb (1,654 kg)
Economy:	11 mpg (3.89 km/l)

Plymouth Road Runner (1973)

Less powerful and less handsome than its predecessors, the later Road Runners nonetheless did have all the right ingredients to turn them into performance machines. The Hemi had been dropped the previous year, but the 440ci (7.2-litre) top engine option came as part of the GTX package and could at least deliver an ultra reliable 280bhp (209kW). This car has been treated to a hefty engine reworking, with an overbore to 446ci (7,308cc), a full balanced rotating assembly, Offenhauser intake and dual Edelbrock four-barrel carburettors. Nitrous adds around 150bhp (112kW) to the set-up to make the car capable of 10-second quarter-miles. To lower power, the rear chassis rails are narrowed so 18.5-inch (470mm) Mickey Thompson tyres can fit under the stock arches. The chassis uses a six-point roll cage, and despite torsion bars up front, a drag-racing set-up is used out back.

Top speed:	135 mph (216 km/h)
0–60 mph (0–96 km/h):	4.9 sec
Engine type:	V8
Displacement:	446 ci (7,308 cc)
Transmission	3-speed auto
Max power:	430 bhp (321 kW) @ 6,200 rpm
Max torque:	515 lb ft (698 Nm) @ 3,800 rpm
Weight:	3,525 lb (1,602 kg)
Economy:	7 mpg (2.48 km/l)

Plymouth Prowler

Massively popular as a concept, the Prowler took three years to make production but when it did, demand was huge, to the point where its $40,000 price quickly doubled on the second-hand market. It was headed by Chrysler design head Tom Gale, himself a hot rodder, who wanted to give the public a new slant on a 1930s hot rod. The idea was to keep it light, with an aluminium chassis to which slender A-arms were attached either end for full independent suspension. At the front, the coilovers were mounted inboard as per race cars, while the rear had a multi-link arrangement. To distribute weight evenly the gearbox was mounted out back. It all added up to neutral handling and supercar cornering. The only slight let down was the power – although the 24v engine was linear in output, it didn't have enough torque to make the Prowler a true hot rod.

Top speed:	140 mph (224 km/h)
0–60 mph (0–95 km/h):	7.0 sec
Engine type:	V6
Displacement:	215 ci (3,523 cc)
Transmission	4–speed auto
Max power:	214 bhp (159 kW) @ 5,850 rpm
Max torque:	221 lb ft @ 3,100 rpm (300 Nm)
Weight:	2,862 lb (1,300 kg)
Economy:	20 mpg (7.08 km/l)

Pontiac Torpedo Eight (1941)

Prior to World War II, Pontiac had long battled with Buick in the intermediate-priced market, but in 1941 it came up with a winner that put it ahead, so much so that the company continued the car's production up until 1948, when many companies were trying to leave their pre-war designs behind. The wide low grille was a sign of things to come in car design, as were the blended-in sealed beam headlamps and tail lights. While still using a separate chassis, the Torpedo did have independent wishbones suspension and telescopic shocks on the rear axle which Pontiac promoted as reducing sway on corners. The engine offered extremely relaxed performance thanks to its low-down torque and almost silent revving. It went well with the car's smooth cruising ability and flat cornering prowess with neutral handling. The interior was a work of art, thanks to hand-made dash details.

Top speed:	88 mph (141 km/h)
0–60 mph (0–96 km/h):	18.9 sec
Engine type:	In-line eight
Displacement:	294 ci (4,817 cc)
Transmission	3-speed manual
Max power:	103 bhp (77 kW) @ 3,500 rpm
Max torque:	190 lb ft (258 Nm) @ 2,200 rpm
Weight:	3,325 lb (1,511 kg)
Economy:	16 mpg (5.66 km/l)

Pontiac Chieftan (1949)

Pontiac was one of the last brands to offer new models following the war, but when it did, it gave them cleaner, more integrated styling with a handsome front fender line which continued down the side to flow into the rear fender. The Chieftan replaced the Torpedo and was lower-slung because of a new chassis design which incorporated an X-brace for improved rigidity. The front suspension featured double wishbones while the rear had leaf springs, but all were designed to be soft to give the Chieftan the best possible ride quality. The straight-eight engine had made its debut in 1933 so was old, but by 1949 it was up in displacement and, thanks to the long-stroke crankshaft, torquey at low revs. The convertible was the most expensive model in 1949, and continues to be the most 'in demand' Pontiac today, with values up to $30,000.

Top speed:	89 mph (142 km/h)
0–60 mph (0–96 km/h):	19.0 sec
Engine type:	In-line eight
Displacement:	249 ci (4,080 cc)
Transmission	4-speed auto
Max power:	104 bhp (76 kW) @ 3,800 rpm
Max torque:	188 lb ft (255 Nm) @ 2,000 rpm
Weight:	3,670 lb (1,668 kg)
Economy:	17 mpg (6.01 km/l)

Pontiac Bonneville (1957)

Performance was fast becoming a major selling point in the 1950s and Pontiac were likely to be left behind if they didn't release a vehicle to capture the public's imagination. In 1956 the company brought in Bunkie Knudson as new General Manager, and he quickly announced the availability of a new model called the Pontiac Bonneville, so called after the Pontiac which made a record-breaking run of 118mph (88km/h) for 24 hours at the Bonneville Salt Flats. The car was launched in 1957 at a NASCAR meeting, where the company showcased its new fuel-injection system. It was only ever a limited edition, with 630 supplied at a very high price, but the customer got a lot for their money. Displacement was up from 316ci (5.2 litres) with a new stroker crank, and the compression ratio was raised. It gave seamless acceleration through the 1956 Hydramatic transmission.

Top speed:	114 mph (182 km/h)
0–60 mph (0–96 km/h):	8.5 sec
Engine type:	V8
Displacement:	370 ci (6,063 cc)
Transmission	3-speed auto
Max power:	315 bhp (235 kW) @ 4,800 rpm
Max torque:	N/A
Weight:	4,285 lb (1,947 kg)
Economy:	14 mpg (4.95 km/l)

Pontiac Bonneville (1959)

Anew style of longer and lower Pontiacs arrived in 1959, and they picked up the brand name from its lacklustre image. The Bonneville felt more sporty to drive compared to older models, thank to its lower seating position and ultra powerful engine. To enhance the car's low stance, the wheels were down in size to 14 inches (355mm) and other styling touches included the now-famous Pontiac split grille, which has been virtually every model from the company since. While the main concentration at the time was on engine power and outward style, Pontiac did have one advance on the suspension and that was the use of coil springs at the rear instead of semi-elliptical units, which improved the ride significantly. While this car had the powerful 389ci (6.3-litre) unit, there was a Tri-Power set-up with three carbs to boost output to 345bhp (257kW), for a sub 7-second 0–60mph (0–96km/h) sprint.

Top speed:	120 mph (192 km/h)
0–60 mph (0–96 km/h):	8.1 sec
Engine type:	V8
Displacement:	389 ci (6,374 cc)
Transmission	3-speed auto
Max power:	300 bhp (224 kW) @ 4,600 rpm
Max torque:	450 lb ft (610 Nm) @ 2,800 rpm
Weight:	4,233 lb (1,924 kg)
Economy:	10 mpg (3.54 km/l)

Pontiac Bonneville (1960)

The new long and lower Bonnevilles had been introduced in 1959 and were acclaimed for their slender, sporty looks and good road-holding. They carried on in similar mechanical guise for 1960, but this was the only year that, styling-wise, the Pontiacs didn't have the split grille. Underneath, the car used a X-braced chassis with unequal-length wishbone front suspension and a live rear axle. Changes were made to the rear suspension with the attachments points of the upper-control arms raised and given stiffer bushings to better locate the axle. Other changes to the drive train included a redesign of the bellhousing to lower the transmission tunnel and give an inch extra room inside the car. The standard engine was again the 389ci (6.3-litre) as in 1959, but the top option was the 10.5:1 compression unit which ran with a high-lift camshaft, less restrictive heads and a Tri-Power intake.

Top speed:	113 mph (181 km/h)
0–60 mph (0–96 km/h):	9.7 sec
Engine type:	V8
Displacement:	389 ci (6,374 cc)
Transmission	3-speed auto
Max power:	318 bhp (237 kW) @ 4,600 rpm
Max torque:	420 lb ft (569 Nm) @ 2,800 rpm
Weight:	4,070 lb (1,850 kg)
Economy:	12 mpg (4.24 km/l)

Pontiac Ventura (1961)

Pontiac were at the forefront of muscle-car production, and nowhere was this more evident than with models such as the Ventura. And being one of the good-looking 'bubble top' cars produced at the time – so called because of their thin pillars and large glass area – the car is in demand as a classic today. It also has Pontiac's famous split grille, which is still used to the present day. This example is barely different from stock, with simple but effective changes to the rolling stock to improve handling and looks. Where it has seen dramatic change is under the hood, with a 1969 400ci (298kW) GTO engine fitted and tuned up for more power. The Ram Air option motor has been fitted with a free-flowing exhaust and the heads have been ported. This puts it in the 14-second range for the quarter-mile, enough to surprise, thanks to the car's sneakily stock appearance.

Top speed:	124 mph (198 km/h)
0–60 mph (0–96 km/h):	6.5 sec
Engine type:	V8
Displacement:	400 ci (6,554 cc)
Transmission	3-speed auto
Max power:	380 bhp (283 kW) @ 5,500 rpm
Max torque:	450 lb ft (610 Nm) @ 3,900 rpm
Weight:	3,687 lb (1,676 kg)
Economy:	11.8 mpg (4.17 km/l)

Pontiac Tempest Le Mans (1962)

Of the three compact cars GM introduced in 1960, the Tempest was the most radical, with its all-independent suspension. It used a rear mounted transaxle for near-perfect weight distribution, which produced exceptional handling for great driver reward. The other advantage with the Tempest was its weight. Although in standard form it came with a 194ci (3.2-litre) slant four engine, it was best with Buick's all-aluminium V8 (later sold to Rover in the UK) which was virtually the same weight as the four-cylinder unit and helped put the Tempest's overall weight under 3000lb (130kg), almost unheard of for a muscle car of that era. The Tempest used Pontiac's famous split grille, albeit in a slightly subdued fashion for this 1962 year, and inside was roomy for a compact, thanks to the flat floor through the lack of a transmission tunnel.

Top speed:	115 mph (184 km/h)
0–60 mph (0–96 km/h):	9.9 sec
Engine type:	V8
Displacement:	215 ci (3,523 cc)
Transmission	3-speed auto
Max power:	190 bhp (142 kW) @ 4,800 rpm
Max torque:	240 lb ft (325 Nm) @ 2,600 rpm
Weight:	2,955 lb (1,343 kg)
Economy:	17 mpg (6.01 km/l)

Pontiac GTO 1964

This model is often referred to as the one which started the muscle-car wars, and it combined a 1964 Tempest body with a 389ci (6.3-litre) V8 to be the 'GTO'. In creating the new model, designers got around a GM ruling which limited its intermediate cars to a maximum engine size of 330ci (5.4 litres). Thus the trend for shoehorning big engines into medium cars began, lasting for almost 10 years before the fuel crisis of 1973. The GTO had a thicker anti-roll bar, stiffer springs, uprated shocks and higher speed rated tyres. The top-option gearbox was the four-speed 'Muncie' that made the most of the huge power output. Drum brakes weren't the greatest attribute of the GTO, but they could be ordered with sintered lining, which helped a little. The biggest advantage was the weight, some 300lb (136kg) lighter than most later muscle cars, making the car very quick off the line.

Top speed:	120 mph (192 km/h)
0–60 mph (0–95 km/h):	6.6 sec
Engine type:	V8
Displacement:	389 ci (6,374 cc)
Transmission	4-speed manual
Max power:	348 bhp (259 kW) @ 4,900 rpm
Max torque:	428 lb ft (579 Nm) @ 3,600 rpm
Weight:	3,126 lb (1,420 kg)
Economy:	14 mpg (5 km/l)

Pontiac Le Mans (1964)

Without the original factory-backed race cars' class constraints, modern drag racers have been able to develop muscle cars further still, and this Le Mans is a prime example. It uses some of the original frame but with the rear rails narrowed in order to fit in the huge racing slicks and custom-fabricated coilover damper suspension and adjustable four-bar locating arms. At the front all unnecessary steel has been stripped out which means no inner fenders. The interior too has been stripped completely, with painted metal left for the floor and door panels. Two lightweight racing bucket seats stand alone inside. The engine comprises a 400ci (6.6-litre) block with 455ci (7.5-litre) crank and Super Duty con-rods, plus 12.5:1 pistons and a huge carburettor that can flow 1150 cubic feet (32 cubic metres) of air per minute. Nitrous oxide adds 150bhp (112kW) while racing.

Top speed:	159 mph (254 km/h)
0–60 mph (0–96 km/h):	3.8 sec
Engine type:	V8
Displacement:	449 ci (7,357 cc)
Transmission	3-speed auto
Max power:	520 bhp (388 kW) @ 5,500 rpm
Max torque:	524 lb ft (710 Nm) @ 4,000 rpm
Weight:	2,501 lb (1,137 kg)
Economy:	5.9 mpg (2.08 km/l)

Pontiac Catalina 2+2 (1965)

As the 1960s went on, mid-sized cars became increasingly popular as they were lighter and therefore responded better to modifications. However, the full-sized machines still had their fans, and that's why Pontiac persevered with their Catalina. The 2+2 performance package included uprated suspension comprising stiffer springs and shocks and thicker front anti-roll bar, a Safe-T-Track differential, and an uprated 421ci (6.8-litre) engine available in three states of tune. The first, rated at 338bhp (252kW), had a single four-barrel carb, while the other two had three-two barrel 'Tri-Power' carb manifolds. These gave out 356bhp (265kW) and 376bhp (280kW), the latter higher due to a less restrictive exhaust system. Though most people regard the GTO as Pontiac's ultimate muscle car, the Catalina remains one of the finest and most in demand.

Top speed:	125 mph (200 km/h)
0–60 mph (0–96 km/h):	7.0 sec
Engine type:	V8
Displacement:	421 ci (6,898 cc)
Transmission	4-speed manual
Max power:	376 bhp (280 kW) @ 5,500 rpm
Max torque:	461 lb ft (625 Nm) @ 3,600 rpm
Weight:	3,748 lb (1,703 kg)
Economy:	12 mpg (4.24 km/l)

Pontiac GTO (1966)

Borrowing a Ferrari name, Pontiac created the GTO (Grand Turismo Omologato) and by 1966 it had more power than anything Italian. The 389ci (6.4-litre) engine gave enough torque to overpower the rear tyres with a mere touch of the throttle, even when fitted with the optional Safe-T-Track limited-slip differential. For 1966 the GTO, having been available since 1964 as a high-performance option, had a new larger and more curvy 'Coke bottle' body style, which improved looks while retaining an aggressive stance. The 389ci (6.4-litre) was standard issue on all GTOs from 1964 to 1967, and to start with the package even had an optional Tri-Power set-up, though multi-carbs were outlawed by GM in mid–1966. Performance parts like the 4.33:1 optional gears and a four-speed Muncie transmission were the things to have, and this model has them all, plus the style of a convertible.

Top speed:	125 mph (200 km/h)
0–60 mph (0–96 km/h):	6.2 sec
Engine type:	V8
Displacement:	389 ci (6,374 cc)
Transmission	4-speed manual
Max power:	360 bhp (268 kW) @ 5,200 rpm
Max torque:	424 lb ft (575 Nm) @ 3,600 rpm
Weight:	3,555 lb (1,615 kg)
Economy:	14 mpg (4.96 km/l)

Pontiac Grand Prix (1967)

The Grand Prix was Pontiac's top-of-the-line car, and was a sales sensation for the company. While they already had a strong muscle image from the GTO, they built the big Grand Prix more for luxury, but it accelerated like a muscle car, thanks to the tuned 400ci (6,554cc) motor under the hood. The luxury was emphasized further with the ride quality, which was possible through coil springs at each corner and a separate chassis. The drum brakes were self-adjusting, but there was also an option of discs up front to stop the 400lb (181kg) leviathan. Externally the car was smoothly styled with a 'Coke bottle' rear which set the fashion that lasted into the 1970s, plus concealed headlights in the trademark Pontiac split grille. Inside there was the choice of three-speed auto or four-speed fully synchronized manual transmission and a luxury leather bench seat, plus wood dash trim.

Top speed:	110 mph (176 km/h)
0–60 mph (0–96 km/h):	9.4 sec
Engine type:	V8
Displacement:	400 ci (6,554 cc)
Transmission	3-speed auto
Max power:	350 bhp (261 kW) @ 5,000 rpm
Max torque:	440 lb ft (596 Nm) @ 3,200 rpm
Weight:	4,005 lb (1,820 kg)
Economy:	15 mpg (5.34 km/l)

Pontiac GTO (1968)

Using what was previously a Ferrari model name, Pontiac created the GTO (Grand Turismo Omologato) and by 1968 it had more power than anything Italian and the handling to match. The torquey 400ci (6.6-litre) engine meant the Safe-T-Track limited-slip differential was essential. For 1968 the GTO, having been out since 1964, had a new body style which improved looks while retaining an aggressive look. It was also slighter shorter in the wheelbase than its predecessor, but kept the separate chassis and body. At the front it used unequal-length A-arms, while the live rear axle used trailing arms and coil springs with separate shocks. Three versions of the engine were available in 1968, the base having 350bhp (261kW), the second featuring a higher lift cam and 360bhp (268kW), and third, the Ram Air II with improved heads and hood cold-air feed, giving 366bhp (273kW).

Top speed:	120 mph (192 km/h)
0–60 mph (0–95 km/h):	6.4 sec
Engine type:	V8
Displacement:	400 ci (6,554 cc)
Transmission:	5-speed manual
Max power:	360 bhp (268 kW) @ 5,400 rpm
Max torque:	445 lb ft (602 Nm) @ 3,800 rpm
Weight:	3,506 lb (1,595 kg)
Economy:	11 mpg (3.9 km/l)

Pontiac GTO Judge

Launched in Carousel Red only paint with 'The Judge' logos on the hood and fenders, you couldn't miss this new GTO. Looks were backed up with a regular 350bhp (261kW) 400ci (6.6-litre) on the base model,while the best Judges got the 366bhp (273kW) Ram Air III engine. Also provided with the car was heavy-duty suspension with stiffer springs and shocks. The standard gear ratio in the rear axle was 3.90:1 with a Safe-T-Track differential, though steeper gears for better acceleration could be ordered. Externally the car was one of the first to use energy-absorbing fenders which would cope with any low-speed knocks. The car was raved about for its interior style, with a very clear dash layout and a useful hood-mounted rev counter. The buckets seats gave good support and the Hurst shifter could bang the four-speed Muncie gearbox into gear without missing a shift.

Top speed:	123 mph (197 km/h)
0–60 mph (0–95 km/h):	6.2 sec
Engine type:	V8
Displacement:	400 ci (6,555 cc)
Transmission:	4-speed manual
Max power:	366 bhp (273 kW) @ 5,400 rpm
Max torque:	445 lb ft (603 Nm) @ 3,600 rpm
Weight:	3,503 lb (1,592 kg)
Economy:	11 mpg (3.9 km/l)

Pontiac Firebird H.O.

The Pontiac Firebird was not regarded as a major contender in the muscle-cars wars, being overshadowed by the Camaro from which it was derived. Arriving in 1968, the base Firebird came with manual steering and brakes, though most buyers opted for power versions of both, which totally transformed the car. Inside it used buckets seats and extra deep-set gauges for a sporty feel. The H.O. model wasn't the most powerful engine available (the 400ci/6.5-litre took that crown) but the 350ci (5.7-litre) did have a long duration camshaft, 10.25:1 compression and big valves to achieve its impressive power. While it was barely slower than the bigger-engined car, it was much cheaper, so was a good seller. The four-speed manual was the gearbox to have, while at the rear the 10-bolt, leaf-sprung axle could be ordered with the Safe-T-Track limited-slip differential and a variety of gear ratios.

Top speed:	114 mph (182 km/h)
0-60 mph (0–95 km/h):	6.9 sec
Engine type:	V8
Displacement:	350 ci (5,735 cc)
Transmission	4-speed manual
Max power:	320 bhp (239 kW) @ 5,000 rpm
Max torque:	380 lb ft (514 Nm) @ 3,400 rpm
Weight:	3,740 lb (1,700 kg)
Economy:	12 mpg (4.2 km/l)

Pontiac Trans Am (1969)

The Trans Am was Pontiac's sporty answer to the Camaro, and was the most sought-after of the all the Firebirds. The sheet metal was based on the Camaro, but a new nose with split grille and double headlamps either side ensured the looks remained pure Pontiac. The car was named after the American race series, so came with all the right components fitted to make it a street racer, uprated springs and shocks and more powerful brakes being just a some of the parts. The owner of this car has gone one step further by fitting rear discs brakes from a 1979 model Trans Am, and there are wide 7x15 inch (178x381mm) rims with 235/60 tyres to take full advantage of the new powertrain. Long gone is the original small-block, in favour of a late-model Tuned Port Injection small-block, which gives as much power but with more miles per gallon and better manners.

Top speed:	140 mph (224 km/h)
0–60 mph (0–96 km/h):	6.8 sec
Engine type:	V8
Displacement:	350 ci (5,735 cc)
Transmission	3-speed auto
Max power:	250 bhp (186 kW) @ 5,000 rpm
Max torque:	295 lb ft (400 Nm) @ 3,650 rpm
Weight:	3,649 lb (1,658 kg)
Economy:	15.7 mpg (5.56 km/l)

Pontiac GTO Judge (1971)

Pontiac were one of the other manufacturers holding onto the muscle era as long as they possibly could before the fuel-conscious early 1970s took over. The GTO name had started when John DeLorean installed a 389ci (6.3-litre) big-block into Pontiac's intermediate Tempest sedan, and the car reached its peak in 1969, but wasn't about to got out without a bang come 1971. The car got a slight restyle around the nose section with a more protruding grilled surround, and used large vents at the front of the hood for the Ram Air intake. The car changed little in the suspension department except for revalved shocks, but wider alloy wheels at 7x14 inches (178x356mm) helped the handling. The interior had individual bucket seats and optional was a hood-mounted rev counter. The new engine was the 455ci (7.4-litre), which lost power through low compression to comply with emissions.

Top speed:	108 mph (173 km/h)
0-60 mph (0–96 km/h):	7.0 sec
Engine type:	V8
Displacement:	455 ci (7,456 cc)
Transmission	3-speed auto
Max power:	335 bhp (250 kW) @ 4,800 rpm
Max torque:	412 lb ft (558 Nm) @ 3,200 rpm
Weight:	3,894 lb (1,770 kg)
Economy:	10.2 mpg (3.61 km/l)

Pontiac GP Hurst SSJ (1972)

The looks might have been a long way from the muscle Pontiacs of the 1960s, but the 1972 Grand Prix at least had some of those classics' traits, thanks to the front V8 and rear-wheel-drive format. This was the third year for Hurst's involvement with the Grand Prix, and their additions included heavy-duty suspension and power front disc brakes, plus on the majority of cars, a Hurst shifted auto gearbox. The standard engine was the 400ci (6,554cc) D-port unit, underrated at 250bhp (186kW) with a dual plane intake and four-barrel carb. Buyers could opt for the mighty 455ci (7.4-litre) which was modified by Hurst Performance Research. It received blueprinting, a more aggressive camshaft and reworked cylinder heads, hence though rated at 250bhp (186kW), it was more like 350bhp (261kW). The interior had a curved dash facing the driver and centre console splitting high-back bucket seats.

Top speed:	125 mph (200 km/h)
0–60 mph (0–96 km/h):	8.0 sec
Engine type:	V8
Displacement:	455 ci (7,456 cc)
Transmission	3-speed auto
Max power:	250 bhp (186 kW) @ 3,600 rpm
Max torque:	375 lb ft (508 Nm) @ 2,400 rpm
Weight:	3,898 lb (1,771 kg)
Economy:	8 mpg (2.83 km/l)

Pontiac Formula 400 (1973)

Many manufacturers had given up with their muscle cars with the advent of stringent emissions laws, but Pontiac persevered with their Firebird and Trans Am models, de-tuning the engines where necessary. The thing was, while bhp was easy to limit with intake and fueling restrictions, torque often survived the changes unaffected, so the cars were still quick off the mark and gave drivers a good 'seat of the pants' feel. This made the Firebirds popular for those who either didn't mind paying extra for fuel or for people who simply wanted them as a second car. They still handled well with unitary construction and uprated double wishbone front suspension (with anti-roll bar) plus a leaf sprung live rear axle, and 11-inch (280mm) front discs helped too, as did 7x14-inch (178x356mm) five-spoke steel wheels. The car kept its energy-absorbing front fender, and even had a cold-air intake hood.

Top speed:	118 mph (188 km/h)
0–60 mph (0–96 km/h):	9.4 sec
Engine type:	V8
Displacement:	400 ci (6,554 cc)
Transmission	3-speed auto
Max power:	230 bhp (172 kW) @ 4,400 rpm
Max torque:	277 lb ft (375 Nm) @ 3,200 rpm
Weight:	3,766 lb (1,711 kg)
Economy:	12.4 mpg (4.39 km/l)

Pontiac Grand Ville (1974)

Pontiac, like many manufacturers, had reduced the number of performance models drastically by the mid-1970s. It had also reduced the number of convertibles it produced down to just one car (from six in the mid-1960s): the Grand Ville. Car peaked in size in the mid-1970s and the Grand Ville was no exception, being just short of 19ft (5.8m) in length and 6.5ft (2m) wide. For the first time ever the cars were fitted with radial tyres, a major development in road holding and safety, and as such the Grand Ville got RTS (Radial Tuned Suspension). Another first was the 5mph (8km/h) fenders which could absorb impacts up to the that speed, while a final bow was the use of leaded fuel which at least gave a modest horsepower increase to the 455ci (7.4-litre) engine. Luxury equipment included the power hood, double bench for six passengers, wood veneer and sound system.

Top speed:	124 mph (198 km/h)
0–60 mph (0–96 km/h):	7.8 sec
Engine type:	V8
Displacement:	455 ci (7,456 cc)
Transmission	3-speed auto
Max power:	250 bhp (186 kW) @ 4,000 rpm
Max torque:	370 lb ft (502 Nm) @ 2,800 rpm
Weight:	4,476 lb (2,034 kg)
Economy:	11 mpg (3.89 km/l)

Pontiac Trans Am SD455 (1974)

If you wanted a muscle car of the old school in 1974, there was only one
manufacturer who you could go to, and that was Pontiac. They offered the
SD455 (Super Duty) in limited numbers (just 953 were made) but the car was built
almost as if the fuel crisis had never happened. Underneath it used a raised
transmission tunnel, so the body could be mounted lower on the suspension, thus
improving the centre of gravity for better handling, and the drive train was pure
muscle, thanks to a 455ci (7.4-litre) with four-bolt main caps, forged pistons and a
massive 800cfm Quadrajet carburettor. Inside it still looked 1970s, but it still
showed the way dash layout was going, with a flat aluminium plate housing
several dials for maximum driver information, plus a sporty three-spoke wheel.
The car's performance meant the limited-slip differential and front disc brakes
were much needed.

Top speed:	132 mph (211 km/h)
0–60 mph (0–96 km/h):	5.4 sec
Engine type:	V8
Displacement:	455 ci (7,456 cc)
Transmission	3-speed auto
Max power:	310 bhp (231 kW) @ 4,000 rpm
Max torque:	390 lb ft (529 Nm) @ 3,600 rpm
Weight:	3,655 lb (1,661 kg)
Economy:	13 mpg (4.60 km/l)

Pontiac Can Am (1977)

Refusing to let go of the notion that people liked their muscle cars, Pontiac developed the Cam Am in 1977 by dropping their 400ci (6,554cc) V8 engine into the Le Mans. The limited-edition car had just 3,177 models made, but they were great performers in their day. While the suspension was conventional, coming from the Le Mans, the Can Am received the RTS (Radial Tuned Suspension) package, and this included stiffer springs and shocks, front and rear anti-roll bars, and steel belted radial tyres. If sold in California the engine was the 185bhp (138kW) 403ci (6.6-litre) Oldsmobile V8, though everywhere else got the W-72 code high-output 400ci (6.5-litre) Pontiac V8 with dual-plane intake manifold and four-barrel carburettor. Inside, the dash housed multiple circular gauges and enclosed the driver. The three-spoke wheel and bucket seats boasted sporting intentions.

Top speed:	120 mph (192 km/h)
0–60 mph (0–96 km/h):	8.6 sec
Engine type:	V8
Displacement:	400 ci (6,554 cc)
Transmission	3-speed auto
Max power:	200 bhp (149 kW) @ 3,600 rpm
Max torque:	325 lb ft (440 Nm) @ 2,400 rpm
Weight:	4,140 lb (1,881 kg)
Economy:	11 mpg (3.89 km/l)

Pontiac Trans Am (1978)

Displaying a large Firebird hood decal meant the 1978 Trans Am had to live up to expectations. The car had already satisfied owners with its handling, which it was praised for back in 1970, but the owner of this car has gone further still to enhance the cornering potential with uprated gas shocks, larger anti-roll bars front and rear, plus lowering springs. The brakes have a rear-disc upgrade and all are now vented. The engine is Pontiac's awesome big-block 455ci (7,456cc), tuned here with an Edelbrock intake, Crane high-lift camshaft, high-flow carburettor and dual exhaust with performance mufflers. The wheels are 8x16-inch (203x406mm) cross-spoke alloys with 255/50ZR rated tyres, a nice compromise between ride quality and handling. A front spoiler with air dam helps airflow over the car instead of underneath, while the rear spoiler provides downforce and stability at speed.

Top speed:	125 mph (200 km/h)
0–60 mph (0–96 km/h):	5.1 sec
Engine type:	V8
Displacement:	455 ci (7,456 cc)
Transmission	3-speed auto
Max power:	350 bhp (261 kW) @ 4,800 rpm
Max torque:	360 lb ft (488 Nm) @ 3,300 rpm
Weight:	3,511 lb (1,596 kg)
Economy:	9 mpg (3.19 km/l)

Pontiac Trans Am Anniversary (1979)

After almost axing the Trans Am in 1972, Pontiac decided to continue with it through the fuel conscious mid-1970s, and eventually they had a best seller late in that decade. The car shown was the 10th Anniversary model, all in silver and featuring the W72 400ci (6.6-litre) V8 plus four-speed Borg Warner Super T10 manual transmission. Though the Trans Am had been redesigned a year before, it featured much the same suspension layout but on the Anniversary model a special upgrade of the springs and shocks took care of cornering, along with 7x15-inch (178x381mm) Turbine alloys and wide radial tyres. Braking was also exceptional, with the four-wheel discs being power assisted. The interior looked ultra-modern for the time, having a machined aluminium dash with seven sport gauges, drilled three-spoke steering wheel, and silver vinyl high-back bucket seats.

Top speed:	125 mph (200 km/h)
0–60 mph (0–96 km/h):	7.0 sec
Engine type:	V8
Displacement:	400 ci (6,554 cc)
Transmission	4-speed manual
Max power:	220 bhp (164 kW) @ 4,000 rpm
Max torque:	320 lb ft (434 Nm) @ 2,800 rpm
Weight:	3,551 lb (1,614 kg)
Economy:	12 mpg (4.25 km/l)

Pontiac Firebird Turbo T/A (1980)

While it looked like the Anniversary model, the Turbo T/A was very different indeed as it used a turbocharged V8 under the hood. The car was deemed good enough to pace that year's Indianapolis 500, and around 7,500 replicas made it on to the road. A WS6 suspension package was optional, and this gave recalibrated shocks and stiffer springs, as was a four-wheel disc brake set-up, which many buyers went for. Pontiac's 400ci (6.5-litre) and Oldsmobiles 403ci (6.6-litre) engines were proving too tough to get through emission, so engineers started out with a 401ci (6.5-litre) from the station wagons, then bolted a turbo to it, lowering the compression in the process to aid reliability. While it took some getting over the lag, the car was great once up to speed. An all-time high in sales was reached this year with 117,109 Trans Am being sold.

Top speed:	116 mph (186 km/h)
0–60 mph (0–96 km/h):	8.2 sec
Engine type:	V8
Displacement:	301 ci (4,932 cc)
Transmission	3-speed auto
Max power:	210 bhp (157 kW) @ 4,000 rpm
Max torque:	345 lb ft (468 Nm) @ 2,000 rpm
Weight:	3,673 lb (1,669 kg)
Economy:	16 mpg (5.66 km/l)

Pontiac Fiero Formula (1988)

Conceived as competition to the forthcoming MR2 from Toyota, Pontiac's Fiero was launched in 1983 and was well designed, and proved a good seller for the company. It even paced the Indianapolis 500 in 1985, which inspired the launch of the GT model with low drag nose from the pace car. The Fiero used mainly parts-bin components, with a Chevrolet Chevette front strut set-up and the front subframe, including transaxle and engine mountings, from GM's X-body cars but adapted for the rear. This planted the engine mid-ships and gave the Fiero great handling. Just two motors were available, the first being the 'Iron Duke' four pot, so called because it was all-iron and ruggedly reliable, and the GM corporate 60-degree V6. The GT got this engine and a whole lot more, but the Formulas were the same in the drive train and suspension, yet slightly faster and cheaper.

Top speed:	120 mph (192 km/h)
0-60 mph (0–96 km/h):	7.4 sec
Engine type:	V6
Displacement:	173 ci (2,834 cc)
Transmission	5-speed manual
Max power:	135 bhp (101 kW) @ 5,200 rpm
Max torque:	170 lb ft (230 Nm) @ 3,600 rpm
Weight:	2,778 lb (1,262 kg)
Economy:	26 mpg (9.20 km/l)

Pontiac Turbo Trans Am (1989)

Pontiac wanted a car to commemorate the first Trans Am put into production in 1969. It had to be powerful, it had to be ground-breaking and, most of all, it had to be a driver's machine. They came up with the Turbo Trans Am, loaded with electrics inside plus a wealth of performance extras. All these 20th anniversary models came with the WS6 handling package which consisted of uprated shocks and springs plus fatter anti-roll bars front and rear. Also fitted was a torque arm for better rear tyre grip and Panhard rod to locate the axle in a sideways direction, both of which benefited the car because it could pull 0.89g in cornering. The powerplant was straight from the not-long departed Buick Grand National and used a Garrett turbo, air-to-air intercooler and electronic ignition for massive power which could only be compared to a big V8, though the V6 was much lighter.

Top speed:	157 mph (251 km/h)
0–60 mph (0–95 km/h):	5.1 sec
Engine type:	V6
Displacement:	231 ci (3,785 cc)
Transmission	4-speed auto
Max power:	255 bhp (190 kW) @ 4,000 rpm
Max torque:	340 lb ft (460 Nm) @ 2,800 rpm
Weight:	3,406 lb (1,548 kg)
Economy:	27 mpg (9.6 km/l)

Pontiac Firebird GTA (1991)

The GTA stood for Gran Turismo Americano and was a development of the original Pontiac GTO name which meant so much to muscle-car enthusiasts. Hence, the GTA for 1987–1992 had to be good. With the 350ci (5.7-litre) high-output engine, it finally got the power that early-1980s versions had lacked, and once again represented a great muscle machine which was quick in a straight line, and also was economical and could handle with the best supercar exotica. Although still a live axle chassis, the rear end was held in check well, thanks to a torque arm, Panhard rod and lower trailing arms. Being on the same platform as the Camaro meant MacPherson struts up front, and disc brakes were fitted all around, completing the very axle package. The engine got Tuned Port Injection which increased power while retaining impressive mpg, considering the car's potential.

Top speed:	150 mph (240 km/h)
0–60 mph (0–96 km/h):	6.7 sec
Engine type:	V8
Displacement:	350 ci (5,735 cc)
Transmission	4-speed auto
Max power:	240 bhp (179 kW) @ 4,400 rpm
Max torque:	340 lb ft (461 Nm) @ 3,200 rpm
Weight:	3,519 lb (1,599 kg)
Economy:	18 mpg (6.37 km/l)

Pontiac Firebird Firehawk

Ex-drag racer Ed Hamburger formed his company Street Legal Performance (SLP) in 1987 and negotiated a deal with GM whereby he'd design a performance package for the Pontiac Firebird. The first SLP 'Firehawk' hit the market in 1992 and by 1995 it was using the 315bhp (235kW) LT1 engine in coupe and convertible bodies. In 1998 this new Firehawk was revealed, featuring the Corvette's all-alloy LS1 engine, only available with the six-speed manual, as this was the only gearbox which could cope with the power. SLP options offered Bilstein Ultra Performance Suspension which got the Firehawk to 0.91g on the skidpad. The styling cleverly incorporated heat-extracting vents in the top of the hood with functional ram air nostrils in the nose. The 9x17-inch (229x432mm) alloys hid 11.8-inch (299mm) vented discs, ABS assisted and completing the car as a devastating all–rounder.

Top speed:	157 mph (251 km/h)
0–60 mph (0–95 km/h):	5.1 sec
Engine type:	V8
Displacement:	350 ci (5,735 cc)
Transmission	6–speed manual
Max power:	327 bhp (244 kW) @ 5,200 rpm
Max torque:	345 lb ft (467 Nm) @ 4,400 rpm
Weight:	3,520 lb (1,600 kg)
Economy:	22 mpg (7.8 km/l)

Pontiac Grand Prix GTP (1999)

While the Grand Prix name had been around for many years, it didn't use much in the way of modern technology nor looks until it switched to front-wheel drive in 1988. It got sporty styling that year, marking it out significantly, and the looks were backed up by performance, thanks to the same basic turbocharged engine as in the fire-breathing Grand Nationals from just a couple of years before. Into the 1990s the car was renamed the GTP instead of Turbo, then in 1994 got new styling, then again in 1996, which has since become the car's most successful guise. In GPX form it used a supercharger but remained front-wheel drive. The suspension had revised geometry with more negative camber on the front wheels to improve cornering. A GM first was the heads-up display, which projected the speed and other functions onto the windshield.

Top speed:	142 mph (227 km/h)
0–60 mph (0–96 km/h):	6.6 sec
Engine type:	V6
Displacement:	231 ci (3,785 cc)
Transmission	4-speed auto
Max power:	240 bhp (179 kW) @ 5,200 rpm
Max torque:	280 lb ft (380 Nm) @ 3,200 rpm
Weight:	3,396 lb (1,543 kg)
Economy:	23 mpg (8.14 km/l)

Porsche 356

Ferry Porsche started something big with the 356. Being the first Porsche-badged car, the prototype first hit the street in 1948 using a VW engine. It made a spring debut at the Geneva Motor Show in 1949 and in 1951 it won its class at Le Mans. An updated 356A appeared with Speedster and Carrera versions in 1955, then came the 356B in 1959 with a facelift and more powerful engines, while the final 356C made an appearance in 1963, only to be replaced by the 911 two years later. The 356 has, like the Beetle, a floorpan chassis with swing axles and torsion bars at the rear, while at the nose, torsion bars are again used with trailing arms. The engine might also have its roots in the air-cooled VW unit, but it's more sophisticated with better balancing, improved flow and the ability to rev more freely. The ultimate variant was the Carrera which came with four cams for 125mph (201km/h) performance.

Top speed:	103 mph (165 km/h)
0–60 mph (0–95 km/h):	13.0 sec
Engine type:	Flat four
Displacement:	96 ci (1,582 cc)
Transmission	4-speed manual
Max power:	75 bhp (56 kW) @ 5,000 rpm
Max torque:	85 lb ft (115 Nm) @ 3,700 rpm
Weight:	2,059 lb (936 kg)
Economy:	25 mpg (8.9 km/l)

Porsche 356 Speedster

In 1952 Porsche produced a few stripped-out 356 American Roadsters which were mainly for racing, but later in 1954 they resurrected the idea in the lightweight Speedster. In 1956 the car received a bigger engine which made it quite a performance model: indeed, it attracted many serious drivers because it was lighter than the hardtop. It used the same pressed-steel floorpan as the 356 Cabriolet, with the rear-mounted engine and transaxle plus torsion bar front suspension and swing axle rear end. The engine in base form produced 70bhp (52kW) but a 'Super Tune' version was available which took it to 88bhp (66kW), but best of all was the Carrera four-cam engine with twin spark plugs which pushed out 115bhp (86kW). The Speedster windshield was around 3 inches (76mm) shorter to save weight, and there was no side glass, plus a very light folding roof.

Top speed:	100 mph (160 km/h)
0–60 mph (0–95 km/h):	11.2 sec
Engine type:	Flat four
Displacement:	96 ci (1,582 cc)
Transmission	4-speed manual
Max power:	70 bhp (52 kW) @ 4,500 rpm
Max torque:	82 lb ft (11 Nm) @ 2,700 rpm
Weight:	1,790 lb (813 kg)
Economy:	26 mpg (9.2 km/l)

Porsche 911 (901 model)

The very first 911 was model was launched at the Frankfurt Motor Show in 1963, but was penned in 1959 to replace what was considered the ageing 'upturned bath' 356 design. Engineers wanted the power of the 356 Carrera engine, so the new car could comfortably top 100mph (160km/h), but without the complexity and expense of multiple cams, so added two cylinders instead. The resultant 122ci (2-litre) flat-six '901' engine was innovative in design, featuring dry sump lubrication and hemispherical combustion chambers. With carburettors it made a reliable 145bhp (108kW). The 1963 911 needed more strength to cope with the bigger, more powerful engine and the designers stiffened the floorpan, added large box-section sills and made the roof a stressed section. MacPherson struts and torsion bars took care of the front while the rear used a trailing-arm layout. It lasted until the 1990s.

Top speed:	132 mph (211 km/h)
0–60 mph (0–95 km/h):	9.0 sec
Engine type:	Flat six
Displacement:	122 ci (1,991 cc)
Transmission	5-speed manual
Max power:	145 bhp (108 kW) @ 6,100 rpm
Max torque:	143 lb ft (194 Nm) @ 4,200 rpm
Weight:	2,360 lb (1,073 kg)
Economy:	19 mpg (6.7 km/l)

Porsche 911 Carrera RS 2.7

Regarded by many Porsche fans as the best-handling 911 ever, the RS 2.7 is one of the finest fettled cars ever to come out of Stuttgart, Germany. Originally there were to be just 500 built for homologation purposes, though this went to 1,500. The car was so radically modified compared to the regular 911 that it had to be built on a separate production line, having a delete list of items like the carpet, sealer, glovebox door and even the coat hooks. Also, the body received treatment with the engine cover and fenders being glass-fibre, while the steel panels and window glass were thinner. Bilsten gas shocks were fitted, along with thicker anti-roll bar, and the RS was given wider Fuchs alloys. The engine was taken out to 164ci (2.7 litres) from 146ci (2.4 litres) and flat top pistons plus fuel injection was fitted. A close-ratio gearbox helped keep the motor in the power band.

Top speed:	148 mph (237 km/h)
0–60 mph (0–95 km/h):	5.9 sec
Engine type:	Flat six
Displacement:	164 ci (2,687 cc)
Transmission	5-speed manual
Max power:	210 bhp (156 kW) @ 6,300 rpm
Max torque:	188 lb ft (255 Nm) @ 5,100 rpm
Weight:	2,160 lb (982 kg)
Economy:	14.7 mpg (5.2 km/l)

Porsche 911 Turbo (1976–1977)

The Turbo version of the 1976–1977 911 was for the rich performance enthusiast after a challenging drive. It was a brave move by Porsche to install the turbo, as only BMW and Chevrolet had tried it on a production model before, though the Stuttgart, Germany-based company did know the turbocharging had strong appeal in its own race programme. It was a single KKK turbo with 12psi boost, but it made the engine so much more punchy that a stronger transmission was required. To get the power down, wider rear arches were also needed in order to get sufficient rubber under them. After 1977 the car's displacement was upped to 201ci (3,293cc) for 300bhp (224kW), but the Turbo had developed a reputation for being a monster, well deserved given the performance and sudden oversteer. The 'whaletail' spoiler, where the intercooler was mounted, also provided downforce at speed.

Top speed:	156 mph (250 km/h)
0–60 mph (0–95 km/h):	4.9 sec
Engine type:	Flat six
Displacement:	183 ci (2,993 cc)
Transmission	4-speed manual
Max power:	234 bhp (174 kW) @ 5,500 rpm
Max torque:	245 lb ft (332 Nm) @ 4,000 rpm
Weight:	2,514 lb (1,143 kg)
Economy:	19 mpg (6.7 km/l)

Porsche 924 Turbo

While the 924 had been the first Porsche to run with a front-engine, rear-wheel drive layout, purists didn't like it because of the involvement with VW/Audi. The car used a 122ci (2-litre) Audi 100 engine, itself was derived from a VW LT van, and didn't look like a Porsche, nor did it go like one. Porsche addressed the car's shortcomings and made it a driver's machine. They fitted a KKK 26 turbocharger and though, like many other turbo cars of the era it suffered from turbo lag, when the boost came in the acceleration was good. Better still was the handling and braking, the former helped by perfect 50:50 weight distribution with the gearbox in the rear transaxle, while the latter was incredible, thanks to massive 11-inch (279mm) discs all around. The body changes were subtle with a NACA-style duct in the hood for the turbo, grilles in the front spoiler and a discreet rear spoiler.

Top speed:	134 mph (214 km/h)
0–60 mph (0–95 km/h):	8.9 sec
Engine type:	In-line four
Displacement:	121 ci (1,985 cc)
Transmission	5-speed manual
Max power:	143 bhp (107 k/W) @ 5,500 rpm
Max torque:	147 lb ft (199 Nm) @ 3,000 rpm
Weight:	2,719 lb (1,236 kg)
Economy:	19.5 mpg (6.9 km/l)

Porsche 928

Intended as a replacement for the 911, the 1977 928 seemed to offer more space, grace and pace. Indeed it did offer the first two, but not in the latter with just 240bhp (179kW) at launch in a much heavier car than the 911. A jump to 300bhp (224kW) in 1979 cured the situation somewhat, but by then it was obvious the 928 wasn't so much a replacement as an extra model in Porsche's line-up. To balance the car, the transmission was put at the rear, while up front an all-new 90-degree V8 started off with single-overhead cams, eventually progressing to a dual-overhead set-up with 32v and 305ci (4,998cc) displacement, in the 1986 S4. Suspension was double wishbones at the front and semi-trailing arms at the rear with diagonal links. The body blended flexible polyurethane fenders into the bodywork, giving the car a smooth look and excellent drag coefficient of 0.39 in 1977.

Top speed:	165 mph (264 km/h)
0–60 mph (0–95 km/h):	5.8 sec
Engine type:	V8
Displacement:	302 ci (4,957 cc)
Transmission	5-speed manual
Max power:	330 bhp (246 kW) @ 4,100 rpm
Max torque:	317 lb ft (429 Nm) @ 4,100 rpm
Weight:	3,449 lb (1,568 kg)
Economy:	12.4 mpg (4.4 km/l)

Porsche 911 Turbo 3.3 SE

While the 1980s Porsche Turbo was phenomenally quick, Porsche went one better with the 1985 SE (Special Equipment). Visual upgrades included the nose with an aerodynamic flat front, deep spoiler and pop-up lamps, while the rear aches had functional engine-cooling vents. The suspension of the standard car was left alone, apart from Bilstein shocks, but the Fuchs alloys were up to 16 inches (406mm) in diameter. The engine received high-performance camshafts, bigger intercooler, re-mapped engine management, and a modified exhaust system for an extra 30bhp (22kW) over the regular Turbo model. Inside, the SE was given air-conditioning, full leather trim, heated adjustable Recaro seats and Blaupunkt sound. The SE had a strictly limited production run so ended in 1986, though in the USA, the SE package remained as a $23,244 option on the Turbo model in 1987.

Top speed:	170 mph (272 km/h)
0–60 mph (0–95 km/h):	5.0 sec
Engine type:	Flat six
Displacement:	201 ci (3,299 cc)
Transmission	4-speed manual
Max power:	330 bhp (246 kW) @ 5,750 rpm
Max torque:	318 lb ft (430 Nm) @ 4,000 rpm
Weight:	3,000 lb (1,363 kg)
Economy:	18 mpg (6.4 km/l)

Porsche 911 Turbo (1990–1995)

A new 911 bodystyle in 1989 saw the Turbo re-launched a year later. It remained rear-wheel drive only, though traction was good because of the engine's weight being over the rear wheels. The new model still demanded respect, however, especially in the wet, even though development engineers at Porsche tamed these later models a little by stiffening the rear suspension and revising the rear trailing arm set-up. Also much better was the MacPherson strut front end, a carry-over from the Carrera 2 of 1989. The brakes were huge for this year, being 12-inch (305mm) vented items with four-piston callipers. Power-assisted steering was required on this model, because despite the weight being at the rear, the wide tyres still made the steering heavy. The engine was still air-cooled with Bosch K-Tronic fuel injection plus a single KKK turbo, with intercooler mounted in the 'whale tail' spoiler.

Top speed:	168 mph (269 km/h)
0–60 mph (0–95 km/h):	4.9 sec
Engine type:	Flat six
Displacement:	201 ci (3,299 cc)
Transmission	5-speed manual
Max power:	315 bhp (235 kW) @ 5,750 rpm
Max torque:	332 lb ft (449 Nm) @ 4,500 rpm
Weight:	3,274 lb (1,488 kg)
Economy:	12.4 mpg (4.4 km/l)

Porsche 968

Carrying on a tradition which had been started by the 924 25 years earlier, the 1991 Porsche 968 offered a budget-priced Porsche to the enthusiast which was far more refined and civilized than any of its ancestors. Too refined and too well-honed for some Porsche's fans' liking, in fact. It used one of the biggest displacement four-cylinder engines in recent production history, which had balancer shafts to run smoothly, plus 16 valves for more performance, in fact over 30bhp (22kW) more than the 944 S2's similar engine. The gearbox was set at the rear to maximize weight-distribution and it balanced the car beautifully. So good was the handling that people remarked it required less driver involvement and hence wasn't a real Porsche. This Club Sport model rectified that, with 17-inch (432mm) wheels, no back seat nor power windows thus saving 117lb (53kg) weight.

Top speed:	150 mph (240 km/h)
0–60 mph (0–95 km/h):	6.1 sec
Engine type:	In-line four
Displacement:	182 ci (2,990 cc)
Transmission	6-speed manual
Max power:	240 bhp (179 kW) @ 6,200 rpm
Max torque:	224 lb ft (303 Nm) @ 4,100 rpm
Weight:	2,943 lb (1,338 kg)
Economy:	19.4 mpg (6.9 km/l)

Porsche 911 Ruf (1997)

A lois Ruf began modifying Porsche 911s in 1977, turning them into the fastest road cars available. In 1987 a Ruf CTR (based on a 911) broke the World Speed Record for a production car by going 211mph (339km/h), and the company has since grown. Ruf specialize in modfying all areas, therefore a 911 from them is a Ruf production car, not a Porsche. This 1997 example got 1.5-inch (38mm) lower suspension, Bilstein shocks, stiffer anti-roll bars and a strut brace. Drive was still via Porsche's permanent 4WD system with viscous coupling and traction control. The flat-six engine had different pistons, modified cylinder heads, more aggressive cams and special KKK turbochargers. Also changed was the stock exhaust for custom Ruf pipes, while a re-mapped engine management system took care of the running. Optional was an electronic clutch, permitting fingertip gear changes.

Top speed:	192 mph (307 km/h)
0–60 mph (0–95 km/h):	3.8 sec
Engine type:	Flat six
Displacement:	220 ci (3,600 cc)
Transmission	6-speed manual
Max power:	490 bhp (365 kW) @ 5,500 rpm
Max torque:	480 lb ft (650 Nm) @ 4,800 rpm
Weight:	3,090 lb (1,404 kg)
Economy:	11 mpg (3.9 km/l)

Porsche 993 Turbo

The 1997 993 Turbo was the last of the 911-shaped cars to use the famous air-cooled flat six, and by then it been bored out to the limit, yet still used just two valves per cylinder. The key to its enormous output was, as ever, turbocharging, though this model was the first to use twin turbos, Porsche again choosing KKK for two smaller units, which virtually eliminated the turbo lag which had been associated with previous models. Aside from the engine refinement, Porsche had also made the power far more useable, thanks to four-wheel drive which had first appeared in the Carrera 4 model of 1989. Cleverly, to make it feel like the old cars, the rear wheels would be driven only in normal situations, but when sensors detected traction was being lost, drive would be fed to the front wheels as well. The 993 goes down as one of many Porsche fans' favourites.

Top speed:	180 mph (288 km/h)
0–60 mph (0–95 km/h):	3.8 sec
Engine type:	Flat six
Displacement:	220 ci (3,600 cc)
Transmission	6-speed manual
Max power:	400 bhp (298 kW) @ 5,750 rpm
Max torque:	400 lb ft (542 Nm) @ 4,500 rpm
Weight:	3,307 lb (1,503 kg)
Economy:	18 mpg (6.4 km/l)

Porsche 911 (1998)

Introduced in 1997, the new 911 followed a tradition dating back to 1963, of a rear-engined sports car with an emphasis on quality and driving pleasure. The sixth-generation version featured an all-new body and a water-cooled flat-six for the first time. While being 122ci (200cc) larger than the former air-cooled unit, it boasted more power and was far quieter, in fact Porsche claimed it took 20 new 911s to make the same noise as one older model. To keep rear weight bias to a minimum and neutralize the handling, the unit was all-alloy and used dual overhead cams with variable valve timing. The platform is a stretched version of the Boxster's and uses Porsche's high-tech MacPherson type struts at the front, with rear double track control arms and multi-link suspension. A stronger bodyshell helped with the torsional rigidity and made the handling the best ever in a 911.

Top speed:	174 mph (278 km/h)
0–60 mph (0–95 km/h):	5.0 sec
Engine type:	Flat six
Displacement:	207 ci (3,387 cc)
Transmission	6-speed manual
Max power:	296 bhp (200 kW) @ 6,800 rpm
Max torque:	258 lb ft (349 Nm) @ 4,600 rpm
Weight:	3,081 lb (1,400 kg)
Economy:	23.3 mpg (8.3 km/l)

Porsche Boxster

Porsche's first new car in 20 years had to do two things: boost the company's flagging profits, and bring a supercar to the masses. It did both successfully, and remained a strong seller into the 21st century. Using Porsche's famed engine layout of six horizontally opposed cylinders, the Boxster's was slightly different being mid-ships, giving near perfect weight distribution. With an output of 204bhp (152kW) at 6,000rpm, the Boxster needs to be revved, and is at its best with the motor near the redline. Being relatively lightweight made the car very responsive in corners and the brilliant steering further enhanced this. The car wasn't just a great driver's machine, however, because with good trunk and hood space, it was practical. The interior went way beyond the dated ergonomics of the 911, while the convertible roof felt like a hardtop in reality, such was the build quality.

Top speed:	149 mph (238 km/h)
0–60 mph (0–95 km/h):	6.9 sec
Engine type:	Flat six
Displacement:	151 ci (2,480 cc)
Transmission	6-speed manual
Max power:	204 bhp (152 kW) @ 6,000 rpm
Max torque:	181 lb ft (245 Nm) @ 4,500 rpm
Weight:	2,756 lb (1,252 kg)
Economy:	23.5 mpg (8.3 km/l)

Range Rover

The original luxury off-roader was launched in 1970 to massive acclaim from the world's press. Not only did it have more agility off road than the Land Rover, thanks to long-travel coil springs instead of leaf springs front and rear, it had much better road manners than anything else in its class, plus it looked and felt almost limo-like inside. At first it was only available as a two-door, but the impracticalities of this soon showed, and by 1981 all models had four doors. The underside was brutally strong, using a separate ladder-style chassis which protected all the major components. Telescopic shocks sat up front while the rear had self-levelling Boge units, and disc brakes were used all around. The engine was the all-aluminium Buick V8, for which Rover had bought the rights back in the 1960s, and it offered the perfect combination of lightweight and plenty of torque.

Top speed:	99 mph (158 km/h)
0–60 mph (0–95 km/h):	12.9 sec
Engine type:	V8
Displacement:	215 ci (3,528 cc)
Transmission	4-speed manual
Max power:	130 bhp (97 kW) @ 5,000 rpm
Max torque:	205 lb ft (277 Nm) @ 3,000 rpm
Weight:	3,864 lb (1,756 kg)
Economy:	17 mpg (6 km/l)

Range Rover Overfinch

While the Range Rover was good, it wasn't quick, for all its V8 thirst. The Rover engine, while being lightweight, just didn't have the torque needed. Under the name Schuler, Overfinch created its first modified Range Rover as early as 1975, but it wasn't until 1982 that production proper began, with the 570T being Overfinch's first Chevy-powered vehicle. As time went by and technology increased, Overfinch added injection on the 570TPi model using Chevrolet's Tuned Port Injection, then produced a very special limited edition 20th Anniversary model with a 380bhp (283 kW) 400ci (6.5-litre) GM V8. In 1998 came the car shown, the 570 HSE, with firmer air suspension, seven seats (the stock had five), a quicker steering ratio, and Bentley turbo tyres. While it has all the extra power, the Overfinch remarkably can achieve the same fuel economy as the stock Range Rover.

Top speed:	130 mph (208 km/h)
0–60 mph (0–95 km/h):	7.2 sec
Engine type:	V8
Displacement:	350 ci (5,733 cc)
Transmission	4-speed auto
Max power:	330 bhp (246 kW) @ 4,700 rpm
Max torque:	425 lb ft (573 Nm) @ 3,150 rpm
Weight:	4,960 lb (2,254 kg)
Economy:	17 mpg (6 km/l)

Reliant Scimitar

Is it a sports car or is it a station wagon? That's the question often levelled at the Scimitar GTE, and the answer remains something of a conundrum. At the rear, the car featured a wide-opening tailgate and the rear seat could be dropped to accommodate long loads, making it surprisingly practical, while it was also extremely comfortable. The well-equipped cabin used parts from several British makers, meaning switchgear was instantly familiar to most buyers. But with a stiff chassis, lightweight glassfibre bodywork and a choice of powerful Ford V6 engines, the Reliant was also incredibly sporty and could cruise all day at speeds in excess of 100mph (160km/h). The car gained Royal approval from Britain's Princess Anne, who was famously a keen advocate of the model. In 1986 Reliant stopped production and sold the rights to a firm which then went bankrupt, but the possibility of new Scimitars becoming available remains.

Top speed:	120 mph (194 km/h)
0–60 mph (0–95 km/h):	8.8 sec
Engine type:	V6
Displacement:	183 ci (2,994 cc)
Transmission:	4-speed man/3-speed auto
Max power:	146 bhp (109 kW) at 5,000 rpm
Max torque:	172 lb ft (233 Nm) at 3,000 rpm
Weight:	2,554 lb (1,149 kg)
Economy:	23 mpg (8.2 km/l)

Renault Dauphine

With cuddly looks and an old-fashioned engine, nobody would have guessed that the Renault Dauphine hid a fantastic chassis. But in reality, it was a great car to drive, thanks to its independent coil-sprung front end and optional hydro-pneumatic rear springing set-up. The best Dauphines were those from the last four years of production, as they came with an excellent all-synchromesh four-speed gearbox and four-wheel disc brakes. Standard cars struggled to reach 80mph (128km/h), but those tuned by French racing firm Gordini were surprisingly quick. A factory sporty version was also offered. The 1093 Rallye was finished in bright blue with garish stripes, and had a top speed of over 100mph (160km/h). It was only offered officially in France and Spain, but many were taken to other countries through private importers.

Top speed:	74 mph (119 km/h)
0–60 mph (0–95 km/h):	28.2 sec
Engine type:	in-line four
Displacement:	52 ci (845 cc)
Transmission:	4-speed manual
Max power:	30 bhp (22 kW) at 4,250 rpm
Max torque:	43 lb ft (58 Nm) at 2,200 rpm
Weight:	1,344 lb (605 kg)
Economy:	30 mpg (10.7 km/l)

Renault 4

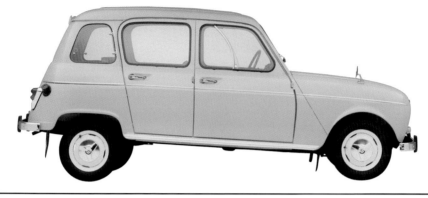

Only the Volkswagen Beetle and Ford Model T have sold in greater numbers than the Renault 4, which was France's best-selling car for almost two decades. Built along similar lines to the Citroen 2CV, it featured a utilitarian interior, odd dashboard-mounted gear lever and flimsy metal bodywork that looked like it was made from corrugated tin. Handling was excellent by virtue of its incredible grip, despite the massive body lean through corners. The 4 was extremely cheap and very practical, making it a big hit with French families, while it was also built in South America, Spain and Portugal to satisfy local demand. As well as a hatchback-cum-station wagon, the R4 could be ordered as a delivery van, pick-up truck and beach buggy. Over eight million were built over 31 years, and French production did not finish until 1992.

Top speed:	68 mph (110 km/h)
0–60 mph (0–95 km/h):	38.1 sec
Engine type:	in-line four
Displacement:	51.5 ci (845 cc)
Transmission:	4-speed manual
Max power:	34 bhp (25 kW) at 5,000 rpm
Max torque:	43 lb ft (58 Nm) at 2,500 rpm
Weight:	1,466 lb (660 kg)
Economy:	30 mpg (10.7 km/l)

Renault 16

The 16 was one of Renault's most significant cars. It was extremely versatile by virtue of its large and practical rear hatchback and fold-flat rear seats, while all-round independent suspension and front disc brakes made it one of the most advanced cars of its era in terms of driver appeal. Interior space was excellent, offering incredible levels of comfort – a feeling enhanced by the car's soft yet stable ride. Its only downfall was its unusual gearbox, operated by a clumsy column lever instead of the floor change favoured by most European motorists. The 16 was the first of a breed – across Europe today, almost 80 per cent of cars sold in its market sector are hatchbacks rather than traditional saloons; and the 16 was the car that started the craze. Almost two million of these front-wheel-drive vehicles were built between 1965 and 1980.

Top speed:	93 mph (150 km/h)
0–60 mph (0–95 km/h):	16.2 sec
Engine type:	in-line four
Displacement:	95 ci (1,565 cc)
Transmission:	4-speed manual
Max power:	70 bhp (52kW) at 5,200 rpm
Max torque:	86 lb ft (117 Nm) at 2,500 rpm
Weight:	2,260 lb (1017 kg)
Economy:	27 mpg (9.6 km/l)

Renault Alpine A110

The Alpine 110 started as a simple lightweight coupe and by sticking to that ideal, with a few tweaks, Renault topped rallying for 10 years. The low weight was partly due to a skinny, yet strong, chassis, made in alloy and using a single spine design with a subframe for the front suspension and more substantial cage for the drive train/suspension out back. Unequal length wishbones were used at the front in conjunction with coil-over-shocks, where the rear again used wishbones but with two coil-over-shocks per side because of the extra weight. Four wheel 10-inch (254mm) disc brakes ensured great stopping power. Because of the low production run, it was only ever produced in lightweight glass-fibre and with the small all-alloy hemi-chambered engine on twin Weber carburettors, was rapid through the bends. It won the World Rally Championship in both 1971 and 1973.

Top speed:	127 mph (203 km/h)
0–60 mph (0–95 km/h):	6.3 sec
Engine type:	In-line four
Displacement:	98 ci (1,605 cc)
Transmission	5-speed manual
Max power:	138 bhp (103 kW) @ 6,000 rpm
Max torque:	106 lb ft (144 Nm) @ 5,000 rpm
Weight:	1,566 lb (712 kg)
Economy:	23.5 mpg (8.3 km/l)

Renault 5 Turbo 2

Renault did two important things with the 1980 R5 Turbo 2. It immediately raised the profile of its brand, plus gave itself a formidable rally car to tackle the Group B class. Just 1,000 road cars homologated the R5 Turbo for competition but 1,300 were made. It had little in common with the standard R5; the suspension was all-new with double wishbones at each end, using torsion bars springs up front but regular rear coils. The engine used the gearbox from the larger Renault 30, but turned around allowing the four-cylinder unit to be mounted midships. The motor featured an alloy head with hemispherical combustion chambers and a Garrett turbo running 12.2psi for the road but more boost and 300bhp (224kW) on rally cars and up to 500bhp (373kW) in the R5 Turbo Evolution. Sensational handling helped give the car great rally success: 250 international wins in four years.

Top speed:	124 mph (198 km/h)
0–60 mph (0–95 km/h):	7.7 sec
Engine type:	In-line four
Displacement:	85 ci (1,397 cc)
Transmission	5-speed manual
Max power:	160 bhp (119 kW) @ 6,000 rpm
Max torque:	158 lb ft (214 Nm) @ 3,500 rpm
Weight:	2,138 lb (972 kg)
Economy:	22 mpg (7.8 km/l)

Renault Alpine V6 GT/Turbo

The GT's origins can be traced back to the early 1970s and the A110 two-seater sportscars which also excelled in racing and rallying. And with Renault's manufacturing might behind the new model, it had everything going for it in 1985, except image. The car used a separate steel backbone chassis with subframes at the front and rear carrying the suspension/steering and engine/'box. Suspension was double wishbone all around which gave very good handling even with rear weight bias split 37:63. The all-aluminium engine had a cam-per-bank and two valves per cylinder in the hemispherical combustion chambers. A short-stroke crankshaft meant the V6 was rev happy, but its real power came through the turbo, which gave great torque at low rpm. This was a great driver's machine, having very controllable handling and a near-perfect driving position.

Top speed:	152 mph (243 km/h)
0–60 mph (0–95 km/h):	6.3 sec
Engine type:	V6
Displacement:	150 ci (2,458 cc)
Transmission	5-speed manual
Max power:	200 bhp (149 kW) @ 5,750 rpm
Max torque:	214 lb ft (289 Nm) @ 2,500 rpm
Weight:	2,600 lb (1,182 kg)
Economy:	25 mpg (8.9 km/l)

Renault Sport Spider

Prior to the Spider's production in 1996, Renault had never produced an open-top two-seater sportscar. The Spider was originally a race machine designed to run in a one-make endurance series across Europe, but such was the demand for it, even without a windscreen to begin with, the decision was made to produce a street-going version. An light chassis of just 176lb (80kg) was made in extruded alloy sheet boxes, while the body panels were all glass-fibre. All suspension joints dismissed rubber bushes in favour of Heim joints, yet the car still managed an above-average ride quality. For power Renault used the 122ci (2-litre) 16-valve unit also used in the Megane, and the long-stroked engine produced impressive torque which the chassis easily handled. The small screen eventually fitted was deemed to ineffective for regular use, so a conventional screen was fitted to 1997 models.

Top speed:	124 mph (198 km/h)
0–60 mph (0–95 km/h):	7.7 sec
Engine type:	In-line four
Displacement:	122 ci (1,998 cc)
Transmission	5-speed manual
Max power:	150 bhp (112 kW) @ 6,000 rpm
Max torque:	140 lb ft (190 Nm) @ 4,500 rpm
Weight:	2,106 lb (957 kg)
Economy:	23.5 mpg (8.3 km/l)

Riley RM Roadster

It might look like the definition of an antique car, but under the skin the Riley RM Roadster was an advanced machine. Built to traditonal methods with a separate chassis and ash-frame bodywork, the RM was Riley's first post-war car, and although the construction might have been old-fashioned, the engine and suspension certainly weren't. Power came from a revvy 1.5-litre twin cam unit that gave it a surprising turn of speed, while a fluent gearchange and hydraulic brakes meant driving quickly was also safe. At the rear, the car had semi-elliptic leaf springs, while independent torsion bars at the front meant it had good roadholding. The RM was a touring car in the most traditional British style, and in drophead form was rightly considered very desirable. However it was not a great export success and as a result the Riley RM series is much prized today.

Top speed:	75 mph (121 km/h)
0–60 mph (0–95 km/h):	25.1 sec
Engine type:	in-line four
Displacement:	91 ci (1,496 cc)
Transmission:	4-speed man
Max power:	54 bhp (40 kW) at 4,500 rpm
Max torque:	76 lb ft (103 Nm) at 3,000 rpm
Weight:	2,688 lb (1,209 kg)
Economy:	20 mpg (7.1 km/l)

Rolls-Royce Phantom III

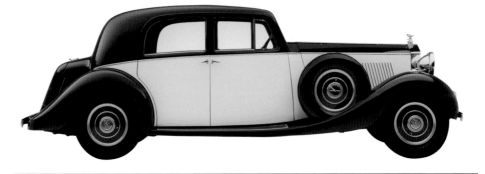

Committed enthusiasts believe the Phantom III to be the last 'true' Rolls-Royce. It was the last car worked on by company founder Henry Royce and retained traditional company virtues such as exclusive coachbuilt bodywork and an interior that was a masterpiece of fine craftsmanship. but it was significant for other reasons, too, not least its all-new V12 engine. Built to compete with successful designs from rivals such as Cadillac and Packard, the 7.3-litre unit was incredibly smooth and refined, while in true Rolls-Royce fashion its power output, estimated by many to be about 160bhp, was kept a closely guarded secret. The Phantom III was also the first Rolls-Royce to use independent front suspension, in the form of a General Motors-designed coil and wishbone set up. Only 710 examples were built between 1936 and the outbreak of war in 1939.

Top speed:	93 mph (150 km/h)
0–60 mph (0–95 km/h):	16.5 sec
Engine type:	V12
Displacement:	448 ci (7,340 cc)
Transmission:	4-speed manual
Max power:	160 bhp (119 kW) at 4,000 rpm
Max torque:	not quoted
Weight:	5,800 lb (2,610 kg)
Economy:	12 mpg (4.3 km/l)

Rolls-Royce Silver Cloud

Until the Silver Cloud debuted in 1955, Rolls-Royce had used external coachbuilders to create the bodywork for its cars. The bodies for the Cloud, however, were constructed in-house. And although it might have looked traditional and old-fashioned, the Cloud was equipped with the latest in automotive technology – including self-levelling suspension, power steering and power-assisted braking. The Mk 2 model, which debuted in 1959, was the first car to use Rolls-Royce's famous 6.2-litre V8 (later 6.7-litres), and even today its power output remains a closely guarded secret, known only to employees of the company. The Silver Cloud was a successful car for Rolls-Royce and its engine and transmission – a General Motors Hydramatic unit – would go on to appear in the company's most successful car ever; the 1965 Silver Shadow.

Top speed:	113 mph (183 km/h)
0–60 mph (0–95 km/h):	11.5 sec
Engine type:	V8
Displacement:	380 ci (6,230 cc)
Transmission:	3-speed auto
Max power:	not quoted
Max torque:	not quoted
Weight:	4,650 lb (2,093 kg)
Economy:	13 mpg (4.6 km/l)

Roush Mustang 1999

Roush and Mustang go back to 1988, when Jack Roush built a 351ci (5.8-litre) twin turbo 400bhp (298kW) Mustang as a 25th Anniversary edition. Due to costs, Ford rejected selling it, but seven years later Roush Performance was formed as an offshoot of Roush Racing, and attention turned to the Mustang again, with thoughts of a high-performance GT for the street. With the advent of the 1999 Mustang, Roush had developed a number of models in various stages of tune and prices. Shown is the Stage II car, which had minor but effective tweaks for more driver involvement. The shocks and springs were uprated and lowered, stiffer anti-roll bars were fitted and Roush control arms bolted in to locate the live rear axle. Brembo13-inch (330mm) vented discs were added at the front and, with the stock ASB, work extremely well. Finishing it off was a full skirt body kit with side exits for exhaust.

Top speed:	150 mph (240 km/h)
0–60 mph (0–95 km/h):	5.8 sec
Engine type:	V8
Displacement:	281 ci (4,606 cc)
Transmission	5-speed manual
Max power:	260 bhp (194 kW) @ 5,250 rpm
Max torque:	302 lb ft (409 Nm) @ 4,000 rpm
Weight:	3,471 lb (1,578 kg)
Economy:	16 mpg (5.7 km/l)

Rover P5B

The P5 was a real landmark car for Rover. As well as being the first model from the British maker to use unitary construction, it was also one of the most stylish cars on the market thanks to the design genius of its creator, David Bache. A svelte-looking Coupé variant joined the line up in 1963 with a chopped roofline to give it a more dynamic appearance, transforming it from a robust luxury saloon into a desirable grand tourer. But the most significant change in the P5's production cycle would come in 1967, after Rover acquired all rights to an alloy V8 engine designed by Buick. The compact unit wasn't popular in the States, but was just the thing Rover needed to move its product range forward. The famous 'Rover V8' went on to power over 70 different series production models, including cars from Land Rover, Morgan and TVR.

Top speed:	110 mph (178 km/h)
0–60 mph (0–95 km/h):	12.4 sec
Engine type:	V8
Displacement:	215 ci (3,528 cc)
Transmission:	3-speed auto
Max power:	161 bhp (120 kW) at 5,200 rpm
Max torque:	210 lb ft (285 Nm) at 2,600 rpm
Weight:	3,479 lb (1,566 kg)
Economy:	20 mpg (7.1 km/l)

Rover P6

By the early 1960s, Rover was in desperate need of a car to shake off its old-fashioned image, so it decided to follow the most modern route possible with the P6. The car was not only a technical masterpiece, but also an incredibly smart piece of design and engineering. The body panels all bolted on to a steel skeleton frame, meaning they didn't have to carry any stress or load, while the De Dion independent rear suspension set-up was more advanced than that of many car on the market today. In-board rear disc brakes, a vacuum-operated brake boost and run-flat tyres were further innovations to be found on the model, which won Europe's inaugural Car of the Year award in 1964. A V8 version debuted in 1968 and was regarded as the ultimate luxury saloon in its day. This was initially only available as an automatic, but the manual 3500S was introduced in 1971.

Top speed:	108 mph (175 km/h)
0–60 mph (0–95 km/h):	11.5 sec
Engine type:	in-line four
Displacement:	121 ci (1,978 cc)
Transmission:	4-speed manual/3-speed auto
Max power:	124 bhp (92 kW) at 5,500 rpm
Max torque:	132 lb ft (179 Nm) at 4,000 rpm
Weight:	2,867 lb (1,290 kg)
Economy:	24 mpg (8.6 km/l)

Rover SD1 Vitesse

A s part of the British Leyland group, Rover launched the SD1 in 1976 and gave it handsome fastback styling which years later was admitted as being inspired by the Ferrari Daytona. The car initially used the Rover V8 engine, which was a version of Buick's all-aluminium unit which had been bought in the early 1960s. While the SD1 sold well into the 1980s, by then it had started to look dated, so it was facelifted in 1982. The following year saw a substantial increase in power with the launch of the Vitesse, which was French for 'speed'. The Vitesse ran the same SD1 layout of front-engine, rear-wheel drive via a live axle, but had lowered and stiffened suspension, uprated front disc brakes, larger alloys and re-calibrated steering. The engine received Lucas electronic fuel injection and the heads had gas flow improvements. In 1986 a Twin Plenum intake upped power over 200bhp (149kW).

Top speed:	135 mph (216 km/h)
0–60 mph (0–95 km/h):	7.1 sec
Engine type:	V8
Displacement:	215 ci (3,528 cc)
Transmission	5-speed manual
Max power:	190 bhp (142 kW) @ 5,280 rpm
Max torque:	220 lb ft (298 Nm) @ 4,000 rpm
Weight:	3,175 lb (1,443 kg)
Economy:	22 mpg (7.8 km/l)

Saab 96

I t might have been odd to look at, but Saab's quirky 96 was in many respects one of the most sensible and practical cars of its day. The 96 used aerospace technology and its unusual curved roofline and sloping tail were based on the cockpit of an aircraft. The 96 was also one of the first cars to use a wind tunnel to improve aerodynamic efficiency. Inside, it had plenty of room for four adults, while the characterful two-stroke engine was free-revving and much livelier than the performance figures would suggest. Later models got a V4 engine co-developed with Ford, giving the 96 the power its excellent chassis deserved. Thanks to its nimble handling and light kerbweight, the 96 was a successful rally car, winning the Monte Carlo in 1962 and 1963. An estate version, the 95, was also offered for sale by Saab.

Top speed:	87 mph (141 km/h)
0–60 mph (0–95 km/h):	21.2 sec
Engine type:	in-line three
Displacement:	51 ci (841 cc)
Transmission:	4-speed manual
Max power:	57 bhp (42kW) at 5,000 rpm
Max torque:	68 lb ft (92 Nm) at 3,500 rpm
Weight:	1,860 lb (837 kg)
Economy:	26 mpg (9.3 km/l)

Saab 99 Turbo

As a standard sedan, the 99 was rather dull and uninviting, but with the clever addition of a turbo, Saab created a cult car. Looking typically heavy (which it was) and clumsy in design, the 99 turbo was surprisingly good to drive with a great ride quality and even inspiring handling. The engine was from, of all places, the Triumph Dolomite range, and for turbocharging Saab simply dropped the compression ratio, fitted a Garrett T3 turbo, and added electronic fuel injection. A five main bearing crank kept it reliable while the driven went through a tough three-row Triplex chain. Suspension comprised a wishbone front end and beam rear located with the aid of a Panhard rod. The set-up was good enough in uprated form for Stig Blomquist to take the Swedish Rally in 1979, in the first turbocharged car to do so. The 99 was later replaced by the even more successful 900 Turbo.

Top speed:	120 mph (192 km/h)
0–60 mph (0–95 km/h):	9.1 sec
Engine type:	In-line four
Displacement:	121 ci (1,985 cc)
Transmission	4-speed manual
Max power:	145 bhp (108 kW) @ 5,000 rpm
Max torque:	174 lb ft (236 Nm) @ 3,000 rpm
Weight:	2,715 lb (1,234 kg)
Economy:	22 mpg (7.8 km/l)

Saab 900 Convertible

Unusual styling has always been a Saab trademark and the company's most successful car, the 1979–93 900, was no exception. With huge bumpers and an oddly-sloped tail, its unconventional looks polarised opinion. But nobody could deny the 900's excellent safety record and impressive build quality, which easily rivalled that of the top German makers. Saab decided to chop the top off the 900 in 1986 and the soft-top model became an instant success, offering all the practicalities and comforts that owners of the saloon were accustomed to alongside an added dash of style and fresh air fun. The roof was designed in the USA and could be raised or lowered electrically, while the lack of a roll-over hoop meant that extra body stiffening was added to the windscreen pillars and floor. Production only finished in 1993 after the sale of almost one million 900s.

Top speed:	131 mph (212 km/h)
0–60 mph (0–95 km/h):	7.5 sec
Engine type:	in-line four
Displacement:	121 ci (1,985 cc)
Transmission:	5-speed manual/4-speed auto
Max power:	160 bhp (119 kW) at 5,300 rpm
Max torque:	201 lb ft (273 Nm) at 3,000 rpm
Weight:	2,833 lb (1,275 kg)
Economy:	24 mpg (8.6 km/l)

Saleen Mustang SSC

Steve Saleen made his name in 1984 racing his own modified Mustang. He produced three examples which got sold, then in 1985 modified and sold a further 139 hatchbacks and two convertibles. In 1986 sales continued to grow so Saleen formed a racing team. By 1989 the race and road experience led to the production of the SSC, or Saleen Super Car. Based on the 5.0L LX, Saleen had modified the suspension by adding stiffer springs and adjustable shocks, and improved the chassis rigidity by fitting a strut brace and 4-point roll cage. A special Saleen leather interior and bodykit finished it all off. In the drive train Saleen took the standard 5.0L and re-worked the heads, increased the throttle body size, got more lift from the cam and increased exhaust flow. The gearbox remained, but the rear end gears were changed for 3.55:1 ratio and discs were added to the rear.

Top speed:	156 mph (250 km/h)
0–60 mph (0–95 km/h):	5.6 sec
Engine type:	V8
Displacement:	302 ci (4,948 cc)
Transmission	5-speed manual
Max power:	290 bhp (216 kW) @ 5,200 rpm
Max torque:	325 lb ft (440 Nm) @ 3,500 rpm
Weight:	3,425 lb (1,556 kg)
Economy:	22 mpg (7.8 km/l)

Saleen Mustang S351 (1995)

While Ford has its top-line Cobra for high-performance junkies, Saleen used their knowledge to go a huge step up with its S351. Started in 1995 with this set-up, the S351 used a truck block but with modifications like aluminium heads, roller rockers, a bigger throttle body, upgraded fuel system, bigger fuel injectors and, best of all, the 'S' in the name stood for supercharged which meant a Vortech 6psi centrifugal blower. To contain the power a Tremec gearbox was fitted, with new rear end gears and an uprated limited-slip differential. The brakes featured huge discs with Alcon four-pot callipers, with 18-inch (457mm) Speedline rims plus 255/35 and 295/35 BF Goodrich tyres. The special Saleen bodykit and graphics weren't matched inside, as it was mostly Mustang, but with the important addition of Recaro seats. Mid-12-second quarter-miles were possible in full street trim.

Top speed:	177 mph (283 km/h)
0–60 mph (0–96 km/h):	4.5 sec
Engine type:	V8
Displacement:	351 ci (5,751 cc)
Transmission	6-speed manual
Max power:	495 bhp (369 kW) @ 5,700 rpm
Max torque:	490 lb ft (664 Nm) @ 3,500 rpm
Weight:	3,450 lb (1,568 kg)
Economy:	11.7 mpg (4.14 km/l)

Saleen Explorer

Steve Saleen's company had been modifying and selling its own Mustang for years before the Explorer came to light in 1990, so it was natural for the company to take on Ford's S.U.V. It was 1996 when they did, after the launch of the Ford Explorer V8 which used the pushrod 5.0L engine. Saleen launched their version in 1998 and concentrated on giving it enhanced driver appeal and a more dynamic road presence, where most 4WD S.U.Vs spent their time. The separate steel chassis and live axle were retained, but stiffer bushes were added throughout the suspension, plus the springs were both lowered and uprated and the shocks re-valved. Thicker anti-roll bars replaced the stock items, and with lightweight magnesium 18-inch (457mm) rims and low-profile tyres, the car could pull 0.80g on the skidpad. Finishing off was a spoiler and, on this model, a supercharger.

Top speed:	125 mph (200 km/h)
0–60 mph (0–95 km/h):	7.9 sec
Engine type:	V8
Displacement:	302 ci (4,948 cc)
Transmission	4-speed auto
Max power:	286 bhp (213 kW) @ 4,500 rpm
Max torque:	333 lb ft (451 Nm) @ 3,200 rpm
Weight:	4,500 lb (2,045 kg)
Economy:	15 mpg (5.3 km/l)

Saleen Mustang (racer)

With an established name on the racing circuit and street in the 1980s, Steve Saleen continued to develop his company. In 1997 his SR Mustang became a force to be reckoned with at Le Mans, then in 1998 in the US Speedvision World Challenge Series, Saleen, in conjunction with Tim Allen from 'Home Improvement', dominated with the 1998 Mustang RRR. Using a stock SN 95 stripped bare, the car received a full tubular spaceframe chassis with double A-arm suspension with Howe springs and Bilstein shocks. The engine was a bored-out Windsor 351ci (5.7-litre) with GT40 aluminium heads, 10:1 compression and a Holley 600cfm carburettor. Carbon-fibre was abundant on the doors, trunk lid, hood, fenders and nose. A brute Jerico gearbox handled the power and remained, and was reliable. In 1998 Terry Borcheller won five races, winning Saleen the manufacturer's trophy.

Top speed:	210 mph (336 km/h)
0–60 mph (0–95 km/h):	3.2 sec
Engine type:	V8
Displacement:	357 ci (5,850 cc)
Transmission	4-speed manual
Max power:	525 bhp (391 kW) @ 6,800 rpm
Max torque:	N/A
Weight:	N/A
Economy:	N/A

Shelby Mustang GT350

Carroll Shelby's started with the powerful Cobra two-seater roadster, but in 1965 he turned his attention to the Mustang at Ford's request. He took the powerful 271bhp (202kW) Mustang as a base and created the GT350. Shelby improved the handling by re-locating the front suspension control arms, fitting stiffer springs and re-valved Koni shocks, and adding rear traction bars. To provide extra stopping power, he used Kelsey-Hayes front discs, and while the rears were drums, they were cooled by air from the functional side scoops. The 289ci (4.7-litre) V8 engine was upped in power with higher compression, a high-lift camshaft, larger valves and a bigger carburettor. The Shelby R was more powerful, but only 37 racers were built, though they did win Sports Car Club of Americas B-production class against Corvettes, Cobras, Ferraris, Cobras, Lotuses and Jaguar E-Types.

Top speed:	131 mph (210 km/h)
0–60 mph (0–95 km/h):	6.2 sec
Engine type:	V8
Displacement:	302 ci (4,948 cc)
Transmission	4-speed manual
Max power:	335 bhp (250 kW) @ 5,200 rpm
Max torque:	325 lb ft (440 Nm) @ 3,200 rpm
Weight:	3,340 lb (1,518 kg)
Economy:	14 mpg (5 km/l)

Shelby Mustang GT350 (1966)

Carroll Shelby turned his tuning skills to the Mustang in 1965. Using the 271bhp (202kW) Mustang as a base, he created the GT350. It had to beat the Corvette in all areas, and so Shelby relocated the front suspension control arms, fitted stiffer springs and Koni shocks for the handling, then put traction control arms at the rear. For better braking he fitted Kelsey-Hayes front discs, and cooled the rear drums with air ducts on the car's side. The 289ci (4.7-litre) V8 engine went through alterations to improve the power, with higher compression, a high-lift camshaft, larger valves in the heads and a bigger carburettor. The higher-spec'd Shelby R was even more powerful, but only 37 were built for racing, though they did win Sports Car Club of America's B-production class against Corvettes, Cobras, Ferraris, Cobras, Lotuses and Jaguar E-Types.

Top speed:	135 mph (216 km/h)
0–60 mph (0–96 km/h):	5.7 sec
Engine type:	V8
Displacement:	289 ci (4,735 cc)
Transmission	4-speed manual
Max power:	350 bhp (261 kW) @ 6,750 rpm
Max torque:	312 lb ft (423 Nm) @ 3,800 rpm
Weight:	2,600 lb (1,181 kg)
Economy:	13.8 mpg (4.89 km/l)

Shelby Mustang GT500 (1969)

If too much power was considered just enough, the Shelby GT500 went overboard when it joined the GT350 in production in 1967. It was a sales success, outselling the smaller-engined model two to one. Based on the standard Mach 1 Mustang, it differed visually with a new grille, different tail lights, Shelby stripes and square tailpipes. Like the Mach 1, the Shelby used the 428 Cobra jet big-block V8 engine, but it had massive handling improvements. Heavy-duty springs and shocks, wider tyres, thicker anti-roll bars and a roll cage to stiffen the shell gave the Shelby great balance. The exclusivity cost though, at three times the price of Ford's regular Mach 1. Although the factory rated the Cobra Jet motor at 335bhp (250kW) to appease insurance companies who were charging $1000 to insure young males, the output was actually closer to 400bhp (298kW).

Top speed:	130 mph (208 km/h)
0–60 mph (0–96 km/h):	5.5 sec
Engine type:	V8
Displacement:	428 ci (7,013 cc)
Transmission	3-speed auto
Max power:	335 bhp (250 kW) @ 5,200 rpm
Max torque:	440 lb ft (596 Nm) @ 3,400 rpm
Weight:	3,100 lb (1,409 kg)
Economy:	8 mpg (2.83 km/l)

Shelby Omni GLH-S (1986)

Compacts made a big impact as soon as the VW Rabbit (Golf in Europe) debuted in 1975. Chrysler fought back in 1977 with its European-acquired Talbot, altering it for the US market and calling it the Omni. It was significant as it was the first front-wheel drive compact from a US manufacturer. Things hotted up when VW launched the GTi, but Dodge fought back with their 1984 134ci (2.2-litre) Omni GLH, tuned by Carroll Shelby. A year on they turbocharged the engine for 146bhp (109kW), then in 1986 released just 500 of their hottest version: the GLH-S. It ran an intercooler and different intake for the extra power and could do the quarter-mile in 14.9 seconds. Strut suspension with uprated springs and shocks made it handle like a dream, but torque steer was a problem under boost, barely controllable with the 205/50 Goodyear Eagle tyres.

Top speed:	130 mph (208 km/h)
0–60 mph (0–96 km/h):	6.4 sec
Engine type:	In-line four
Displacement:	135 ci (2,212 cc)
Transmission	5-speed manual
Max power:	175 bhp (130 kW) @ 5,200 rpm
Max torque:	168 lb ft (227 Nm) @ 3,600 rpm
Weight:	2,300 lb (1,045 kg)
Economy:	20 mpg (7.08 km/l)

Shelby Charger GLH-S

The name Carroll Shelby is synonymous with performance cars, so as power became important again in the 1980s, he was called upon by Chrysler to inject some life into the rather lame Charger range of 1986 and 1987, which were by then devoid of a V8 and rear-wheel drive in favour of a four-cylinder and front-wheel drive, thus leaving them in direct competition with the compact imports. Shelby took the 146bhp (109kW) engine and added an air-to-air intercooler to the turbo plus equal-length intake runners. Koni shocks were fitted at each corner with lowering springs, and alloys with low-profiles were added for improved handling. The owner of this car has gone a step further with the engine by changing the pistons, strengthening the rotating assembly, gas-flowing the head and adding four extra injectors. Power is sufficient to give 13-second quarter-miles times.

Top speed:	125 mph (200 km/h)
0–60 mph (0–95 km/h):	5.4 sec
Engine type:	In-line four
Displacement:	134 ci (2,200 cc)
Transmission	5-speed manual
Max power:	289 bhp (215 kW) @ 6,200 rpm
Max torque:	274 lb ft (371 Nm) @ 3,700 rpm
Weight:	2,483 lb (1,128 kg)
Economy:	18 mpg (6.4 km/l)

Shelby Dakota

For the majority of the 1980s the compact Dodge Ram Mini pick-up was actually a Mitsubishi truck, simply re-badged for sale in the USA. That changed in 1987 when Dodge brought out their home-grown Dakota to replace it. It was bigger than most of its rivals plus ran a 238ci (3.9-litre) V6. Two years later Dodge offered a Sport version of the same truck, with blacked-out trim and alloys. Carroll Shelby decided to go one further when he offered his Shelby Dakota later that same year, by removing the V6 and squeezing in Chrysler's 318ci (5.4-litre) V8, giving it way more power. But it wasn't all about acceleration, because Shelby also added stiffer springs and dampers, Goodyear Eagle tyres and a limited-slip differential for the rear live axle. A sport steering wheel plus Shelby trim inside finished it off as a new breed of sport truck.

Top speed:	119 mph (190 km/h)
0–60 mph (0–95 km/h):	8.5 sec
Engine type:	V8
Displacement:	318 ci (5,211 cc)
Transmission	4-speed auto
Max power:	175 bhp (130 kW) @ 4,000 rpm
Max torque:	270 lb ft (366 Nm) @ 2,000 rpm
Weight:	3,610 lb (1,641 kg)
Economy:	15 mpg (5.3 km/l)

Shelby/Cooper King Cobra

British racer John Cooper had introduced his mid-engined race car in 1958, but it wasn't until 1963 that Carroll Shelby, in his search for the quintessential race-car design, chose it to shoehorn in an American V8. The chassis was strong but very light being of tubular construction, with the engine and transmission forming part of the structure for extra rigidity. Double A-arms, anti-roll bars and disc brakes sat at either end and the whole body was hand-formed in aluminium. The engine was massively tuned, and a full balancing and blueprinting job was carried out to cope with the racing use. Compression was raised to 10.5:1 for more power, and four twin Weber downdraught carburettors gave the car immense pulling power, even from low rpm. In the space of 2 years, just 12 cars were made and only 3 are known to survive, making them incredibly valuable today.

Top speed:	176 mph (282 km/h)
0–60 mph (0–95 km/h):	3.5 sec
Engine type:	V8
Displacement:	289 ci (4,735 cc)
Transmission	4-speed manual
Max power:	400 bhp (298 kW)@ 6,800 rpm
Max torque:	345 lb ft (467 Nm) @ 4,000 rpm
Weight:	1,400 lb (636 kg)
Economy:	10 mpg (3.5 km/l)

Studebaker Champion (1951)

Often described by people as the car which didn't know which way it was going – due to the wraparound rear screen which could have been the windshield – the Studebaker Champion was designed by famed stylist Raymond Loewy. He took a lot of his influence from the aircraft industry, and nowhere was this more evident than with the bullet nose which even carried a small spinning propeller early in production. This car has been substantially modified since those days, with a revised and strengthened chassis, Mustang II independent front suspension and a Chrysler rear axle on lowered leaf springs. A tuned Mopar 360 sits under the hood and is mated to a Chrysler Torqueflite gearbox with shift-improvement kit. The body has been treated to shaving off any superfluous trim, and the door handles now open on electric solenoid locks operated by remote control.

Top speed:	115 mph (184 km/h)
0–60 mph (0–96 km/h):	9.8 sec
Engine type:	V8
Displacement:	360 ci (5,899 cc)
Transmission	3-speed auto
Max power:	244 bhp (182 kW) @ 4,200 rpm
Max torque:	290 lb ft (393 Nm) @ 3,000 rpm
Weight:	2,690 lb (1,222 kg)
Economy:	17 mpg (6.01 km/l)

Studebaker Golden Hawk (1956)

The Golden Hawk, like its Studebaker sister models the Sky Hawk and Flight Hawk, was based on the original 1953 Starlight body, and so retained its single-piece rear window as opposed to the '52 model's four-piece panoramic item. The '56 Golden Hawk could be identified by its small upright glass-fibre fins on the top of the rear fenders and, being a top model, it shared the glitzy President Classic's wide grooved horizontal aluminium trim mouldings above the rocker panels. It was the most powerful of all Studebakers this year by some margin, so featured power brakes and 7-inch (178mm) wide tyres to make full use of the V8's torque. The car came as a two-door hardtop coupe only to emphasis its sporting nature, but came only with the Twin Drive automatic gearbox from Packard, who'd been in control since '53. In 1957 the Golden Hawk was supercharged and made over 300bhp (223kW).

Top speed:	109 mph (174 km/h)
0-60 mph (0–96 km/h):	9.5 sec
Engine type:	V8
Displacement:	352 ci (5,768 cc)
Transmission	3-speed auto
Max power:	275 bhp (205 kW) @ 4,600 rpm
Max torque:	300 lb ft (406 Nm) @ 2,800 rpm
Weight:	3,360 lb (1,527 kg)
Economy:	15 mpg (5.31 km/l)

Stutz Bearcat (1914)

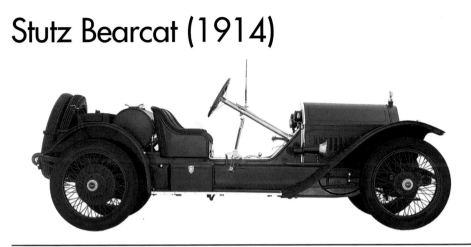

Fundamentally a road-going race car, the Bearcat was developed from Stutz's Indy racer which came 11th in 1911 at the very first Indy 500. The race car inspired Harry Clayton Stutz to start production, and he was clever in the design of his Bearcat, make it lightweight and with good weight distribution to make the car handle, albeit it had standard wooden 'cart' wheels, though wire-spoked rims were optional. The Bearcat had a basic but strong twin rail design, and used the engine solid-mounted to make it a stressed member, a trick that's still used in racing cars today. The gearbox was mounted at the rear as part of the transaxle, helping offset the huge cast-iron engine's weight up front. The car could easily cruise at 60mph (96km/h), making it the supercar of its day. In 1915 Erwin 'Cannonball' Baker crossed America in one, doing 3,700 miles (5,953km) at 13.7mph (22km/h), without proper roads.

Top speed:	80 mph (128 km/h)
0–60 mph (0–96 km/h):	N/A
Engine type:	In-line four
Displacement:	390 ci (6,3902 cc)
Transmission	3–speed manual
Max power:	60 bhp (44 kW) @ 1,500 rpm
Max torque:	N/A
Weight:	2,500 lb (1,136 kg)
Economy:	13.8 mpg (4.88 km/l)

Subaru SVX

The SVX is a curious car in that it came out of the blue from Subaru. Though the company had previously produced their XT Coupe which ran from 1985 to 1990, the car was not a beauty, yet in most ways the 1991 SVX made up for that with Italian styling. Uniquely it used glass all around with hidden pillars, which gave it great visibility for such a low-slung supercar. The SVX's drive train was another one-off, featuring a flat-six engine mounted at the front and driving all four wheels. The torque was automatically split between front and rear wheels depending on grip, and MacPherson struts at each corner helped with space allocation for the 4WD set-up. Handling was superb and the traction phenomenal, with minimal body roll in corners. Alas, sales weren't good for the car, even when cheaper models were introduced, and by 1996 it had gone.

Top speed:	144 mph (230 km/h)
0–60 mph (0–95 km/h):	7.6 sec
Engine type:	Flat six
Displacement:	202 ci (3,318 cc)
Transmission	4-speed auto
Max power:	230 bhp (172 kW) @ 5,400 rpm
Max torque:	228 lb ft (309 Nm) @ 4,400 rpm
Weight:	3,614 lb (1,642 kg)
Economy:	22 mpg (7.8 km/l)

Subaru Impreza rally car

Subaru started making an impression on the World Rally Championship with its 1990 4WD turbo Legacy. When the 1994 Impreza was introduced, they used it because it was both lighter and smaller, thus more nimble. The road was so good that the rally car remained very similar in layout, having MacPherson struts all around but fully adjustable. Vented discs with four-pot callipers at each corner ensured superb braking while the 4WD system remained 50:50 split in torque. A tubular roll cage strengthened up the stock body and gave the required safety. The flat-four engine received new engine management but was limited to 300bhp (223kW) as per the FIA World Rally regulations, and used a three-way catalytic converter to conform to emissions standards. This car is Colin McRae's WRC-winning car which made him the first British champion and Subaru's first champion also.

Top speed:	140 mph (224 km/h)
0–60 mph (0–95 km/h):	3.2 sec
Engine type:	Flat four
Displacement:	122 ci (1,994 cc)
Transmission	6-speed sequential
Max power:	300 bhp (223 kW) @ 5,500 rpm
Max torque:	348 lb ft (471 Nm) @ 4000 rpm
Weight:	2,711 lb (1,232 kg)
Economy:	N/A

Subaru Impreza Turbo

For many the Impreza Turbo was the car of the 1990s. It made its debut in Japan in 1992, with the engine from the bigger Legacy, a car which had already proven itself in rally competition. The Impreza hit the UK market in 1994 , the same time as Colin McRae romped home to win the World Rally Championship in one. From there the model has gone from strength to strength, and it's easy to see why. Though the interior is bland and the exterior barely more dynamic, the driving experience has sold this car to thousands. With limpet-like grip in corners, the handling is nothing short of sensational, while the punch from the turbo is virtually lag-free, partly down to the high compression ratio of 9.5:1. Four-wheel discs with ABS make for excellent braking, while the 4WD split torque evenly front/rear, unless conditions change, whereby it alters the split to where the grip is best.

Top speed:	143 mph (229 km/h)
0–60 mph (0–95 km/h):	6.4 sec
Engine type:	Flat four
Displacement:	122 ci (1,994 cc)
Transmission	5-speed manual
Max power:	208 bhp (155 kW) @ 5,600 rpm
Max torque:	214 lb ft (289 Nm) @ 4,000 rpm
Weight:	2,879 lb (1,308 kg)
Economy:	29 mpg (10.35 km/l)

Sunbeam Alpine

The Sunbeam Talbot 90 saloon was an atrractively styled sedan with a well-appointed interior. It was a comfortable and well-respected tourer, but its lack of image meant that sales were slow. In order to boost the car's showroom appeal, Sunbeam's owner, the Rootes Group, decided to create the Alpine – a stylish two-door drophead based on the running gear and chassis of the Talbot. While it was always too heavy and ponderous to be regarded as a sports car, the Alpine was nonethless a competent and desirable touring car, with a well-insulated cabin, beautifully-trimmed interior and gorgeous, curvy styling, penned by American designer Raymond Loewy. The bodies were built independently by HJ Mulliner of Birmingham, England, and transported to Rootes Group's nearby plant in Coventry for final assembly.

Top speed:	98 mph (158 km/h)
0–60 mph (0–95 km/h):	14.8 sec
Engine type:	in-line four
Displacement:	138 ci (2,267 cc)
Transmission:	4-speed manual
Max power:	80 bhp (60 kW) at 4,400 rpm
Max torque:	122 lb ft (166 Nm) at 2,400 rpm
Weight:	2,856 lb (1,285 kg)
Economy:	24 mpg (8.6 km/l)

Sunbeam Tiger

With V8s being fitted to many sportscars, Sunbeam were only trying what many others had done by 1964. They took their four-cylinder Alpine, which usually had a 91ci (1.4-litre) engine, and fitted a Ford V8. Being a British company, Ford had no problem selling their Mustang's 260ci (4.6-litre) V8 and the unit fitted well. The Alpine bodyshell needed little work in order to take the new larger engine, the most notable change being a switch to rack and pinion steering, as the standard recirculating ball system got in the way. Also, the engine left no room for the battery so that had to be mounted in the trunk. The chassis was very strong, featuring an X-brace design welded to the body and carrying wishbone suspension at the front and a live axle rear on leaf springs. All the spring rates and shocks were uprated, but on twisty streets, the car would show its limitations.

Top speed:	117 mph (187 km/h)
0–60 mph (0–95 km/h):	9.7 sec
Engine type:	V8
Displacement:	289 ci (4,735 cc)
Transmission	4-speed manual
Max power:	164 bhp (122 kW) @ 4,400 rpm
Max torque:	258 lb ft (349 Nm) @ 2,200 rpm
Weight:	2,644 lb (1,201 kg)
Economy:	14.7 mpg (5.25 km/l)

Suzuki Cappuccino

Japanese tax breaks for cars under 660cc were the main reason for the Cappuccino's existence. Until then, most cars offered in the sector were tiny city hatchbacks designed for commuters, but offering little in the way of driver appeal. The Cappuccino, though, would change all that. Equipped with a revvy little turbocharged three-pot engine capable of over 9,000rpm, it offered surprising performance from such a tiny unit, while the stunning styling looked fantastic despite the car's minusucule dimensions. It was a hoot to drive, too. With its engine mounted longitudinally and supplying drive to the rear wheels, the Suzuki had near perfect 50:50 weight distribution, giving it excellent poise and handling balance, while a snappy gearshift and direct steering added to its driver appeal. Just over 1000 were exported to the UK, with a handful being sold in Europe between 1993 and 1995.

Top speed:	87 mph (141 km/h)
0–60 mph (0–95 km/h):	10.0 sec
Engine type:	in-line three
Displacement:	40 ci (658 cc)
Transmission:	5-speed manual
Max power:	64 bhp (48 kW) at 6,500 rpm
Max torque:	76 lb ft (103 Nm) at 3,500 rpm
Weight:	1,543 lb (694 kg)
Economy:	33 mpg (11.8 km/l)

Talbot Sunbeam Lotus

Chrysler bought the British Rootes and French Simca groups in 1967 as part of its foray into Europe. It produced the Avenger from 1976 to 1979 and it was a shorter version of that car's wheelbase under the Talbot Sunbeam. It was called a Talbot by then because Chrysler sold its Europe operation to Peugeot in 1978, and Talbot was part of Simca. As a celebration of the takeover, in conjunction with Lotus, Peugeot produced this new hot hatch in 1979. Lotus used the all-alloy, twin-cam from their own Elite, but with extra crank stroke for another 10.5ci (172cc), plus twin Weber carbs. Uprated and lowered springs and shocks were added to the simple MacPherson strut front and trailing arm-located live rear axle, and 6x13-inch (152x330mm) alloys added. Also fitted were bucket seats and 5-speed gearbox. This very capable car won the 1981 World Rally Championship, beating Audi's Quattro.

Top speed:	121 mph (194 km/h)
0–60 mph (0–95 km/h):	7.4 sec
Engine type:	In-line four
Displacement:	133 ci (2,174 cc)
Transmission	5-speed manual
Max power:	150 bhp (112 kW) @ 5,750 rpm
Max torque:	150 lb ft (203 Nm) @ 4,500 rpm
Weight:	2,116 lb (962 kg)
Economy:	22 mpg (7.8 km/l)

Tatra T613

Czechoslovakian manufacturer Tatra was nothing if not proud of its ability to be unconventional, and the T613 proved that point perfectly. Enormous and arguably ungainly in appearance, the T613 was designed with government officials and seriously wealthy businessmen in mind. But although it looked like a conventional three-box saloon, the engine was hidden in the back, almost directly above the rear axle in order to alleviate handling problems previously associated with rear-engined Tatras. What's more, the quad-cam V8 unit was air-cooled, giving it a distinctive exhaust note. Although sold in strictly limited numbers, as few people in what was then Czechoslovakia could afford such an elaborate machine, it enjoyed a production run of 23 years, manufacture finally ending in 1998 when the company folded.

Top speed:	115 mph (184 km/h)
0–60 mph (0–95 km/h):	12.0 sec
Engine type:	air-cooled V8
Displacement:	213 ci (3,495 cc)
Transmission:	5-speed manual
Max power:	165 bhp (123 kW) at 4,400 rpm
Max torque:	150 lb ft (204 Nm) at 2,800 rpm
Weight:	4,104 lb (1,846 kg)
Economy:	16 mpg (5.7 km/l)

Toyota MR2

When Toyota first debuted their mid-engined Toyota MR2 to the world's press in 1984, journalists couldn't believe something with such basic suspension could handle so well. But it did, and was incredibly nimble because of its lightweight construction. When the second-generation car hit the market in 1990, it was heavier so lost that razor-sharp feel of the early car, but at the same time became more civilized and was, ultimately, built better. The new car retained the handling of the first through use of MacPherson struts all around, but was less twitchy on the limit as mid-engined cars are prone to be. The 122ci (2-litre) engine used twin camshafts and a variable induction system to increase high rpm output whilst retaining reasonable low rpm power. Discs that were slightly larger at the rear accompanied slightly larger rear tyres too, all in an effort to balance the car perfectly.

Top speed:	128 mph (205 km/h)
0–60 mph (0–95 km/h):	8.1 sec
Engine type:	In-line four
Displacement:	122 ci (1,998 cc)
Transmission	5-speed manual
Max power:	173 bhp (129 kW) @ 7,000 rpm
Max torque:	137 lb ft (185 Nm) @ 4,800 rpm
Weight:	2,833 lb (1,288 kg)
Economy:	23.5 mpg (8.39 km/l)

Toyota Supra Turbo

T he Supra name first appeared in the Celica range on the Celica Supra, which
unlike the other four-cylinder cars in the range had a 171ci (2.8-litre) straight
six twin-cam motor with 168bhp (125kW). By 1986 the two names had separated
again and the Supra was completely re-styled. Its engine was taken out to 183ci (3
litres) and with 24 valves, power was up to 200bhp (149kW). Three years later
Toyota hotted the car up with an intercooled turbo for 232bhp (173kW) and much
improved mid-range torque. This turned the car from cruising GT to street monster;
Toyota had well and truly put the Supra into supercar territory. Wishbone
suspension plus fattened anti-roll bars gave it good handling. The brakes were 11-
inch (279mm) vented discs with ABS. Power steering was essential, and the car was
better with the standard five-speed manual, though four-speed auto was popular.

Top speed:	144 mph (230 km/h)
0–60 mph (0-95 km/h):	6.5 sec
Engine type:	In-line six
Displacement:	180 ci (2,954 cc)
Transmission	4-speed auto
Max power:	232 bhp (173 kW) @ 5,600 rpm
Max torque:	254 lb ft (344 Nm) @ 4,000 rpm
Weight:	3,535 lb (1,606 kg)
Economy:	24 mpg (8.5 km/l)

Toyota Celica All-Trac

Toyota built a 4WD turbo version of their Celica in order to homologate it for world rallying. It first appeared in 1988 as the GT-Four, which in street-going form produced 185bhp (138kW) with its boosted 16v four-cylinder. The Celica was already a great handling front-wheel drive vehicle, and the extra two wheels driving made it even more memorable, if expensive. In 1990 Toyota launched the All-Trac, with more power and active suspension. This did very well in rallying in the early 1990s, winning many races and eventually taking the World Rally Championship in 1993. By then the car was both quick and very reassuring on fast, twisty streets. The hood had a huge intake for the intercooler and the turbo used a clever method of smoothing flow with two different-sized ports for the exhaust. Power on street cars could be 300bhp (224kW); the excellent chassis easily coped.

Top speed:	136 mph (218 km/h)
0–60 mph (0–95 km/h):	6.7 sec
Engine type:	In-line four
Displacement:	122 ci (1,998 cc)
Transmission	5-speed manual
Max power:	200 bhp (149 kW) @ 6,000 rpm
Max torque:	200 lb ft (271 Nm) @ 3,200 rpm
Weight:	3,218 lb (1,463 kg)
Economy:	24 mpg (8.5 km/l)

Toyota MR2 Turbo

The 1990 version of the MR2 was further improved with more refinement and power, and with a turbocharger attached to the 122ci (2-litre) 16v four-cylinder unit, output was 200bhp (149kW) and 200lb ft (279Nm) torque, making the car more like a mini Ferrari. Yet the engine remained very useable throughout, thanks to a variable induction system, and of course being a Toyota, it was ultra-reliable. All the power was put down by capably by a limited-slip differential. The 1990 MR2 Turbo used MacPherson struts and anti-roll bars front and rear, and to overcome twitchy handling experienced on earlier models, later cars were fitted with both taller tyres and fatter rears, which worked well with the 42:58 front/rear weight distribution. The car was very controllable even in hard acceleration out of corners. Vented discs all around meant braking was also superb, with no fade under heavy use.

Top speed:	144 mph (230 km/h)
0–60 mph (0-95 km/h):	6.2 sec
Engine type:	In-line four
Displacement:	122 ci (1,998 cc)
Transmission:	5-speed manual
Max power:	200 bhp (149k kW) @ 6,000 rpm
Max torque:	200 lb ft (271 Nm) @ 3,200 rpm
Weight:	2,888 lb (1,313 kg)
Economy:	27 mpg (9.6 km/l)

Toyota Celica GT

T he Celica went from a live axle rear-wheel drive configuration to front-wheel
drive in 1986. Toyota also slotted in a high-revving, smooth four-cylinder motor
which in US version put out just 130bhp (97kW) but in Europe had 147bhp (110kW).
In 1990 the car was updated, then again in 1994 with the swoopy shape shown here.
By the mid-1990s the car's sporting prowess had been well established as Carlos
Sainz had taken home the World Rally Championship in a Celica earlier that
decade. The independent suspension layout, being MacPherson struts all around
with anti-roll bars, was retained for the new model, as were the 10-inch (254mm)
four-wheel disc brakes with ABS. New alloys with low-profile tyres ensured
excellent cornering speed. The 16v engine used dual-phase intake system, which
used a shorter intake once the revs climbed above 5,000rpm, for extra power.

Top speed:	131 mph (210 km/h)
0–60 mph (0–95 km/h):	8.3 sec
Engine type:	In-line four
Displacement:	134 ci (2,200 cc)
Transmission	5-speed manual
Max power:	130 bhp (97kW) @ 5,400 rpm
Max torque:	145 lb ft (196 Nm) @ 4,400 rpm
Weight:	2,580 lb (1,173 kg)
Economy:	26 mpg (9.2 km/l)

Triumph TR3

Although the first Triumph TR model was the TR2, it was the TR3 that was the first genuinely sporting offering. It was little different from the TR2 in appearance, with only an egg-crate style grille and chromed wheels distinguishing it from the earlier model, but it had a completely different charcter from the driver's seat. Equipped with a 2.0-litre four-cylinder engine lifted from the Standard Vanguard, it delivered enough power to give it seriously quick acceleration for its day and the ability to cruise at over 100mph (160km/h), while Girling disc brakes meant it was capable of slowing down adequately as well. The TR3 was the car that finally brought success to Triumph in the strategically important American market, and it would go on to spawn a glorious line of revered TR sports cars. In 1957 a revamped version was produced, the TR3A, with a full-length grille.

Top speed:	106 mph (172 km/h)
0–60 mph (0–95 km/h):	11.4 sec
Engine type:	in-line four
Displacement:	121 ci (1,991 cc)
Transmission:	4-speed manual
Max power:	100 bhp (74 kW) at 5,000 rpm
Max torque:	117 lb ft (159 Nm) at 3,000 rpm
Weight:	2,200 lb (990 kg)
Economy:	31 mpg (11 km/l)

Triumph TR5

Much like the TR3 was almost a facsimile of the TR2, the TR5 looked pretty much identical to the TR4A that preceded it. But the TR5's biggest difference was hidden under the long bonnet, with a new 2.5-litre (152ci) six-cylinder fuel-injected engine installed. The result was a car that delivered blistering performance and a fantastic exhaust note, while other changes included more powerful brakes, stiffer rear suspension and a more comfortable and safety-conscious cabin. The TR4A's bonnet bulge was retained, although it wasn't needed, for effect. Unfortunately for Triumph, the Lucas fuel-injection system fitted to home market cars failed to meet stringent emmisions legislation in the USA, so cars destined for the States came with Zentih carburettors instead. These less powerful machines were rebadged as TR250s.

Top speed:	107 mph (173 km/h)
0–60 mph (0–95 km/h):	10.6 sec
Engine type:	in-line six
Displacement:	152 ci (2,498 cc)
Transmission:	4-speed manual
Max power:	111 bhp (83 kW) at 4,500 rpm
Max torque:	152 lb ft (206 Nm) at 3,000 rpm
Weight:	2,350 lb (1,058 kg)
Economy:	23 mpg (8.2 km/l)

Triumph TR6

For many enthusiasts the 1969 TR6 was the last Triumph TR. It might have been crude and old fashioned, but it rewarded drivers who knew its limits. The styling was by Karmann of Germany, and now enthusiasts regard this as a classic look thanks to wraparound rear lights and the bold, aggressive front.   Underneath it had a separate chassis with double wishbones at the front and a trailing arm independent rear which, though better than previous live axles TRs, still wasn't that great so Triumph gave the TR6 wide tyres to help. The straight-six engine was a development of the former four-cylinder cast-iron unit from the early 1960s and hence was no technical revelation in design; however, it did use Lucas mechanical fuel injection which improved power, but at the cost of reliability at low speeds. The TR6 lasted until 1976, and remained on the market when the TR7 was launched.

Top speed:	119 mph (190 km/h)
0–60 mph (0–95 km/h):	8.4 sec
Engine type:	In-line six
Displacement:	152 ci (2,498 cc)
Transmission	4-speed manual
Max power:	150 bhp (112 kW) @ 5,500 rpm
Max torque:	164 lb ft (222 Nm) @ 3,500 rpm
Weight:	2,473 lb (1,124 kg)
Economy:	16.8 mpg (6 km/l)

Triumph Stag

The Triumph Stag was out on its own in the market when it appeared in 1970. There was nothing quite like the grand touring four-seater convertible, but it embodied the British Leyland spirit of setting trends and not following them. The theory behind the car worked well, in that it used a new, small-capacity SOHC V8, unitary construction for extra chassis strength, independent front and rear suspension and an Italian-involved design. Unfortunately, reliability problems on the engine with overheating and head gasket failures meant many replacement motors under warranty, and when the car hit the US market in 1971, its reputation had already started to tarnish. Two years on saw a MkII version produced with a more refined V8, better steering, five-spoke alloys and improved seating, but by then the damage was done, and the Stag was doomed by 1977.

Top speed:	118 mph (189 km/h)
0–60 mph (0-95 km/h):	9.3 sec
Engine type:	V8
Displacement:	183 ci (2,997 cc)
Transmission	4-speed manual
Max power:	145 bhp (108 kW) @ 5,500 rpm
Max torque:	170 lb ft (230 Nm) @ 3,500 rpm
Weight:	2,795 lb (1,270 kg)
Economy:	22 mpg (7.8 km/l)

Triumph Dolomite Sprint

In 1965 Triumph brought out their one and only front-wheel drive car, the 1300, and though it was styled by Italian House Michelotti it looked rather dumpy, but inside was at least luxurious for the money and so sold well. The car was re-styled for 1970 and given rear-wheel drive, and it came in both Toledo and 1500 guises, the 1500 being slightly longer in the tail and featuring double headlamps. The 1973 Dolomite was simply an upgraded 1500 and came with had the new generation 113ci (1.8-litre) four cylinder, which for the Sprint only was given a 16-valve head working with one camshaft. The TR6's gearbox was needed to cope with the extra power made. The Dolomite had firmer suspension which made it into a good quality sports saloon, and it won the 1974 British Saloon Car Championship with Andy Rouse behind the wheel. Production ended in 1980, with just short of 23,000 made.

Top speed:	115 mph (184 km/h)
0–60 mph (0–95 km/h):	8.8 sec
Engine type:	In-line four
Displacement:	122 ci (1,998 cc)
Transmission	5-speed manual
Max power:	127 bhp (95 kW) @ 5,700 rpm
Max torque:	122 lb ft (165 Nm) @ 4,500 rpm
Weight:	2,300 lb (1,045 kg)
Economy:	25 mpg (8.9 km/l)

Triumph Spitfire

Starting with the chassis of the humble Herald, Triumph pulled off a brilliant feat of engineering to create the little Spitfire, its new budget sports car launched in 1962. By chopping the chassis and clothing it in a beautiful body styled by Italian Michelotti, the Spitfire emerged as one of the prettiest small sports cars on the road. That, coupled to a choice of free-revving Herald-derived engines, a snappy gearshift and a quicker steering rack made the Spitfire one of the most desirable cars of its day. The fact it was cheap to buy and the one-piece lift-up bonnet meant servicing was simple made it even more popular, despite the fact that its Herald rear suspension made it difficult to handle when cornering at speed. With three restyles, the Spitfire lasted in production for 18 years and achieved considerable sales success, with over 300,000 sold across Europe, Australasia and the USA.

Top speed:	97 mph (157 km/h)
0–60 mph (0–95 km/h):	13.6 sec
Engine type:	in-line four
Displacement:	79 ci (1,296 cc)
Transmission:	4-speed manual
Max power:	75 bhp (56kW) at 6,000 rpm
Max torque:	75 lb ft (102 Nm) at 4,000 rpm
Weight:	1,680 lb (756 kg)
Economy:	30 mpg (10.7 km/l)

Triumph TR7

The TR7 changed perceptions of Triumph's previously macho TR sports car range. Designed by Harris Mann, who also penned the disastrous Austin Allegro and BL Princess, it had controversial wedge-shaped lines that you either loved or hated, while unlike previous TRs it was offered at launch as a fixed-head coupé only. Power came from a 2.0-litre slant-four engine, but although Triumph had fitted the first 16-valve cylinder head to this engine in the Dolomite Sprint, the TR7 got an eight-valve unit instead as the 16v wouldn't fit underneath the steeply raked front end. Early cars were badly built and much criticised, but a far better looking convertible model finally arrived in 1979. The following year, the TR8, powered by the venerable alloy Rover V8 engine, was introduced for the American market, but it was too late to rescue flagging sales, and the TR7 died a year later.

Top speed:	110 mph (178 km/h)
0–60 mph (0–95 km/h):	11.2 sec
Engine type:	slant-four
Displacement:	122 ci (1,998 cc)
Transmission:	4-speed manual/5-speed manual/3-speed auto
Max power:	90 bhp (67 kW) at 5,000 rpm
Max torque:	106 lb ft (144 Nm) at 3,000 rpm
Weight:	2,240 lb (1,008 kg)
Economy:	33 mpg (11.8 km/l)

Triumph TR8

In the same way that British Leyland (BL) livened up the MGB by fitting a V8, so the Triumph TR7 was improved with one. The TR7 appeared in 1975 but with the 122ci (2-litre) only producing 92bhp (69kW). In the US market, for which the TR8 was intended, the car needed more power. To satisfy demand, British Leyland slotted in their Rover V8, which was all-aluminium, so weighed a similar amount to the four-cylinder TR7 engine. The new car used MacPherson strut front and a four-link rear suspension which improved handling over the TR6 model. The spring rates were slightly too soft, giving more of a leisurely touring ride quality than firm sportscar feel, but there was no doubt about performance, as the V8 made the car 12 seconds quicker to 100mph (160km/h) than the 2-litre. Due to BL strikes and production delays it was two years late, never making the impact it should have.

Top speed:	120 mph (192 km/h)
0–60 mph (0–95 km/h):	8.4 sec
Engine type:	V8
Displacement:	215 ci (3,528 cc)
Transmission	5-speed manual
Max power:	148 bhp (110 kW) @ 5,100 rpm
Max torque:	180 lb ft (243 Nm) @ 3,250 rpm
Weight:	2,620 lb (1,190 kg)
Economy:	20 mpg (7.1 km/l)

Tucker Torpedo

It was a fairy tale that went disastrously wrong. Millionnaire Preston Tucker, a car industry man through-and-through, decided that America needed an advanced and modern car that would wow the world, and secured the backing of several well-heeled investors to help fund the project. The Torpedo was unveiled in 1948 and caused quite a stir, with its striking styling, amazing aerodynamics, rubber-sprung suspension and distinctive middle headlight, which turned with the steering wheel to help drivers see round corners. But in reality, the Torpedo was a financial disaster that took far too long to develop, and the project was aborted when Preston Tucker was indicted on fraud charges. He was later acquitted, but investors lost confidence and the project stalled after just 37 cars were made, although a further 14 were constructed from leftover parts.

Top speed:	120 mph (193 km/h)
0–60 mph (0–95 km/h):	10.1 sec
Engine type:	in-line six
Displacement:	335 ci (5,491 cc)
Transmission:	4-speed manual
Max power:	166 bhp (124 kW) at 3,200 rpm
Max torque:	not quoted
Weight:	4,235 lb (1,906 kg)
Economy:	13 mpg (4.6 km/l)

TVR 450 SEAC

TVR's theory of putting a lot of power into a relatively lightweight body has won many fans and produced some stunning machines. The 450 SEAC, one of their most brutal-looking cars with performance to match, was produced from 1988 to 1991. In TVR tradition the chassis is tubular steel with a central backbone and outriggers along the sills to provide side impact protection. Independent suspension all around using double wishbones at the front and lower wishbones at the rear provided a nimble, if firm, ride. The body was made from glass-fibre composite and the engine is all-aluminium; as such the car is only just over a ton so has an excellent power-to-weight ratio. The powerplant is a heavily modified version of the Rover V8, the TVR's being bored and stroked to give an extra litre displacement and fitted with Lucas L-Type electronic fuel injection.

Top speed:	165 mph (264 km/h)
0–60 mph (0–95 km/h):	4.7 sec
Engine type:	V8
Displacement:	271 ci (4,441 cc)
Transmission	5-speed manual
Max power:	320 bhp (239 kW) @ 5,700 rpm
Max torque:	310 lb ft (420 Nm) @ 4,000 rpm
Weight:	2,315 lb (1,052 kg)
Economy:	16 mpg (5.7 km/l)

TVR Tuscan (racer)

Chairman of TVR, Peter Wheeler, described the Tuscan racer as 'very frightening', which was no understatement, given its incredible power. The car came about as the 420 SEC was banned from competition because it was beating all its competition. TVR responded by creating its own one-make racer series, with the Tuscan announced as the new car everyone would compete in. The first meeting was in 1989 and was deemed a huge success because of the close racing and the skill required from the drivers. The Tuscan used a backbone chassis, but with double wishbones at the rear instead of trailing arms. Huge disc brakes were fitted to withstand hard use, and racers were allowed changes only to the spring rates, anti-roll bars and shocks. The mandatory engine was TVR's modified version of a Rover V8, using four Dellorto carbs and a strengthened bottom end.

Top speed:	165 mph (264 km/h)
0–60 mph (0–95 km/h):	3.6 sec
Engine type:	V8
Displacement:	271 ci (4,441 cc)
Transmission	5-speed manual
Max power:	400 bhp (298 kW) @ 7,000 rpm
Max torque:	361 lb ft (489 Nm) @ 5,500 rpm
Weight:	1,765 lb (802 kg)
Economy:	N/A

TVR Griffith

The 1992 Griffith's rounded and smooth shape took over the wedge-shaped TVRs of the 1980s to much public enthusiasm. Underneath it used the ultra-stiff steel backbone chassis which extended to the side sills, with the entire frame being plastic-coated to prevent corrosion. Twin wishbones front and rear created an independent suspension which was a marvel, though the TVR took some taming thanks to a heavy clutch and no power steering at first. Ever-accessible oversteer was just a prod of the throttle away despite a Quaife limited-slip differential used in a beefed-up Sierra rear housing. The latest tune of Rover V8 up front was by then sporting (in the 1993 Griffith 500) over double the original engine's 1960's output and an equally spectacular torque figure. Cleverly, the motor was mounted far back in the chassis to provide a near equal front/rear weight distribution.

Top speed:	161 mph (258 km/h)
0–60 mph (0–95 km/h):	4.3 sec
Engine type:	V8
Displacement:	305 ci (4,997 cc)
Transmission	5-speed manual
Max power:	340 bhp (253 kW) @ 5,500 rpm
Max torque:	351 lb ft (475 Nm) @ 4,000 rpm
Weight:	2,370 lb (1,077 kg)
Economy:	13.1 mpg (4.6 km/l)

TVR Chimaera

The 1993 Chimaera was built as a milder version of the Griffith, but was still a formidable roadster thanks to the lightweight construction. It used a steel backbone chassis with side rails to provide impact protection which was strong and transmitted no cowl shake. Wishbone suspension was used front and rear as were four-wheel discs brakes, but the handling was good, thanks to 50:50 weight distribution, achieved by setting the engine well back. The steering was, like other TVRs, a very quick rack and pinion. The engine was a developed version of Rover's all-aluminium V8, and TVR modified theirs by increasing the compression ratio to 9.8:1, then mapping their own engine management to help power delivery. By 1995 there was a 305ci (5-litre) version of the Chimaera available, which took power up to 340bhp (253kW) and the 0–60mph (0–95km/h) down to 4.1 seconds.

Top speed:	158 mph (253 km/h)
0–60 mph (0–95 km/h):	5.2 sec
Engine type:	V8
Displacement:	241 ci (3,950 cc)
Transmission	5-speed manual
Max power:	240 bhp (179 kW) @ 5,250 rpm
Max torque:	270 lb ft (366 Nm) @ 4,000 rpm
Weight:	2,260 lb (1,027 kg)
Economy:	23 mpg (8.2 km/l)

TVR Cerbera 4.5

The 1997 Cerbera continued in TVR's tradition of producing lightweight sportscars and developed their modern range, started with the Griffith in 1991. Conventional underneath, it used TVR's strong backbone chassis with double wishbones and anti-roll bars front and rear, though softer spring rates were used to make it more comfortable than former models. At first the car had a 224ci (4-litre) straight-six producing 365bhp (272kW). This new engine was quickly followed by a new all-alloy V8, with a flat plane crank to promote rpm, one camshaft per bank and dry sump lubrication. There were two versions of the V8: 256ci (4.2-litre) with 349bhp (260kW); and this 275ci (4.5-litre) with 420bhp (313kW). Huge vented discs with racing four-piston callipers could stop the car from 60mph (95km/h) in just 2.8 seconds. The body had electronic door buttons under the door mirror.

Top speed:	168 mph (269 km/h)
0–60 mph (0–95 km/h):	4.1 sec
Engine type:	V8
Displacement:	273 ci (4,475 cc)
Transmission	5-speed manual
Max power:	420 bhp (313 kW) @ 6,750 rpm
Max torque:	380 lb ft (514 Nm) @ 5,500 rpm
Weight:	2,598 lb (1,180 kg)
Economy:	19.3 mpg (6.8 km/l)

Ultima Spyder

The first Ultima was built in 1986 and entered the British Kit Car Championship, which it won twice. By 1992 the car had been so finely honed in MkIII guise that it made sense for Ultima to offer it as a road car for track day/autocross use. The inspiration for the Ultima was Group C2 racing cars of the 1980s, used at events like Le Mans 24 hours. In 1993, once the MkIV Ultima was thoroughly proven, it was re-bodied with the new Spyder roadster. The car was mid-engined, as per all Ultimas, and ran a tubular steel perimeter chassis with integral roll bar and composite bodywork. Double wishbone suspension was fitted at either end, along with a low-geared steering rack and 12-inch (305mm) four-wheel AP racing vented discs. Though various engine options were available, the one to go for was the small-block Chevy. This one has Chevy's H.O. unit, with a Porsche 911 transaxle.

Top speed:	170 mph (272 km/h)
0–60 mph (0–95 km/h):	3.8 sec
Engine type:	V8
Displacement:	350 ci (5,733 cc)
Transmission	5-speed manual
Max power:	345 bhp (257 kW) @ 5,600 rpm
Max torque:	379 lb ft (513 Nm) @ 3,600 rpm
Weight:	2,180 lb (991 kg)
Economy:	18 mpg (6.4 km/l)

Vauxhall/Opel Calibra Turbo

The Calibra was welcomed by all when it debuted at the Frankfurt Motor Show, Germany, in 1989. It was a clever piece of design too, as Vauxhall had simply based it on their Vectra/Cavalier sedan yet managed to create one of the most aerodynamic production cars in the world. The range-topper that came early in 1990 was the 122ci (2-litre) 16-valve 150bhp (112kW) model, which finally brought the former dull-driving model to life. With the Cavalier/Vectra having been successful with 4WD, the company decided to install it on the Calibra and to distance the car from the sedan, they added a turbo which pushed power beyond 200bhp (149kW). The chassis handled it well, and the grip from the 4WD system was incredible, though it would start to understeer on the limit. While other turbo 4WD rally refugees were faster, none could match the bargain price of the Calibra.

Top speed:	150 mph (240 km/h)
0–60 mph (0–95 km/h):	6.3 sec
Engine type:	In-line four
Displacement:	122 ci (1,998 cc)
Transmission	6-speed manual
Max power:	201 bhp (150 kW) @ 5,600 rpm
Max torque:	207 lb ft (280 Nm) @ 2,400 rpm
Weight:	3,100 lb (1,409 kg)
Economy:	25 mpg (8.9 km/l)

Vector W8

Amerca's answer to the likes of Lamborghini and Ferrari was a long time in the
making. Debuted in Los Angeles in 1977 as 'the fastest car in the world', the
Vector W2 eventually saw launch in 1990 as the W8, with a Donovan-designed
aluminium small-block V8 displacing 348ci (5,703cc) based on Chevrolet's Corvette
engine. Two years later came the WX3 model, which utilized twin turbos on the
same engine to produce an astonishing 1100bhp (820kW). Sadly, the tiny company
never did enjoy particularly spectacular success and the total built to date numbers
less than 50. What a package you got though, with a mid-engined aerodynamic
body, lightweight composite panels, an aluminium chassis and huge ABS-assisted
disc brakes to pull the car down from its top speed of 218mph (350km/h). This was a
hypercar in the true sense, being fast, expensive and extremely rare.

Top speed:	195 mph (312 km/h)
0–60 mph (0–95 km/h):	4.1 sec
Engine type:	V12
Displacement:	348 ci (5,707 cc)
Transmission	3-speed auto
Max power:	492 bhp (367 kW) @ 7,000 rpm
Max torque:	428 lb ft (580 Nm) @ 5,200 rpm
Weight:	3,308 lb (1,504 kg)
Economy:	8.4 mpg (3 km/l)

Venturi 260

France's only supercar manufacturer, Venturi, started manufacturing in 1984 and tested Peugeot's four-cylinder turbo engines at first. However, they eventually went for Renault's GTA V6, and full production began in 1986 with two models, the 210 and 260 (bhp output). The 260 used a backbone chassis with the glass-fibre composite body bonded to it to form a stiff monocoque. The suspension had double wishbones up front and a sophisticated multi-link rear. The PRV V6, so called because both Peugeot, Renault and Volvo use it, started off as a 153ci (2.5-litre) but was increased in 1990 then again to 183ci (3 litres) in 1994. Venturi modified the all-alloy unit with new pistons, camshafts, high compression and a new exhaust. Extra power came through an intercooled Garrett turbo. The car combined leech-like grip, controllable oversteer, sharp steering and incredible braking power.

Top speed:	168 mph (269 km/h)
0–60 mph (0–95 km/h):	5.3 sec
Engine type:	V6
Displacement:	174 ci (2,849 cc)
Transmission	5-speed manual
Max power:	260 bhp (194 kW) @ 5,500 rpm
Max torque:	318 lb ft (431 Nm) @ 2,000 rpm
Weight:	2,867 lb (1,303 kg)
Economy:	19.6 mpg (7 km/l)

Venturi Atlantique

The Atlantique was produced after a Thai consortium took over Venturi in 1996. It used a similar layout to most mid-engined cars, with a backbone steel chassis supporting double wishbones at the front and a multi-link rear, plus coil springs and telescopic shocks all around. Large vented discs handled the braking and anti-lock was standard. The car developed quickly, thanks to composite plastic bodywork, which is one of the strongest of its kind. It also boasts a very slippery drag coefficient of just 0.31. While the V6 was familiar to Venturis of the past, the Atlantique's owed little to the previous motor except in layout. It is all-aluminium and has quad cams plus 24 valves. Sequential fuel injection is state-of-the-art, but the real key to the V6's power is the twin intercooled turbos which have variable internal geometry to maintain near-maximum power across the rev range.

Top speed:	174 mph (278 km/h)
0–60 mph (0–95 km/h):	5.3 sec
Engine type:	V6
Displacement:	180 ci (2,946 cc)
Transmission	5-speed manual
Max power:	302 bhp (225 kW) @ 5,500 rpm
Max torque:	298 lb ft (403 Nm) @ 2,500 rpm
Weight:	2,750 lb (1,250 kg)
Economy:	24 mpg (8.5 km/l)

Volvo 120 Series

Known universally as the 'Amazon', but never sold under the name because
moped manufacturer Kriedler owned the trademark, the 120-Series was a
significant car in motoring history. It was the first vehicle ever to be fitted with
safety belts, while its inherent toughness meant it was also regarded as a car that
would last for years. Early models were slow and had an awkward three-speed
transmission, but later examples were much better, with a choice of two larger
engines and an all-syncromesh four-speed gearbox. Although it looked big and
heavy, the 120 was a surprisingly agile car to drive, while its mechanical solidity
meant it was also a successful rally car – a tradition that continues to this day with
its popularity in historic events. A sports version was released in 1966 badged as
the 123GT. Production of the 120 ended in the summer of 1969.

Top speed:	100 mph (162 km/h)
0–60 mph (0–95 km/h):	14.9 sec
Engine type:	in-line four
Displacement:	108 ci (1,778 cc)
Transmission:	4-speed manual
Max power:	90 bhp (67 kW) at 5,000 rpm
Max torque:	105 lb ft (142 Nm) at 3,500 rpm
Weight:	2,380 lb (1,071 kg)
Economy:	27 mpg (9.6 km/l)

Volvo P1800

With Volvo's reputation for solidity and stunning styling from Italian design
house Frua, the Volvo P1800 should have been a remarkable success. But it
was haunted by early build and reliability problems. A lack of space at Volvo's
factory in Sweden, coupled to limited projected sales, meant that manufacture of
the P1800 was franchised out to British sports car maker Jensen. The English firm
agreed to assemble the car if it was supplied in component form, so Volvo
outsourced manufacture of the body pressings to Pressed Steel Limited of Linwood,
Scotland. The bodies were freighted to Jensen, but some weren't properly treated
against rust and rot was always a P1800 problem. Later cars were called 1800E and
had a 2.0-litre fuel-injected engine, while an unusual 1800ES sports estate was
offered for the final three years of production.

Top speed:	105 mph (170 km/h)
0–60 mph (0–95 km/h):	14.0 sec
Engine type:	in-line four
Displacement:	109 ci (1,780 cc)
Transmission:	4-speed manual
Max power:	100 bhp (74.5 kW) at 5,500 rpm
Max torque:	108 lb ft (147 Nm) at 4,000 rpm
Weight:	2,404 lb (1,081 kg)
Economy:	20.5 mpg (7.3 km/l)

Volvo 262 Coupé

If you were looking for excitement in your driving during the 1970s, then Volvo was probably the last manufacturer you'd consider buying from. The Swedish firm decided it was time to rid itself of its dowdy image while also celebrating its 50th anniversary, so it asked Italian styling house Bertoné to create a coupé version of the dull but popular 260 Sedan. The 262C was at least distinctive, although its low-cut roof looked at odds with its otherwise boxy styling, which remained largely unchanged from the saloon. It was well-equipped, however, with pleated leather seat trim, wooden door cappings, air conditioning and a full-length Webasto sunroof. The aluminium V6 engine provided plenty of power and good refinement, but the 262C could never be considered sporting as it felt too big and heavy. It was primarily intended for the US market.

Top speed:	109 mph (176 km/h)
0–60 mph (0–95 km/h):	11.1 sec
Engine type:	V6
Displacement:	163 ci (2,664 cc)
Transmission:	4-speed manual/3-speed auto
Max power:	125 bhp (93 kW) at 5,750 rpm
Max torque:	150 lb ft (204 Nm) at 2,750 rpm
Weight:	3,120 lb (1,404 kg)
Economy:	20 mpg (7.1 km/l)

Volvo V70 T5

When the 850 arrived in 1992 it dispelled the myth that Volvos were boring, especially in the case of the T5. That car quickly became a commercial success, but in the fast-changing 1990s a new shape was needed just four years later and Volvo came up with the S70 and V70, 'S' for 'sedan' and 'V' for 'vagen', or wagon. The body was of unitary construction and had a rubber-mounted subframe to isolate major components such as the engine, transmission, strut suspension and steering. The rear used a multi-link arrangement, while the brakes were 11-inch (279mm) discs all around. Few companies use five-cylinder engines but Volvo has mastered it and in the smooth V70 this was obvious. Power was upped through twin camshafts, four valves per cylinder and sequential fuel injection. The compression was low to allow for the turbo which pushed power to 247bhp (184kW) in Europe.

Top speed:	152 mph (243 km/h)
0–60 mph (0–95 km/h):	6.9 sec
Engine type:	In-line five
Displacement:	141 ci (2,319 cc)
Transmission	5-speed manual
Max power:	236 bhp (176 kW) @ 5,100 rpm
Max torque:	244 lb ft (330 Nm) @ 2,100 rpm
Weight:	3,371 lb (1,532 kg)
Economy:	25 mpg (8.9 km/l)

Volvo C70 T5

Debuted in 1996 at the Paris Motor Show, the C70 a demonstrated a radical departure from regular Volvos. It used the same five-cylinder drive train as the V70 T5, and although much of the suspension hardware was derived from the V70 sedan also, F1 racing team TWR were commissioned to fine-tune the set-up for its new purpose. It retained Volvo's Delta Link rear which allowed the back wheels to turn fractionally to aid handling. The engine was all-aluminium and featured Motronic fuel injection plus a high-pressure turbo. The only gearbox available was an auto but it had settings for sports, economy and winter. As always with Volvos there were several safety features such as EBD (electronic brake distribution) and SIPS (side impact protection system), but it managed to combine luxury as well with wood, leather and a very quiet interior, thanks to a drag coefficient of just 0.29.

Top speed:	155 mph (248 km/h)
0–60 mph (0–95 km/h):	6.3 sec
Engine type:	In-line five
Displacement:	141 ci (2,319 cc)
Transmission	5-speed manual
Max power:	236 bhp (176 kW) @ 5,100 rpm
Max torque:	243 lb ft (329 Nm) @ 2,700 rpm
Weight:	3,365 lb (1,529 kg)
Economy:	18 mpg (6.4 km/l)

Volvo S80 T6

Volvo's reputation for building boxy tanks belongs in the history books. The handsome S80, with its high sculptured waistline, was one of the finest vehicles ever to come out of the Gothenburg, Sweden, factory and its performance variant, the T6, looked more dynamic than any Volvo previous. Launched in 1998, the car was strong and safe in Volvo tradition, and handled well, thanks to MacPherson front struts and a multi-link rear. Its cornering and ride-quality was superb, enough to prove competition to BMW and Mercedes. Unusually, the straight-six 171ci (2.8-litre) engine was mounted transversely, the first car to use such a layout in over a decade. It used twin turbos for the incredible power output, with 280lb ft (379Nm) torque at 2,000–5,000rpm. This power was helped down by traction control and a limited-slip differential with viscous coupling. Top speed was electronically limited.

Top speed:	150 mph (240 km/h)
0–60 mph (0–95 km/h):	6.7 sec
Engine type:	In-line five
Displacement:	170 ci (2,783 cc)
Transmission	4-speed auto
Max power:	268 bhp (200 kW) @ 5,400 rpm
Max torque:	280 lb ft (379 Nm) @ 2,000 rpm
Weight:	3,580 lb (1,627 kg)
Economy:	26 mpg (9.2 km/l)

VW Beetle Cabrio

Volkswagen's first collaboration with Karmann was to create a convertible version of the Beetle and put it into series production. The soft-top Bug was unveiled in 1949 and went into production straight away, although unusually conversion specialists Hebmüller also offered a chopped Beetle for the first four years. After that, the Karmann derivative was the only soft-top available and remained in production for over 30 years, undergoing the same mechanical changes and minor facelifts as the saloon car on which it was based. Such was the quality of Karmann's engineering that, with the roof raised, the Convertible was actually quieter than the sedan on the road, although rear visibility was hampered by a small plastic window that was prone to discolouration over time. The Karmann Beetles all carried the coachbuilder's own badge rather than that of Volkswagen.

Top speed:	63 mph (101 km/h)
0–60 mph (0–95 km/h):	not quoted
Engine type:	flat-four
Displacement:	69 ci (1,131 cc)
Transmission:	4-speed manual
Max power:	25 bhp (19 kW) at 3,300 rpm
Max torque:	49 lb ft (66 Nm) at 2,000 rpm
Weight:	1,652 lb (743 kg)
Economy:	30 mpg (10.7 km/l)

VW Karmann Ghia

The humble Volkswagen Beetle had already hit it big in the States when the German manufacturer was approached by coachbuilders Karmann with a proposal to turn it into an attractive coupé. While a sporty Beetle variant was never on VW's agenda, the designs (by Ghia of Italy) were so pretty that it was decided to put the car into production. The car's slippery shape lent itself well to the Beetle's wheelbase, but although it looked like a sports car the Karmann Ghia made do with the standard air-cooled mechanical layout of its sedan cousin. Even though the engine was uprated four times during its 19-year production cycle, the Karmann Ghia never went or handled like a sports car, but those sinewy looks and a reputation for being mechanically unburstable meant it was perennially a good seller. The Cabriolet remains the most sought-after model.

Top speed:	87 mph (141 km/h)
0–60 mph (0–95 km/h):	21.7 sec
Engine type:	flat-four
Displacement:	91 ci (1,493 cc)
Transmission:	4-speed manual
Max power:	45 bhp (33kW) at 3,800 rpm
Max torque:	83 lb ft (113 Nm) at 2,000 rpm
Weight:	1,930 lb (869 kg)
Economy:	25 mpg (8.9 km/l)

VW Type 3 Fastback

Despite the massive success of the Beetle, Volkswagen relied on a one-car model range right up until 1961, when it finally took the decision to expand its line-up. The next car to emerge from its Wolfsburg factory in Germany was the 1500 Sedan, also known as the Type 3. Although it was styled like a conventional car, with a large nose and aerodynamic curves, the Type 3 retained VW's established mechanical layout, with an air-cooled flat-four engine mounted adrift of the rear axle and an expanded Beetle floorpan. The engine was increased in size to 1,584cc in 1965 and the car became known as the VW 1600TL, while a conventional two-door saloon was also introduced. It never achieved the sales success of the Beetle, but 1.5 million were made over a 12-year period. The car had luggage space in the front and rear, the latter alongside the engine.

Top speed:	105 mph (170 km/h)
0–60 mph (0–95 km/h):	10.4 sec
Engine type:	flat four
Displacement:	108 ci (1,776 cc)
Transmission:	4-speed manual
Max power:	83 bhp (62 kW) at 4,700 rpm
Max torque:	70 lb ft (95 Nm) at 2,400 rpm
Weight:	2,150 lb (968 kg)
Economy:	28 mpg (10.0 km/l)

VW Beetle

During the 1970s when the drag-racing scene of the USA was dominated by muscle cars, VWs began to make an appearance on the West Coast tracks. With companies such as Empi and Scat providing aftermarket VW performance parts, and individuals like Gene Berg who was at the forefront of tuning the flat four, the VWs started to embarrass many quick muscle cars with crazy quarter-miles times of 12 seconds. This was almost unheard from engines as small as 122ci (2 litres), but it sparked a craze in tuning VWs. That craze continues today and this Beetle is a British street/strip racer. It retains the Beetle floorpan, but has lowered suspension and uprated shocks. The all-alloy engine comprises a custom-machined block, race spec heads, dual 2-inch (52mm) carbs and a custom grind cam, all driving through a modified gearbox. With slick tyres the car can run low 12-second quarter-miles.

Top speed:	133 mph (212 km/h)
0–60 mph (0–95 km/h):	5.2 sec
Engine type:	Flat four
Displacement:	146 ci (2,398 cc)
Transmission	4-speed manual
Max power:	210 bhp (157 kW) @ 7,000 rpm
Max torque:	180 lb ft (244 Nm) @ 4,800 rpm
Weight:	1,629 lb (740 kg)
Economy:	18 mpg (6.4 km/l)

VW Scirocco

By rights, the VW Scirocco should never have been built. At the time of its development, Volkswagen was busy designing the Golf and had far more important considerations with what would be its most important model since the original Beetle. The design for the Scirocco was carried out by Guigiaro while styling the Golf, and although VW liked it, there wasn't the money to develop the car further. Unperturbed, Guigiaro went to Karmann, which agreed to engineer the bodyshell to take Golf mechanical components. Ironically, the Scirocco was finished before the Golf and went on sale three months earlier. VW's early concerns were unfounded, as it remained in production for 17 years and sold over half a million units, proving profitable for all concerned. In 1977 the car had a facelift, and a Mk II version appeared in 1981.

Top speed:	99 mph (160 km/h)
0–60 mph (0–95 km/h):	10.2 sec
Engine type:	in-line four
Displacement:	105 ci (1,715 cc)
Transmission:	4-speed manual
Max power:	76 bhp (57 kW) at 5,500 rpm
Max torque:	89 lb ft (121 Nm) at 3,000 rpm
Weight:	1,933 lb (870 kg)
Economy:	30 mpg (10.7 km/l)

VW Golf GTi

When Volkswagen launched the Golf GTi in 1975, it created a new breed of car called the hot hatch, or sport compact. VW combined serious performance – the GTi could out-pace and out-handle most sportscars of the time – with the practicality of a small family car and thus opened a very lucrative market. The GTi looked different from the regular Golf by fitting wider wheels and tyres, which necessitated flared plastic arches, plus it had slightly lowered suspension all around and used a front chin spoiler. Bilstein shocks and a rear anti-roll bar made for terrific handling while the brakes were simple but effective with discs front and drums rear. The engine started out as a 91ci (1.5-litre) four-cylinder, transversely mounted for front-wheel drive, but soon went to 109ci (1.7 litres). Bosch fuel injection allowed the power to be developed while retaining excellent refinement.

Top speed:	107 mph (171 km/h)
0–60 mph (0–95 km/h):	9.8 sec
Engine type:	In-line four
Displacement:	97 ci (1,588 cc)
Transmission	5-speed manual
Max power:	110 bhp (82 kW) @ 6,100 rpm
Max torque:	100 lb ft (135 Nm) @ 5,000 rpm
Weight:	1,904 lb (865 kg)
Economy:	25 mpg (8.9 km/l)

VW Corrado VR6

Volkswagen's Corrado was one of the best-handling front-wheel drive cars in the world. Based on the excellent Golf MkII platform, it was never intended as a replacement for the VW's ailing Scirocco because it was far too good for that. The Corrado got revised spring and shock rates and with its front heavy weight bias (64:36) was brilliant through corners, suffering virtually no understeer. The chassis was so good that it easily handled the powerful VR6, launched in 1992. The engine used a very narrow 'V' (15 degrees) to make it compact, and although it had been used in the Golf before, for the Corrado it was bored out an extra 4.2ci (70cc) for more power, plus the compression was raised to 10:1. A subtle form of traction-control was used, so when a wheel was spinning, the brake on it would come on until its speed matched the other side. Other tricks included a self-raising spoiler.

Top speed:	140 mph (224 km/h)
0–60 mph (0–95 km/h):	6.8 sec
Engine type:	V6
Displacement:	170 ci (2,792 cc)
Transmission	5-speed manual
Max power:	178 bhp (132 kW) @ 5,800 rpm
Max torque:	177 lb ft (240 Nm) @ 4,200 rpm
Weight:	2,810 lb (1,277 kg)
Economy:	28 mpg (10 km/l)

Watson Roadster (1960)

Indy racing is part of the US culture, and in the early 1960s A.J. Watson dominated the manufacturing of the cars, at a time when Formula One machines were just starting to influence design. Watson's history goes back to 1950 when, as a mechanic, he built his own car for the Indy 500 which Dick Rathmann drove. In 1954 Watson got his break with the John Zink Jnr team, and a year later his modified version of the Frank Kurtis-built roadster won the Indy 500. This 1960 example is typical of his racers, with a basic chassis with front/rear solid axles but torsion bar suspension that could be tweaked by the driver whilst going along. The Offenhauser Sprint and Champ car engine was offset to the left to make the car turn naturally in that direction, and gearbox only needed two speeds due to the massive torque available low down, plus the car's light weight.

Top speed:	175 mph (280 km/h)
0–60 mph (0–96 km/h):	3.3 sec
Engine type:	In-line four
Displacement:	252 ci (4,129 cc)
Transmission	2-speed manual
Max power:	400 bhp (298 kW) @ 6,600 rpm
Max torque:	N/A
Weight:	1,600 lb (727 kg)
Economy:	N/A

Westfield SEiGHT

Chris Smith started Westfield in the UK in 1982, building a one-off Lotus XI replica for a US customer which later went into production as the Westfield XI. Though a Lotus Seven replica followed in 1984, a lawsuit filed by Caterham Cars, which had the rights to the Lotus Seven, forced him to re-style his cars, and by 1988 he'd created the SE and SEi. In 1991 his models had developed further and the ultimate SE variant was born: the SEiGHT. The chassis for this car was made in square section steel tubing which was heavily triangulated, and it ran high up inside the bodywork as there was no requirement for doors. The V8 was an all-aluminium Rover, stroked to 238ci (3,900cc) and at first featuring SU carbs, though later versions had fuel injection and either 198bhp (148kW) or 273bhp (203kW). Double wishbones suspension front and rear and quick steering made it a driver's machine.

Top speed:	139 mph (222 km/h)
0–60 mph (0–95 km/h):	4.3 sec
Engine type:	V8
Displacement:	240 ci (3,946 cc)
Transmission	5-speed manual
Max power:	273 bhp (203 kW) @ 5,750 rpm
Max torque:	265 lb ft (359 Nm) @ 4,750 rpm
Weight:	1,521 lb (691 kg)
Economy:	24 mpg (8.5 km/l)

Willys 65-Knight (1925)

Willys prided themselves on building quality cars, and it was this, plus a number of special design points, which made the company's 65-Knight a great seller in the 1920s. Whereas engines had been rough and noisy up until this point in the majority of machines, Willys added internal balancing which comprised two extra cylinders rotating in the opposite direction to the main engine. Also, it used sleeve valves which improved the seal of the combustion as carbon built up inside the engine, thus giving the car more power as it used it, which independent testing endorsed. It also produced plenty of torque which meant the drive could get away with the minimum gear changes for an almost effortless drive. The sedan was one of few hardtops built at the time, and it maximized internal space, plus had 'suicide' style opening rear doors to ease passenger entry.

Top speed:	60 mph (96 km/h)
0–60 mph (0–96 km/h):	31.0 sec
Engine type:	In-line four
Displacement:	186 ci (3,047 cc)
Transmission	3–speed manual
Max power:	40 bhp (30 kW) @ 2,600 rpm
Max torque:	N/A
Weight:	3,060 lb (1,390 kg)
Economy:	16 mpg (5.6 km/l)

Willys Coupe

In the 1960s when drag-racing really caught on in the USA, pre-war cars were cheap and plentiful and popular as a basis for 'Gassers'. These used large V8s run on pump gas and ran high in order to fit both large wheel in the rear and the big motor up front without any body modifications. The 1940–1941 Willys was a Gasser favourite, but as drag-racing came on, aerodynamics became more important and so the cars sat lower. Street rodders started using the Willys body from the 1960s, but they became most popular in the 1980s and 1990s. This car is typical of the best produced, using a strong ladder frame style chassis, off of which a custom double wishbone suspension hangs at the front, and a four-bar linked live axle sits at the rear. A blown Chrysler Hemi engine gives power for 10-second quarters.

Top speed:	150 mph (240 km/h)
0–60 mph (0–95 km/h):	3.4 sec
Engine type:	V8
Displacement:	392 ci (6,423 cc)
Transmission	3-speed auto
Max power:	700 bhp (522 kW) @ 6,800 rpm
Max torque:	509 lb ft (689 Nm) @ 3,200 rpm
Weight:	2,872 lb (1,305 kg)
Economy:	5 mpg (1.7 km/l)

Willys Jeep (1941)

When the US Army needed an all-purpose in World War II, Bantam came up with the right 4WD design but production was also given to both Ford and Willys. Each company produced virtually the same vehicle, though Willys produced the most with 361,349, Ford being second with 277,896, and Bantam last with just 2,675. The frame was simple but very rugged and everything had to be bolt-on for ease of maintenance. Fully floating Spicer axles were used at either end with multi-leaf springs for durability and strength to carry heavy loads as these cars were adapted to many uses. As the idea was to keep the components simple and reliable, the engine was a four-cylinder unit with high torque and low output. The Jeep could pull up steep inclines, thanks to a two-speed transfer case and minimal bodywork overhang which allowed approach and departure angles of 45 degrees.

Top speed:	62 mph (99 km/h)
0–60 mph (0–96 km/h):	30 sec
Engine type:	In-line four
Displacement:	134 ci (2,195 cc)
Transmission	3-speed manual
Max power:	60 bhp (45 kW) @ 3,600 rpm
Max torque:	105 lb ft (142 Nm) @ 2,000 rpm
Weight:	2,453 lb (1,115kg)
Economy:	13.8 mpg (4.88 km/l)

Zimmer Quicksilver (1988)

Zimmer was a well-known van conversion company who in 1980 decided to produce a nostalgia coupe called the Golden Spirit. It used Ford running gear and that decade produced sales of 1,500. In 1986 GM designer Don Johnson penned the striking Quicksilver for the company, and while it was first shown that summer, it didn't start production until 1987. The car was based on the Pontiac Fiero so, unusually for a large coupe, it had its engine mid-mounted and handling was very good. The long nose was purely there for styling and was deceptive as there was no huge engine under it, though it did give incredible luggage space. The retro-styling also featured with the massive chrome fenders, as a nod to the glitzy cars like Lincolns and Cadillacs of the 1970s. The front suspension used wishbones, while the rear had struts, and discs front and rear uprated the braking.

Top speed:	121 mph (193 km/h)
0–60 mph (0–96 km/h):	9.7 sec
Engine type:	V6
Displacement:	173 ci (2,834 cc)
Transmission	3-speed auto
Max power:	140 bhp (104 kW) @ 5,200 rpm
Max torque:	170 lb ft (230 Nm) @ 3,600 rpm
Weight:	2,920 lb (1,327 kg)
Economy:	24 mpg (8.50 km/l)

Index

Index

Index

Index

Index

Index

Index

Index

Index

Index

Index

Index

Index

Index